Sunbeam
Owners
Workshop
Manual

by J H Haynes
Member of the Guild of Motoring Writers
and Peter G Strasman

Models covered

Sunbeam 1.0 LE,LS and GL, 928 cc
Sunbeam 1.3 LS and GL, 1295 cc
Sunbeam 1.6 GL, S, GLS and Ti, 1598 cc

Does not cover Sunbeam Lotus

ISBN 0 85696 807 2

ABCDE
FG

Haynes Publishing Group
Sparkford Nr Yeovil
Somerset BA22 7JJ England

Haynes Publications, Inc
861 Lawrence Drive
Newbury Park
California 91320 USA

Acknowledgements

Thanks are due to the Talbot Motor Company Ltd for the provision of technical information, and to Castrol Limited who supplied lubrication data. The Champion Sparking Plug Company supplied the illustrations showing the various spark plug conditions. The bodywork repair photographs used in this manual were provided by Lloyds Industries Limited who supply 'Turtle Wax', 'Dupli-Color Holts' and other Holts range products.

Special thanks are due to all those people at Sparkford who helped in the production of this manual, particularly Brian Horsfall and Les Brazier who carried out the mechanical work and took the photographs respectively, Lee Saunders who planned the layout of each page and Chris Rogers who edited the text.

About this manual

Its aim

The aim of this manual is to help you get the best value from your car. It can do so in several ways. It can help you decide what work must be done (even should you choose to get it done by a garage), provide information on routine maintenance and servicing, and give a logical course of action and diagnosis when random faults occur. However, it is hoped that you will make full use of the manual by tackling the work yourself. On simpler jobs it may even be quicker than booking the car into a garage, and having to go there twice, to leave and collect it. Perhaps most important, a lot of money can be saved by avoiding the costs the garage must charge to cover its labour and overheads.

The manual has drawings and descriptions to show the function of the various components so that their layout can be understood. Then the tasks are described and photographeded in a step-by-step sequence so that even a novice can do the work.

Its arrangement

The manual is divided into thirteen Chapters, each covering a logical sub-division of the vehicle. The Chapters are each divided into consecutively numbered Sections and the Sections into paragraphs (or sub-sections), with decimal numbers following on from the Section they are in eg 5.1, 5.2, 5.3 etc.

It is freely illustrated, especially in those parts where there is a detailed sequence of operations to be carried out. There are two forms of illustration; figures and photographs. The figures are numbered in sequence with decimal numbers, according to their position in the Chapter: eg Fig. 6.4 is the 4th drawing/illustration in Chapter 6. Photographs are numbered (either individually or in related groups) the same as the Section or sub-section of the text where the operation they show is described.

There is an alphabetical index at the back of the manual as well as a contents list at the front.

References to the 'left' or 'right' of the vehicle are in the sense of a person in a seat facing towards the front of the vehicle.

Whilst every care is taken to ensure that the information in this manual is correct no liability can be accepted by the authors or publishers for loss, damage or injury caused by any errors in, or omissions from, the information given.

Introduction to the Sunbeam

The Sunbeam is only available as a three-door 'hatchback' saloon but with choices of both engine size and trim specification.

There are two basic engine types and three engine sizes used throughout the range. The smallest engine (930 cc) is a development of the Hillman Imp single overhead camshaft engine which has been suitably modified and is mounted in the front of the car. The two larger engines (1295 cc and 1598 cc) are well proven and taken from the Talbot (formerly Chrysler and Hillman) Avenger range. The 930 cc and 1295 cc models are only available with manual transmission, whereas the 1598 cc models can be specified with the optional automatic transmission.

The car should prove mechanically reliable, as it largely comprises components which have been used in other models over a numer of years. It is a solidly constructed vehicle, surprisingly heavy for its size and engine capacity. This should make for safety on the road and ensure a long life.

Maintenance and overhaul are simple and straightforward operations, thanks to the rear wheel drive design, and plenty of room is provided within the engine compartment for access to regularly serviced items.

Contents

4

Three-quarter front view of 1.6 litre Sunbeam

General dimensions, weights and capacities

Dimensions

Overall length	150.7 in (3829 mm)
Overall width	63.1 in (1603 mm)
Overall height	54.9 in (1395 mm)
Wheelbase	95.0 in (2413 mm)

Kerb weight (unladen)

	To 1979		1980 on	
	lb	kg	lb	kg
1.0 LS	1792	813	1803	818
1.0 GL	1808	820	1828	829
1.3 LS	1936	878	1947	883
1.3/1.6 GL	1951	885	1971	894
1.6S	1993	904	–	–
1.6 GLS	–	–	2026	919

Add 29.1 lb (13 kg) if equipped with automatic transmission

Maximum roof rack load .... 100 lb (45 kg)

Capacities

Fuel tank:	
To 1979	9 gallons (41 litres)
1980 on	10 gallons (45 litres)
Cooling system:	
930 engine	8 pints (4.5 litres)
1300/1600 engine	13 pints (7.3 litres)
Engine oil:	
930 engine	5.25 pints (3.0 litres)
1300/1600 engine	7.0 pints (4.0 litres)
Manual gearbox	3 pints (1.7 litres)
Automatic transmission	10.5 pints (6.0 litres)
Rear axle	1.5 pints (0.85 litres)

Buying spare parts and vehicle identification numbers

Buying spare parts

Spare parts are available from many sources, for example: Talbot garages, other garages and accessory shops, and motor factors. Our advice regarding spare part sources is as follows:

Officially appointed Talbot garages – This is the best source of parts which are peculiar to your car and are otherwise not generally available (eg complete cylinder heads, internal gearbox components, badges, interior trim etc). It is also the only place at which you should buy parts if your car is still under warranty – non-Talbot components may invalidate the warranty. To be sure of obtaining the correct parts it will always be necessary to give the storeman your car's vehicle identification number, and if possible, to take the old part along for positive identification. Remember that many parts are available on a factory exchange scheme – any parts returned should always be clean! It obviously makes good sense to go straight to the specialists on your car for this type of part for they are best equipped to supply you.

Other garages and accessory shops – These are often very good places to buy materials and components needed for the maintenance of your car (eg oil filters, spark plugs, bulbs, fan belts, oils and greases, touch-up paint, filler paste etc). They also sell general accessories, usually have convenient opening hours, charge lower prices and can often be found not far from home.

Motor factors – Good factors will stock all of the more important components which wear out relatively quickly (eg clutch components, pistons, valves, exhaust systems, brake cylinders/pipes/hoses/seals/shoes and pads etc). Motor factors will often provide new or reconditioned components on a part exchange basis – this can save a considerable amount of money.

Vehicle identification numbers

As already stated, when ordering new parts it is essential that the storeman has full information about your particular model. He cannot guarantee to supply you with the correct part unless you give him the vehicle identification number and/or the engine number as applicable.

The service plate and the vehicle identification plate are fitted to the bonnet locking platform.

The vehicle specification code is contained within the vehicle service number appearing on the service plate. The 12th to 15th characters inclusive make up the code, and their significance is as follows:

12th character (engine specification)

Code letter	Capacity (cc)	Compression ratio	Carburettor
C	930	High	1.50
D	1300 (restricted output)	High	1.50
H	1600	High	Twin Weber
J	1300	Low	1.50
K	930	High (uprated)	1.50
R	1300	High	1.50
S	1300	High	1.75
T	1600	High	1.50
U	1600	Low	1.50
V	1300	Low	1.50
W	1600	High	1.75

13th character (rear axle ratio)

Code number	Ratio
1	4.38 : 1
3 or 4	4.11 : 1
5 or 6	3.89 : 1
7 or 8	3.70 : 1
9 or 0	3.54 : 1

14th character (brakes and suspension)

Code	Brakes	Suspension
A, Q, X or 6	Standard	Standard
B, R, Y or 7	Standard	Heavy duty
C, E or G	With rear wheel anti-lock*	Heavy duty
D, F or H	With rear wheel anti-lock*	Standard

Pressure conscious reducing valve (PCRV) incorporated in braking system

15th character (market code)

Code	Market
H	Domestic
E	Right-hand drive export
X	Left-hand drive export

The engine number of 930 cc models is stamped on the cylinder block just above the starter motor location. In the case of 1300 and 1600 cc models it will be found on the right-hand side of the cylinder block, just below No 3 spark plug.

The series of vehicle is indicated by the second character of the vehicle service number appearing on the service plate.

The vehicle identification plate provides the vehicle identification number (VIN) required for legal documentation, eg vehicle registration.

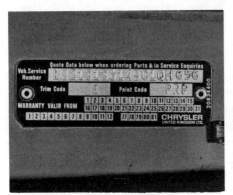

Vehicle service plate (typical)

Location of engine number (930 cc)

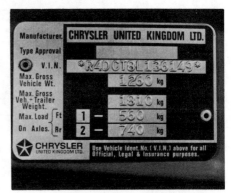

Vehicle identification plate (typical)

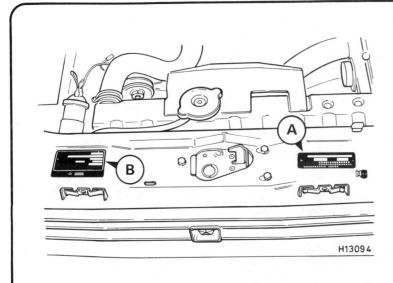

Location of service plate (A) and vehicle identification plate (B)

Tools and working facilities

Introduction

A selection of good tools is a fundamental requirement for anyone contemplating the maintenance and repair of a motor vehicle. For the owner who does not possess any, their purchase will prove a considerable expense, offsetting some of the savings made by doing-it-yourself. However, provided that the tools purchased are of good quality, they will last for many years and prove an extremely worthwhile investment.

To help the average owner to decide which tools are needed to carry out the various tasks detailed in this manual, we have compiled three lists of tools under the following headings: *Maintenance and minor repair, Repair and overhaul,* and *Special.* The newcomer to practical mechanics should start off with the *Maintenance and minor repair* tool kit and confine himself to the simpler jobs around the vehicle. Then, as his confidence and experience grows, he can undertake more difficult tasks, buying extra tools as, and when, they are needed. In this way, a *Maintenance and minor repair* tool kit can be built-up into a *Repair and overhaul* tool kit over a considerable period of time without any major cash outlays. The experienced do-it-yourselfer will have a tool kit good enough for most repair and overhaul procedures and will add tools from the *Special* category when he feels the expense is justified by the amount of use to which these tools will be put.

It is obviously not possible to cover the subject of tools fully here. For those who wish to learn more about tools and their use there is a book entitled *How to Choose and Use Car Tools* available from the publishers of this manual.

Note: *The nuts and bolts used on the Sunbeam models are a mixture of AF and metric sizes. The mechanical components and assemblies (engine, transmission, rear axle) drawn from the Avenger, have fixings of AF sizes.*

Maintenance and minor repair tool kit

The tools given in this list should be considered as a minimum requirement if routine maintenance, servicing and minor repair operations are to be undertaken. We recommend the purchase of combination spanners (ring one end, open-ended the other); although more expensive than open-ended ones, they do give the advantages of both types of spanner.

Combination spanners - 6, 7, 8, 9, 10, 11, 12, 13 & 18 mm
Combination spanners - $\frac{5}{16}$, $\frac{7}{16}$, $\frac{1}{2}$, $\frac{9}{16}$, $\frac{5}{8}$, $\frac{11}{16}$, $\frac{3}{4}$ in AF
Adjustable spanner - 9 inch
Engine sump/gearbox/rear axle drain plug key (where applicable)
Spark plug spanner (with rubber insert)
Spark plug gap adjustment tool
Set of feeler gauges
Brake adjuster spanner (where applicable)
Brake bleed nipple spanner
Screwdriver - 4 in long x $\frac{1}{4}$ in dia (flat blade)
Screwdriver - 4 in long x $\frac{1}{4}$ in dia (cross blade)
Combination pliers - 6 inch
Hacksaw, junior
Tyre pump
Tyre pressure gauge
Grease gun (where applicable)
Oil can
Fine emery cloth (1 sheet)
Wire brush (small)
Funnel (medium size)

Repair and overhaul tool kit

These tools are virtually essential for anyone undertaking any major repairs to a motor vehicle, and are additional to those given in the *Maintenance and minor repair* list. Included in this list is a comprehensive set of sockets. Although these are expensive they will be found invaluable as they are so versatile - particularly if various drives are included in the set. We recommend the $\frac{1}{2}$ in square-drive type, as this can be used with most proprietary torque wrenches. If you cannot afford a socket set, even bought piecemeal, then inexpensive tubular box spanners are a useful alternative.

The tools in this list will occasionally need to be supplemented by tools from the *Special* list.

Sockets (or box spanners) to cover range in previous list
Reversible ratchet drive (for use with sockets)
Extension piece, 10 inch (for use with sockets)
Universal joint (for use with sockets)
Torque wrench (for use with sockets)
'Mole' wrench - 8 inch
Ball pein hammer
Soft-faced hammer, plastic or rubber
Screwdriver - 6 in long x $\frac{5}{16}$ in dia (flat blade)
Screwdriver - 2 in long x $\frac{5}{16}$ in square (flat blade)
Screwdriver - 1$\frac{1}{2}$ in long x $\frac{1}{4}$ in dia (cross blade)
Screwdriver - 3 in long x $\frac{1}{8}$ in dia (electricians)
Pliers - electricians side cutters
Pliers - needle nosed
Pliers - circlip (internal and external)
Cold chisel - $\frac{1}{2}$ inch
Scriber (this can be made by grinding the end of a broken hacksaw blade)
Scraper (this can be made by flattening and sharpening one end of a piece of copper pipe)
Centre punch
Pin punch
Hacksaw
Valve grinding tool
Steel rule/straight edge
Allen keys
Selection of files
Wire brush (large)
Axle-stands
Jack (strong scissor or hydraulic type)

Special tools

The tools in this list are those which are not used regularly, are expensive to buy, or which need to be used in accordance with their manufacturers' instructions. Unless relatively difficult mechanical jobs are undertaken frequently, it will not be economic to buy many of these tools. Where this is the case, you could consider clubbing together with friends (or a motorists' club) to make a joint purchase, or borrowing the tools against a deposit from a local garage or tool hire specialist.

The following list contains only those tools and instruments freely available to the public, and not those special tools produced by the vehicle manufacturer specifically for its dealer network. You will find occasional references to these manufacturers' special tools in the text of this manual. Generally, an alternative method of doing the job without the vehicle manufacturer's special tool is given. However, sometimes, there is no alternative to using them. Where this is the case and the relevant tool cannot be bought or borrowed you will have to entrust the work to a franchised garage.

Valve spring compressor
Piston ring compressor
Balljoint separator
Universal hub/bearing puller
Impact screwdriver
Micrometer and/or vernier gauge

Carburettor flow balancing device (where applicable)
Dial gauge
Stroboscopic timing light
Dwell angle meter/tachometer
Universal electrical multi-meter
Cylinder compression gauge
Lifting tackle (photo)
Trolley jack
Light with extension lead

Buying tools

For practically all tools, a tool factor is the best source since he will have a very comprehensive range compared with the average garage or accessory shop. Having said that, accessory shops often offer excellent quality tools at discount prices, so it pays to shop around.

Remember, you don't have to buy the most expensive items on the shelf, but it is always advisable to steer clear of the very cheap tools. There are plenty of good tools around at reasonable prices, so ask the proprietor or manager of the shop for advice before making a purchase.

Care and maintenance of tools

Having purchased a reasonable tool kit, it is necessary to keep the tools in a clean serviceable condition. After use, always wipe off any dirt, grease and metal particles using a clean, dry cloth, before putting the tools away. Never leave them lying around after they have been used. A simple tool rack on the garage or workshop wall, for items such as screwdrivers and pliers is a good idea. Store all normal spanners and sockets in a metal box. Any measuring instruments, gauges, meters, etc, must be carefully stored where they cannot be damaged or become rusty.

Take a little care when tools are used. Hammer heads inevitably become marked and screwdrivers lose the keen edge on their blades from time to time. A little timely attention with emery cloth or a file will soon restore items like this to a good serviceable finish.

Working facilities

Not to be forgotten when discussing tools, is the workshop itself. If anything more than routine maintenance is to be carried out, some form of suitable working area becomes essential.

It is appreciated that many an owner mechanic is forced by circumstances to remove an engine or similar item, without the benefit of a garage or workshop. Having done this, any repairs should always be done under the cover of a roof.

Wherever possible, any dismantling should be done on a clean flat workbench or table at a suitable working height.

Any workbench needs a vice: one with a jaw opening of 4 in (100 mm) is suitable for most jobs. As mentioned previously, some clean dry storage space is also required for tools, as well as the lubricants, cleaning fluids, touch-up paints and so on which become necessary.

Another item which may be required, and which has a much more general usage, is an electric drill with a chuck capacity of at least $\frac{5}{16}$ in (8 mm). This, together with a good range of twist drills, is virtually essential for fitting accessories such as wing mirrors and reversing lights.

Last, but not least, always keep a supply of old newspapers and clean, lint-free rags available, and try to keep any working area as clean as possible.

Spanner jaw gap comparison table

Jaw gap (in)	Spanner size
0·250	$\frac{1}{4}$ in AF
0·277	7 mm
0·313	$\frac{5}{16}$ in AF
0·315	8 mm
0·344	$\frac{11}{32}$ in AF; $\frac{1}{8}$ in Whitworth
0·354	9 mm
0·375	$\frac{3}{8}$ in AF
0·394	10 mm
0·433	11 mm
0·438	$\frac{7}{16}$ in AF
0·445	$\frac{3}{16}$ in Whitworth; $\frac{1}{4}$ in BSF
0·472	12 mm
0·500	$\frac{1}{2}$ in AF
0·512	13 mm
0·525	$\frac{1}{4}$ in Whitworth; $\frac{5}{16}$ in BSF
0·551	14 mm
0·563	$\frac{9}{16}$ in AF
0·591	15 mm
0·600	$\frac{5}{16}$ in Whitworth; $\frac{3}{8}$ in BSF
0·625	$\frac{5}{8}$ in AF
0·630	16 mm
0·669	17 mm
0·686	$\frac{11}{16}$ in AF
0·709	18 mm
0·710	$\frac{3}{8}$ in Whitworth; $\frac{7}{16}$ in BSF
0·748	19 mm
0·750	$\frac{3}{4}$ in AF
0·813	$\frac{13}{16}$ in AF
0·820	$\frac{7}{16}$ in Whitworth; $\frac{1}{2}$ in BSF
0·866	22 mm
0·875	$\frac{7}{8}$ in AF
0·920	$\frac{1}{2}$ in Whitworth; $\frac{9}{16}$ in BSF
0·938	$\frac{15}{16}$ in AF
0·945	24 mm
1·000	1 in AF
1·010	$\frac{9}{16}$ in Whitworth; $\frac{5}{8}$ in BSF
1·024	26 mm
1·063	$1\frac{1}{16}$ in AF; 27 mm
1·100	$\frac{5}{8}$ in Whitworth; $\frac{11}{16}$ in BSF
1·125	$1\frac{1}{8}$ in AF
1·181	30 mm
1·200	$\frac{11}{16}$ in Whitworth; $\frac{3}{4}$ in BSF
1·250	$1\frac{1}{4}$ in AF
1·260	32 mm
1·300	$\frac{3}{4}$ in Whitworth; $\frac{7}{8}$ in BSF
1·313	$1\frac{5}{16}$ in AF
1·390	$\frac{13}{16}$ in Whitworth; $\frac{15}{16}$ in BSF
1·417	36 mm
1·438	$1\frac{7}{16}$ in AF
1·480	$\frac{7}{8}$ in Whitworth; 1 in BSF
1·500	$1\frac{1}{2}$ in AF
1·575	40 mm; $\frac{15}{16}$ in Whitworth
1·614	41 mm
1·625	$1\frac{5}{8}$ in AF
1·670	1 in Whitworth; $1\frac{1}{8}$ in BSF
1·688	$1\frac{11}{16}$ in AF
1·811	46 mm
1·813	$1\frac{13}{16}$ in AF
1·860	$1\frac{1}{8}$ in Whitworth; $1\frac{1}{4}$ in BSF
1·875	$1\frac{7}{8}$ in AF
1·969	50 mm
2·000	2 in AF
2·050	$1\frac{1}{4}$ in Whitworth; $1\frac{3}{8}$ in BSF
2·165	55 mm
2·362	60 mm

A Haltrac hoist and gantry in use during a typical engine removal sequence

Jacking and towing

Jacking

Four jacking points are provided below the body sills, two at either side of the car. The jacking points are basically holes formed in the body stiffening member, into which the domed lifting pad of the scissor type jack fits.

The spare wheel, jack, jack handle, wheel brace, and hub cap removing tool are located at the rear of the car under the load floor.

To operate the jack place it in position under the jacking point. Insert the hooked end of the jack handle through the ring on the jack screw. Turn the jack handle in a clockwise direction to raise the car and vice versa to lower it. For safety reasons chock one of the roadwheels remaining in contact with the ground and also apply the handbrake. Never get underneath the car while it is jacked up unless an additional form of support is provided such as axle stands or packing blocks.

Towing

The 'eyes', as shown in the accompanying photographs, are primarily fitted for lashing the vehicle down during transportation, but it is permissible to use these 'eyes' for straight line towing in emergency conditions. The 'eyes' should not be used for suspending the car during towing or for recovering the vehicle, eg from a ditch.

If your Sunbeam is an automatic version and is being towed by another vehicle then the following points should be noted:

(a) If the transmission is in order place the selector lever in N, add 2 pints (1 litre) of automatic transmission fluid to supplement the normal quantity and do not exceed a road speed of 30 mph (48 kph) or a towing distance of 30 miles (48 kilometres). Drain off the excess automatic transmission fluid after rectification of the fault.

(b) Where the automatic transmission is faulty, the car must either be towed with the rear wheels clear of the ground, the propeller shaft disconnected from the final drive flange and supported, or the propeller shaft removed completely. Where the propeller shaft is removed completely it will be necessary to seal the end of the extension housing to prevent the loss of transmission fluid and to prevent dirt entering.

Finally it should be remembered before towing commences that there will be no servo assistance of the brakes without the engine running and that the ignition key should be in position 'I' (steering column unlocked).

Towing loads

Braked

930 engine	1213 lb (550 kg)
1300 engine	1500 lb (680 kg)
1600 engine	1764 lb (800 kg)

Unbraked

All models	937 lb (425 kg)

Wheel changing jack in position

Using hub cap removal tool

Location of spare wheel and jack

Front towing hook

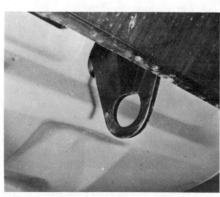
Rear towing hook

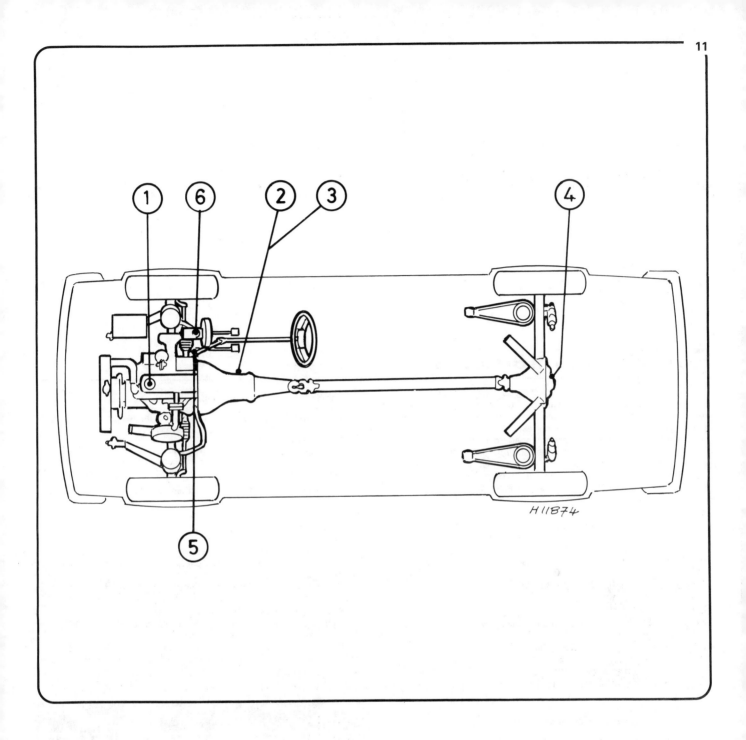

H11874

Recommended lubricants and fluids

Component	Lubricant type or specification	Castrol product
1 Engine	Multigrade engine oil	Castrol GTX
2 Manual gearbox	Multigrade engine oil	Castrol GTX
3 Automatic transmission	Shell Donax automatic transmission fluid	Castrol TQF
4 Rear axle	SAE 90EP hypoid gear oil	Castrol Hypoy
5 Steering gear	SAE 90EP hypoid gear oil	Castrol Hypoy
6 Brake master cylinder	SAE J1703 hydraulic fluid	Castrol Girling Universal Brake & Clutch Fluid

Note: *The above are general recommendations only. Lubrication requirements vary from territory to territory and depend on vehicle usage. If in doubt, consult the operators handbook supplied with the vehicle, or your nearest dealer.*

Routine maintenance

Maintenance is essential for ensuring safety and desirable for the purpose of getting the best in terms of performance and economy from your car. Over the years the need for periodic lubrication – oiling, greasing, and so on – has been drastically reduced if not totally eliminated. This has unfortunately tended to lead some owners to think that because no such action is required, components either no longer exist, or will last for ever. This is a serious delusion. It follows therefore that the largest initial element of maintenance is visual examination. This may lead to repairs or renewals.

Every 250 miles (400 km) or weekly – whichever comes first

Steering
    Check tyre pressures
    Examine tyres for wear or damage

Brakes
    Check brake fluid level and top up if necessary
    Try an emergency stop
    Check the handbrake on a steep incline

Lights and electrical components
    Check the operation of all lights, instruments and controls

Engine compartment
    Check the level of oil in the engine sump
    Check the level of coolant in the radiator
    Check the battery electrolyte level
    Top up washer fluid reservoir

Every 5000 miles (8000 km) or 6 months – whichever comes first

---

    Change engine oil and renew oil filter
    Check front brake pad thickness
    Clean and adjust spark plugs

Every 10 000 miles (16 000 km) or 12 months – whichever comes first

---

Engine
    Renew air cleaner element
    Clean flame trap for crankcase ventilation
    Clean fuel pump filter and sediment chamber

    Top up the carburettor damper with oil
    Check carburettor settings
    Check and, if necessary, adjust valve clearances (ohv models only)
    Check ignition timing and reset if necessary
    Renew spark plugs
    Clean and examine ignition HT leads

Clutch
    Check clutch pedal free play and reset pedal height if necessary

Brakes
    Inspect brake pipes, hoses, calipers and wheel cylinders for condition and leakages
    Check rear brake lining thickness
    Check handbrake ratchet for wear and handbrake lever travel
    Examine handbrake cable for fraying and corrosion
    Check that the brake master cylinder filler cap vent hole is clear

Steering and suspension
    Examine all the steering linkages, rods, joints, bushes and rubber boots for signs of wear or deterioration
    Examine the front suspension balljoints for wear
    Examine the dampers/struts for leakage and deterioration of mounting rubbers

Checking a tyre pressure

Checking brake hydraulic fluid level

Topping up engine oil (930 engine)

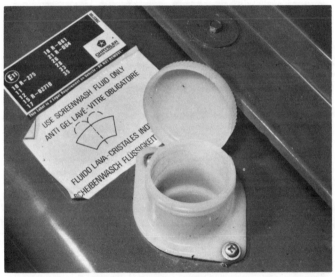

Screen washer fluid filler

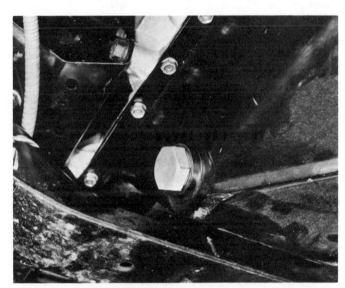

Sump drain plug

Topping up the manual gearbox

Rear axle filler plug

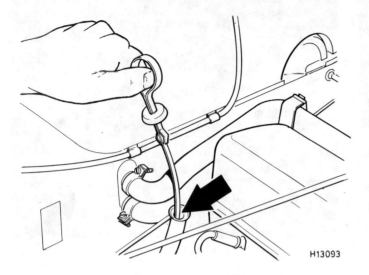

H13093

Checking the fluid level (automatic transmission)

Wheels
Check wheel nuts for tightness

Electrical
Clean battery terminals, clamp and carrier. Smear parts with petroleum jelly

General mechanical
Check cooling and fuel systems for leaks
Check condition of water, fuel, vacuum and oil hoses and clips
Examine the exhaust system for security, condition and gas leaks
Check steering rack, engine, gearbox and final drive for leaks

Body
Clean door drain holes and heater intake drain
Examine safety belts for condition and operation
Check and, if necessary, top up gearbox and final drive
Check and, if necessary, top up automatic transmission (where applicable)
Lubricate accelerator linkage and pivots
Lubricate door and bonnet hinges and catches
Lubricate clutch and brake pedal pivots

Operation check
Brakes and steering
Clutch and manual gearbox
Automatic gearbox (shift speeds – adjust cable if necessary)

Every 20 000 miles (32 000 km) or 2 yearly – whichever comes first

---

Engine
Renew air cleaner element
Check valve clearances (930 ohc engine)

Suspension
Adjust front hub endfloat

Brakes
Bleed old fluid from system and recharge with new fluid

Cooling system
Every two years in the autumn, renew anti-freeze mixture

Every 40 000 miles (64 000 km) or every 4 years – whichever comes first

---

Suspension
Clean out all lubricant from front hub, repack and adjust

Brakes
Renew all hydraulic assembly rubber seals

Chapter 1 Part A 930 engine

For modifications, and information applicable to later models, see Supplement at end of manual

Contents

Specifications

Engine (general)

Type	4 cylinder in-line, overhead camshaft
Capacity	56.6 in³ (928 cc)
Bore	2.756 in (70.0 m)
Stroke	2.374 in (60.3 m)
Compression ratio	9.0:1
Power output (max)	42 DIN bhp at 5000 rpm
Torque (max)	51 lbf ft at 2600 rpm
Firing order	1-3-4-2 (No 1 at timing cover end)
Engine rotation	Clockwise (viewed from timing cover)
Compression pressure at cranking speed	180 to 195 lbf/in² (12.4 to 13.1 bar)

Cylinder block

Material	Aluminium alloy with cast iron liners
Cylinder bore diameters:	
Grade A	2.7553 to 2.7556 in (69.985 to 69.992 mm)
Grade B	2.7556 to 2.7559 in (69.992 to 70.000 mm)
Grade C	2.7559 to 2.7562 in (70.000 to 70.007 mm)
Cylinder bore oversizes	+ 0.015 in (0.381 mm) + 0.030 in (0.762 mm)

Crankshaft

Main bearing running clearance	0.0010 to 0.0027 in (0.025 to 0.069 mm)
Endfloat	0.002 to 0.010 in (0.05 to 0.25 mm)
Thrust washer oversize	+ 0.005 in (0.127 mm)
Big-end running clearance	0.0010 to 0.0027 in (0.025 to 0.069 mm)
Big-end side clearance	0.012 to 0.016 in (0.305 to 0.411 mm)
Main journal diameter	1.8750 to 1.8755 in (47.625 to 47.638 mm)

Crankpin diameter	1.6245 to 1.6250 in (41.262 to 41.275 mm)
Crank grinding undersizes	0.020 in (0.508 mm), 0.040 in (0.1016 mm)

Pistons

Piston to bore clearance	0.0010 to 0.0016 in (0.025 to 0.041 mm)
Piston diameters:	
Grade A	2.7540 to 2.7543 in (69.951 to 69.959 mm)
Grade B	2.7543 to 2.7546 in (69.959 to 69.967 mm)
Grade C	2.7546 to 2.7549 in (69.967 to 69.975 mm)
Grade D	2.7549 to 2.7552 in (69.975 to 69.982 mm)
Piston grades A and B are only fitted during production	
Piston oversizes	+ 0.015 in (0.381 mm) + 0.030 in (0.762 mm)
Piston ring end gap	0.008 to 0.013 in (0.203 to 0.330 mm)
Gudgeon pin offset	0.040 in (1.016 mm)
Gudgeon pin fit	Thumb pressure at 68°F (20°C)

Camshaft

Valve timing:	
Inlet opens	27° BTDC
Inlet closes	61° ABDC
Exhaust opens	55° BBDC
Exhaust closes	9° ATDC
Camshaft journal diameter	0.9370 to 0.9375 in (23.800 to 23.813 mm)
Bearing running clearance	0.0002 to 0.0018 in (0.005 to 0.046 mm)
Camshaft endfloat	0.002 to 0.007 in (0.051 to 0.178 mm)

Cylinder head and valves

Cylinder head material	Aluminium alloy
Maximum reduction of cylinder head depth during refacing	0.005 in (0.127 mm)
Valve seat angle	45°
Valve guide bore	0.2810 to 0.2815 in (7.14 to 7.15 mm)
Valve guide outside diameter:	
Standard	0.5016 to 0.5020 in (12.74 to 12.75 mm)
Oversizes	+ 0.001 in (0.025 mm). + 0.003 in (0.076 mm)
Interference fit	0.0008 to 0.002 in (0.02 to 0.05 mm)
Valve clearances (Cold):	
Inlet	0.006 to 0.008 in (0.15 to 0.20 mm)
Exhaust	0.008 to 0.010 in (0.20 to 0.25 mm)
Valve face angle	45°
Valve seat width	0.057 in (1.45 mm)
Inlet valve:	
Head diameter	1.200 to 1.204 in (30.480 to 30.582 mm)
Stem diameter	0.2785 to 0.2790 in (7.074 to 7.087 mm)
Stem to guide clearance	0.002 to 0.003 in (0.051 to 0.076 mm)
Exhaust valve:	
Head diameter	1.062 to 1.066 in (26.975 to 27.076 mm)
Stem diameter	0.2775 to 0.2780 in (7.048 to 7.061 mm)
Stem to guide clearance	0.003 0.004 in (0.076 to 0.102 mm)
Valve seat inserts:	
Outside diameter:	
Inlet	1.3395 to 1.3405 in (34.023 to 34.049 mm)
Exhaust	1.1275 to 1.1285 in (28.639 to 28.664 mm)
Oversizes	+ 0.002 in (0.050 mm), + 0.005 in (0.127 mm)
Interference fit	0.0025 to 0.0045 in (0.063 to 0.114 mm)
Valve springs:	
Type	Single coil
Free length	1.54 in (39.12 mm)
Fitted length	1.12 in (28.45 mm)
Tappets:	
Diameter	1.000 to 1.010 in (2.54 to 25.65 mm)
Length	0.715 to 0.735 in (18.2 to 18.7 mm)

Lubrication system

Oil pump type	Rotor
Oil pressure (hot) at 50 mph (80 km/h)	30 lbf/in² (2 bar)
Oil capacity	5.25 pints (3.0 litres)

Torque wrench settings

	lbf ft	Nm
Stud tightening	6	8
Alternator to mounting bracket	16	22
Camshaft bearing cap	5	7
Camshaft cover screws	5	7
Carburettor to manifold	8	11
Chain tensioner bolts	5	7
Cylinder head to timing cover bolts	15	20
Engine front mounting to crossmember	27	37

Fuel pump mounting nuts	15	20
Manifold nuts to cylinder head	15	20
Oil filter base to crankcase	15	20
Oil pump mounting nuts	5	7
Tappet guide housing nuts	5	7
Timing cover to crankcase	15	20
Oil drain pipe to crankcase	8	11
Oil pressure gauge adaptor to block	32	44
Oil pressure gauge sender unit to adaptor	10	14
Oil pressure switch to adaptor	4	6
Alternator bracket to cylinder block	15	20
Alternator bracket to timing cover	15	20
Camshaft sprocket to camshaft	19	26
Connecting rod cap bolts	18	25
Crankshaft pulley bolt	32	44
Cylinder head bolts	36	49
Engine rear mounting to body	12	16
Engine rear mounting to extension housing	26	35
Flywheel bolts	40	54
Engine front mounting bracket to crankcase (plain bolts)	34	46
Engine front mounting bracket to crankcase (Durlock bolts)	44	60
Engine front mounting to bracket	15	20
Main bearing cap bolts	40	54
Oil filter base to crankcase	15	20
Sump screws	5	7
Thermostat housing bolts	15	20
Water pump bolts to timing cover	16	22
Water pump screws to impeller housing	11	15

1 General description

The engine is of the four cylinder in-line, overhead camshaft type, the cylinder block, cylinder head, timing cover and camshaft cover being of light alloy construction. Non-removable cast iron cylinder liners are used. Three crankshaft main bearings are incorporated with crankshaft endfloat being controlled by semi-circular thrust washers. Aluminium pistons are fitted to connecting rods which have big-end mating faces 50° to the vertical, to permit easy removal through the cylinder bores.

The overhead camshaft is supported in three bearings and is driven by a single roller chain, this being tensioned automatically. Valve clearances are set by steel shims placed between the valve stems and the tappets.

The oil pump is driven at half engine speed by a gear on the front end of the crankshaft. The oil pump driveshaft incorporates an extension to drive the distributor.

2 Major operations possible with engine fitted

The following work can be carried out with the engine still in position in the car.

Removal and refitting of:

(a) The engine front and rear mountings
(b) The cylinder head and camshaft
(c) The sump
(d) The pistons and connecting rods
(e) The oil pump and oil filter
(f) The timing cover, chain and tensioner

3 Major operations requiring engine or gearbox removal

1 The crankshaft and main bearings can only be removed if the engine is first withdrawn.
2 The flywheel or the rear crankshaft oil seal can be reached either by removing the engine, or by leaving the engine in position and removing the gearbox.
3 If the engine is removed for major or complete dismantling, it is recommended that the ancillary components are first removed. These include the following and reference should be made to the Chapters indicated for complete removal and dismantling procedures:

Starter motor (Chapter 10)

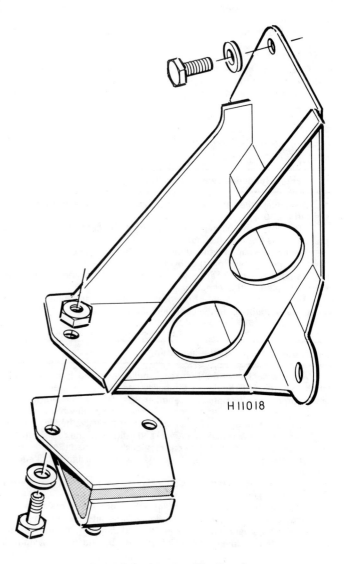

H 11018

Fig. 1.1 Engine mounting (front)

Alternator (Chapter 10)
Water pump (Chapter 2)
Distributor (Chapter 4)
Spark plugs (Chapter 4)
Clutch assembly (Chapter 5)
Fuel pump (Chapter 3)
Manifolds (Chapter 3)
Carburettor (Chapter 3)

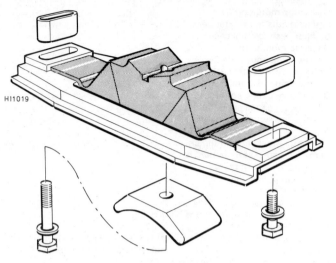

Fig. 1.2 Engine mounting (rear)

4 Engine mountings – removal and refitting

Front mountings

1   Place the car over an inspection pit, or raise the front on axle stands or on ramps.
2   Unscrew and remove the nuts and washers that secure the mountings to the crossmember.
3   Release the clip that secures the clutch cable to the mounting bracket.
4   Support the weight of the engine under the sump, using a jack and a block of wood as an insulator.
5   Unbolt the engine mounting bracket from the cylinder block and remove the mounting assembly. On the right-hand side of the engine the jack will have to be raised a little higher, to allow the engine mounting stud to clear the front crossmember.
6   Refitting is a reversal of removal, but the type of bolt used to attach the mounting bracket to the cylinder block should be noted. On earlier cars, bolts and plain washers are used. Thread locking compound must be applied to these bolt threads. On later cars, 'Durlock' bolts are used which incorporate serrated integral locking flanges. This type of bolt does not require thread locking compound.

Rear mounting

7   To remove the rear mounting, loosen the centre bolt that holds the rear mounting to the gearbox extension housing.
8   Support the gearbox on a jack and then remove the centre bolt and rebound plate.
9   Unscrew the two securing bolts and remove the mounting assembly.
10   Refitting is a reversal of removal.

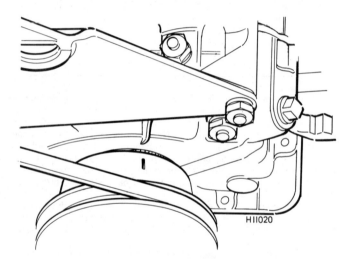

Fig. 1.3 Alignment of timing marks

5 Camshaft cover – removal and refitting

1   Disconnect the vacuum pipe that runs between the distributor and the carburettor.
2   Disconnect the oil separator pipe from the camshaft cover, also the fuel pipes from the fuel pump.
3   Release the clips that hold the coolant hose to the camshaft cover. Move the hose away from the cover.
4   Remove the camshaft cover nuts and washers and remove the cover complete with fuel pump.
5   Refitting is a reversal of removal, but always use a new gasket if there is any doubt about the condition of the original one.

6 Camshaft – removal and refitting

1   Apply a socket to the crankshaft pulley bolt and turn the crankshaft until the TDC marks on the pulley and timing cover are in alignment; then turn the crankshaft another 90°. This will ensure that the pistons are all at a position approximately half way down the cylinder bores. This operation is necessary to prevent the valve heads contacting the piston crowns during removal and refitting of the camshaft.
2   Remove the camshaft cover as previously described (Section 5).
3   The chain tensioner should now be restrained using a tool similar to the one shown (photo).
4   Flatten the camshaft sprocket lockplate tab and then remove the sprocket bolt, lockwasher and plain washer (photo).
5   Withdraw the camshaft sprocket, taking great care not to let the positioning dowel in the camshaft flange drop into the timing cover. Disengage the chain from the sprocket and drape the chain over the side of the timing cover, holding it in position by attaching a weight to it with a piece of wire.
6   Mark the camshaft bearing caps as to their relative positions and

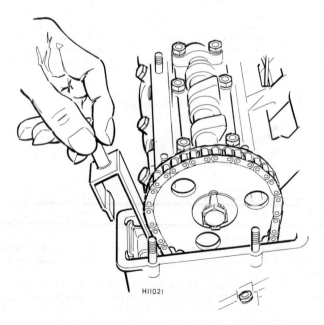

Fig. 1.4 Inserting timing chain restraining tool

6.3 Timing chain tensioner blade located in upper slide

6.4 Camshaft sprocket, bolt and lockplate

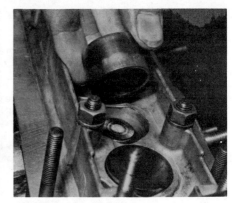
6.8 Withdrawing a tappet

6.9 Withdrawing a tappet shim

6.12A Camshaft bearing shell

6.12B Refitting camshaft

6.17 Camshaft sprocket alignment marks

7.8 Oil drain pipe

7.11 Removing tappet guide housing

7.17 Cylinder block O-ring seal

7.18 Refitting cylinder head

7.22 Tightening a cylinder head bolt

then release the cap securing nuts evenly, a turn at a time.
7   Lift off the bearing caps and shells and remove the camshaft. Extract the lower bearing shells.
8   If necessary, the tappets can be withdrawn from their guides in the lower bearing housing using a suction cap (valve grinding tool) (photo).
9   Retrieve the shim located between the tappet and valve stem. It is very important that the tappets and shims are kept in their original order for refitting (see Section 9) (photo).
10   All the dismantled components should now be examined for wear or damage and renovation carried out as described in Section 25 of this Chapter.
11   To refit the camshaft, refit the shims and tappets and check that the pistons are still at their previously set positions.
12   Apply engine oil to the camshaft bearings and journals. Refit the lower shells and the camshaft, followed by the upper shells and caps (photos).
13   Tighten the cap nuts to the specified torque, evenly and progressively.
14   At this stage, it is recommended that the camshaft sprocket is temporarily fitted without the chain, and the camshaft rotated to check the tappet clearances as described in Section 9.
15   Remove the camshaft. Rotate the crankshaft until the TDC marks on the pulley and timing cover are in alignment; feeding the chain through as the crankshaft is turned.
16   Refit the camshaft with the dowel peg at the top. Lubricate the bearings and journals, refit the bearing upper shells and caps in their correct positions. Tighten the cap nuts evenly and progressively to the specified torque.
17   Fit the camshaft sprocket, without the bolt, and then turn the sprocket and camshaft until the scribed lines on the sprocket are in alignment with the top flange of the timing cover (photo).
18   Pull the sprocket from the camshaft and then engage it within the loop of the timing chain in such a position that the sprocket can be refitted to the camshaft without altering the alignment described in the preceding paragraph.
19   Fix the sprocket bolt (finger tight) with a new tab washer and plain washer.
20   Remove the timing chain restraining tool. Check that the crankshaft and camshaft are still in their correct positions, reposition if necessary.
21   Tighten the sprocket bolt to the specified torque and bend up both tabs on the lockplate. If the flats on the bolt do not align with the tabs, tighten the bolt further.
22   Refit the camshaft cover as described in Section 5.

7   Cylinder head – removal and refitting

If the engine is in the car, carry out the following preliminary operations (paragraphs 1 to 8).
1   Drain the cooling system and disconnect the brake servo vacuum hose from the inlet manifold.
2   Release the throttle cable support bracket and disconnect the inner throttle cable from the carburettor.
3   Disconnect the choke inner and outer cables.
4   Disconnect the vacuum advance pipe from the carburettor. Remove the air cleaner.
5   Disconnect the spark plug leads. Disconnect the coolant hose from the camshaft cover and then disconnect the hose from the cylinder head.
6   Disconnect the heater hose from the cylinder head.

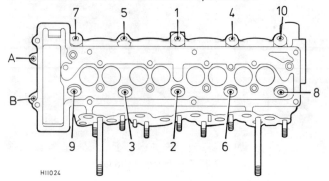
Fig. 1.5 Cylinder head bolt tightening sequence

7   Disconnect the exhaust downpipe from the manifold.
8   Remove the oil drain pipe that runs between the cylinder head and the crankcase (photo).
9   Remove the camshaft cover and the camshaft as described in Sections 5 and 6.
10   Extract the tappets and shims, keeping them in their exact original order.
11   Unscrew the nuts and remove the tappet guide housing (photo).
12   Remove the two nuts that secure the cylinder head to the timing cover (A and B in Fig. 1.5), then release the cylinder head bolts evenly. Commence at the end bolts and work towards the centre. It is important that the bolt lengths and their locations are noted as each one is withdrawn. It is suggested that a paper copy of the new cylinder head gasket is taken and the bolts pushed through the paper in their appropriate positions.
13   Hold the timing chain fully extended and then lift the cylinder head, allowing the chain to pass through the aperture at the front of the head. The cylinder head will come away complete with carburettor and manifolds.
14   Remove and discard the cylinder head gasket and O-ring seal.
15   To refit the cylinder head, first make sure that the timing marks on the crankshaft pulley and engine front cover are in alignment (No 1 position at TDC).
16   Make sure that the cylinder head and cylinder block mating faces are absolutely clean and then locate a new cylinder head gasket on the block.
17   Grease a new O-ring and locate it in its cylinder block recess (photo).
18   Support the timing chain vertically, passing it through the aperture in the cylinder head as the cylinder head is lowered into position (photo).
19   Drape the chain over the side of the aperture.
20   Fit the timing chain tensioner restraining tool (see paragraph 3, Section 6).
21   Dip the cylinder head bolts in clean engine oil and allow them to drain. Screw in the bolts finger tight, ensuring that the bolts, which are of differing lengths, are located in their original positions. The longest bolt goes into the right-hand rear hole and the four shortest bolts in the remaining holes on the right-hand side.
22   Tighten the bolts progressively, in the sequence shown in Fig. 1.5, to their specified torque (photo).
23   Refit the washers and nuts to the timing cover studs (A and B in Fig. 1.5) and tighten to the specified torque.
24   Refit the tappet guide housing, tightening the nuts to the specified torque.
25   Refit the tappet shims and tappets to their original locations.
26   Refit the camshaft and cover after reference to Sections 5 and 6.
27   Reconnect and refit all the components listed in paragraphs 1 to 8 if the engine is in the car. Refill the cooling system.
28   At the end of the first 1000 miles (1600 km) the cylinder head bolts should be rechecked for the correct torque loading with the engine cold.
29   Unless the special tool (RG 355) is available, the camshaft will have to be removed for access to some of the bolts.
30   Working to the sequence given in Fig. 1.5, loosen the first bolt slightly and then retighten to the specified torque. Repeat on the remaining bolts.

8   Cylinder head – dismantling, decarbonising and reassembly

1   With the cylinder head removed from the engine, unbolt and remove the manifolds.
2   Unscrew and remove the sparking plugs.
3   Place the cylinder head on the bench and tap each valve spring cap with a mallet to free the split cotters.
4   Now use a valve spring compressor to compress the first valve spring until the split cotters can be extracted. Remove the spring compressor and then take off the valve spring cap, the spring and the valve stem oil seal. Note that the inlet valve stem oil seals have clips on them (photo).
5   Remove the valve. As the valves must be kept in their original fitted sequence, use a rack or card with holes punched in it and numbered 1 to 8 to keep them in order.
6   Repeat the operations on the remaining valves.
7   With the cylinder head off, carefully remove, with a wire brush and

8.4 Compressing a valve spring

8.13 Refitting a valve

8.14A Inlet valve oil seal

8.14B Valve spring and cap

9.7 Checking a valve clearance

9.11 Valve clearance adjusting shim

blunt scraper, all traces of carbon deposits from the combustion spaces and ports. The valve head stems and valve guides should also be freed of any carbon deposits. Wash the combustion spaces and ports down with petrol and scrape the cylinder head surface free of any foreign matter with a brass scraper, or one made of a similar soft metal.

8   Clean the pistons and top of the cylinder bores. If the pistons are still in the block then it is essential that great care is taken to ensure that no carbon gets into the cylinder bores, as this could scratch the cylinder walls or cause damage to the piston and rings. To ensure this does not happen, first turn the crankshaft so that two of the pistons are at the top of their bores. Stuff rag into the other two bores or seal them off with paper and masking tape. The waterways should also be covered with small pieces of masking tape to prevent particles of carbon entering the cooling system and damaging the water pump.

9   The cylinder head should now be examined in conjunction with the advice given in Section 25. If the valve seats and guides and the valves themselves are in good condition, then the valves should be ground in the following way.

10 Smear a trace of coarse carborundum paste on the seat face and apply a suction grinder tool to the valve head. With a semi-rotary motion, grind the valve head to its seat, lifting the valve occasionally to redistribute the grinding paste. When a dull matt surface finish is produced on both the valve seat and the valve, wipe off the paste and repeat the process with fine carborundum paste, lifting and turning the valve to redistribute the paste as before. A light spring placed under the valve head will greatly ease the operation. When a smooth unbroken ring of light grey matt finished is produced on both valve and valve seat faces, the grinding operation is completed.

11 Scrape away all carbon from the valve head and the valve stem. Carefully clean away every trace of grinding compound, taking great care to leave none in the ports or in the valve guides. Clean the valves and valve seats with a paraffin soaked rag, then with a clean rag, and finally, if an air line is available, blow the valves, valve guides and valve ports clean.

12 To reassemble the cylinder head, apply engine oil to the stem of the first valve to be fitted.

13 Refit the valve into its guide (photo).

14 Refit the oil seal, the spring and the cap (photos).

15 Compress the valve spring and refit the split collets in the cut-out in the valve stem. Slowly release the compressor, taking care that the split collets are not displaced.

16 Repeat the refitting operations on all the remaining valves. Make sure that the valves are returned to the seats into which they were ground.

17 Place the cylinder head on the bench and tap the top of each valve spring with a hammer and block of wood, to settle the components.

18 Refit the manifolds, using new gaskets, and tightening the bolts to the specified torque.

19 Refit the spark plugs.

9   Valve clearances – checking and adjusting

1   The valve adjustment MUST be made with the engine cold. The importance of correct valve clearances cannot be overstressed as they vitally affect the performance of the engine.

2   If the clearances are set too open, the efficiency of the engine is reduced as the valves open later and close earlier than was intended. If, on the other hand the clearances are set too close, there is a danger that the stems will expand upon heating and not allow the valves to close properly; this will cause burning of the valve head and seat and possible warping.

3   To check valve clearances it will be necessary to remove the cambox cover. If the engine is in the car this can be done by referring to Section 5.

4   Clearances are checked with a feeler gauge between the tappet flat face and the heel of the cam (opposite side of the cam to the peak), when the cam peak is pointing toward the centre of the valve cover (if it were fitted).

5   Using the following sequence all clearances can be checked in only two complete revolutions of the crankshaft:

Valve	Cam
No 1 Cyl Exhaust valve	No 2
No 2 Cyl Inlet valve	No 3
No 3 Cyl Exhaust valve	No 6
No 1 Cyl Inlet valve	No 1

No 4 Cyl Exhaust valve	*No 8*
No 3 Cyl Inlet valve	*No 5*
No 2 Cyl Exhaust valve	*No 4*
No 4 Cyl Inlet valve	*No 7*

The correct clearances are given in the Specifications Section.

6   The engine may be rotated by using a suitable spanner on the camcase pulley bolt head. If for some reason the valve clearances are being checked when the timing chain is disconnected, then the camshaft can be turned by temporary refitment of the camshaft sprocket. However, it is extremely important that all pistons are half-way down their cylinders, otherwise a valve may contact a piston. To accomplish this, turn the engine 90° either way from TDC.

7   The clearance is measured by sliding a feeler gauge blade between the heel of the camshaft and the top of the tappet (photo).

8   If it is found when checking the valve clearances that some exceed or are smaller than the permitted clearances, then it will be necessary to re-shim the tappet pistons. Instructions are given in the following paragraphs.

9   Write down the numbers 1 to 8 across the top of a sheet of paper. Measure the clearance of each valve and write it down under its number, eg 0.006 for No 1 valve, 0.009 for No 2 and so on.

10   Next work out what should be added or subtracted from each clearance to bring it within tolerance. For example, an inlet valve with a clearance of 0.010 in will need 0.002 or 0.003 in added to the tappet shim to bring it back to the correct clearance. Similarly, if the valve clearance were 0.004 in then 0.002 to 0.003 would need to be subtracted from the thickness of the tappet shim. Write down the addition or subtraction for each valve beneath its number.

11   To remove the shims, the camshaft must be withdrawn as described in Section 6. Extract the tappet and the shim from each position and record the thickness engraved on one of the faces of the shim (photo).

12   If the marking has been erased due to wear, measure the thickness using a micrometer and mark the shim with a piece of tape (photo).

13   When the thickness of every shim has been recorded, add or subtract the thickness needed to bring the clearance for each shim within tolerance. For example, it has already been decided that 0·003 in should be added to the shim to bring a clearance within tolerance. When the shim was removed it was found to be 0·095 in in thickness. Therefore, the shim needed to obtain the correct clearance for this particular valve is one of 0·098 in thickness.

14   When the correct thickness of the shim has been determined for each valve, the correct shims can be purchased from your Chrysler dealer. Beneath is an example of what your calculations should look like for one valve.

Valve No 1 Inlet (correct clearance 0.0060 to 0.008 in)

Existing clearance	*0.010 in*
Thickness to be added to tappet shim to bring clearance within tolerance	*0.003 in*
Thickness of existing shim	*0.093 in*
Thickness of shim required to bring clearance within tolerance	*0.096 in*

In this case a shim of 0·096 in thickness should be substituted for the existing shim.

15   When the new shims have been obtained, place them in their correct tappet pistons. Take great care to ensure that they do go into the correct tappet pistons, because if they are incorrectly fitted your work will be nullified.

16   Refit the camshaft in position as described in Section 6. Recheck the valve clearances to ensure that they are all correct. Refit the camshaft sprocket, cambox, fuel pipes, etc, as necessary.

10   Timing cover, chain and tensioner – removal and refitting

1   If the engine is in the car, carry out the following preliminary operations (to paragraph 4).

2   Disconnect the battery and drain the cooling system.

3   Remove the radiator assembly and the alternator.

4   Drain the engine oil, disconnect the front mountings and raise the engine about ¾ in (19·0 mm), using a hoist to avoid obstructing the sump, which is to be removed later.

5   Remove the cylinder head as described in Section 7, using the timing chain tensioner restrainer.

6   Remove the distributor cap and leads.

7   Release the bolts that secure the water pump to the timing cover and swing the water pump to one side.

8   Release the crankshaft pulley bolt. This can usually be unscrewed if a socket and bar are fitted to it and the bar struck a sharp blow. This will cause the tab on the lockwasher to shear at the same time. The tab is otherwise very difficult to bend back. If this method of releasing the bolt is not successful, the flywheel starter ring gear can be jammed after removing the starter, or the crankshaft secured by placing a wooden block between one of the crankshaft webs and the side of the crankcase, after first having drained the engine oil and removed the sump.

9   Remove the crankshaft pulley, using two levers behind it if necessary, and then retrieve the broken locking tab.

10   Drain the engine oil and remove the sump.

11   Unscrew and remove the timing cover nuts.

12   Withdraw the timing chain tensioner restrainer and pull off the timing cover complete with oil pump and distributor.

13   To remove the timing chain tensioner, release the securing bolts and withdraw the tensioner blade, the spring and the bracket.

14   To remove the timing chain damper, release the securing nuts and bolts and withdraw it.

15   Remove the timing chain from the crankshaft sprocket. If necessary, the skew gear and the sprocket can be removed from the front end of the crankshaft using a two-legged puller.

16   Inspect all components for wear or damage as described in Section 25.

17   Commence reassembly by refitting the sprocket to the crankshaft using hand pressure. Fit the oil pump skew gear so that the key engages and then drive it tight against the sprocket using a piece of tubing (photos).

18   Engage the timing chain with the crankshaft sprocket teeth.

19   If the timing chain damper was removed, refit it inside the timing cover and tighten the securing bolts.

20   Refit the tensioner assembly insert the bolts and lockplate (photo).

21   Tighten the bolts and then bend over the corners of the lockplate (photo).

22   Examine the timing cover oil seal. It is recommended that it is renewed as a matter of routine whenever a major overhaul is carried out. Removal and refitting of the oil seal can be done using a piece of suitable diameter tubing. Smear the inner and outer edges of the new seal with grease before refitting.

23   Check the oil seal contact surface of the pulley for scoring. Light grooves can be polished away using abrasive paper, but severe wear can only be eradicated by renewing the pulley.

24   Refit a new oil seal at the oil passage that runs between the timing cover and oil seal (photo).

25   Check that the mating faces of the timing cover and the cylinder block are perfectly clean.

26   Fit a new timing cover gasket in position on the cylinder block.

27   Check that No 1 piston is at TDC. If it is not, temporarily refit the crankshaft pulley and turn the pulley by hand.

28   Set the refitting position of the oil pump and distributor driveshafts, by turning the distributor rotor until its contact end is at 45° to a line drawn between the two flange mounting bolt holes.

29   Refit the timing cover without disturbing the O-ring seal. As the cover is fitted, the oil pump gear will mesh with the skew gear on the crankshaft and the distributor rotor will turn to take up one of the following positions according to make of distributor; (i) opposite No 1 spark plug segment in the distributor cap (Lucas) or, (ii) in alignment with the notch in the distributor body (Bosch).

30   If the distributor was removed from the timing cover after dismantling, the timing cover must be refitted after setting the oil pump driveshaft in accordance with (A) Fig. 1.6. As the cover is refitted, the oil pump driveshaft dog will turn and take up the position shown in (B). Refit the distributor as described in Chapter 4, Section 4 (photo).

31   Refit and tighten the timing cover nuts to the specified torque.

32   Refit the sump (Section 11).

33   Refit the crankshaft pulley, a new lockplate and screw in the bolt. Tighten the bolt to the specified torque, preventing the crankshaft turning as described in paragraph 8. Bend down the locking tab (photo).

34   Refit the water pump, alternator and drivebelt. Refit the cylinder head (Section 7) (photos).

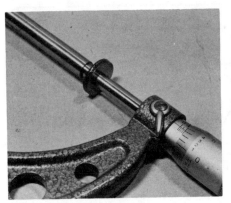
9.12 Measuring shim thickness

10.17A Crankshaft timing sprocket

10.17B Oil pump skew gear fitted to crankshaft

10.20 Timing chain and tensioner

10.21 Timing chain tensioner bolts and lockplate

10.24 Timing cover oil passage seal

10.30 Refitting the timing cover

10.33 Crankshaft pulley and bolt

10.34A Water pump and drive pulley

10.34B Alternator rear mounting bracket

10.34C Alternator in position

10.34D Drivebelt refitted

24

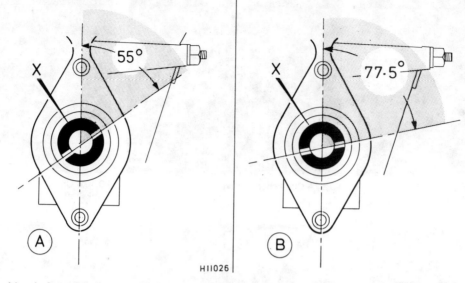

Fig. 1.6 Oil pump driveshaft setting diagrams (Sec. 10) A Setting before installing pump. B Setting after installing pump. X Larger segment

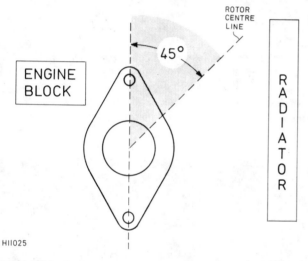

Fig. 1.7 Distributor rotor positioning diagram for correct setting of oil pump driveshaft (Sec. 10)

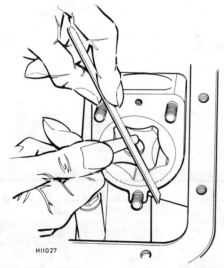

Fig. 1.9 Checking oil pump rotor endfloat (Sec. 13)

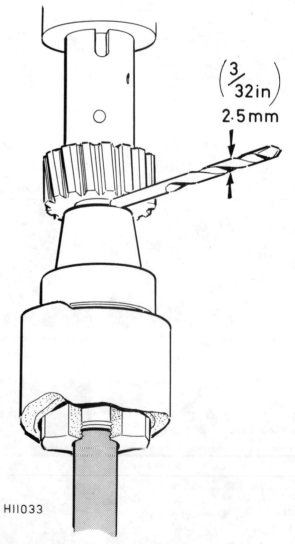

Fig. 1.8 Supporting oil pump spindle and using a drill to locate driven gear (Sec. 13)

11.7 Refitting the sump

12.3 Oil pump and pick-up filter

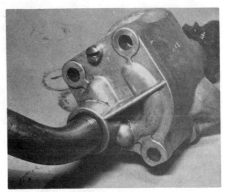
13.1 Oil pump showing baseplate screw

35 If the engine is in the car, refit the radiator and hoses and lower the engine onto its mountings.
36 Refill the cooling system and the crankcase.
37 Connect the battery.
38 After starting the car and running to operating temperature, check the ignition timing (Chapter 4, Section 5).

11 Sump – removal and refitting

1 If the engine is in the car, carry out the preliminary operations described up to paragraph 4.
2 Place the car over an inspection pit, or raise the front end on axle stands or on ramps.
3 Disconnect the battery.
4 Release the front mountings and raise the engine about ¾ in (19·0 mm) by placing a jack under the gearbox.
5 Drain the engine oil.
6 Unscrew and remove the sump bolts and lower the sump. If this is done carefully, the gasket can probably be salvaged for further use. If it breaks or tears, renew it.
7 Refitting is a reversal of removal (photo).

12 Oil pump – removal and refitting

1 Apply a socket to the crankshaft pulley bolt. Turn the crankshaft until the timing marks are in alignment (TDC) and the distributor rotor is pointing towards No 1 segment in the distributor cap.
2 Remove the sump as described in Section 11.
3 Unscrew and remove the three securing nuts and withdraw the oil pump (photo).
4 To refit the oil pump, clean both flange mating surfaces and fit a new joint gasket.
5 Check that the engine is still set with No 1 piston at TDC and the timing marks aligned.
6 Hold the oil pump ready for refitting onto its mounting studs and then turn the driveshaft so that the drive dog takes up position (A) in Fig. 1.6. Refit the oil pump. The dog will now be in position (B), the shaft having turned by the meshing of the oil pump gears.
7 If the distributor is still in position when the oil pump is refitted, make sure that the drive dogs engage and then when the pump is fully home, check that the distributor rotor is opposite No 1 segment in the distributor cap. If it is not, withdraw the pump and adjust the position of the oil pump driveshaft.
8 Tighten the oil pump nuts to the specified torque, refit the sump and fill the engine with oil.

13 Oil pump – overhaul

1 With the pump removed from the engine as described in the preceding Section, extract the screw that secures the baseplate and pick-up assembly (photo).
2 Turn the pump upside down and remove the baseplate (photo).
3 Turn the pump over, holding the internal components in position

by hand. Shake the pump to eject the outer rotor. Do not drop the outer rotor as it is glass hard and is easily fractured. Refit the outer rotor, chamfered end first (photo).
4 Clean all components free from oil and inspect for wear or scoring.
5 The pump can be checked to see if it is still serviceable in the following way.
6 The rotor endfloat can be checked by placing a straight edge across the pump face and inserting a feeler gauge between the straight edge and the rotor end faces. The clearance must not exceed 0·003 in (0·075 mm).
7 Again using a feeler gauge, check the clearance between the tips of the lobes of the inner and outer rotors. This should not exceed 0.006 in (0.15 mm) (photo).
8 Finally, check the clearance between the outer rotor and the pump body. This should not exceed 0·008 in (0.2 mm) (photo).
9 If any of the foregoing checks indicates wear is greater than permissible, renew the pump complete.
10 If the oil pump driven gear must be removed, carefully remove the peening from one side of each pin. Drive out the pins.
11 Press the spindle from the gear using a press or extractor.
12 When refitting the driven gear, it is essential that the end of the spindle is supported, not the inner rotor. Using a 3/32 in (2·5 mm) diameter twist drill as a gauge positioned on the pump body, press the gear onto the spindle until it just contacts the drill. Make sure that the pin holes line up.
13 The pin holes will now have to be drilled using a ⅛ in (3·2 mm) diameter drill. Peen new pins in position.
14 Commence reassembly by applying engine oil to the rotors.
15 Refit the baseplate/pick-up assembly without gasket or jointing compound. Make sure that the filter screen is perfectly clean.
16 It should be noted that a new oil pump driven gear is only supplied with a matching drive gear for the crankshaft.

14 Pistons and connecting rods – removal, dismantling, reassembly and refitting

1 Remove the cylinder head and sump as previously described in this Chapter.
2 Scrape away any carbon ring from the top of the cylinder bores; also carefully remove the wear ridge if one can be felt, otherwise the piston rings will not pass over it when they are being pushed out of the bores.
3 Turn the crankshaft until the first piston is at its lowest position in the cylinder bore.
4 Now check that the big-ends and their caps are numbered. If they are not, dot punch the connecting rod and cap at adjacent points, numbering 1 to 4 from the front of the engine.
5 Note also towards which side of the engine the markings face, so that the rods will be refitted the correct way round.
6 Remove the big-end bolts, cap and bearing shell. Keep the shell with the cap if it is to be used again (photo).
7 Push the connecting rod and piston out of the top of the cylinder block. If the shell is displaced from the rod, retrieve it and place it in the connecting rod recess.
8 Repeat the operations on the remaining pistons and connecting rods.

9   Inspect and renovate the components as described in Section 25.

10   The piston rings can be removed using a twisting action. It will be found an easy job if two or three feeler blades are first slid behind the ring and positioned at equidistant points round the piston. Always remove the top ring first, and slide all rings from the top of the piston, never from the bottom.

11   To disconnect the connecting rod from the piston, extract the circlip from both ends of the gudgeon pin. Warm the piston in hot water until the gudgeon pin can be pushed out.

12   To reassemble, fit a new circlip into the groove of one of the piston bosses.

13   Warm the piston and hold the piston and connecting rod in their correct relative positions. Push the gudgeon pin into position until the pin contacts the circlip in the opposite piston boss. Refit the second circlip.

14   The alignment of the piston to the rod is critical. With the word 'FRONT' on the piston crown towards the front of the engine, the larger portion of the big-end shell bearing recess at the base of the rod must be towards the distributor (photo).

15   Check that the piston ring grooves and oilways are thoroughly clean and unblocked. Piston rings must always be fitted over the head of the piston and never from the bottom.

16   The easiest method to use when fitting rings is to wrap a feeler gauge round the top of the piston and place the rings one at a time, starting with the bottom oil control ring, over the feeler gauge.

17   The feeler gauge, complete with ring, can then be slid down the piston over the other piston ring grooves until the correct groove is reached. The piston ring is then slid gently off the feeler gauge into the groove.

18   An alternative method is to fit the rings by holding them slightly open with the thumbs and both of your index fingers. This method requires a steady hand and great care as it is easy to open the ring too much and break it.

19   Refer to Section 25 for details of testing the rings in the bores and grooves before refitting.

20   The top and bottom piston rings can be fitted either way up, but

the second ring must be fitted with its step at the bottom.

21   Stagger the piston ring gaps at equidistant points round the piston, lubricate the rings liberally and then fit a piston ring compressor.

22   Turn the crankshaft to bring No 1 journal to its lowest point. Oil the cylinder bores.

23   Refit the first piston/rod assembly into the cylinder bore, until the base of the ring compressor is resting squarely on the top of the cylinder block. Check that the 'FRONT' mark on the piston crown is towards the front of the engine (photo).

24   Rest the wooden handle of a hammer on the piston crown. Give a sharp blow to the head of the hammer with the hand to drive the assembly into the block. The piston ring compressor will be ejected as the piston enters the bore.

25   Refit the bearing shell into the rod recess and then draw the rod down into contact with the crankshaft journal.

26   Refit the shell to the big-end cap. Refit the cap and then insert new bolts and tighten them to the specified torque (photos).

27   Refit the remaining three piston/connecting rod assemblies in the same way.

28   Turn the crankshaft to check for smooth rotation.

29   Refit the sump and cylinder head as described in earlier Sections of this Chapter.

15   Engine – methods of removal

The engine can be removed leaving the gearbox in the car, or by removing the complete engine with gearbox and separating them once they are withdrawn. Both methods are described in the following Sections.

16   Engine (without gearbox) – removal and refitting

1   Disconnect the battery.

2   Drain the cooling system (Chapter 2).

3   Mark the position of the bonnet hinges and remove the bonnet.

4   Disconnect the throttle and choke cables.

5   Disconnect the fuel inlet pipe from the fuel pump.

6   Disconnect the brake servo hose from the inlet manifold.

7   Disconnect the distributor vacuum hose from the carburettor.

8   Disconnect the exhaust downpipe from the manifold.

9   Disconnect the electrical leads from the starter motor, the oil pressure sender unit and the coolant temperature sender unit.

10   Move the spring clip and withdraw the multi-plug from the rear of the alternator.

11   Disconnect the coil high tension lead, also the distributor multi-plug.

12   Disconnect the coolant outlet hose at the cylinder head and release the hose from the cam box by prising off the clips (photo).

13   Working under the car, disconnect the coolant inlet hose from the water pump.

14   Disconnect the clutch cable from the release fork arm.

15   Disconnect the engine front mountings from the crossmember.

16   Unbolt and remove the cover from the lower half of the clutch bellhousing. It is possible for these cover bolts to foul the anti-roll bar when being withdrawn. In this case, raise the engine slightly by levering it between the bellhousing and the anti-roll bar.

17   Unscrew and remove the lower bellhousing to engine bolts, also the starter motor lower mounting bolt.

18   Resume operations within the engine compartment by disconnecting the leads from the radiator fan motor and the temperature sensor switch.

19   Remove the radiator, fan and bracket assembly, complete with top and bottom hoses attached.

20   Disconnect the heater hoses at the cylinder head and bypass pipe.

21   Unscrew and remove the starter motor upper bolt and withdraw the starter motor.

22   Release the reversing lamp switch leads from their clip. Loosen the two top clutch bellhousing to engine bolts.

23   Suitable lifting gear should now be attached to the engine. It is recommended that a lifting sling or chain should be connected to the hole in the engine front plate, then passed under the neck of the exhaust manifold, round the rear of the engine block and up underneath the heater pipe on the cylinder head (photo).

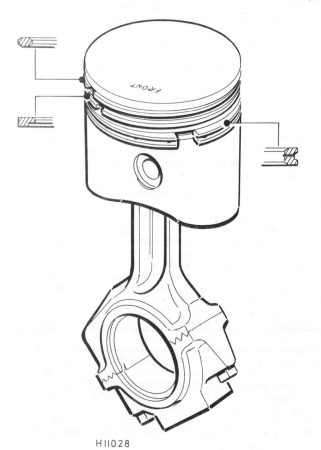

H11028

Fig. 1.10 Piston to connecting rod assembly diagram and piston ring fitting arrangement (Sec. 14)

13.2 Oil pump baseplate removed

13.3 Removing oil pump outer rotor

13.7 Checking oil pump rotor lobe clearance

13.8 Checking oil pump outer rotor to body clearance

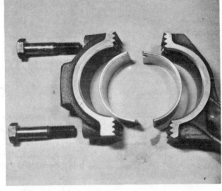
14.6 Connecting rod big-end components

14.14 Piston crown markings

14.23 Piston with piston ring compressor

14.26A Fitting a big-end cap

14.26B Connecting rod big-end cap fitted

16.12 Coolant outlet hose

16.23 Engine front plate

17.2 Engine earth strap

24 Support the weight of the gearbox by placing a jack under the clutch bellhousing.
25 Take the weight of the engine, so that the two bellhousing upper bolts can be removed. Continue to raise the engine until the engine mounting studs clear the crossmember.
26 Pull the engine forward off the gearbox input shaft. Take care not to displace the gearbox jack. Hoist the engine from the engine compartment (photo).
27 Refitting is a reversal of removal, but to make the work easier, observe the following points.
28 Remove the engine flexible mounting from the right-hand support bracket.
29 Check that the two dowels are fitted in the rear face of the cylinder block.
30 If the clutch assembly has been removed and refitted, make sure that the driven plate has been centralised (Chapter 5).
31 As the engine is mated with the input shaft, turn the crankshaft slightly to engage the splines. Do this by applying a socket to the crankshaft pulley bolt.
32 Once the engine has been refitted, check that the earth strap is reconnected under the starter motor upper mounting bolt.
33 Adjust the clutch pedal height (Chapter 5).
34 Refill the cooling system (Chapter 2).
35 Refill the engine with oil, if drained.

17 Engine (with gearbox) – removal and refitting

1 Carry out the operations described in paragraphs 1 to 11 in the preceding Section.
2 Disconnect the earth lead that runs from the starter motor upper bolt to the body (photo).
3 Disconnect the battery lead from the starter motor.
4 Remove the cylinder head oil drain pipe.
5 Working inside the car, if the car does not have a centre console, extract the four screws from the gear lever gaiter. Raise the gaiter and extract the three screws that hold the gear lever cover. Remove the gear lever.
6 If the car is fitted with a centre console, release the locknut and remove the gear knob. Disconnect the leads from the electric clock (if fitted). Extract the five screws and remove the centre console. Remove the console fixing bracket, the insulating pad and gaiter. Extract the gear lever screws and remove the gear lever.
7 Place the car over an inspection pit, or raise the car both at the front and the rear and support it securely on axle stands.
8 Unbolt and remove the propeller shaft guard.
9 Remove the propeller shaft as described in Chapter 7.
10 Disconnect the speedometer cable and the reversing lamp switch wires from the gearbox.
11 Disconnect the clutch cable from the release lever.
12 Remove the nuts that secure the front mountings to the crossmember.
13 Support the gearbox with a jack and then remove the bolts that hold the rear mounting crossmember to the body.
14 Again working within the engine compartment, extract the reversing lamp switch wires from their clip on the clutch bellhousing.
15 Connect a suitable hoist, as described in paragraph 23 of Section 5, and take the weight of the engine.
16 Lower the jack under the gearbox until the engine and gearbox are at a steeply inclined angle.
17 Lift the engine and gearbox from the car.
18 Refitting is a reversal of removal, but on completion remember to adjust the clutch, refill the cooling system (and oil if drained), and reconnect the battery.

18 Engine/gearbox – separation and reconnection

1 With the engine and gearbox removed complete from the car, the first job is to clean away all external dirt and grease. A water-soluble solvent, or paraffin and a stiff brush are both suitable for this work.
2 Support the engine and gearbox using blocks of wood. Remove the cover from the lower face of the clutch bellhousing.
3 Remove the starter motor and the bellhousing to engine bolts.
4 Support the weight of the gearbox and withdraw it, in a straight line, from the engine.

Fig. 1.11 Sealing rear main bearing cap (Sec. 19)

5 Reconnection is a reversal of separation, but make sure that the alignment dowels are in position on the cylinder block mating face and, if the clutch assembly has been disturbed, that the driven plate has been centralised (Chapter 5).

19 Crankshaft and bearings – removal and refitting

1 Remove the engine as described in the earlier Section of this Chapter.
2 Remove the cylinder head (Section 7).
3 Remove the sump (Section 11).
4 Remove the timing chain cover, chain and tensioner (Section 10).
5 Remove the clutch assembly and unbolt and remove the flywheel (Section 20).
6 Unbolt and remove the big-end caps. Number them carefully if they are not already marked and keep the bearing shells with their respective caps.
7 If the piston and connecting rods are not to be removed (see Section 14) the rods can be left in their disconnected positions in the bores.
8 Release the main bearing cap bolts evenly, noting the cap markings and which way round they are fitted. If there is any doubt, identify them by dot punching the caps and the adjacent crankcase webs.
9 Remove the caps and lift the crankshaft from the crankcase.
10 Extract the bearing upper shells, identifying them in respect of location (using a piece of adhesive tape) if they are to be used again.
11 Remove and discard the crankshaft rear oil seal.
12 Inspect the condition of all components and renovate in conjunction with Section 25 of this Chapter.
13 Before refitting the crankshaft, probe the oil holes in the crankshaft and crankcase with a piece of wire. Remove all sealant from the rear main bearing cap and oil seal recess.
14 Locate the bearing shells in the crankcase recesses (photo).
15 Stick the two semi-circular thrust washers into the recesses on either side of the centre main bearing web in the crankcase, using thick grease. Note the oil grooves face outward (photo).
16 Oil the crankcase bearing shells liberally and then lower the crankshaft into position (photo).
17 Refit the front and centre main bearing caps with their shells. Refit the bolts and tighten to the specified torque.
18 Refit a new crankshaft rear oil seal, so that its lip is towards the front of the engine. Apply grease to the seal lips (photo).
19 Refit the rear main bearing cap and tighten the bolts to the specified torque (photo).
20 Using recommended sealant (Hylosil), apply the nozzle of the tube to the groove at each side of the rear main bearing cap. Inject the sealant until a drop of sealant emerges from between the bearing cap

19.14 Main bearing shell in crankcase

19.15 Crankshaft thrust washer

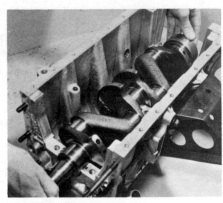
19.16 Refitting crankshaft

19.18 Crankshaft rear oil seal

19.19 Fitting rear main bearing

20.5 Flywheel refitted

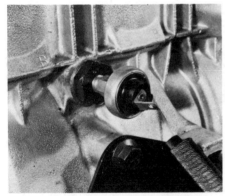
22.5 Oil pressure warning lamp switch

23.5 Oil filter

24.5 Oil filter base removed

24.8 Oil filter base refitted

25.8 Cylinder bore grading marks

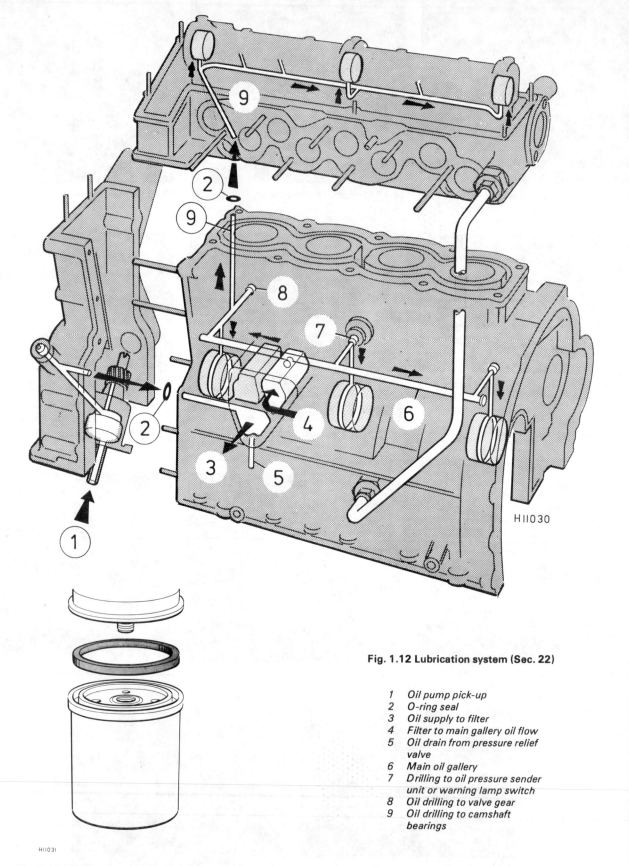

H11030

Fig. 1.12 Lubrication system (Sec. 22)

1   Oil pump pick-up
2   O-ring seal
3   Oil supply to filter
4   Filter to main gallery oil flow
5   Oil drain from pressure relief
     valve
6   Main oil gallery
7   Drilling to oil pressure sender
     unit or warning lamp switch
8   Oil drilling to valve gear
9   Oil drilling to camshaft
     bearings

H11031

Fig. 1.13 Oil filter and sealing ring (Sec. 22)

and block.
21 Refit the connecting rods to their crankpins.
22 Refit the flywheel and the clutch.
23 Refit the timing cover and components.
24 Refit the sump and cylinder head and refit the engine.

20 Flywheel – removal and refitting

1 If the engine has been removed, then obviously access to the clutch and flywheel is immediate. If the flywheel is to be removed without the prior need for engine withdrawal, then it is easier to remove the gearbox (Chapter 6) leaving the engine in position in the car.
2 Mark the relative position of the clutch cover to the flywheel and then remove the clutch.
3 Unscrew the flywheel bolts evenly and progressively and lift the flywheel from the dowel on the crankshaft mounting flange.
4 Inspect the condition of the starter ring gear, also the spigot bearing in the centre of the crankshaft rear flange and renovate as described in Section 25.
5 Refitting is a reversal of removal. Tighten the flywheel bolts to the specified torque (photo).

21 Crankshaft rear oil seal – renewal with engine in position in car

1 Remove the gearbox (Chapter 6), the clutch (Chapter 5) and flywheel (Section 20).
2 Prise the oil seal from its recess and clean the recess thoroughly.
3 Grease the new seal and push it into position using hand pressure.
4 Using the old seal as a drift, tap the new seal fully home in its seating.
5 Refit the flywheel, clutch and gearbox.

22 Lubrication system – description

1 Oil is drawn from the sump through a gauze filter and pressurised by a rotor type oil pump mounted in the timing cover. The pump is driven by a gear on the front end of the crankshaft.
2 Oil pressure is regulated by a regulator valve in the oil filter base.
3 The oil flow is through a cartridge type full-flow filter to the main oil gallery and through drillings for the crankshaft main bearings.
4 The connecting rod crankpins are supplied with oil through drillings in the crankshaft webs.
5 The oil pressure sender unit is screwed into a drilling that is an extension from the drilling to the centre main bearing (photo).
6 The camshaft bearings and valve gear are supplied with oil through a drilling from the front main bearing.
7 The tappets are lubricated from the camshaft bearings.
8 The timing chain, tensioner and sprockets are lubricated by oil draining from the front of the cylinder head. There is also an oil drain pipe that runs between the cylinder head and the crankcase, to take excess oil from around the valve gear.
9 Splash lubrication is provided for the cylinder bores, the gudgeon pins, cams and tappets, the valve stems, timing chain tensioner, chain, sprockets and oil pump drive gear.

23 Oil filter cartridge – renewal

1 It is usual to renew the oil filter at the same time as the engine oil is changed.
2 Drain the engine oil first and refit the drain plug.
3 Place a container below the oil filter and unscrew the cartridge. If it is stuck tight, use a chain or strap wrench. If such a tool is not available, a screwdriver can be driven through one side of the cartridge so that it emerges from the opposite side and the screwdriver then used as a lever to unscrew the cartridge.
4 Discard the old filter and clean the contact surface on the cylinder block.
5 Smear the rubber sealing ring on the new filter with engine oil and screw it into position as tightly as possible *using hand pressure only* (photo).

6 Refill the engine with oil, adding an extra pint (0·57 litres) for absorption by the new filter.
7 Start the engine. It will take a few seconds for the oil warning lamp to go out (or oil pressure to register on the gauge). This will happen when the new filter is filled with oil.

24 Oil filter base and relief valve – removal and refitting

1 Place a container below the filter.
2 Unscrew and remove the nut and bolts that hold the base to the engine.
3 Withdraw the filter base and discard the gasket.
4 If the relief valve is to be dismantled it is recommended that it is released before the filter base is removed, as it is very tight.
5 With the filter base removed, unscrew and remove the relief valve (photo).
6 The valve cannot be dismantled, but it can be washed in paraffin whilst holding the piston off its seat with a plunger, provided it is dried thoroughly before refitting.
7 Screw the valve into the base finger tight.
8 Refit the filter base, using a new gasket smeared sparingly with jointing compound (photo).
9 Tighten the filter base bolts and nut and the relief valve to the specified torque.

25 Examination and renovation

1 Full dismantling procedures have been included in the earlier Sections of this Chapter, but unless any fault is immediately apparent or previously known, the dismantled components should be inspected as described in the following paragraphs:

Crankshaft
2 Examine the crankpin and main journal surfaces on the crankshaft for scoring or scratches that may be present. Check the ovality of the crankpins and main journals at different positions with a micrometer. If more than 0·001 in (0·0254 mm) out of round, the crankpins and journals will have to be reground. Also check the journals in the same fashion. On highly tuned engines the centre main bearing has been known to break up. This is not always immediately apparent, but slight vibration in an otherwise normally smooth engine and a very slight drop in oil pressure under normal conditions are clues. If the centre main bearing is suspected of failure it should be immediately investigated by dropping the sump and removing the centre main bearing cap. Failure to do this will result in a badly scored centre main journal. If it is necessary to regrind the crankshaft and fit new bearings, your local Chrysler garage or engineering works will be able to decide how much metal to grind off and the correct undersize shells to fit. If the spigot bearing in the crankshaft rear flange is worn, extract it with a suitable puller and press in a new one. The bearing is pre-packed with grease and requires no further lubrication.

Big-end and main bearings
3 Big-end bearing failure is accompanied by a noisy knocking from the crankcase and a slight drop in oil pressure. Main bearing failure is accompanied by vibration, which can be quite severe as the engine speed rises and falls, and a drop in oil pressure. Bearings which have not broken up, but are badly worn will give rise to low oil pressure and some vibration. Inspect the big-ends, main bearings and thrust washers for signs of general wear, scoring, pitting and scratches. The bearing should be matt grey in colour. With lead bronze bearings, should a trace of copper colour be noticed the bearings are badly worn, as the lead bearing material has worn away to expose the indium underlay. Renew the bearings if they are in this condition or if there is any sign of scoring or pitting. If you are not sure how worn the bearings are take them to the stores at your local garage and compare them with new ones.
4 The undersizes available are designed to correspond with the regrind sizes ie 0·010 in (0·254 mm) bearings are correct for a crankshaft reground 0·010 in (0·254 mm) undersize. The bearings are in fact slightly more than the stated undersize as running clearances have been allowed for during their manufacture.
5 Examine the mating faces of the big-end caps to see if they have ever been filed in a mistaken attempt to take up wear. If so, the offend-

ing rods must be renewed.

6   Check the alignment of the rods visually, and if misaligned take the rods to your local Chrysler agent for checking on a special jig.

Cylinder bores, pistons and piston rings

7   The cylinder block is of aluminium alloy formed round cast iron liners. The liners cannot be removed but they can be rebored to accept oversize pistons.

8   Cylinder bores are graded A, B or C and marked externally at the centre of the block (photo).

9   Pistons are graded A, B C or D and marked on the piston crown. Details of cylinder bore diameters, piston diameters and clearances are given in the Specifications.

10   The cylinder bores must be examined for taper, ovality, scoring and scratches. Start by carefully examining the top of each bore. If they are at all worn a very slight ridge will be found on the thrust side. This marks the top of the piston ring travel. The owner will have a good indication of bore wear prior to dismantling the engine or removing the cylinder head. Excessive oil consumption accompanied by blue smoke from the exhaust is a sure sign of worn cylinder bores and piston rings.

11   Measure the bore diameter just under the ridge with a micrometer and compare it with the diameter at the bottom of the bore, which is not subject to wear. If the difference between the two measurements is more than 0·006 in (0·15 mm), then it will be necessary to fit special pistons and rings or to have the cylinders rebored and fit over-size pistons.

12   If the bores are slightly worn but not so badly worn as to justify reboring them, then special oil control rings and pistons can be fitted which will restore compression and stop the engine burning oil. Several different types are available and the manufacturer's instructions concerning their fitting must be followed closely.

13   If new pistons or rings are being fitted and the bores have not been reground, it is essential to slightly roughen the hard glaze on the sides of the bores. This process is called 'glazebusting'. With a partly worn piece of No 1 or 1½ grade emery paper, gently rub the interior of the bore, working up and down and rotating on each bore until the entire cylinder wall is criss-crossed with abrasions.

14   An easier way to carry out this task is to make a mandrel about 10 in (250 mm) long with a slot 2 in (50 mm) long in one end, from a piece of welding rod, or similar, of approximately $\frac{3}{16}$ in (5 mm) thickness. Mount a piece of emery paper (1 to 1½ grade) slightly wider than the bore in the mandrel slot. Place the unslotted end of the mandrel in the chuck of an electric drill and work up and down each bore with the emery paper for about two minutes.

15   Pistons are available in oversizes as shown in the Specifications Section but in practice, the reborers will normally supply matching pistons of the correct grading to give the specified clearance in the new bores.

16   If the old pistons are to be refitted, carefully remove the piston rings and then thoroughly clean them. Take particular care to clean out the piston ring grooves. At the same time do not scratch the aluminium in any way. If new rings are to be fitted to the old pistons then the top ring should be stepped, so as to clear the ridge left in the bore above the previous top ring. If a normal but oversize new ring is fitted, it will hit the ridge and break because the new ring will not have worn in the same way as the old, which will have worn in unison with the ridge.

17   Before fitting the rings on the pistons each should be inserted approximately 2¼ in (60 mm) down the cylinder bore and the end gap measured with a feeler gauge. This should be between 0·008 in and 0·013 in. It is essential that the gap should be measured at the bottom of the ring travel, as if it is measured at the top of a worn bore and gives a perfect fit, it could easily seize at the bottom. If the ring gap is too small, rub down the end of the ring with a very fine file until the gap, when fitted, is correct. To keep the rings square in the bore for measurement, line each up in turn by inserting an old piston in the bore upside down and use the piston to push the ring down about 2¼ in (60 mm). Remove the piston and measure the piston ring gap.

18   When fitting new pistons and rings to a rebored engine, the piston ring gap can be measured at the top of the bore as the bore will not now taper. It is not necessary to measure the side clearance in the piston ring grooves with the rings fitted, as the groove dimensions are accurately machined during manufacture. When fitting new oil control rings to pistons it may be necessary to have the grooves widened by machining to accept the new wider rings. In this instance the manufacturers representative will make this quite clear, and will supply

the address to which the pistons must be sent for machining.

Camshaft and camshaft bearings

19   The camshaft bearings are not subject to heavy wear and it is therefore, difficult to tell when they should be renewed. However, it is a good idea to renew them as a matter of course on a major overhaul.

20   The camshaft bearings are renewable in pairs, like the other plain bearings in the engine. They require no special fitting and are therefore new bearings simply substituted for the old ones. Bearing caps or shells should **not** be filed.

21   The camshaft itself should show no signs of wear but if very slight scoring on the cams is noticed, the score can be removed by very gentle rubbing down with a very fine emery cloth. The greatest care should be taken to keep the cam profiles smooth and not to break through the case hardening. If the cam lobes are worn it is more satisfactory to buy a new camshaft.

Timing chain, sprockets and tensioner

22   The timing chain sprockets will be well worn if their teeth are hooked in appearance.

23   To check the chain for wear, hold it horizontally with the link plates to top and bottom. Support the chain with a finger at each end and if the chain takes on a deeply bowed appearance, it is badly worn.

24   The tensioner slipper should be renewed if it is deeply grooved or scored.

Tappets

25   Examine the bearing surface of the tappets which lie beneath the camshaft. Any indentation in this surface or any cracks indicate serious wear and the tappets should be renewed. It is most unlikely that the sides of the tappets will prove worn but it they are a very loose fit in their bores and can readily be rocked, they should be exchanged for new units. It is very unusual to find any wear in the tappets and any wear present is likely to occur only at very high mileages.

Valves, valve seats and guides

26   Examine the heads of the valves for pitting and burning, especially the head of the exhaust valves. The valves seatings should be examined at the same time. If the pitting on valve and seat is very slight, the marks can be removed by grinding the seats and valves together with coarse, and then fine, valve grinding paste (refer to Section 8). Where bad pitting has occured to the valve seats if will be necessary to recut them and fit new valves. If the valve seats are so worn that they cannot be recut, then it will be necessary to fit new valve seat inserts. These latter two jobs should be entrusted to the local Chrysler agent or engineering works. In practice it is very seldom that the seats are so badly worn that they require renewal. Normally, it is the exhaust valve that is too badly worn for renewal and the owner can easily purchase a new set of valves and match them to the seats by valve grinding.

27   Examine the valve guides internally for wear. If the valves are a very loose fit in the guides and there is the slightest suspicion of lateral rocking using a new valve, then new guides will have to be fitted. If the valve guides have been removed, compare them internally by visual inspection with a new guide as well as testing them for rocking with a new valve. If new valve guides are needed this is a job for your Chrysler garage or engineering works.

28   The valve springs should be renewed if the engine has covered 30 000 miles (48 000 km) since the last major overhaul.

Flywheel

29   If the teeth on the flywheel starter ring are badly worn, or if some are missing, then it will be necessary to remove the ring. After drilling a hole as large as possible between the base of two teeth (this hole should almost penetrate to the flywheel) split the ring with a cold chisel.

30   The new ring should be heated in an oven (not direct flame) to a temperature of 428°F (220°C). Most domestic ovens can achieve this temperature.

31   When the ring is uniformly heated, place the ring on the flywheel with the chamfered sides of its teeth facing the clutch side of the flywheel. Gently tap the ring into place against its locating face on the flywheel. As the ring cools it will contract until it gets a firm and permanent grip on the flywheel.

32   If the clutch mating surface of the flywheel is scored, or there are a number of tiny cracks caused by overheating, it may be possible to

have the surface refinished. If, however, very much metal has to be removed to achieve worthwhile results, the flywheel will have to be renewed.

26 Engine reassembly – general

1 Precise reassembly is described in the foregoing Sections, but the following general operations should be carried out in advance of reassembly.
2 To ensure maximum life with minimum trouble from a rebuilt engine, not only must everything be correctly assembled, but all the parts must be spotlessly clean, all the oilways must be clear, locking washers and spring washers must always be fitted where indicated and all bearing and other working surfaces must be thoroughly lubricated during assembly. Before assembly begins renew any bolts or studs, the threads of which are in any way damaged, and whenever possible use new spring washers.
3 Apart from your normal tools, a supply of clean rag, an oil can filled with engine oil (an empty plastic detergent bottle thoroughly cleaned and washed out will invariably do just as well), a new supply of assorted spring washers and a set of new gaskets should be gathered together. A torque wrench is essential as the engine is largely made from aluminium. If a torque wrench cannot be bought then one must be borrowed, otherwise trouble will be experienced after a few thousand miles through aluminium components distorting.

4 If the engine has been completely stripped, the following reassembly sequence is recommended.

(a) Crankshaft
(b) Flywheel
(c) Pistons/connecting rods
(d) Oil pump
(e) Sump
(f) Timing chain, tensioner and cover
(g) Cylinder head
(h) Camshaft
(j) Ancillary components (clutch, oil filter, alternator etc)

27 Initial start-up after major overhaul

1 Adjust the throttle speed screw to provide a faster than normal idling speed. This will offset the stiffness of the engine, due to new components being fitted.
2 Start the engine and check for oil and water leaks.
3 Run the engine until normal operating temperature is reached and then adjust the slow-running.
4 Dependent upon the number of new internal components which have been fitted, the engine speed should be restricted for the first few hundred miles. It is recommended that the engine oil and filter are changed after the initial 1000 miles (1600 km) running.

28 Fault diagnosis – engine

Symptom	Reason/s
Engine will not turn over when starter switch is operated	Flat battery Bad battery connections Bad connections at solenoid switch and/or starter motor Defective starter motor
Engine turns over normally but fails to start	No spark at plugs No fuel reaching engine Too much fuel reaching the engine (flooding)
Engine starts but runs unevenly and misfires	Ignition and/or fuel system faults Incorrect valve clearances Burnt out valves Worn out piston rings
Lack of power	Ignition and/or fuel system faults Incorrect valve clearances Burnt out valves Worn out piston rings
Excessive oil consumption	Oil leaks from crankshaft, rear oil seal, timing cover gasket and oil seal, rocker cover gasket, oil filter gasket, sump gasket, sump plug washer Worn piston rings or cylinder bores resulting in oil being burnt by engine Worn valve guides and/or defective inlet valve stem seals
Excessive mechanical noise from engine	Wrong valve clearances Worn crankshaft bearings Worn cylinders (piston slap) Slack or worn timing chain and sprockets

Note: *When investigating starting and uneven running faults do not be tempted into snap diagnosis. Start from the beginning of the check procedure and follow it through. It will take less time in the long run. Poor performance from an engine in terms of power and economy is not normally diagnosed quickly. In any event the ignition and fuel systems must be checked first before assuming any further investigation needs to be made*

Chapter 1 Part B   1300 and 1600 engines

Contents

Specifications

Engine (general)

Type . . . .   Four cylinder in-line overhead valve
Capacity:
    1300 engine . . . .   79.0 in³ (1295 cm³)
    1600 engine . . . .   97.5 in³ (1598 cm³)
Bore:
    1300 engine . . . .   3.09 in (78.6 mm)
    1600 engine . . . .   3.44 in (87.3 mm)
Stroke . . . .   2.625 in (66.7 mm)
Compression ratio:
    High compression (hc) 8.8:1
    Low compression (lc) 7.8:1

Power output (max):	**1.50 carburettor**	**1.75 carburettor**
1300 engine	59 DIN bhp at 5000 rpm	N/A
1600 engine	69 DIN bhp at 4800 rpm	80 DIN bhp at 5400 rpm
Torque (max):	**1.50 carburettor**	**1.75 carburettor**
1300 engine	69 lbf ft at 2600 rpm	N/A
1600 engine	91 lbf ft at 2900 rpm	86 lbf ft at 4400 rpm

Firing order . . . .   1–3–4–2 (No 1 at timing cover end)
Engine rotation . . . .   Clockwise (viewed from timing cover)
Compression pressure at cranking speed:
    High compression with 1.50 carb . . . .   160 to 180 lbf/in² (11.0 to 12.4 bar)
    High compression with 1.75 carb . . . .   150 to 170 lbf/in² (10.3 to 11.7 bar)
    Low compression with 1.50 carb . . . .   150 to 160 lbf/in² (10.3 to 11.0 bar)

Cylinder block
Material . . . .   Cast-iron

Cylinder bore diameters:	**1300 engine**	**1600 engine**
Grade A	3.0945 to 3.0949 in	3.4384 to 3.4388 in
	(78.600 to 78.610 mm)	(87.335 to 87.346 mm)
Grade B	3.0949 to 3.0953 in	3.4388 to 3.4392 in
	(78.610 to 78.621 mm)	(87.346 to 87.356 mm)
Grade C	3.0953 to 3.0957 in	3.4392 to 3.4396 in
	(78.621 to 78.631 mm)	(87.356 to 87.366 mm)
Grade D	3.0957 to 3.0963 in	3.4396 to 3.4402 in
	(78.631 to 78.646 mm)	(87.366 to 87.381 mm)

Cylinder bore oversize .... + 0.030 in (+ 0.762 mm)
Cylinder liner outside diameter:
   1300 engine .... 3.241 to 3.242 in (82.32 to 82.34 mm)
   1600 engine .... 3.587 to 3.588 in (91.11 to 91.13 mm)
Interference fit in block .... 0.002 to 0.004 in (0.050 to 0.100 mm)

Crankshaft
Main bearing running clearance .... 0.0008 to 0.0028 in (0.020 to 0.07 mm)
Endfloat .... 0.002 to 0.008 in (0.05 to 0.20 mm)
Thrust washer oversize .... + 0.005 in (+ 0.127 mm)
Big-end running clearance .... 0.0009 to 0.0024 in (0.02 to 0.06 mm)
Big-end side clearance .... 0.007 to 0.019 in (0.18 to 0.48 mm)
Main journal diameters:
   Class A .... 2.1245 to 2.1252 in (53.962 to 53.980 mm)
   Class B .... 2.1145 to 2.1152 in (53.708 to 53.726 mm)
Crankpin diameter:
   Class A .... 1.9995 to 2.0000 in (50.787 to 50.800 mm)
   Class B .... 1.9895 to 1.9900 in (50.533 to 50.546 mm)
Crank grinding undersizes .... 0.010 in (0.254 mm) – Class A only: 0.020 in (0.508 mm);
0.040 in (1.016 mm)

Pistons and rings
Piston to bore clearance .... 0.0029 to 0.0037 in (0.07 to 0.09 mm)
Maximum piston weight difference .... 0.3 oz (8.8 g)

Piston diameters:	**1300 engine**	**1600 engine**
Grade A	3.0912 to 3.0916 in	3.4351 to 3.4355 in
	(78.517 to 78.527 mm)	(87.252 to 87.262 mm)
Grade B	3.0916 to 3.0920 in	3.4355 to 3.4359 in
	(78.527 to 78.537 mm)	(87.262 to 87.272 mm)
Grade C	3.0920 to 3.0924 in	3.4359 to 3.4363 in
	(78.537 to 78.547 mm)	(87.272 to 87.282 mm)
Grade D	3.0924 to 3.0928 in	3.4363 to 3.4367 in
	(78.547 to 78.557 mm)	(87.282 to 87.292 mm)
Grade E	3.0928 to 3.0932 in	3.4367 to 3.4371 in
	(78.557 to 78.567 mm)	(87.292 to 87.302 mm)

Piston grades A and B are only fitted during production
Piston oversize .... 0.030 in (0.0762 mm)
Piston ring gap:
   Top compression .... 0.014 to 0.019 in (0.36 to 0.48 mm)
   2nd compression and oil control:
      1300 engine .... 0.009 to 0.014 in (0.23 to 0.36 mm)
      1600 engine .... 0.020 to 0.025 in (0.25 to 0.38 mm)
Gudgeon pin:
   Type .... Fully floating
   Fit .... Thumb pressure at 68°F (20°C)

Camshaft
Valve timing:
   1300 hc and lc, 1600 hc ('hi-torque'), all with 1.50 carburettor:
      Inlet opens .... 38° BTDC
      Inlet closes .... 66° ABDC
      Exhaust opens .... 72° BBDC
      Exhaust closes .... 20° ATDC
   1300 engine with 1.75 carburettor:
      Inlet opens .... 44° BTDC
      Inlet closes .... 78° ABDC
      Exhaust opens .... 69° BBDC
      Exhaust closes .... 23° ATDC
   1600 lc, 1600 hc (excluding 'hi-torque') with 1.50 carburettor:
      Inlet opens .... 44° BTDC
      Inlet closes .... 86° ABDC
      Exhaust opens .... 66° BBDC
      Exhaust closes .... 20° ATDC
Camshaft journal diameter:
   Front bearing .... 1.9345 to 1.9352 in (49.136 to 49.154 mm)
   Centre bearing .... 1.7470 to 1.7477 in (44.374 to 44.392 mm)
   Rear bearing .... 1.5595 to 1.5602 in (39.611 to 39.629 mm)

Camshaft bearing running clearance .... 0.0013 to 0.003 in (0.033 to 0.076 mm)
Camshaft endfloat .... 0.002 to 0.008 in (0.05 to 0.20 mm)

Cylinder head and valves
Cylinder head material .... Cast iron
Maximum reduction of cylinder head depth during refacing .... 0.005 in (0.127 mm)
Valve seat angle .... 45°
Valve guide bore:
    Standard .... 0.3125 to 0.3135 in (7.937 to 7.962 mm)
    Oversizes .... + 0.003 in (0.076 mm) – production only; + 0.015 in (0.381 mm); + 0.030 in (0.762 mm)
Valve clearances (Hot or Cold):
    1.50 carburettor:
        Inlet .... 0.008 in (0.20 mm)
        Exhaust .... 0.016 in (0.40 mm)
    1.75 carburettor:
        Inlet .... 0.010 in (0.25 mm)
        Exhaust .... 0.016 in (0.40 mm)
Valve face angle .... 44° 40'
Valve seat width (minimum) .... 0.114 in (2.9 mm)
Inlet valve head diameter:
    1300 engine .... 1.448 in (36.78 mm)
    1600 engine .... 1.498 in (38.05 mm)
Exhaust valve head diameter:
    1300 engine .... 1.228 in (31.19 mm)
    1600 engine .... 1.228 in (31.19 mm)
Inlet valve stem diameter:
    Standard .... 0.3110 to 0.3115 in (7.889 to 7.912 mm)
    Oversizes .... + 0.003 in (0.076 mm) - production only; + 0.015 in (0.381 mm); + 0.030 in (0.762 mm)
Inlet valve stem to guide clearance .... 0.001 to 0.0025 in (0.025 to 0.064 mm)
Exhaust valve stem diameter:
    Standard .... 0.3095 to 0.3100 in (7.861 to 7.874 mm)
    Oversizes .... As for inlet valves
Exhaust valve stem to guide clearance .... 0.0025 to 0.004 in (0.064 to 0.102 mm)
Valve springs:
    Type .... Single coil with 1.50 carburettor; double coil with 1.75 carburettor
Free length:
    Single .... 1.592 in (40.44 mm)
        Double (inner) .... 1.260 in (32.00 mm)
        Double (outer) .... 1.592 in (40.44 mm)
    Fitted length:
        Single .... 1.331 in (33.80 mm)
        Double (inner) .... 1.373 in (34.90 mm)
        Double (outer) .... 1.154 in (29.31 mm)

Lubrication system
Oil pump type .... Rotor
Oil pressure (hot) at 50 mph (80 km/h): .... 50 to 60 lbf/in^2 (3.4 to 4.1 bar)
Oil capacity .... 7 pints (4.0 litres)

Torque wrench settings

	lbf ft	Nm
Cylinder head bolts and nuts	60	82
Camshaft thrust plate bolts	9	12
Timing chain tensioner bolts	7	10
Bellhousing to engine bolts	34	46
Clutch to flywheel bolts	16	22
Crankshaft pulley bolt	50	68
Driveplate to torque converter	34	46
Driveplate to crankshaft	42	57
Engine mounting bracket to block	17	23
Rear mounting to extension housing (manual)	26	35
Rear mounting to extension housing (automatic)	15	20
Rear mounting crossmember to bodyframe	12	16
Exhaust manifold bolts	16	22
Flywheel bolts	40	54
Fuel pump bolts	10	14
Main bearing cap bolts	52	71
Oil pump bolts	7	10
Rocker cover screws	7	10
Rocker pedestal bolts	17	23
Starter motor bolts	34	46
Timing cover setscrews	13	18
Camshaft sprocket bolt	34	46
Water pump bolts	13	18
Connecting rod big-end nuts	30	41
Engine front mounting to crossmember	27	37
Sump drain plug	37	50

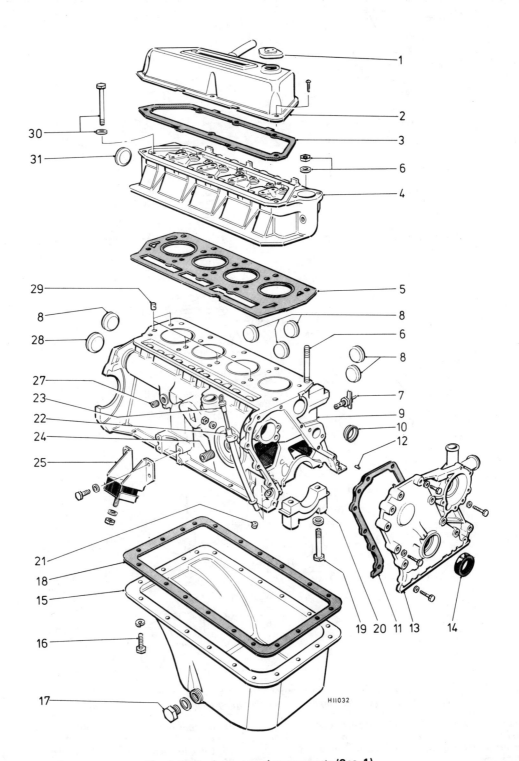

Fig. 1.14 Engine external components (Sec. 1)

1 Oil filler cap	9 Cylinder block	17 Sump drain plug	25 Front mounting
2 Rotor cover	10 Plug	18 Gasket	27 Blanking plug
3 Gasket	11 Gasket	19 Main bearing cap bolt	28 Camshaft blanking plug
4 Cylinder head	12 Dowel	20 Main bearing cap	29 Coolant jets
5 Gasket	13 Timing cover	21 Blanking plug	30 Cylinder head bolt & washer
6 Stud, nut and washer	14 Oil seal	22 Dipstick guide tube	31 Core plug
7 Cylinder block drain tap	15 Sump	23 Dipstick	
8 Core plugs	16 Sump screw	24 Oil filter sleeve	

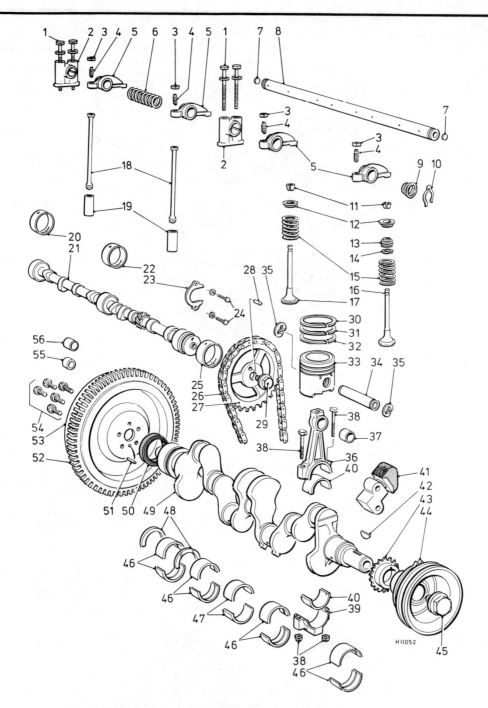

Fig. 1.15 Engine internal components – 1.5 carburettor type (Sec 1)
Note: 1.75 carburettor engine has double timing chain and dual valve springs

1 Rocker pedestal bolts	17 Exhaust valve	32 Oil control ring	46 Main bearings
2 Pedestal	18 Pushrod	33 Piston	47 No 3 main bearing (without oil groove)
3 Rocker arm adjuster locknut	19 Valve lifter tappet	34 Gudgeon pin	48 Thrust washers
4 Adjuster screw	20 Camshaft rear bearing	35 Circlip	49 Crankshaft
5 Rocker arm	21 Camshaft	36 Connecting rod	50 Rear oil seal
6 Coil spring	22 Camshaft centre bearing	37 Small-end bush	51 Dowel
7 Rocker shaft end plugs	23 Camshaft thrust plate	38 Big-end bolts and nuts	52 Starter ring gear
8 Rocker shaft	24 Screws	39 Connecting rod cap	53 Flywheel
9 End conical springs	25 Camshaft front bearing	40 Shell bearing	54 Flywheel bolts
10 Clip	26 Timing chain	41 Timing chain tensioner	55 Spigot bush (input shaft – manual gearbox)
11 Valve cotters	27 Camshaft sprocket	42 Woodruff key	56 Spigot bush (torque converter – automatic transmission)
12 Valve spring cap	28 Dowel	43 Crankshaft sprocket	
13 Inlet valve oil seal	29 Camshaft sprocket bolt	44 Pulley	
14 Oil seal retainer	30 Top compression piston ring	45 Pulley bolt	
15 Valve spring	31 2nd piston ring		
16 Inlet valve			

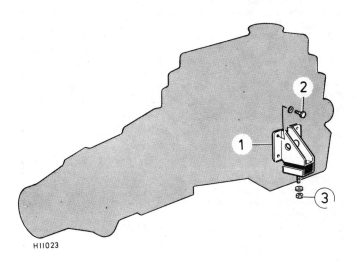

Fig. 1.16 Engine front mounting (Sec. 4)

1   Bracket
2   Securing bolt
3   Nut

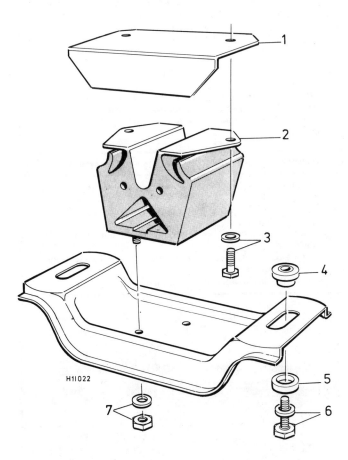

Fig. 1.17 Engine rear mounting (automatic transmission) (Sec. 4)

1   Restrainer plate   5   Collar
2   Mounting   6   Bolt and washer
3   Bolt and washer   7   Nut and washer
4   Insulator

1   General description

The engine is of the four cylinder in-line overhead valve type. The difference in displacement between the 1300 and the 1600 engine is achieved by an increase in the cylinder diameter, the stroke remaining the same on both engines. The material for the cylinder head and the block is cast iron. The cylinder bores and the cam follower (tappet) bores are machined directly in the block.

The crankshaft is supported in five main bearings, endfloat being controlled by semi-circular thrust washers located on the upper half of the rear main bearing. The gudgeon pins are of fully floating type retained by circlips in the piston bosses.

On engines equipped with 1.50 carburettors, a single type timing chain is used, whilst on those 1300 HC engines equipped with a 1.75 carburettor, a Duplex type chain is fitted. The valve guides are integral with the cylinder head and will accept oversize valves after reaming. Only the inlet valves are fitted with oil seals. Engines generally have single type valve springs, except those with a 1.75 carburettor which have double springs. The camshaft runs in three renewable bearings pressed into the cylinder block. The rear bearing aperture is sealed with a cup type plug.

2   Major operations possible with engine fitted

The following operations (Sections 4 to 14) can be carried out with the engine still in position in the car:

(a)   Renewal of the engine mountings
(b)   Cylinder head – removal and refitting
(c)   Sump – removal and refitting
(d)   Pistons and connecting rods – removal and refitting
(e)   Renewal of crankshaft thrust washers
(f)   Renewal of timing cover oil seal
(g)   Timing cover, chain and sprockets – removal and refitting
(h)   Camshaft – removal and refitting
(j)   Oil pump – removal and refitting

3   Major operations requiring engine or transmission removal

1   The crankshaft and main bearings can only be removed if the engine is first withdrawn from the car.
2   The flywheel and rear oil seal can be reached either by removing the engine or by leaving the engine in position and removing the gearbox.
3   If the engine is removed for major or complete dismantling, it is recommended that the ancillary components are first removed. These include the following, and reference should be made to the Chapters indicated for complete removal and dismantling procedures:

Starter motor (Chapter 10)
Alternator (Chapter 10)
Water pump (Chapter 2)
Distributor (Chapter 4)
Spark plugs (Chapter 4)
Clutch assembly (Chapter 5)
Fuel pump (Chapter 3)
Manifolds (Chapter 3)
Carburettor (Chapter 3)

4   Engine mountings – removal and refitting

Front mountings
1   Place the car over an inspection pit, or raise the front of the car on axle stands.
2   Unscrew and remove the nut that screws the mounting to the crossmember.
3   Position a block of wood under the sump and then, using a jack, support the weight of the engine.
4   Disconnect the clutch cable clip from the engine mounting bracket.
5   Extract the four bolts that hold the mounting to the crankcase and remove the mounting.

Rear mounting (manual transmission)

6   Support the weight of the transmission, using a jack and a block of wood as an insulator.
7   Release the bolt that secures the mounting to the extension housing.
8   Remove the centre bolt and rebound plate, and then unbolt the complete mounting assembly from the body members.

Rear mounting (automatic transmission)

9   Support the weight of the transmission but do not place the jack under the sump pan of the transmission.
10 Refer to Fig. 1.17. Unscrew and remove the two nuts and washers (8) that hold the mounting pad to the crossmember.
11 Unscrew and remove the bolts (10) and remove the crossmember. Note carefully the position of the insulators (7) and collars (9).
12 Extract the bolts (6) and remove the mounting pad and restrainer plate.

All mountings

13 Refitting of the front and rear mountings is a reversal of removal, tightening all nuts and bolts to the specified torque.

5   Cylinder head – removal and refitting

1   If the engine is in the car, carry out the following preliminary work (to paragraph 13).
2   Drain the cooling system.
3   Disconnect the battery.
4   Disconnect the top hose from the thermostat housing. Release the hose at the radiator and turn it through 180°.
5   Disconnect the crankcase vent hose from the rocker cover.
6   Disconnect the brake servo hose from the inlet manifold.
7   Disconnect the distributor vacuum pipe from the carburettor.
8   Disconnect the cable and throttle controls from the carburettor, also the fuel pipe.
9   Disconnect the spark plug leads and the lead from the temperature sender unit.
10 On cars equipped with automatic transmission, remove the downshift cable bracket and disconnect the downshift cable.
11 Disconnect the exhaust downpipe from the manifold and support the exhaust pipe.
12 Release the heater hoses from their cylinder head clips.
13 Disconnect the heater hoses at the cylinder head and water pump and tie them to the right-hand side of the engine compartment.
14 Undo the eight bolts and washers that hold the four rocker pedestals to the top of the cylinder head and lift off the rocker shaft, rocker arms and pedestals.
15 Lift out the pushrods and put them into a piece of pierced cardboard, the holes numbered one to eight, so that each pushrod can be identified to its relative rocker arm and tappet.
16 Slacken off the ten cylinder head holding-down bolts and nuts in the reverse order of the tightening sequence, ie work from the outside towards the centre.

17 The cylinder head should now lift off easily. If not, try turning the engine over by the flywheel (with the spark plugs in position) so that compression in the cylinders can force it upwards. A few smart taps with a soft-headed mallet or wood cushioned hammer may also be needed. Under no circumstances whatsoever try to prise the head off by forcing a lever of any sort into the joint. This can cause damage to the machined surfaces of the block and cylinder head.
18 Before refitting the cylinder head, make sure that the cylinder head and block mating surfaces are absolutely clean and free from carbon deposits.
19 Clean out the bolt holes, as any oil left in them can create sufficient hydraulic pressure to crack the block when the bolts are screwed in.
20 Position a new gasket on the top of the block, so that the identifying marks on the gaskets are in the right-hand corner nearest No 1 spark plug and visible from above (photo).
21 Lower the cylinder head onto the block, passing it onto the studs that are used instead of bolts in positions 7 and 10 on the bolt tightening diagram (photo).
22 Lubricate the bolt threads with engine oil and screw them into position finger tight.
23 Fit the lifting brackets to the two studs and screw on the nuts.
24 Tighten the nuts and bolts to the specified torque in stages, as shown in the Specifications Section. Work to the tightening sequence shown (photo).
25 Refit the pushrods into their original positions (photo).
26 Release the rocker arm adjuster screw locknuts and then unscrew the adjuster screws several turns.
27 Place the rocker shaft in position, engage the adjuster screw ball ends in the pushrod depressions. Lubricate the rocker pedestal bolts and screw them into position. Tighten the bolts progressively to the specified torque. On no account overtighten these bolts (photo).
28 Adjust the valve clearances as described in Section 8.
29 If the engine is in the car, reverse the operations described in paragraphs 1 to 13.
30 It is recommended that the torque of the cylinder head bolts is checked after the engine has been run to normal operating temperature. The rocker shaft will have to be removed to reach some of the bolts unless the special tool (RG556) is to hand. Check each bolt in sequence by unscrewing it one quarter of a turn and then tightening it to the specified torque. Check and adjust the valve clearances on completion.

6   Rocker shaft assembly – dismantling and reassembly

1   With the rocker shaft removed, push out the locating sleeve from the front pedestal.
2   Extract and remove the spring clip and conical spring from each end of the rocker shaft.
3   Pull the components from the rocker shaft, keeping them in their originally fitted order.
4   Examine the dismantled components in conjunction with the information given in Section 25.
5   Reassembly is a reversal of dismantling.

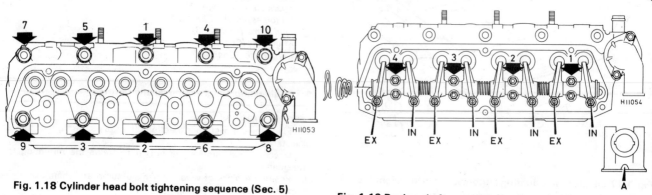

Fig. 1.18 Cylinder head bolt tightening sequence (Sec. 5)

Fig. 1.19 Rocker shaft assembly details and valve identification (Sec. 6)

A Boss on pedestal towards rear of engine

5.20 Positioning new cylinder head gasket

5.21 Lowering cylinder head onto block

5.24 Torque tightening cylinder head bolts

5.25 Refitting the pushrods into their original positions

5.27 Fitting the rocker shaft in position

7.1a Compressing a valve spring

7.1b Removing split collets from valve stem groove

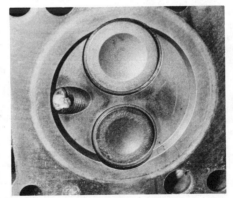
7.6 Cylinder head after decarbonisation

7.15 Fitting new oil seal or inlet valve

7.16 Fitting valve spring, collar and cap

7.19a Fitting new inlet/exhaust manifold gasket

7.19b Refitting inlet/exhaust manifold

7   Cylinder head – dismantling, decarbonising and reassembly

1   The valves can be removed from the cylinder head by the following method. Compress each spring in turn with a valve spring compressor, until the two halves of the split conical collets can be removed. Release the compressor and remove the spring, shroud and valve (photos).

2   If, when the valve spring compressor is screwed down, the valve spring retaining cap refuses to free to expose the split collet, do not continue to screw down on the compressor as there is a likelihood of damaging it.

3   Gently tap the top of the tool directly over the cap with a light hammer. This will free the cap. To avoid the compressor jumping off the valve spring retaining cap when it is tapped, hold the compressor firmly in position on hand.

4   Slide the rubber oil control seal off the top of each inlet valve stem and then drop out each valve through the combustion chamber.

5   It is essential that the valves are kept in their correct sequence unless they are so badly worn that they are to be renewed. If they are going to be kept and used again place them in a sheet of card having eight holes numbered 1 to 8 corresponding with the relative positions the valves were in when fitted. Also keep the valve springs, washers etc in the correct order.

6   With the valves removed, carefully clean off, with a wire brush and blunt scraper, all traces of carbon deposits from the combustion spaces and the ports. The valve head stems and valve guides should also be freed from any carbon deposits. Wash the combustion spaces and ports down with petrol and scrape the cylinder head surface free of any foreign matter with the side of a steel rule, or a similar article (photo).

7   Clean the pistons and top of the cylinder bores. If the pistons are still in the block, then it is essential that great care is taken to ensure that no carbon gets into the cylinder bores, as this could scratch the cylinder walls or cause damage to the piston and rings. To ensure this does not happen, first turn the crankshaft so that two of the pistons are at the top of their bores. Stuff rag into the other two bores or seal them off with paper and masking tape. The waterways should also be covered with small pieces of masking tape, to prevent particles of carbon entering the cooling system and damaging the water pump.

8   Before removing the carbon, press a little grease into the gap between the cylinder walls and the two pistons that are to be worked on. With a blunt scraper carefully scrape away the carbon from the piston crown, taking great care not to scratch the aluminium. Also scrape away the carbon from the surrounding lip of the cylinder wall. When all carbon has been removed, scrape away the grease which will now be contaminated with carbon particles, taking care not to press any into the bores. To assist prevention of carbon build-up the piston crown can be polished with a metal polish.

9   Remove the rags or masking tape from the other two cylinders and turn the crankshaft, so that the two pistons which were at the bottom are now at the top. Place rag or masking tape in the cylinders that have been decarbonised and proceed as just described.

10   The cylinder head should now be examined in conjunction with the advice given in Section 25. If the valve seats and guides and the valves themselves are in good condition, then the valves should be ground in the following way, after first removing the manifolds and spark plugs.

11   Smear a trace of coarse carborundum paste on the seat face and apply a suction grinder tool to the valve head. With a semi-rotary motion, grind the valve head to its seat, lifting the valve occasionally to redistribute the grinding paste. When a dull matt even surface finish is produced on both the valve seat and the valve, then wipe off the paste and repeat the process with fine carborundum paste, lifting and turning the valve to redistribute the paste as before. A light spring placed under the valve head will greatly ease this operation. When a smooth unbroken ring of light grey matt finish is produced, on both valve and valve seat faces, the grinding operation is completed.

12   Scrape away all carbon from the valve head and the valve stem. Carefully clean away every trace of grinding compound, taking great care to leave none in the ports or in the valve guides. Clean the valves and valve seats with a paraffin soaked rag, then with a clean rag, and finally, if an air line is available, blow the valves, valve guides and valve ports clean.

13   To reassemble the cylinder head, first check the number on the end of the valve stem. Your Talbot dealer will be able to tell you from his parts list whether the valve stems are standard or oversize. This is important in order that the correct inlet valve oil seals are purchased. These are identified in the following way:

    Seal with plain surface . . . . Standard stem or + 0.003 in
                                          (0.076 mm) oversize
    Seal with four equally . . . . . +0.015 in (0.38 mm) oversize
    spaced pips
    Seal with projecting ring . . +0.030 in (0.76 mm) oversize

14   Apply engine oil to the first valve stem and insert it into its guide.

15   As No 1 valve is an inlet valve, fit a new oil seal of correct size (see paragraph 13) (photo).

16   Fit the valve spring. Fit the valve spring retaining cap and then, using a valve spring compressor, fit the split collets into their valve stem cut-outs. Release the compressor gently, taking care not to displace the collets (photo).

17   Refit the remaining valves, making sure that they are returned to the seats into which they were ground and remembering to fit the oil seals to the inlet valves.

18   Place the cylinder head on the bench and tap the top of each valve spring with a hammer and block of wood, to settle the components.

19   Refit the manifolds, using new gaskets and tightening the bolts to the specified torque (photos).

20   Refit the spark plugs.

8   Valve clearances – checking and adjusting

1   The valve clearances can be set with the engine either hot or cold but never when it is only warm. Remove the rocker cover.

2   Apply a spanner or socket to the crankshaft pulley bolt and turn the crankshaft until No 1 piston is at TDC on its compression stroke. This is signified when the exhaust valve on No 4 cylinder is just closing and the TDC mark on the pulley is aligned with the mark on the timing cover.

3   Check both the clearances of the valves on No 1 cylinder, remembering that the inlet and exhaust valve clearances are different (see Specifications).

4   To adjust the clearance, release the adjuster screw locknut and turn the screw until the appropriate feeler blade is a stiff sliding fit between the end of the valve stem and the heel of the rocker arm (photo).

5   Tighten the locknut whilst holding the screw still with a screwdriver. Re-check the clearance (photo).

6   Turn the crankshaft through 180° (half a turn) and adjust both valve clearances on No 3 cylinder.

7   Turn the crankshaft through 180° (half a turn) when No 4 piston will be at TDC (marks in alignment). Check and adjust both valve clearances on No 4 cylinder.

8   Turn the crankshaft through 180° (half a turn) and check and adjust both valve clearances on No 2 cylinder.

9   Refit the rocker cover, using a new gasket if the original one is deformed or over compressed.

9   Timing cover, chain and tensioner – removal and refitting

1   If the engine is in the car, carry out the following preliminary work (to paragraph 5).

2   Drain the cooling system and then raise the rear of the car. This will help to prevent any coolant remaining in the cylinder block from entering the engine and mixing with the oil when the water pump is removed.

3   Disconnect the battery.

4   Remove the electric radiator fan/motor assembly.

5   Remove the alternator and drivebelt.

6   Remove the water pump and then disconnect the heater hose and the radiator bottom hose from their timing cover ends.

7   Disconnect and remove the starter motor.

8   Jam the flywheel starter ring gear with a cold chisel, or similar tool inserted between a tooth and the edge of the starter motor aperture.

9   Unscrew and remove the crankshaft pulley bolt and then withdraw the pulley.

10   Remove the sump stiffener brackets and the four bolts that hold the sump to the timing cover.

11   Loosen the sump bolts at both sides, to allow the front edge of the sump to drop away slightly from the bottom face of the timing cover.

12   Unscrew and remove the timing cover bolts. These bolts vary in length and it is suggested that a paper replica of the new timing cover

43

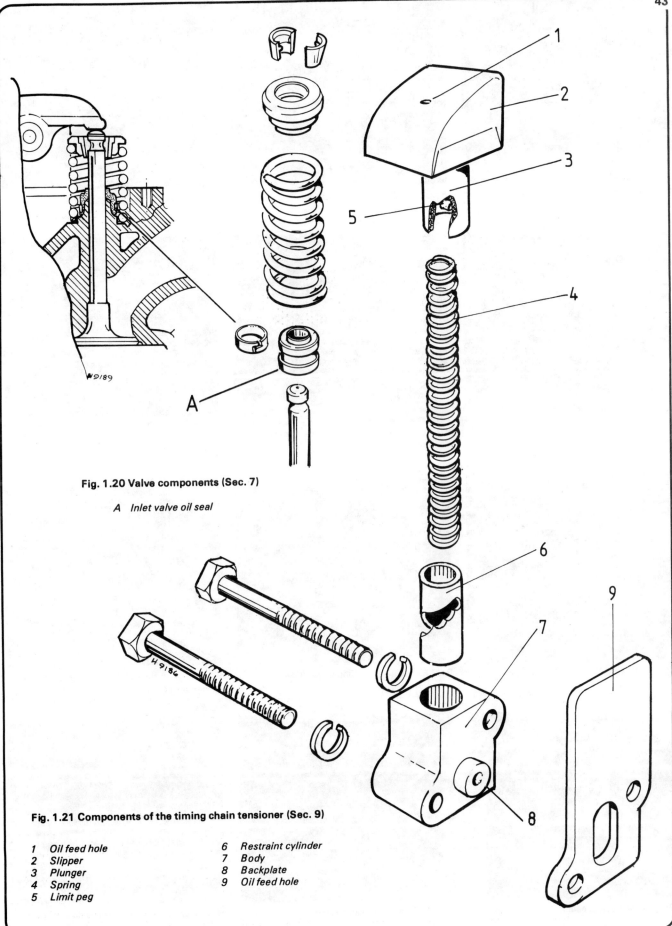

Fig. 1.20 Valve components (Sec. 7)

A   Inlet valve oil seal

Fig. 1.21 Components of the timing chain tensioner (Sec. 9)

1   Oil feed hole
2   Slipper
3   Plunger
4   Spring
5   Limit peg
6   Restraint cylinder
7   Body
8   Backplate
9   Oil feed hole

8.4a Releasing rocker arm adjustment locknut

8.4b Checking a valve clearance

8.5 Tightening adjusting screw locknut

9.20 Positioning the timing chain and sprockets

9.22 Crankshaft and camshaft sprockets in position

9.25a Bolting timing chain tensioner in position

9.25b Releasing tensioner slipper head

9.28 Fitting a new timing cover gasket

9.29a Ensure the old timing cover seal is driven out squarely

9.29b Fit the new oil seal to the timing cover

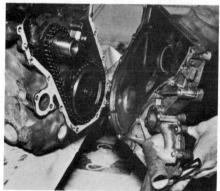
9.30 Refitting the timing cover

10.6 Positioning new sump gasket

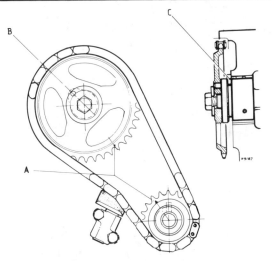

Fig. 1.22 Timing marks in alignment

A Sprocket timing marks   C Camshaft thrust plate
B Locating dowel

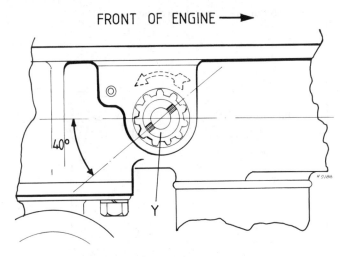

FRONT OF ENGINE ➝

40°

Y

Fig. 1.23 Correct setting of distributor drive dog after oil pump refitted with No 4 piston at TDC (Sec. 11)
Y is larger segment of drive dog

gasket is made and the bolts pushed through it in their relative positions.
13 Withdraw the timing cover. The cover is aligned on dowels so do not attempt to tap it sideways to release it.
14 The tensioner can be removed by pressing the slipper and body together, and then unscrewing and removing the securing bolts. Withdraw the tensioner and backplate.
15 Release the slipper head slowly from the tension of its spring and remove the slipper and restraint cylinder from the body.
16 To remove the timing chain and sprockets unscrew the bolt, with plain washer, that holds the camshaft sprocket to the camshaft.
17 Use two levers to remove the sprocket.
18 Withdraw the timing chain, complete with both camshaft and crankshaft sprockets.
19 Examine all components for wear in conjunction with the information given in Section 25.
20 Commence refitting by starting the crankshaft sprocket onto its Woodruff key. Now turn the camshaft by gripping the sprocket until the Woodruff key is exactly at the top (photo).
21 Engage the timing chain with the teeth of the crankshaft sprocket. Fit the crankshaft sprocket within the loop of the chain, so that when the camshaft sprocket is refitted, the sprocket timing marks are closest together and lie on a line drawn through the two sprocket centres, with the driving side of the chain taut.
22 Push the two sprockets into position, making sure that the camshaft sprocket dowel engages. Ensure this by turning the camshaft as necessary. Use only hand pressure to fit the sprockets (photo).
23 Check the timing marks are in alignment and then tighten the sprocket bolt to the specified torque.
24 To refit the chain tensioner, first depress the restraint cylinder into the plunger at the same time turning it clockwise, until the limit stop engages in the recess in the upper face of the helix. The restraint cylinder should now protrude by about $\frac{1}{8}$ in (3 mm).
25 Offer the tensioner assembly and backplate to the cylinder block. Refit and tighten the securing bolts. Depress the slipper head to release the restraint mechanism. Do not press the timing chain inwards after this stage, as the tensioner plunger could then move out beyond its normal position. The chain will automatically tension itself once the engine is started (photo).
26 Stuff a piece of rag into the aperture that runs between the timing case and the sump to prevent any dirt entering. Clean the cover mating face on the front of the cylinder block.
27 Remove the rag and apply jointing compound to the upper surface of the exposed sump gasket. Should the gasket be damaged, then the engine oil will have to be drained, the sump removed and a new gasket fitted.
28 Stick a new timing cover gasket to the front face of the cylinder block (photo).
29 Unless the timing cover oil seal has only recently been fitted, it should be renewed now. Drive out the old one and refit the new, using a suitable piece of tubing. Make sure that the lip of the seal faces

inwards and grease the lip liberally (photos).
30 Refit the timing cover, the crankshaft pulley and bolt (photo).
31 If the engine is in the car, reverse the operations described in paragraphs 2 to 5.

10 Sump – removal and refitting

1   Place the car over an inspection pit, or raise the front end by placing a jack under the crossmember.
2   Drain the engine oil.
3   Unbolt and remove the sump stiffener brackets, retaining any shims, if fitted.
4   Unscrew and remove the sump setscrews and lower the sump.
5   Before refitting the sump, take the opportunity to clean the gauze filter on the oil pump pick-up pipe.
6   Stick a new gasket into position, using a few dabs of thick grease on the crankcase flange (photo).
7   Refit the sump and stiffener brackets. Tighten the sump setscrews and the stiffener bracket to sump bolts before tightening the bolts that hold the stiffener brackets to the clutch housing (photo).
8   Refill the engine with oil.

11 Oil pump – removal and refitting

1   Disconnect the battery.
2   Remove the distributor cap. Using a ring spanner or socket on the crankshaft pulley bolt, turn the crankshaft until the distributor rotor is pointing at No 4 spark plug lead segment in the distributor cap (when in position). The TDC timing marks on the front of the engine should also be in alignment.
3   Remove the distributor as described in Chapter 4.
4   Remove the sump as described in the preceding Section.
5   Unscrew and remove the oil pump (three bolts) from inside the crankcase.
6   Before refitting the oil pump, clean the gauze filter and the pump and crankcase mating faces.
7   Check that the engine is still at TDC (No 4 piston on compression).
8   Hold the oil pump in its approximate fitted position and turn the driven gear, so that the larger segment of the driving dog is towards the front of the engine.
9   Refit the pump but before tightening the bolts, check that the distributor driving dog has moved to the position shown. A little trial and error with positioning of the oil pump driving gear may be needed before the correct setting is achieved (photo).
10 Refit the sump and fill the engine with oil.
11 Fit the distributor cap, connect the battery and check the ignition timing on completion.

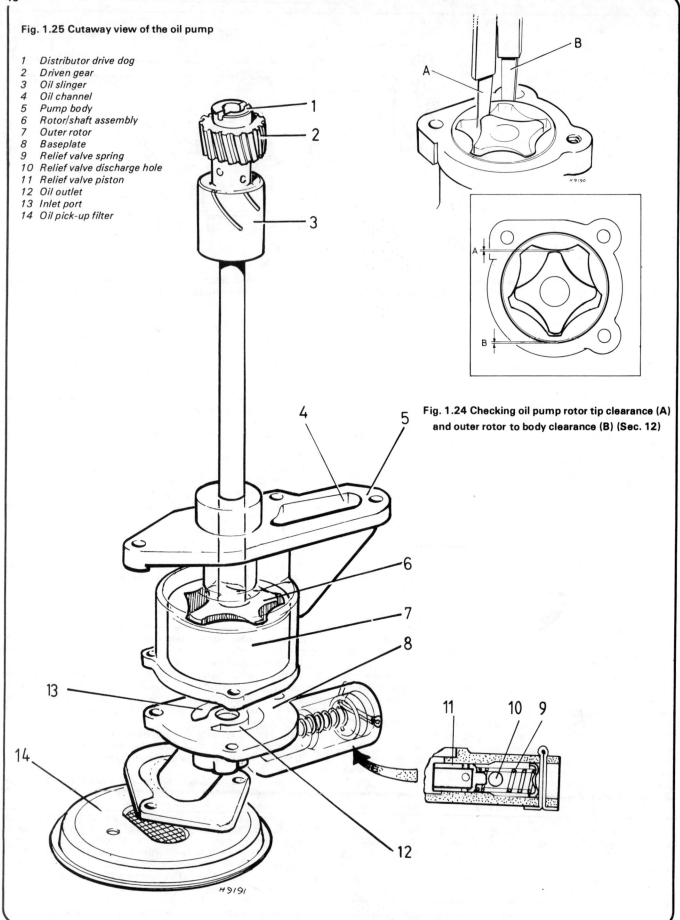

Fig. 1.25 Cutaway view of the oil pump

1 Distributor drive dog
2 Driven gear
3 Oil slinger
4 Oil channel
5 Pump body
6 Rotor/shaft assembly
7 Outer rotor
8 Baseplate
9 Relief valve spring
10 Relief valve discharge hole
11 Relief valve piston
12 Oil outlet
13 Inlet port
14 Oil pick-up filter

Fig. 1.24 Checking oil pump rotor tip clearance (A) and outer rotor to body clearance (B) (Sec. 12)

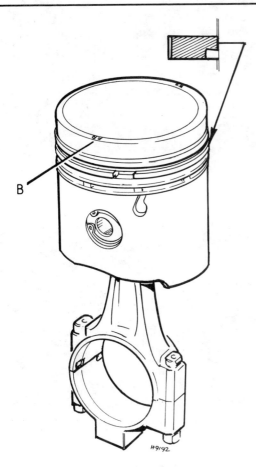

Fig. 1.26 Piston assembled to connecting rod (Sec. 14)

B indicates letters FR towards front of engine

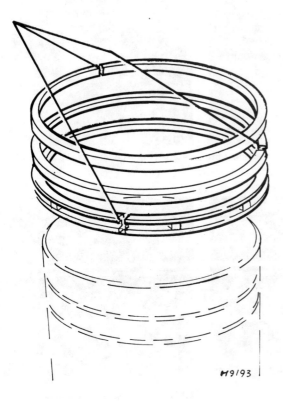

Fig. 1.27 Piston ring gaps staggered (Sec. 14)

12 Oil pump – overhaul

1   If the oil pump is worn it is best to purchase a new or reconditioned unit, as to rebuild the oil pump is a job that calls for engineering shop facilities.
2   To check if the pump is still serviceable, first check if there is any slackness in the spindle bushes, and then remove the bottom cover held by three screws.
3   Allow the outer rotor ring to fall out under its own weight, but do not drop it as there is a possibility of it cracking.
4   Clean all traces of oil from the mating faces of the rotors and pump. Refit the outer rotor ring, ensuring that its chamfered end is towards the gear end of the pump.
5   With a feeler gauge and straight edge, check the clearance between the end faces of the inner and outer rotor rings and the pump body. The permissible gap is between 0.001 in (0.025 mm) and 0.003 in (0.075 mm).
6   Check with a feeler gauge, the side clearance between the top of the inner and outer lobes as shown at 'A' in Fig. 1.35. The permissible gap is between 0.001 in (0.025 mm) and 0.006 in (0.15 mm).
7   Then check the clearance between the inside of the pump body and the outside of the outer rotor as shown at 'B' in Fig. 1.35. The permissible gap is between 0.005 in (0.125 mm) and 0.008 in (0.20 mm).
8   If any of the measurements taken are outside the permitted clearances then it will be necessary to fit a replacement pump.
9   The oil pressure relief valve incorporated in the base of the pump normally requires no attention and is not adjustable.

13 Camshaft and tappets – removal and refitting

1   If the engine is in the car, carry out the preliminary operations described (to paragraph 5).
2   Drain the cooling system.
3   Drain the engine oil.
4   Remove the front radiator grille.
5   Remove the radiator and the radiator fan (Chapter 2).
6   Remove the cylinder head (Section 5).
7   Lift out each of the tappets (cam followers), marking each one with a piece of adhesive tape to identify its refitted position.
8   Remove the timing cover, chain and sprockets (Section 9).
9   Remove the sump, oil pump and the distributor (Sections 10 and 11).
10   Disconnect the engine front mountings from the crossmember and then jack up the front of the engine (under the crankcase front flange), so that the camshaft can be withdrawn through the radiator grille aperture.
11   Unscrew and remove the camshaft thrust plate bolts and withdraw the camshaft, taking great care not to damage the bearings as the cams and the gears pass through them (photo).
12   Refitting is a reversal of removal. Oil the bearing surfaces first and when refitted, check the camshaft endfloat. If it is not within the tolerance specified, renew the thrust plate (photos).

14 Pistons and connecting rods – removal, dismantling, reassembly and refitting

1   Remove the cylinder head and the sump as previously described in this Chapter.
2   Scrape away any carbon ring from the top of the cylinder bores, also carefully remove the wear ridge if one can be felt, otherwise the piston rings will not pass over it when they are being pushed out of the bores.
3   Turn the crankshaft until the first piston is at its lowest position in the cylinder bore.
4   Now check that the big-ends and their caps are numbered. If they are not, dot punch the connecting rod and cap at adjacent points, numbering them 1 to 4 from the front of the engine.
5   Note also towards whch side of the engine the markings face, so that the rods will be refitted the original way round.
6   Remove the big-end nuts, cap and bearing shell. Keep the shell with the cap if it is to be used again.
7   Push the connecting rod and piston out of the top of the cylinder

10.7 Tightening the sump screws evenly

11.9 Tightening the oil pump bolts

13.11 The camshaft thrust plate

13.12a Inserting the camshaft into the crankcase

13.12b Tightening the thrust plate bolts

14.15 Piston/connecting rod locating mark

14.24 Driving piston into bore

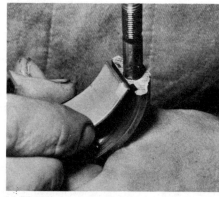
14.25 Fitting bearing shell into connecting rod recess

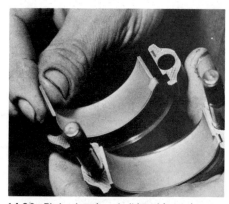
14.26a Fitting bearing shell into big-end cap

14.26b Lubricating crankpin journals

14.26c Fitting a connecting rod cap

20.12 Ensure cleaness of crankcase

block. If the shell is displaced from the rod, retrieve it and place it in the connecting rod recess.

8   Repeat the operations on the remaining pistons and connecting rods.

9   Inspect and renovate the components as described in Section 25.

10   The piston rings can be removed using a twisting action. It will be found an easy job if two or three feeler blades are first slid behind the ring and positioned at equidistant points around the piston. Always remove the top ring first and slide all rings from the top of the piston, never from the bottom.

11   To disconnect the connecting rod from the piston, extract the circlip from both ends of the gudgeon pin. Warm the piston in hot water until the gudgeon pin can be pushed out.

12   To reassemble, fit a new circlip into the groove in one of the piston bosses.

13   Warm the piston and hold the piston and the connecting rod in their correct relative positions. Push the gudgeon pin into position until the pin contacts the circlip in the opposite piston boss. Fit the second circlip.

14   The alignment of the piston to the rod can be made either way round, provided the letters 'FR' on the piston crown are positioned towards the front of the engine when refitted in the cylinder block.

15   It is to be preferred that the connecting rods are refitted in the same relative position as was originally the case, with the dot punching to face the side recorded at dismantling. The rod and cap marks should be adjacent. Provided that the shell locating grooves in the big-end and cap are on the same side, the rod can be fitted to the piston either way round (photo).

16   Check that the piston ring grooves and oilways are thoroughly clean and unblocked. Piston rings must be fitted very carefully as they are extremely brittle.

17   Using the three feeler blades as for removal, slide the bottom oil control ring over and down the blades until it locates in the lower groove of the piston.

18   Use the same method to refit the second compression ring and then the top compression ring.

19   The top oil control rings can be refitted either way up, but the second ring must be fitted so that its step is downward.

20   Refer to Section 25 for details of testing the fit of piston rings in the cylinder bores and piston grooves.

21   Stagger the piston ring end gaps at equidistant points round the piston, lubricate the rings liberally and then fit a piston ring compressor.

22   Turn the crankshaft to bring No 1 journal to its lowest point (BDC). Oil the cylinder bores.

23   Refit the first piston/rod assembly into the cylinder bore until the base of the ring compressor is resting squarely on the top of the cylinder block. Check that the 'FR' mark on the piston crown is towards the front of the engine.

24   Rest the wooden handle of a hammer on the piston crown. Give a sharp blow to the head of the hammer with the hand to drive the assembly into the block. The piston ring compressor will be ejected as the piston enters the bore (photo).

25   Fit the bearing shell into the rod recess and then draw the rod down into contact with the crankshaft journal (photo).

26   Fit the shell to the big-end cap, refit the cap. Use new nuts on the big-end bolts and tighten them to the specified torque (photos).

27   Repeat the operations on the remaining three piston/rod assemblies.

28   Turn the crankshaft to check for smooth rotation.

29   Refit the sump and cylinder head, as described in earlier Sections of this Chapter.

15 Engine – methods of removal

The engine can be removed leaving the transmission in the car or the combined engine/transmission can be removed as an assembly.

16 Engine (without transmission) – removal and refitting

1   Disconnect the battery.

2   Drain the cooling system.

3   Mark the position of the bonnet hinges. Unbolt and, with the help of an assistant, remove the bonnet.

4   Disconnect the vacuum pipe from the air cleaner and remove the air cleaner.

5   Disconnect the throttle choke controls, and the downshift cable on cars with automatic transmission.

6   Disconnect the fuel pipe from the fuel pump inlet and detach the pipe from its timing cover clip.

7   Disconnect all electrical leads including those to the alternator, radiator fan temperature sensor, fan, water temperature sender unit, oil warning lamp, oil pressure sender unit, starter motor and distributor. Disconnect the high tension lead from the coil.

8   Disconnect the radiator bottom hose from the water pump and the top hose from the cylinder head.

9   If the car is equipped with automatic transmission, disconnect the oil cooler pipes from the base of the radiator. Cap the open pipe ends to prevent the entry of dirt.

10   Remove the radiator/fan assembly.

11   Disconnect the brake servo vacuum hose from the inlet manifold.

12   Release the heater hoses from their cylinder head clips.

13   Disconnect the heater hoses from the cylinder head and water pump and tie them to one side of the engine compartment.

14   Disconnect the battery lead from the starter motor.

15   Remove the top mounting bolt from the starter motor.

16   On cars with automatic transmission, disconnect the filler tube support strap.

17   Place a support under the exhaust pipe and then disconnect the downpipe from the manifold.

18   Remove the bolt from the rear of the exhaust flange and the two upper bolts that secure the clutch bellhousing or torque converter housing to the engine.

19   Place the car over an inspection pit, or raise the front end under the crossmember and support securely on stands.

20   Working under the car, detach the clutch cable from the clip on the engine front mounting bracket.

21   Unbolt the front mountings from the crossmember.

22   Remove the sump stiffener brackets (where fitted).

23   Remove the shield from the lower front face of the clutch bellhousing or torque converter housing (automatic transmission).

24   Remove the starter motor.

25   On cars with automatic transmission, unscrew and remove the four bolts that hold the torque converter and engine driveplate together. These bolts are accessible through the aperture left by removal of the shield from the lower front face of the torque converter housing. The crankshaft will have to be turned, however, to bring each bolt into view for removal.

26   Unscrew and remove the remaining bolts that hold the clutch bellhousing or torque converter to the cylinder block.

27   Support the transmission on a jack using a block of wood as an insulator.

28   Fit suitable lifting gear to the engine and raise it until the front mounting studs clear the crossmember.

29   On cars with manual transmission, pull the engine forward until it clears the gearbox input shaft and then raise the engine and remove it from the car.

30   On cars with automatic transmission, the torque converter must remain in engagement with the transmission. Have an assistant apply pressure to the torque converter in a rearward direction as the engine is pulled forward.

31   To refit the engine first check that the two positioning dowels are located in the rear face of the cylinder block.

32   Lower the engine into position and guide it so that the input shaft splines of the gearbox enter the splines on the clutch driven plate. If the clutch has been disturbed, make sure that it has been centralised as described in Chapter 5. If the splines do not engage, turn the crankshaft pulley bolt slightly until they do.

33   Push the engine fully into contact with the clutch bellhousing and insert the top two bolts. Check that the clutch cable lies between the engine front mounting and the cylinder block before lowering the mounting studs into their holes in the crossmember.

34   On cars with automatic transmission, make sure that the torque converter is fully rearwards. If the converter was displaced at the time of engine removal, loss of transmission fluid will have occurred and the torque converter must be pushed to the rear and at the same time turned to fully engage the oil pump drive tangs in the transmission. Engage the driveplate with the torque converter and the engine block with the torque converter housing. Refit the driveplate bolts and the engine to converter housing bolts.

35   The rest of the refitting operations are a reversal of removal.

17 Engine (with transmission) – removal and refitting

1   Carry out the operations described in paragraphs 1 to 17 in the preceding Section.

Manual gearbox

2   Working inside the car, remove the console (if fitted) and the gear lever.

3   Disconnect the clutch cable from the clutch lever and from the engine mounting bracket. Disconnect the reverse lamp switch leads.

Automatic transmission

4   Disconnect the oil cooler pipes from the transmission, catch the fluid in a container and cap the open pipe ends.

5   Disconnect the selector linkage rod from the lever on the side of the transmission.

6   Disconnect the leads from the inhibitor switch.

All transmissions

7   Place the car over an inspection pit, or raise the rear on ramps or axle stands.

8   Remove the propeller shaft (Chapter 7).

9   Disconnect the speedometer cable from the transmission.

10   Unscrew and remove the stabilizer bar brackets from the bodyframe, also the two nuts that secure the two engine front mountings to the crossmember.

11   Support the transmission on a jack (**not** placed under the sump pan – automatic transmission).

12   Disconnect the rear mounting and then using a hoist attached to the two heater hose clip brackets, simultaneously raise the hoist and lower the transmission jack, until the engine/transmission can be removed from the engine compartment at an angle of about 45°.

13   Refitting is a reversal of removal. On cars with a manual gearbox, adjust the clutch and on all models, check the oil levels in engine and transmission.

18 Engine/manual gearbox – separation and reconnection

1   With the engine and gearbox removed from the car, the first job is to clean away all external dirt and grease. A water soluble solvent, or paraffin, and a stiff brush are both suitable for this work.

2   Support the engine and gearbox using blocks of wood and then remove the cover from the lower face of the clutch bellhousing.

3   Remove the starter motor and the bellhousing to engine bolts.

4   Support the weight of the gearbox and withdraw it in a straight line from the engine.

5   Reconnection is a reversal of separation, but make sure that the alignment dowels are in position on the cylinder block mating face. If the clutch assembly has been disturbed, make sure that the driven plate has been centralised (Chapter 5).

19 Engine/automatic transmission – separation and reconnection

1   Clean away external dirt as described in paragraph 1 of the preceding Section.

2   Support the transmission and engine on blocks and remove the cover from the lower face of the torque converter housing.

3   Remove the starter motor and the bolts that hold the torque converter housing to the engine.

4   Through the aperture left by the removal of the cover from the torque converter housing, unscrew and remove the bolts that secure the driveplate to the torque converter. These bolts are brought into view one at a time by turning the crankshaft pulley bolt.

5   Support the weight of the transmission and, with an assistant applying pressure to the front face of the torque converter to keep it in complete engagement with the transmission, withdraw the transmission from the engine.

6   Reconnection is a reversal of separation, but again keep the torque converter fully to the rear during mating of the engine and transmission.

20 Crankshaft and main bearings – removal and refitting

1   Remove the engine as described in earlier Sections of this Chapter.

2   Remove the cylinder head (Section 5).

3   Remove the sump (Section 10), oil pump (Section 11) and the distributor.

4   Remove the timing chain cover, chain and tensioner (Section 9).

5   Remove the clutch assembly and unbolt and remove the flywheel (Section 21) or driveplate (automatic transmission).

6   Unbolt the big-end caps. Number them carefully if they are not already marked and keep the bearing shells with their respective caps.

7   If the pistons and connecting rods are not to be removed, the rods can be left in their disconnected positions in the cylinder bores. Take care however that the big-end bolts do not scratch the crankshaft bearing surfaces or the cylinder walls.

8   Release the main bearing cap bolts evenly; note the cap markings and which way round they are fitted.

9   Remove the main bearing caps and lift the crankshaft from the crankcase.

10   Extract the bearing upper shells, identifying their location (using a piece of adhesive tape with their numbered position marked on it) if they are to be used again.

11   Remove and discard the crankshaft rear oil seal.

12   Inspect the condition of all components and renovate in conjunction with Section 25 of this Chapter (photo).

13   Before refitting the crankshaft, probe the oil holes in the crankshaft and crankcase with a piece of wire. Remove all old sealant from the rear main bearing cap and oil seal aperture.

14   Locate the bearing shells in the crankcase recesses. The shell for the centre main bearing does not have a groove (photo).

15   Using a dab of grease, stick the thrust washer one to each side of the rear main bearing crankcase web, so that the oil grooves are visible when the washers are refitted (photo).

16   Oil the crankcase bearing shells liberally and then lower the crankshaft into position (photo).

17   Fit the bearing shells to the main bearing caps and fit the caps Nos 1, 2, 3 and 4. Tighten the bolts to the specified torque (photos).

18   Using a bar as a lever against one of the crankshaft webs, first move the crankshaft fully in one direction and then check the clearance between the semi-circular thrust washer and the crankshaft journal flange.

19   Now move the crankshaft fully in the opposite direction and then check the clearance at the opposite thrust washer.

20   If the endfloat is outside the permitted tolerance (see Specifications) the thrust washers will have to be changed.

21   Smear the lips of a new rear oil seal with grease and fit the seal, so that its lip is towards the front of the engine.

22   Refit the rear main bearing cap, making sure that the oil seal remains squarely in its recess. Tighten the bolts to the specified torque.

23   Using recommended sealant (Hylosil) apply the nozzle of the tube to the groove at each side of the rear main bearing cap. Inject the sealant until a drop emerges from between the bearing cap and the cylinder block.

24   Refit the connecting rods to their crankpins.

25   Refit the flywheel (or driveplate – automatic transmission) and the clutch (manual transmission).

26   Refit the timing components and cover.

27   Refit the sump and cylinder head and refit the engine.

21 Flywheel (or driveplate – automatic transmission) – removal and refitting

1   If the engine has been removed, then obviously access to the flywheel (or driveplate) is immediate. If the flywheel (or driveplate) is to be removed without the prior need for engine withdrawal, then it is easier to remove the transmission (Chapter 6) leaving the engine in position in the car.

2   On cars with a manual gearbox, mark the relative position of the clutch cover to the flywheel and then remove the clutch.

3   Unbolt and remove the flywheel (or driveplate).

4   Inspect the condition of the starter ring gear and renovate as described in Section 25.

5   With the flywheel (or driveplate) removed, take the opportunity to

20.14 Lubricating upper half of main bearing shells

20.15 Fitting the crankshaft rear main bearing thrust washers

20.16 Lowering crankshaft into position

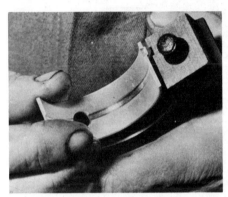
20.17a Fitting bearing shell into main bearing cap

20.17b Fitting main bearing cap

21.6 Torque tightening the flywheel bolts

check the spigot bearing in the centre of the crankshaft rear flange and renew if worn.
6   Refitting is a reversal of removal. Tighten the securing bolts to the specified torque (photo). When fitting the clutch, align the marks made prior to removal.

22 Crankshaft rear oil seal – renewal with engine in position in car

1   Remove the gearbox or automatic transmission (Chapter 6).
2   On cars with a manual gearbox, remove the clutch and flywheel.
3   On cars with automatic transmission, remove the driveplate.
4   Prise the rear oil seal from its recess and clean the recess thoroughly.
5   Grease the new seal and push it into position using hand pressure.
6   Using the old seal as a drift, tap the new seal fully home in its seating.
7   Refit the flywheel (or driveplate), the clutch (if applicable) and transmission.

23 Lubrication system – description

1   A forced feed system of lubrication is used, with oil circulated to all the engine bearing surfaces under pressure by a pump which draws oil from the sump under the crankcase. The oil is first pumped through a full flow oil filter.
2   From the filter, oil flows into a main oil gallery; this is cast integrally into the cylinder block. From this gallery, oil is fed via oilways in the block to the crankshaft main bearings and then from the main bearings along oilways in the crankshaft to the connecting rod bearings. From the same gallery, oilways carry the oil to the camshaft bearings.
3   From the front camshaft bearing, a further oilway passes oil to a gallery in the cylinder head. This gallery delivers oil through the hollow rocker shaft which contains a number of small holes to lubricate the rocker pivots. The tappets are lubricated by oil returning from the rocker gear via the pushrods and is not under pressure. Once oil has

passed through the bearings and out, it finds its own way by gravity back to the sump.
4   If the filter gets blocked, oil will continue to flow because a bypass valve will open, permitting oil to circulate past the filter element. Similarly, any blockage in oilways (resulting in greatly increased pressure) will cause the oil pressure relief valve to operate, returning oil direct to the sump.
5   Oil pressure when hot should be as specified. This pressure is measured after oil has passed through the filter. As the oil pressure warning light only comes on when the pressure is as low as 3-5 lbs/sq in, it is most important that the filter element is regularly changed and the oil changed at the recommended intervals, in order that the lubrication system remains clean.
6   Should the warning light ever come on when the engine is running at any speed above idling, stop at once and investigate otherwise serious bearing and cylinder damage may result.

24 Oil filter cartridge – renewal

1   It is usual to renew the oil filter at the same time at the engine oil is changed.
2   In which case, drain the engine oil first and refit the sum drain plug.
3   Place a container below the oil filter and unscrew the cartridge. If it is stuck tight, use a chain or strap wrench. If such a tool is not available, a screwdriver can be driven through one side of the cartridge so that it emerges from the opposite side and the screwdriver then used as a lever to unscrew the cartridge.
4   Discard the old filter and clean the contact surface on the cylinder block.
5   Smear the rubber sealing ring on the new filter with engine oil and screw it into position as tightly as possible *using hand pressure only*.
6   Refill the engine with oil, adding an extra pint (0.57 litres) for absorption by the new filter.
7   Start the engine. It will take a few seconds for the oil warning lamp to go out. This will happen when the new filter is filled with oil.

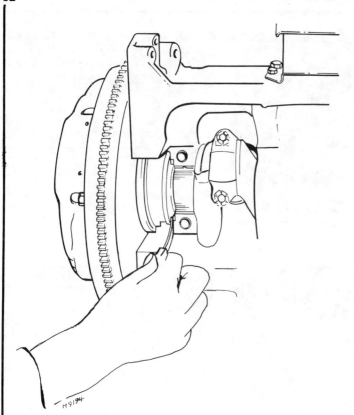

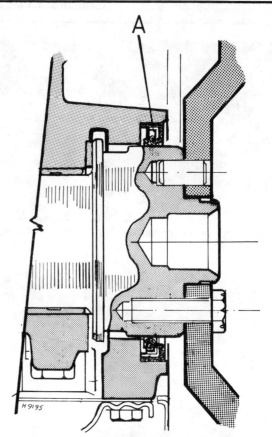

Fig. 1.28 Checking crankshaft endfloat (Sec. 20)

Fig. 1.29 Crankshaft rear oil seal (Sec. 20)

A denotes seal lip towards front of engine

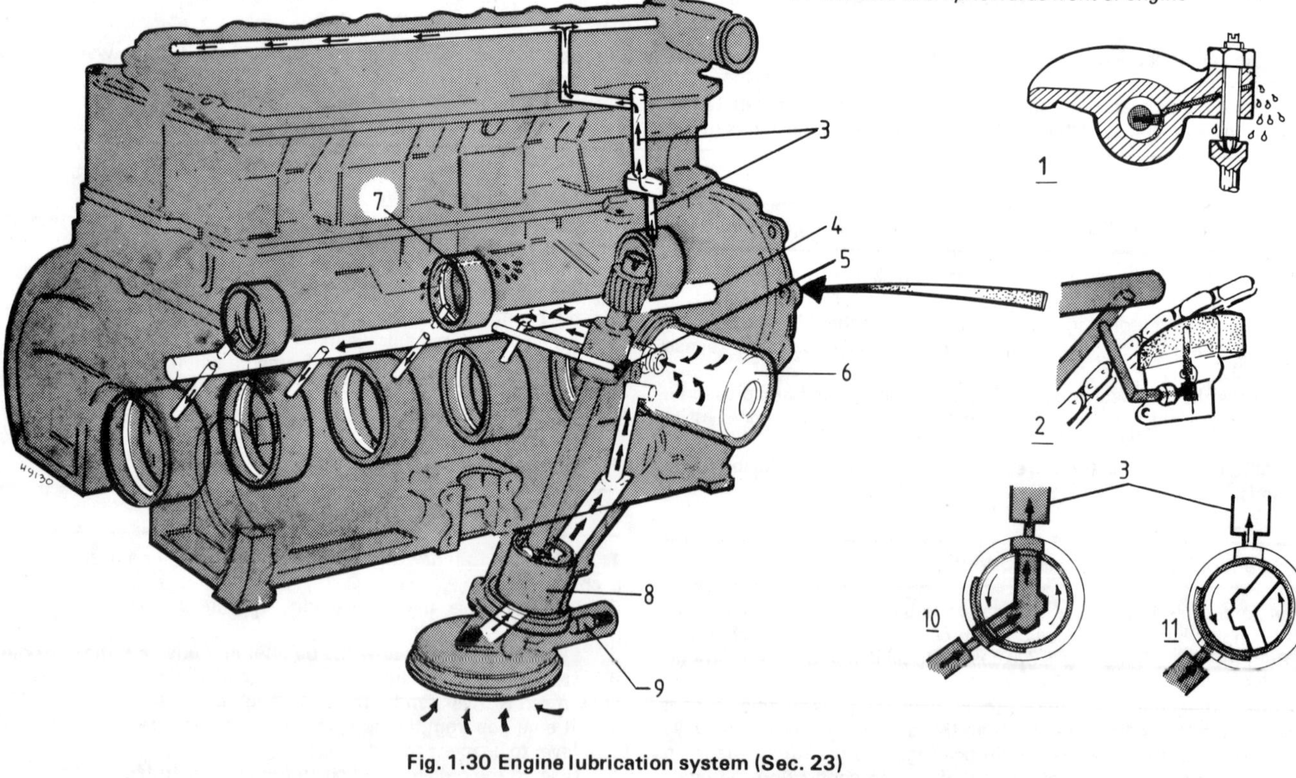

Fig. 1.30 Engine lubrication system (Sec. 23)

1	Oil flow rocker shaft to pushrod cup	7	Camshaft centre bearing oil grooves
2	Oil flow to timing chain tensioner and chain	8	Oil pump
3	Oil flow to rocker shaft	9	Oil pressure relief valve
4	Main oil gallery	10	Camshaft front journal oil drillings
5	Drilling to sender unit (oil pressure gauge or light)	11	Oil flow to rocker shaft interrupted by rotation of camshaft front journal
6	Oil filter		

25 Examination and renovation

1 Full dismantling procedures have been included in the earlier Sections of this Chapter, but unless any fault is immediately apparent or previously known, the dismantled components should be inspected as described in the following paragraphs.

Crankshaft

2 Examine all the crankpins and main bearing journals for signs of scoring or scratches. If all surfaces are undamaged check next that all the bearing journals are round. This can be done with a micrometer or caliper gauge, taking readings across the diameter at six or seven points for each journal. If you do not own or know how to use a micrometer, take the crankshaft to your local engineering works and ask them to check it for you.

3 If the crankshaft is ridged or scored it must be reground. If the ovality exceeds 0.001 in (0.0254 mm) on measurement, and there are signs of scoring or scratching on the surfaces, regrinding may be necessary. It would be advisable to ask the advice of the engineering works to whom you would entrust the work of regrinding in such instances.

4 If the spigot bearing in the crankshaft rear flange is worn, extract it with a suitable puller and press in a new one. The bearing is pre-packed with grease and requires no further lubrication.

Big-end and main bearings

5 Big-end bearing failure is normally indicated by a pronounced knocking from the crankcase and a slight drop in oil pressure. Main bearing failure is normally accompanied by vibration, which can be quite severe at high engine speed, and a more significant drop in oil pressure.

6 The shell bearing surfaces should be matt grey in colour with no sign of pitting or scoring.

7 Replacement shell bearings are supplied in a series of sizes dependent on the degree of regrinding that the crankshaft requires. The engineering works regrinding the crankshaft will normally supply the correct shells with the reground crank. Make sure that bearing shells renewed are to standard dimensions if the crankshaft has not been reground.

8 Examine the mating faces of the big-end caps to see if they have ever been filed in a mistaken attempt to take up the wear. If so, the offending rods must be renewed. Check the alignment of the rods visually, and if misaligned take the rods to your local Talbot agent for checking on a special jig.

Cylinder bores, pistons and piston rings

9 Cylinder blocks are identified by the letters (SB) – 1300 engines or (LB) – 1600 engines, cast on the block above the engine front mounting bracket on the manifold side of the block.

10 Cylinder bores are graded A, B, C or D. The grade letters are stamped on two vertical machined faces at the front and rear of the block, just below the gasket joint on the manifold side of the engine.

11 Pistons are similarly graded, the grade letter being stamped on the edge of the crown. Details of cylinder bore diameters, piston diameters and clearances are given in the Specifications.

12 The bores must be checked for ovality, scoring, scratching and pitting. Starting from the top, look for a ridge where the top piston ring reaches the limit of its upward travel. The depth of this ridge will give a good indication of the degree of wear and can be checked with the engine in the car and the cylinder head removed. Other indications are excessive oil consumption and a smoky exhaust.

13 Measure the bore diameter across the block and just below any ridge. This can be done with an internal micrometer. Compare this with the diameter of the bottom of the bore, which is not subject to wear. If no micrometer measuring instruments are available, use a piston from which the rings have been removed and measure the gap between it and the cylinder wall with a feeler gauge.

14 If the difference in bore diameters at top and bottom is 0.010 in (0.2540 mm) or more, then the cylinders need reboring. If less than 0.010 in (0.2540 mm) then the fitting of new and special rings to the pistons can cure the trouble.

15 If the cylinders have already been bored out to their maximum, it is possible to have liners fitted. This situation will not often be encountered.

16 If the bores are slightly worn and it is decided to fit new rings, then the manufacturers' special instructions should be closely followed.

17 When new rings or pistons are fitted into old bores, it is essential to remove or roughen the hard glaze that will be found on the sides of the bores. This process is called 'glaze busting'. Using a piece of fine glasspaper, gently rub the bore, working up and down and rotating the cloth first one way and then the other.

18 Pistons are available in oversizes as shown in the Specifications Section, but in practice, the reborers will normally supply matching pistons of the correct grading to give the specified clearance in the new bores.

19 If the original pistons are to be refitted, carefully remove the piston rings and thoroughly clean them. Take particular care to clean out the piston ring grooves. A piece of an old broken ring is useful for this. Do not damage the aluminium piston in the process of cleaning.

20 To check the existing rings, place them in the cylinder bore and press each one down in turn to the bottom of the stroke. In this case a distance of $2\frac{1}{2}$ inches (65 mm) from the top of the cylinder will be satisfactory. Use an inverted piston to press them down square. With a feeler gauge, measure the gap for each ring which should be as given in the Specifications at the beginning of this Chapter. If the gap is too large, the rings will need renewal.

21 Check also that each ring gives a clearance in the piston groove according to the Specifications. If the gap is too great, new pistons and rings will be required. However, independent specialist producers of pistons and rings can normally provide the rings required separately. If new pistons and rings are being obtained, it will be necessary to have the ridge ground away from the top of each cylinder bore. If specialist oil control rings are being obtained from an independent supplier, the ridge removal will not be necessary as the top rings will be stepped to provide the necessary clearance. If the top ring of a new set is not stepped it will hit the ridge made by the former ring and break.

22 If new pistons are obtained the rings will be included, so it must be emphasised that the top ring be stepped if fitted to an un-reground bore (or worn, ridged bore).

23 The new rings should be placed in the bores as described in paragraph 20 and the gap checked. Any gaps that are too small should be increased by filing one end of the ring with a fine file. Be careful not to break the ring as they are brittle (and expensive). On no account make the gap less than specified. If the gap should close when under normal operating temperatures the ring will break.

24 The groove clearance of new rings in old pistons should be within the specified tolerances. If it is not enough, the rings could stick in the piston grooves causing loss of compression. The piston grooves in this case will need turning out to accept the new rings.

Camshaft and camshaft bearings

25 With the camshaft removed, examine the bearings for signs of obvious wear and pitting. If there are signs, then the three bearings will need renewal. This is not a common requirement and to have to do so is indicative of severe engine neglect at some time. As special removal and refitting tools are necessary to do this work properly it is recommended that it is done by a specialist. Check that the bearings are located properly, so that the oilways from the bearing housings are not obstructed. Reaming is not required after fitting the bearings.

26 The camshaft itself should show no marks on either the bearing journals or the profiles. If it does, it should be renewed. Examine the skew gear for signs of wear or damage. If this is badly worn it will mean renewing the camshaft.

27 The thrust plate (which also acts as the locating plate) should not be ridged or worn in any way. If it is, renew it.

Timing chain, sprockets and tensioner

28 Examine the teeth of both sprockets for wear. Each tooth is the shape of an inverted 'V' and if the driving (or driven) side is concave in shape, the tooth is worn and the sprocket should be renewed. The chain should also be renewed if the sprocket teeth are worn or if the tensioner adjustment is fully taken up. It is sensible practice to renew the chain anyway.

29 Examine the rubber slipper head of the tensioner for wear or score marks. If the head is worn more than 0.050 in (1.30 mm), or any score marks are present, renew the head. It is normal to renew the slipper head when fitting a new chain.

Rockers and rocker shaft

30 Thoroughly clean out the rocker shaft, remembering that it carries the oil that lubricates the rockers, valves, pushrods and tappets. Check that the oil holes in the shaft are quite clear. Check the shaft for

straightness by rolling it on a piece of plate glass. It is most unlikely that it will deviate from normal, but, if it does, then a new shaft should be obtained. The surface of the shaft should be free from any worn ridges caused by the rocker arms. If any wear is present (especially on the underside) renew the shaft. Wear is only likely to have occurred if the rocker shaft oil holes have become blocked.

31 Check the rocker arms for wear of the rocker bushes, for wear at the rocker arm face that bears on the valve stem, and for wear of the adjusting ball-ended screws. Wear in the rocker arm bush can be checked by gripping the rocker arm tip and holding the rocker arm in place on the shaft, noting if there is any lateral rocker arm shake. If shake is present, and the arm is very loose on the shaft, remedial action must be taken.

32 Check the tip of the rocker arm, where it bears on the valve head, for cracking or serious wear on the case hardening. If none is present re-use the rocker arm. Check the lower half of the ball on the end of the rocker arm adjusting screw. On high mileage engines wear on the ball and top of the pushrod is easily noted. Renew the adjusting screw and the pushrod if wear is uneven, or the end of the adjusting screw ball is flattened.

Tappets

33 Examine the bearing surface of the tappets that lie on the camshaft. Any indentation in this surface, or any cracks, indicate serious wear and the tappets should be renewed. Thoroughly clean them out, removing all traces of sludge. It is most unlikely that the sides of the tappets will prove worn, but, if they are a very loose fit in their bores and can readily be rocked, they should be exchanged for new units. It is very unusual to find any wear in the tappets and any present is likely to occur only at very high mileages.

Valves, valve seats and guides

34 Examine the heads of the valves for pitting, splits and burning, especially the heads of the exhaust valves. The valve seatings should be examined at the same time. If the pitting on the valve and seat is very slight the marks can be removed by grinding the seats and valves together with coarse, and then fine, valve grinding paste.

35 Where bad pitting has occurred to the valve seats it will be necessary to recut them and fit new valves. If the valve seats are so worn that they cannot be recut, then it will be necessary to fit new valve seat inserts. These latter two jobs should be entrusted to the local Talbot agent or engineering works. In practice it is very seldom that the seats are so badly worn that they require renewal. Normally, it is the valve that is too badly worn for refitting and the owner can easily purchase a new set of valves and match them to the seats by valve grinding (see Section 7).

36 Examine the valve guides internally for wear. If the valves are a very loose fit in the guides and there is evidence of lateral rocking, even when a new valve is inserted into the guide, then the valve guides must be reamed to the specified oversize and oversize valves fitted. Some engines have oversize valves fitted during production and this can be ascertained by looking at the two lugs adjacent to the manifold. No figure marked on the lugs indicates that the engine is fitted with standard valves.

37 The valve springs should be renewed if the engine has covered 30 000 miles (48 000 km) since the last major overhaul.

38 The inlet valves are fitted with stem oil seals (see Section 7).

Flywheel (or driveplate – automatic transmission)

39 If the teeth of the flywheel starter ring are badly worn, or if some are missing, then it will be necessary to remove the ring and fit a new one.

40 Split the ring with a cold chisel after making a cut with a hacksaw blade between two teeth. Take great care not to damage the flywheel during this process.

41 Check that the mating surfaces of the new ring and the flywheel are clean and free from burrs and heat the starter ring in an oven set at 428°F (220°C). Most domestic ovens can be heated to 550°F. Place the ring in the oven for 30 minutes. Do not exceed the recommended temperature or the temper of the ring will be lost, causing rapid wear.

42 Remove the heated ring from the oven with two pairs of pliers and fit the ring to the flywheel, so that the gear teeth chamfers are towards the flywheel and clutch face side.

43 The ring should be tapped gently down onto its register and left to cool naturally. The contraction of the metal on cooling will ensure that it is a secure and permanent fit.

44 On cars equipped with automatic transmission, the starter ring gear is a shrink fit on the inertia ring which itself is part of the torque converter. It is recommended that the fitting of a new starter ring gear is left to your dealer or automatic transmission specialist, but, if you do decide to do the work yourself, take care not to damage the inertia ring or torque converter. The best way to remove the old ring is to drill two $\frac{1}{8}$ in (3.0 mm) holes at the root of a tooth, almost through the ring gear, then split the gear with a cold chisel and hammer.

45 After heating the new ring gear, refit it to the torque converter inertia ring, so that the tooth chamfer is facing the front of the torque converter when the torque converter is in position in the car.

46 On cars with manual transmission, the flywheel clutch mating surface should be smooth and free from tiny cracks due to overheating, or any grooving caused by rivets on a worn driven plate.

47 If either of these conditions is observed it may be possible to have the surface refinished but if much metal has to be removed to achieve satisfactory results, the flywheel will have to be renewed.

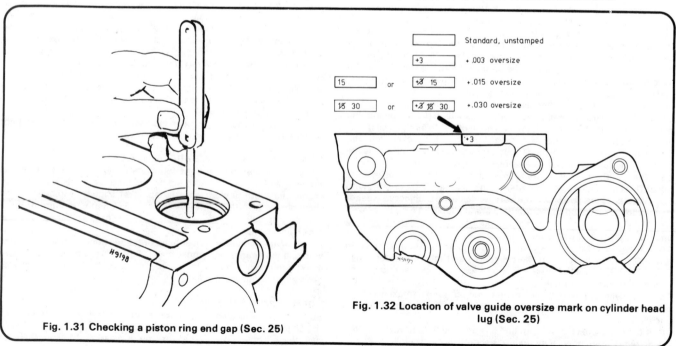

Fig. 1.31 Checking a piston ring end gap (Sec. 25)

Fig. 1.32 Location of valve guide oversize mark on cylinder head lug (Sec. 25)

26 Engine reassembly – general

1   Precise reassembly is described in the foregoing Sections, but the following general operations should be carried out in advance of reassembly.
2   To ensure maximum life with minimum trouble from a rebuilt engine, not only must everything be correctly assembled, but everything must be spotlessly clean, all the oilways must be clear, locking washers and spring washers must always be fitted where indicated and all bearing and other working surfaces must be thoroughly lubricated during assembly.
3   Before assembly begins renew any bolts or studs, if the threads are in any way damaged, and whenever possible use new spring washers.
4   Apart from your normal tools, a supply of clean rag, an oil can filled with engine oil, a supply of new assorted spring washers, a set of new gaskets and a torque wrench should be collected together.
5   If the engine has been completely stripped, the following reassembly sequence is recommended.

    (a) Crankshaft
    (b) Flywheel
    (c) Piston/connecting rods
    (d) Camshaft and tappets
    (e) Oil pump
    (f) Sump
    (g) Timing chain, tensioner and cover
    (h) Cylinder head
    (j) Rocker shaft assembly
    (k) Ancillary components (clutch, alternator, oil filter etc)

27 Initial start-up after major overhaul

1   Adjust the throttle speed screw to provide a faster than normal idling speed. This will offset the stiffness of new components.
2   Start the engine and check for oil and water leaks.
3   Run the engine until normal operating temperature is reached and then adjust the slow running. Check the tightness of the cylinder head bolts.
4   Dependent upon the number of new internal components which have been fitted to the engine, the speed should be restricted for the first few hundred miles.
5   It is recommended that the engine oil and filter are changed and the valve clearances checked after the initial 1000 miles (1600 km) running.

28 Fault diagnosis – engine

Refer to Section 28 of Part 1 of this Chapter.

Chapter 2 Cooling system

For modifications, and information applicable to later models, see Supplement at end of manual

Contents

Specifications

Type . . . .
Thermo syphon with belt-driven water pump. Electric cooling fan on all models excpet certain 1300/1600 versions operating in hot climates or used for towing

Radiator cap
Rating . . . .   15 lbf/in² (1 bar)

Electric fan operating range
Switches on . . . .   187°F (86°C)
Switches off . . . .   180°F (82°C)

Thermostat opening temperature
930 standard engine . . . .   180°F (82°C)
1300/1600 engines (extra hot climate) . . . .   180°F (82°C)
All other engines . . . .   190°F (88°C)

Belt tension . . . .
$\frac{1}{2}$ in (12 mm) deflection at centre of longest run of belt

Coolant capacity
930 engine . . . .   8 pints (4.5 litres)
1300/1600 engine . . . .   13 pints (7.3 litres)

Torque wrench settings

	lbf ft	Nm
Alternator mountings	16	22
Alternator adjuster link	9	12
Temperature sender unit (engine)	14	19
Water pump Taptite screws (930 engine)	15	20
Water pump to timing cover (930 engine)	16	22
Water pump to timing cover (1300/1600 engine)	13	17

1 General description

The cooling system on all models is of the pressurised type, using a radiator, water pump and fan. The standard method of cooling is by means of an electric fan. On 1300/1600 engined models operating in hot climates or used for towing, it is recommended that the belt-driven

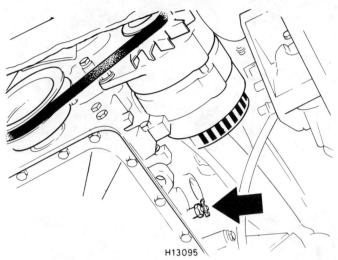

H13095

Fig. 2.1 Cylinder block drain tap (1300/1600 models) (Sec. 3)

type of fan is fitted and the electric type disconnected or removed. The belt-driven type of fan is available as a service part or supplied as part of the tow bar kit.

The electric fan is directly connected to the battery and it can operate at any time if the engine temperature is high enough, even without the ignition being switched on. Remember this when carrying out work in the engine compartment if the engine is hot.

2 Cooling system – maintenance

1   At weekly intervals, check the level of coolant in the radiator. The coolant should be within 1 in (25·4 mm) of the bottom of the filler neck.

2   It is preferable to check and top up the cooling system when the engine is cold. If it must be done hot, then cover the filler cap with a thick cloth and turn it anti-clockwise very slowly to its first stop. Allow the pressure in the radiator to escape slowly. When the hissing has stopped, depress the cap and turn it fully anti-clockwise and remove it. Never add cold water to a hot engine, it may crack the castings.

3   Periodically, check the hoses and clips for security, leaks and deterioration generally.

4   In the autumn, remove the radiator grille and brush away flies and dirt from the front of the radiator, using a soft brush.

3 Cooling system – draining, flushing and refilling

1   The cooling system should be drained, flushed and refilled under either of the following circumstances: Either every two years for renewal of the antifreeze mixture or whenever the coolant appears dirty or rusty in colour.

2   Set the heater controls to *'hot'*, remove the radiator cap and open the radiator and cylinder block drain taps (photos).

3   When the coolant has drained, insert a cold water hose in the filler neck of the radiator and flush the system through, until the water runs clear.

4   With severely contaminated systems, reverse flush by disconnecting the radiator bottom hose and inserting the cold water hose in the open end of the radiator hose. Disconnect the radiator top hose from the engine and then turn on the water pressure. Flush until the water runs out clear.

5   Once the system is clean, allow all the water to drain out and then close the taps finger tight. Reconnect the radiator hoses if these were disconnected.

6   Refill the system through the radiator filler cap making sure that the heater controls are set to *'hot'*. Use only antifreeze or inhibiting mixture as described in the next Section, never plain water. If possible, use rain water to add to the antifreeze mixture and for topping up.

7   On some models, a bleed valve is incorporated in the heater pipe crossover tube. If this is released, any air trapped in the heater will be expelled (photo).

8   Start the engine, run it for a few minutes, varying its speed, switch off and then top up to the specified coolant level. Refit the radiator cap.

4 Coolant mixtures

1   In cold climates, the use of antifreeze mixture is essential during the winter period. The mixture should also remain in the system during the summer months, to act as a corrosion inhibitor.

2   The use of plain water should never be entertained in the 930 engine, as even if an antifreeze mixture is not required because of favourable climatic conditions, an inhibitor must be used to prevent corrosion in the all-aluminium engine.

3   Top quality antifreeze products are suitable for use in all engine types (cast-iron or aluminium). If at all doubtful as to the product's compatibility, choose one to the following specificion:

> *930 engine*   to BS 3150
> *1300/1600 engines*   to BS3151 or 3152

4   Before adding antifreeze to the system, check all hose connections and check the tightness of the cylinder head bolts, as such solutions are searching. The cooling system should be drained and partially refilled with clean water as previously explained, before adding antifreeze (photo).

5   The quantity of antifreeze which should be used for various levels of protection is given in the table below, expressed as a perercentage of the system capacity.

Antifreeze volume	Protection to	Safe pump circulation
25%	–26°C (– 15°F)	–12°C (10°F)
30%	–33°C (–28°C)	–16°C (3°F)
35%	–39°C (–38°F)	–20°C (–4°F)
40%	–41°C (–42°F)	–23°C (–10°F)
50%	–47°C (–53°F)	–37°C (–35°F)

6   Where the cooling system contains an antifreeze solution, any topping up should be done with a solution made up in similar proportions to the original in order to avoid dilution.

7   Do not spill antifreeze onto any paintwork, it may damage it.

5 Radiator cap

1   The radiator filler cap has two functions; to maintain the system pressure and to prevent coolant loss through the overflow pipe. A spring-loaded pressure valve is incorporated in the filler cap, together with a vacuum valve which opens when the coolant temperature falls to allow air to enter the radiator through the overflow pipe.

2   Any doubts about the operation of the cap can only be checked out by your dealer using a pressure tester.

3   Always renew a filler cap with one marked with the identical pressure rating.

6 Radiator – removal, repair and refitting

1   Drain the cooling system as previously described. Retain the coolant in a clean container if it is clean and fresh enough for further use.

Cars with electric fan

2   Disconnect the battery.

3   Disconnect the top and bottom hoses from the radiator.

4   Disconnect the two-pin plugs from the temperature sensing unit and from the fan motor.

5   On models equipped with automatic transmission, disconnect the fluid cooler pipes from the base of the radiator and plug or cap the pipes and holes.

6   Extract the bolt that secures the radiator to the front panel. Support the electric fan assembly and unscrew the three securing bolts from the fan supports.

7   Remove the complete radiator assembly, taking care not to spill any residual antifreeze coolant mixture onto the paintwork.

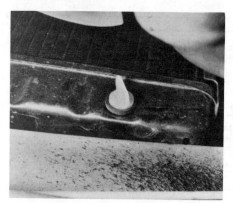
3.2A Radiator drain tap

3.2B Cylinder block drain tap (930 engine)

3.7 Heater air bleed valve (930 engine)

4.4 Tightening a radiator top hose clip (930 engine)

6.13 Electric fan sensing unit

7.3 Fan to radiator mounting bracket (930 engine)

8.4 Thermostat, housing cover and gasket (930 engine)

8.9 Thermostat in position in housing cover (930 engine)

9.4 Water pump removed from impeller housing (930 engine)

9.6A Cylinder block to water pump impeller housing (930 engine)

9.6B Water pump lower hose connections (930 engine)

9.8 Rear view of water pump impeller housing (930 engine)

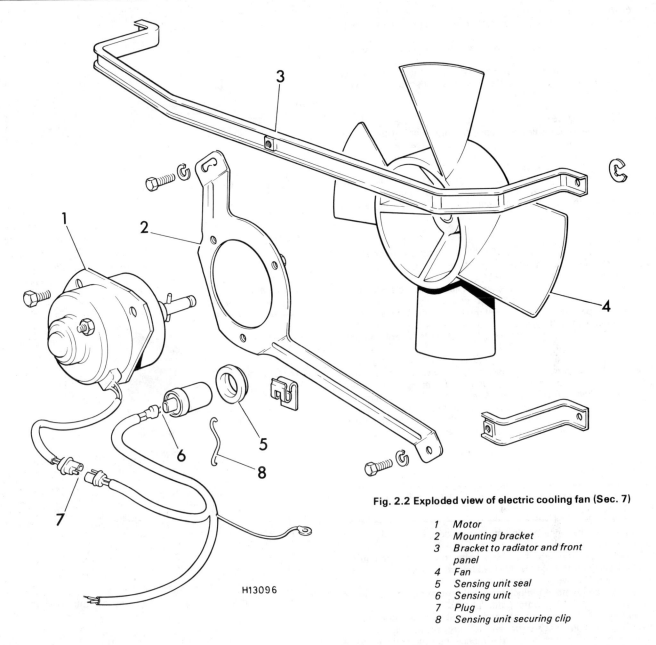

H13096

Fig. 2.2 Exploded view of electric cooling fan (Sec. 7)

1   Motor
2   Mounting bracket
3   Bracket to radiator and front
    panel
4   Fan
5   Sensing unit seal
6   Sensing unit
7   Plug
8   Sensing unit securing clip

Cars with belt-driven fan

8   Drain the cooling system as previously described and disconnect the top and bottom radiator hoses from the radiator.
9   On models equipped with automatic transmission, disconnect the oil cooler pipes from the base of the radiator. Plug the open ends of the pipes and the holes in the radiator.
10   If a radiator cowl is fitted, extract the cowl securing bolts and lift the cowl to the rear over the fan blades.
11   Unscrew and remove the four bolts that secure the radiator to the front panel and lift out the radiator.

All models

12   If the radiator is leaking, it is recommended that a new or reconditioned one is obtained, or the faulty one repaired by a specialist. Soldering a radiator is a difficult job and unless the heat required is applied very locally to perfectly clean metal, is rarely successful.
13   Before discarding a radiator, prise off the clip, and withdraw the electric fan sensing unit from its rubber sealing ring in the base of the radiator (see also Section 13) (photo).
14   Unbolt and remove the electric fan assembly.
15   Refitting of the radiator is a reversal of removal. On completion,

refill the cooling system as described in Section 3 and check and top up the fluid in the automatic transmission (if fitted).

7   Electric cooling fan – removal and refitting

1   Disconnect the battery.
2   Disconnect the two-pin plug from the fan motor.
3   Suppport the weight of the fan motor and mounting bracket and extract the two mounting bracket bolts. Withdraw the assembly from below the front of the car (photo).
4   Refitting is a reversal of removal, but do not tighten the bracket bolts until the fan has been pulled as far from adjacent components as is possible.
5   Faulty fan components should be renewed not repaired.

8   Thermostat – removal, testing and refitting

1   A faulty thermostat can cause overheating or slow warm-up. It will also affect the performance of the heater.

930 engine

2 Completely drain the cooling system as described earlier in this Chapter.
3 Disconnect the radiator bottom hose from the base of the water pump.
4 Extract the two securing bolts and withdraw the cover/inlet pipe assembly, complete with thermostat, from the underside of the water pump (photo).

1300/1600 engines

5 Remove the radiator cap and open the drain tap on the cylinder block. Drain off about three pints of coolant into a clean vessel.
6 Extract the two bolts that secure the thermostat housing cover to the front end of the cylinder head.
7 Lift the thermostat cover, move it to one side (top radiator hose still attached) and extract the thermostat. If it is stuck tightly in its seat, do not attempt to lever it out but cut round its edge using a sharp pointed knife.

All models

8 To test whether the unit is serviceable, suspend the thermostat by a piece of string in a pan of water being heated. Using a thermometer, with reference to the opening and closing temperature in Specifications, its operation may be checked. The thermostat should be renewed if it is stuck open or closed, or it fails to operate at the specified temperature. The operation of a thermostat is not instantaneous and sufficient time must be allowed for movement during testing. Never refit a faulty unit, leave it out if no replacement is available immediately.
9 Refitting is a reversal of the removal operations, using a new gasket smeared with jointing compound. Refill the cooling system on completion. **Note:** *On 930 engines, new water pumps are supplied with securing bolt holes untapped. When connecting the thermostat cover to a new pump body or the pump body to the impeller housing, the special screws supplied should be wound in to the specified torque and they will form their own threads. These special self-tapping screws may be used repeatedly, provided their threads are undamaged (photo).*

---

9 Water pump (930 engine) – removal, dismantling, reassembly and refitting

1 Completely drain the cooling system as described earlier in this Chapter.
2 Slacken the alternator mounting bolts, push the alternator in towards the engine and slip the drivebelt from the pulley.
3 Unbolt and remove the water pump pulley.
4 Unscrew and remove the bolts that hold the pump to the impeller housing and withdraw the water pump (photo).
5 Normally, this amount of dismantling is all that is required but if the impeller housing must also be removed, proceed as follows.
6 Disconnect all the hoses from the impeller housing and thermostat housing (photos).
7 Disconnect the wire from the temperature sender unit.
8 Unscrew and remove the three mounting nuts and withdraw the impeller/thermostat housing from below the car (photo).
9 Provided the rear face of the pulley mounting hub is supported, the impeller spindle can be pressed out of the hub. New water pumps are supplied without a pulley mounting hub and the old hub must be pressed onto the impeller spindle until the chamfer on the spindle is just visible. Make sure to support the inner end of the impeller spindle when pressing on the hub.
10 Refitting of the water pump is a reversal of removal but make sure that the mating surfaces are quite clean. Use a new gasket smeared with jointing compound and tighten all bolts to the specified torque.
11 Refill the cooling system and then fit and adjust the drivebelt as described in Section 11.

---

10 Water pump (1300/1600 engine) – removal and refitting

1 Completely drain the cooling system.
2 Slacken the alternator mounting bolts, push the alternator in towards the engine and slip the drivebelt from the pulley.

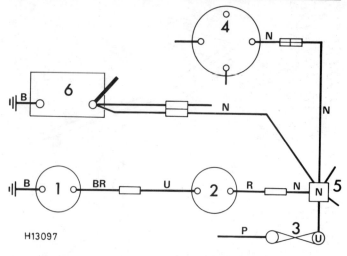

Fig. 2.3 Electric cooling fan wiring circuit (Sec. 7)

1 Sensing unit
2 Fan motor
3 Fuse number four
4 Ignition switch
5 Internal connection
6 Battery

Wiring colour code
B = Black
N = Brown
P – Purple
R = Red
U = Blue

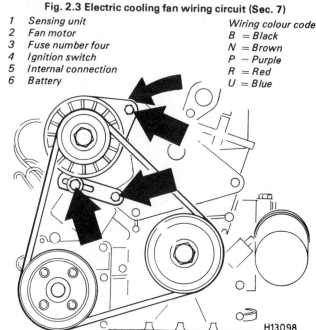

Fig. 2.4 Alternator mountings and adjuster link (930 engine) (Sec 11)

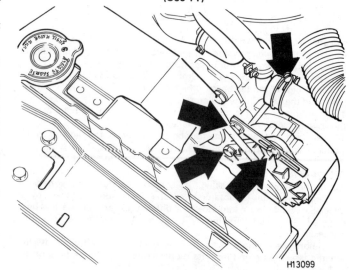

Fig. 2.5 Alternator mountings and adjuster link (1300/1600 engines) (Sec 11)

11.2 Tensioning a drivebelt

12.2 Water temperature gauge sender unit located in rear of water pump impeller housing (930 engine)

13.3 Electric fan sensing unit, cable plug and radiator bottom hose

3   If a belt-driven fan is fitted, remove the fan blades, pulley and spacer.
4   Unscrew and remove the five water pump mounting bolts. These are of different lengths and it is a good plan to push them into a sheet of paper in the same relative position as they are fitted.
5   Withdraw the water pump. This is a very tight fit on its locating dowels and may need tapping off forwards, **never** sideways, to remove it.
6   On cars with an electric fan, the belt pulley fitted to the water pump should now be removed.
7   New water pumps are supplied complete with pulley mounting hub, repair kits are not available.
8   Refitting is a reversal of removal, making sure that the mating surfaces are quite clean. Use a new gasket smeared with jointing compound and tighten the bolts to the specified torque; except the alternator adjuster strap bolt which should be left finger tight.
9   Refill the cooling system, refit the drivebelt and adjust as described in Section 11.

11 Drivebelt – adjusting tension and renewal

1   The drivebelt on all models is used to drive the alternator and water pump from the pulley on the front of the crankshaft.
2   The belt is correctly tensioned when it can be deflected with thumb pressure at the centre of its longest run through $\frac{1}{2}$ in (12·0 mm) (photo).
3   Adjustment is carried out by releasing the alternator mounting bolts and the adjuster strap bolts and moving the alternator in towards or away from the engine until the tension is correct. It will be an easier operation if the mounting bolts are only released enough to enable the alternator to pivot stiffly.
4   On 1300 and 1600 engines, if the coolant is hot, release the radiator cap carefully, as described in Section 2, to release the system internal pressure. This is necessary to avoid the curious feature of these engines, which causes the coolant to escape up the threads of the inner bolt on the adjuster strap as the bolt is unscrewed.
5   Tighten the adjuster strap bolts and alternator mountings on completion.
6   To renew a drivebelt, always slacken the alternator mountings and push the alternator as far towards the engine as possible. It will then be found quite easy to slip the belt over the pulley rim. Never attempt to prise a belt over a pulley rim without first having slackened the alterator mountings.

12 Water temperature sender unit

1   On 930 engines, the unit is screwed into the rear face of the water pump impeller housing.
2   Remove it by unscrewing it, having first drained the cooling system completely (photo).
3   On 1300 and 1600 engines, the sender unit is located just below the thermostat housing at the front of the cylinder head. Removal is similar to that described for the smaller engine, except that only about four pints of coolant need be drained.

13 Water temperature sensing unit (electric fan) – removal, testing and refitting

1   Disconnect the battery.
2   Drain the cooling system completely.
3   Disconnect the two-pin plug from the sensing unit which is located in the base of the radiator (photo).
4   Prise off the sensing unit retaining clip and then carefully prise the unit from its rubber seal.
5   If the unit is suspected of being faulty, connect it in series with a battery and test bulb and place the unit in cold water. If the test bulb lights up, renew the unit.
6   Now heat the water uniformly, until at the specified temperature (see Specification Section) the light comes on. This will correspond to the radiator fan 'cut-in' temperature. If the bulb does not light up at all or does so at a very different temperature, renew the unit.
7   Refit the unit by reversing the removal operations, but apply a smear of liquid detergent to ease the entry of the unit into the rubber seal.

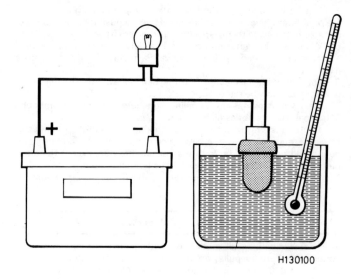

H130100

Fig. 2.6 Electric fan sensing unit test circuit (Sec. 13)

14 Fault diagnosis – cooling system

Symptom	Reason(s)
Overheating	Low coolant level
	Slack fan belt
	Radiator pressure cap faulty or of wrong type
	Defective water pump
	Cylinder head gasket blowing
	Radiator core clogged
	Radiator blocked
	Binding brakes
	Bottom hose or tank frozen
	Electric fan not cutting in due to defective sensing unit or disconnected wire
	Abuse of automatic transmission
Engine running too cool	Defective thermostat
	Faulty water temperature gauge
	Faulty electric fan from sensing unit causing excessive operation
Loss of coolant	Leaking radiator or hoses
	Cylinder head gasket leaking
	Leaking cylinder block core plugs
	Faulty radiator filler cap or wrong type fitted

Chapter 3 Fuel and exhaust systems

For modifications, and information applicable to later models, see Supplement at end of manual

Contents

Specifications

Fuel pump

Type	Mechanical, driven from camshaft
Pressure at zero output:	
930 cc engine (Unitac)	170 to 240 millibars (2.5 to 3.5 lbf/in^2)
1300 and 1600 cc engines (RAI).....................	240 to 345 millibars (3.5 to 5.0 lbf/in^2)
Fuel tank capacity	9 Imp gals (41 litres)

Fuel octane rating

97 (4 star)

Carburettor (8 series, except Sweden)

Engine	Specification No*	Carburettor type
(a) 930	S3892B	Zenith 1.50 CD3
(b) 1300 HC	S3911B	Zenith 1.50 CD3
(c) 1300 LC	S3912B	Zenith 1.50 CD3
(d) 1300 HC	S3908B	Zenith 1.75 CD3
(e) 1600 HC	S3914B	Zenith 1.50 CD3
(f) 1600 LC	S3913B	Zenith 1.50 CD3

*Specification No stamped on metal tag attached to cover screw

Carburettor specifications

As listed in above section:

	Needle type	Piston spring	Cam type	Fast idle gap in (mm)	Idling speed (rpm)
(a)	B5EK	blue	G	0.025 to 0.030 (0.6 to 0.75)	820 to 880
(b)	B5DU	blue	M	0.025 to 0.035 (0.6 to 0.9)	770 to 830
(c)	B5DK	blue	M	0.025 to 0.035 (0.6 to 0.9)	770 to 830
(d)	B1EB	none	VA	0.025 to 0.035 (0.6 to 0.9)	870 to 930
(e)	B5EE	blue	M	0.025 to 0.035 (0.6 to 0.9)	770 to 830 *
(f)	B5DK	blue	M	0.025 to 0.035 (0.6 to 0.9)	770 to 830

* *Automatic transmission selector lever in N (where applicable)*

CO content at idling	1.5 to 2.5%

Torque wrench settings

	lbf ft	Nm
Air cleaner to carburettor	5	7
Carburettor to inlet manifold	8	11

Exhaust pipe to manifold:		
930 cc engines	9	12
1300 and 1600 cc engines	28	38
Fuel pump to camshaft cover (930 cc engines)	15	20
Fuel pump to cylinder block (1300 and 1600 cc engines)	10	13.5
Fuel tank to body	11	15
Manifolds to cylinder head:		
930 cc engines	15	20
1300 and 1600 cc engines	16	21.5

1 General description

The fuel system comprises a nine gallon (41 litre) fuel tank, a mechanically operated fuel pump and a Zenith (Stromberg) constant depression carburettor.

The fuel tank is positioned below the rear load floor panel and is held in position by nuts and bolts. The filler pipe neck is detachable from the tank and at its upper end passes through the right-hand rear wing panel. The combined fuel outlet and sender unit is located in the upper face of the fuel tank. Fuel tank ventilation is via the filler cap which incorporates spring loaded pressure and vacuum valves. The fuel tank is positively sealed when the cap is fitted.

The mechanical fuel pump is mounted either on the cambox (930 cc engine) or the crankcase (1300/1600 cc engines) and is operated by an eccentric formed on the camshaft. Located in the fuel pump is a nylon filter screen and access is gained via a sediment cap.

The air cleaner fitted to all models is of the renewable paper element type, and incorporates an air temperature control device in the interests of maintaining fuel economy and reducing exhaust emission levels during the engine's warm-up period. A positive crankcase ventilation system is fitted, the crankcase fumes being routed through the air cleaner to the combustion chamber where they are burnt off in the normal combustion process.

2 Air cleaner – description and operation

This type of air cleaner incorporates a control flap which admits warm air from an exhaust manifold heated stove under certain operating conditions. It provides an initial rapid warm-up of the air intake and maintains the air temperature between 25°C and 33°C (76°F and 91°F); this permits earlier choke closure and a resulting improvement in fuel consumption.

The control flap is operated by a vacuum energised diaphragm 'motor', the supply of vacuum being governed by a heat sensitive bi-metallic strip mounted in the thermal sensor. Air passing through the air cleaner is brought into contact wih the bi-metallic strip which then reacts, according to air temperature, to operate the control flap. On 930 cc models the thermal sensor has an additional dual sensitive bi-metallic spring which operates a spigot valve located in the brass 'leg' between the thermal sensor and the diaphragm motor.

The vacuum supply tubes to the thermal sensor and the diaphragm 'motor' are connected to the inlet manifold for vacuum source, and this enables the system to be sensitive to throttle butterfly opening positions. If full acceleration is required during the warm-up

period, the control flap will admit cold air in greater volume and the normal temperature control will be temporarily overridden. On 930 cc models there is a delay before the control flap is moved to the cold air position during wide throttle openings at air intake temperatures below 13°C (54°F) and this is caused by the dual sensor. Operation of the dual sensor unit is identical to the single sensor during the warm-up and thermal control periods, the spigot valve is held off its seat by the vacuum inside the sensor unit.

Should the system develop a fault, first inspect all the vacuum pipes for security and fractures. The diaphragm 'motor' can be checked by removing the vacuum pipe from the inlet manifold to the thermal sensor, and connecting it from the inlet manifold to the diaphragm 'motor'. With the engine running the hot air valve flap should open fully. If the control flap and diaphragm 'motor' are still satisfactory, suspect the thermal sensor, which should be checked for blockage of the vacuum restrictor holes and air cleaner supply holes. Make sure that the vacuum relief ball is not sticking to the valve seat.

3 Air cleaner – removal, refitting and servicing

Note: *On 930 cc engine models it is important that the brass connection of the dual sensor unit is coupled to the vacuum motor (photo).*
1   Pull off the vacuum sensor pipe and the rubber crankcase ventilation hose at the inlet manifold connections.
2   Remove the bolts, washers and insulators that secure the air cleaner assembly to the carburettor flange.
3   Lift the air cleaner away from the carburettor and disconnect the attached metallised flexible tube at the exhaust manifold 'stove' (photo).
4   To dismantle the air cleaner pull off the vacuum pipe at the diaphragm motor, remove the single securing screw and prise the cover from the air cleaner body.
5   The filter element and rubber sealing rings can now be removed. Examine the filter element and if it is found to be very dirty renew it. It is recommended that the element is cleaned at 5000 mile (8000 km) intervals and renewed at 10 000 mile (16 000 km) intervals. However, if the car is being driven in very dusty conditions, then it will be found necessary to renew the filter element much earlier than the mileage specified (photo).
6   The paper element may be cleaned by using a compressed air jet in the reverse direction to air flow (outwards, from the centre of the filter element). Finally tap the element gently to remove any adhering particles.
7   When either cleaning or renewing the filter element, wipe out the

3.0 Attachment of vacuum pipes to air cleaner (930 engines)

3.3 Removing air cleaner (930 cc engine)

3.5 Air cleaner showing element

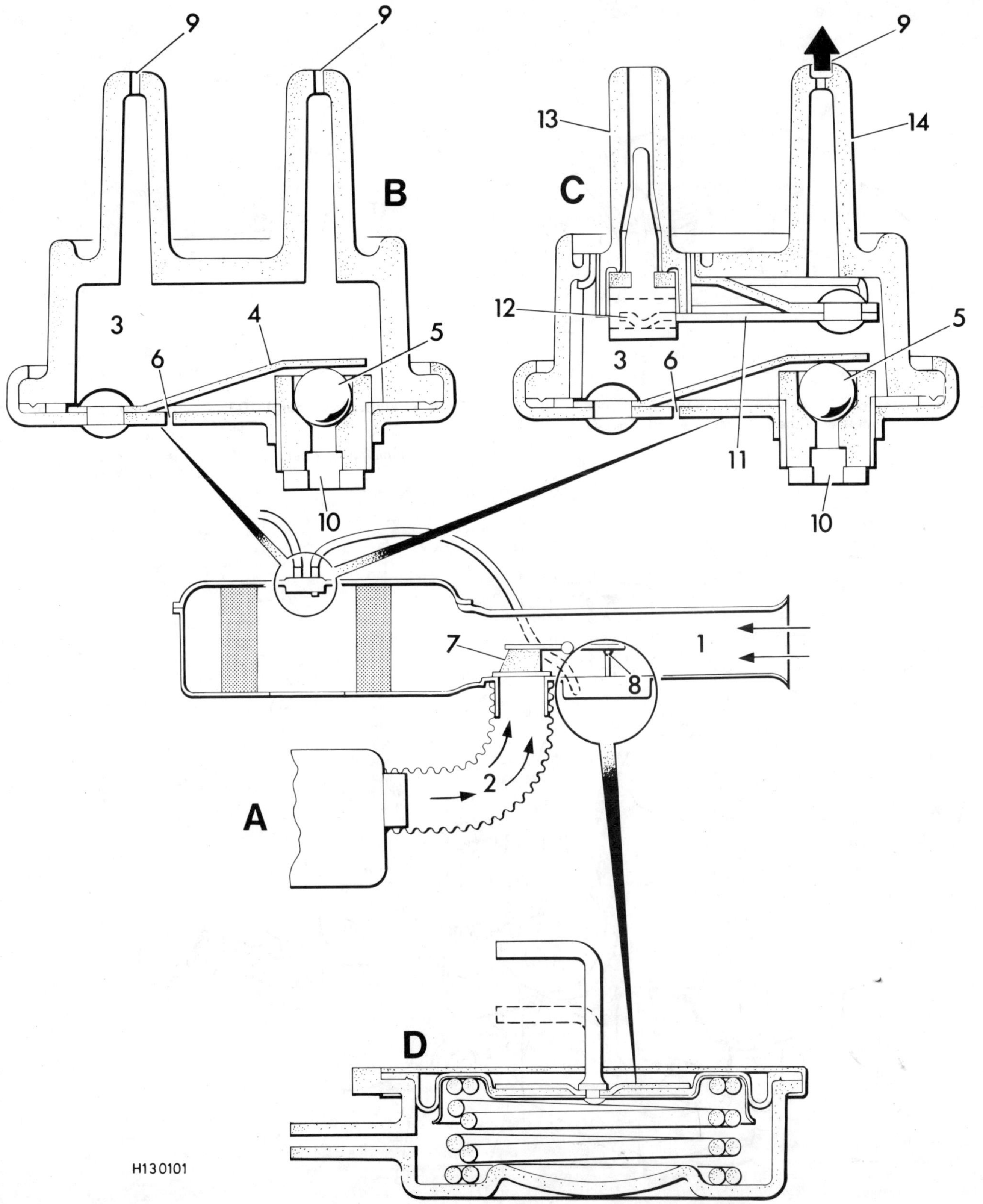

Fig. 3.1 Schematic layout of the air temperature control system (single sensor as fitted to 1300/1600 models and dual sensor as fitted to 930 models) (Sec. 2)

A Stove	3 Vacuum chamber	9 Vacuum restrictor holes	12 Spigot valve
B Single sensor	4 Bi-metallic strip	10 Air admission hole in vacuum relief valve	13 Brass leg which is connected to diaphragm motor
C Dual sensor	5 Vacuum relief ball valve	11 Bi-metallic strip of spigot valve	14 Nylon leg which is connected to inlet manifold
D Diaphragm motor	6 Air admission hole		
1 Air cleaner intake	7 Dual flap valve		
2 Heated air tube	8 Diaphragm motor pivot		

H130101

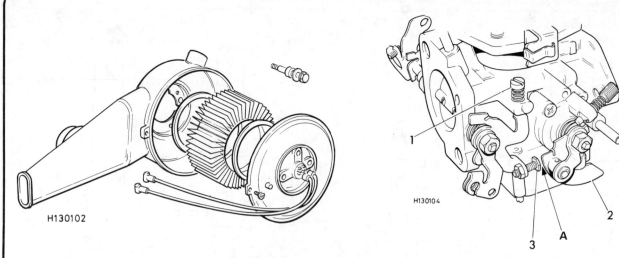

H130102

H130104

Fig. 3.2 Typical air cleaner assembly (type shown is fitted to models with the 1·75 carburettor) (Sec. 3)

Fig. 3.3 Zenith (Stromberg) CD3 carburettor adjustment screws (Sec. 4)

1 Slow running adjustment screw
2 Fast idle cam
3 Fast idle screw
A Fast idle screw to cam gap

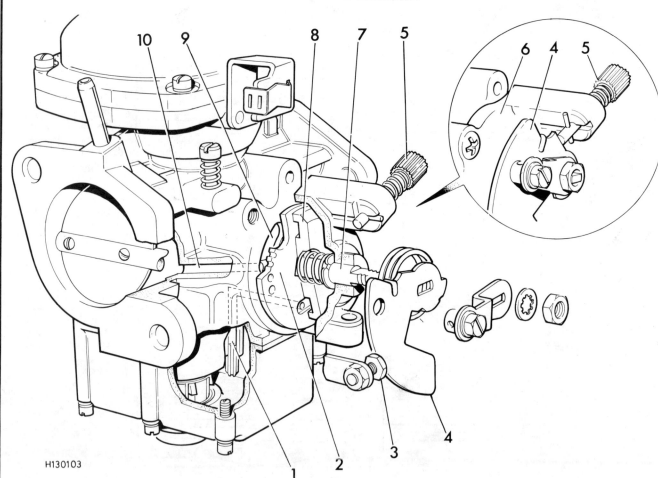

H130103

Fig. 3.4 Zenith (Stromberg) CD3 starter assembly details (Sec. 4)

1 Fuel feed drilling to starter assembly
2 Metering holes in disc valve
3 Fast idle Adjustment screw
4 Fast idle cam
5 Starter assembly two-position stop (inset shows the normal position of the stop.)
6 Starter assembly outer housing
7 Disc valve spindle
8 Starter assembly disc valve
9 Port feed by metering holes in disc valve
10 Fuel feed from port 9 to throttle bore.

interior of the air cleaner casing and cover with a clean rag, taking care to prevent dirt deposits getting into the small air bleed hole or the vacuum relief valve body of the sensor unit.

8   Refit the element with the sealing rings placed one either side of it and refit the cover.

9   Refitting of the air cleaner is the reverse of the removal procedure. It is recommended that the gasket located between the air cleaner and carburettor is renewed. Where the air cleaner of a 930 cc model is being refitted remember to connect the vacuum pipes correctly (see note at the beginning of this Section).

4   Carburettor – description and operation

This is a constant depression type of carburettor fitted with a separate starter assembly. The design permits the use of a variable choke and a needle which moves in a single jet to provide a fuel/air mixture to meet all conditions of engine operation. An external view of the carburettor starter assembly is shown in Fig. 3.4.

The float is made from a synthetic material and cannot be punctured. When the engine is not operating the air valve piston rests on the carburettor body. When the choke control is operated, the cam rotates the throttle and operates the starter assembly disc valve, to meter extra fuel required for cold starting and running. Immediately the engine fires, the air valve piston is lifted by air pressure to a position dependent upon trottle opening. At idling speed the air valve piston is lifted by air pressure. The jet to needle annulus area is then set by the needle adjustment, so that in conjunction with the slow running setting, correct idling is obtained. Above idling speed, the needle and piston are raised by air pressure acting on the underside of the diaphragm. Above the diaphragm there exists a lower pressure (partial inlet manifold vacuum). Operating the throttle raises and lowers it to give the necessary fuel/air ratio and constant air speed over the jet orifice to ensure good fuel atomisation. The hydraulic damper prevents sudden rising of the air valve piston during acceleration, when temporary mixture enrichment is required. The flexible diaphragm provides an air seal and locates the air piston. Fuel flow to the float chamber is controlled by a needle valve which is closed by a float when fuel rises to the correct level. The float chamber is vented to the inside of the air filter mounting flange and fuel reaches the jet through drillings.

Cold starting requires an initial rich mixture, together with a means of progressively weakening the mixture, plus a throttle opening mechanism for fast idling. The starter assembly provides these conditions and is situated behind the fast idle cam. The disc valve controls the extra fuel needed for cold starting. This fuel is fed through a channel from the float chamber, through the disc valve, through a further channel and into the throttle body between the air valve piston and the throttle valve. Immediately the engine starts, the air valve piston rises sufficiently to provide the air needed for engine operation to continue. The two-position stop is provided to permit all, or some, of the disc valve metering holes to be used, dependent upon ambient temperatures. For normal conditions, the position of the stop shown (inset) in Fig. 3.4 is correct. Below −23°C (−10°F) use the alternative stop position. As the choke is pushed home, the number of holes metering fuel through the disc valve decreases, until finally the disc valve is blanked off and no fuel passes to the throttle bore. There is no separate idling circuit, the fuel/air mixture and quantity depends upon the throttle opening set by the slow running adjustment screw.

Part and full throttle driving causes the air valve piston to rise and fall by action of the throttle, which in turn controls the metering of fuel by varying the annular discharge as the differing profile of the needle passes up and down in the jet orifice. The needle is spring loaded and biased to one side so that it always rubs on the side of the jet. By using a biased needle, effect on mixture will always be a known constant. When the air flow under the air valve piston reaches a certain speed, according to the position of the carburettor butterfly valve, a depression is caused above the diaphragm to cause the air valve piston to lift and float on air pressure. The position of the air valve piston is dependent on the throttle opening and the consequent air flow and depression above the diaphragm. The air valve piston movement is also controlled by a return spring (if fitted). Sudden acceleration, with attendant inrush of air, could cause a weakening of the mixture. This is overcome by the provision of the hydraulic damper piston which restricts the upward movement of the air valve piston. Downward motion of this component is not restricted.

5   Carburettor – adjustments

1   The carburettor fitted to all models is of the tamperproof, emission control type. The mixture setting is set during production and can only be altered using a special service tool CC 0027. While it is emphasised that any variation to the mixture setting should only be carried out when absolutely essential, it must be realised that no two engines are exactly the same and slight mixture adjustment may be required, especially after the first few thousand miles of operation. Adjustment may also be required after major overhaul or dismantling of the carburettor (photos).

2   In many operating territories, adjustment of the carburettor may only be carried out in conjunction with a CO meter (exhaust gas analyser). This is described in method 1 in the following paragraphs.

3   Where such regulations do not apply, the carburettor may be adjusted as described in method 2.

Method 1

4   First check that the ignition timing is correct, the valve clearances are adjusted in accordance with the specification and the engine is in a good state of overhaul generally. Make sure that the air cleaner is in clean condition.

5   Run the car on the road until the engine is at normal operating temperature. Open the bonnet immediately the car is stopped to prevent excessive under-bonnet temperatures occurring.

6   Connect a supplementary tachometer to the engine. This must not be of the type triggered by the coil low tension circuit.

7   Start the engine and adjust the idling speed to the specification by turning the slow running adjustment screw.

8   Connect the exhaust gas analyser to the car in accordance with the manufacturers' instructions and using the special service tool, adjust the mixture until the CO reading is between 1.5 and 2.5%.

9   The service tool comprises an inner and outer member. To use the tool, first remove the carburettor damper and then insert the tool into the depression chamber. Engage the outer member of the tool with the piston guide rod and the slot in the inner member with the needle carrier.

10   Turn the inner member of the tool a maximum of $\frac{1}{4}$ of a turn in either direction until the CO level comes within the specified limits. Hold the outer member quite still while the inner member is being turned, otherwise the flexible diaphragm will be damaged.

11   If the carburettor is excessively out of adjustment or has just been reassembled, set the needle to the datum position initially by turning the inner member of the service tool fully clockwise to the upper limit of its travel and then anti clockwise $1\frac{7}{8}$ turns exactly. The turns can be calculated by observing the position of the cranked end of the inner member of the tool.

12   Turning the tool inner member clockwise raises the needle and richens the mixture. Turning the tool anti-clockwise lowers the needle and weakens the mixture.

13   It is recommended that between each adjustment of the needle, the tool is withdrawn, the damper oil topped up and the damper refitted. The engine should then be started and run for half a minute to stabilise the carburettor. The engine will normally have to be switched off to remove the tool and to refit the damper, as the engine will almost certainly stall otherwise.

Method 2

14   The procedure is very similar to that described in the preceding paragraphs. First set the inner member of the service tool fully clockwise, so that the needle is at the upper limit of its travel, then turn it anti-clockwise exactly $1\frac{7}{8}$ turns. The needle is now in its datum position.

15   Adjust the tool a $\frac{1}{4}$ turn in either direction to give the best idling quality and road performance. Confirmation of the mixture may also be obtained by inspection of the sparking plug condition (see Chapter 4) and the interior colour of the exhaust tail pipe. Adjustment of the needle within the limits specified, in conjunction with a tuning device such as a combustion chamber flame viewer or a vacuum gauge, is to be recommended.

Fast idle adjustment

16   After setting the mixture it may be found necessary to re-adjust the engine idling speed.

17   Stop the engine and ensure that the choke control is pushed fully in and the fast idle cam is against its stop. Using a feeler gauge,

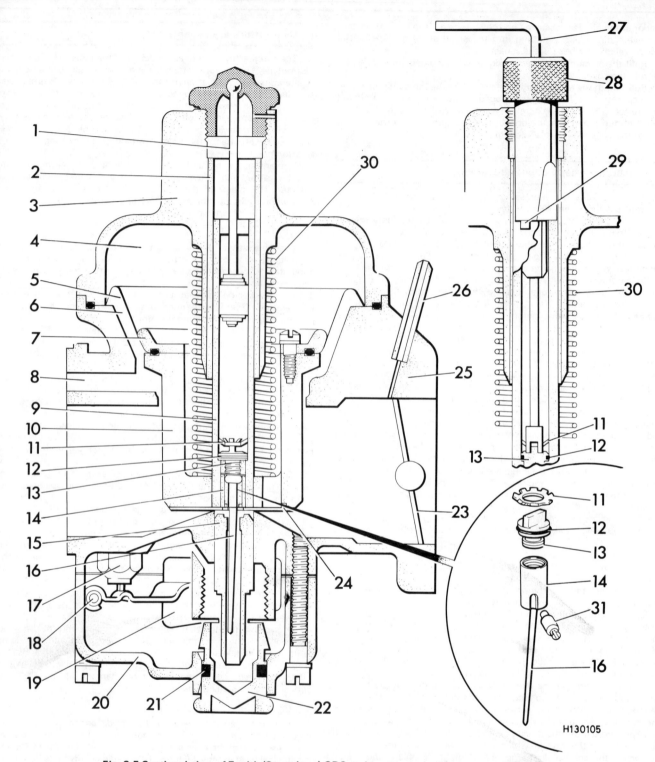

Fig. 3.5 Sectional view of Zenith (Stromberg) CD3 carburettor and adjustment tool (Sec. 5)

1 Air valve piston hydraulic damper
2 Sleeve
3 Cover
4 Depression chamber
5 Flexible diaphragm
6 Air space
7 Diaphragm retaining ring
8 Air passage
9 Air valve piston guide spindle
10 Air valve piston
11 Metering needle adjustment retainer
12 O-ring seal
13 Metering needle adjustment screw
14 Metering needle holder and bias spring
15 Fixed metering jet
16 Metering needle
17 Fuel inlet needle valve
18 Float pivot
19 Float
20 Float chamber
21 O-ring seal
22 Plug
23 Throttle valve
24 Depression feed hole
25 Carburettor body
26 Vacuum (distributor) advance connection
27 Inner component of adjustment tool
28 Outer component of adjustment tool
29 Locating peg
30 Air valve piston return spring
31 Metering needle spring loaded locating screw

H130105

5.1A View of carburettor showing starter device

5.1B View of carburettor showing throttle valve

6.3A Distributor vacuum pipe connection at carburettor

6.3B Carburettor throttle cable and choke wire

6.3C Carburettor throttle lever return spring

6.3D Carburettor ready for removal

6.8 Carburettor damper

8.3 Removing fuel pump cover (930 engine)

9.2 Removing fuel pump (930 engine)

measure the clearance between the fast idle cam and the head of the fast idle adjusting screw. Refer to the Specifications section and check that this clearance is within the limits stated. Adjustment, where necessary, of the gap, is simply carried out by loosening the locknut and altering the effective length of the adjuster screw.

18 It should be noted that any adjustment made to the normal idling speed will always alter the fast idle speed.

6 Carburettor – removal and refitting

1 Remove the air cleaner assembly as described in Section 3.
2 Disconnect the fuel pipe and plug its end to prevent any fuel syphoning out and the possible ingress of dirt.
3 Pull off the vacuum pipe connection and disconnect the choke and throttle cables. Where automatic transmission is fitted it will be necessary to disconnect the downshift cable. Unhook the throttle valve return spring (photos).

4 Remove the securing nuts and washers and remove the carburettor.
5 Before refitting the carburettor, check that both the carburettor flange and manifold flange faces are clean and not distorted.
6 Fit a new gasket and slide the carburettor onto its mounting studs.
7 Secure the carburettor using the washers and nuts, but remember to tighten the nuts evenly to the recommended torque setting.
8 Reconnect the various cables and hoses and top-up the damper unit, using the correct grade of oil which should be as used in the engine (photo).
9 Refit the air cleaner assembly and check the various carburettor adjustments (see Section 5 for details).

7 Carburettor – dismantling and reassembly

1 Diaphragm renewal may be carried out without removing the carburettor from the engine.

2   Remove the crosshead screws that retain the depression cover and lift the cover off.

3   Lift out the air valve piston complete with the diaphragm and retaining ring.

4   Remove the retaining ring screws, ring and diaphragm.

5   Fit the new diaphragm, taking great care to ensure that the locating tag engages with the mating cut-out in the flange, as shown in Fig. 3.6.

6   Complete dismantling and cleaning can only be carried out after removal of the carburettor from the engine. Unscrew and remove the six screws holding the float chamber to the carburettor body and remove the float chamber and its gasket.

7   Remove the hydraulic damper, invert the carburettor and drain out the oil.

8   Remove the screws retaining the depression cover and lift off the cover.

9   Withdraw the air valve piston, needle and diaphragm assembly.

10 Using a tyre pump blow air into the fuel feed hole to the starter assembly, at the same time move the starter assembly over the whole range of its movement with its travel stop in the fully raised (extreme cold) position.

11 Clean the components of the carburettor in fuel or paraffin only.

12 Before reassembly invert the carburettor and measure the height from the face of the carburettor body to the bottom of each float. If this dimension is not between 16–17 mm (0.624–0.663 in) then bend the float arm extension that contacts the float needle. When making adjustments ensure that the float arm is maintained at right angles to the float centre-line.

13 Refit the float chamber to the carburettor body using a new gasket.

14 The needle assembly can be removed by fitting the carburettor adjusting tool into the piston guide rod and turning the inner member in an anti-clockwise direction, as viewed from above. Continue turning until the needle is released from the adjuster. Now remove the needle holder retaining screw and withdraw the needle assembly.

15 Refitting of the needle assembly is the reverse of the removal procedure. It should be noted that the groove in the needle holder should be aligned with the retaining screw.

16 Refit the jet holder retaining screw but only screw it in a few threads and then fit the carburettor adjusting tool.

17 Apply very light inward pressure to the needle holder and at the same time turn the inner member of the adjusting tool in a clockwise direction (as viewed from above), to locate the jet holder in the adjuster.

18 Place a suitable straight edge such as a steel rule, against the bottom of the piston and continue turning the inner member of the adjusting tool until the 'Delrin' washer is flush with the bottom of the piston, as shown in Fig. 3.7. This procedure adjusts the needle to the basic setting position.

19 The remainder of the reassembly is now a reverse of the dismantling procedure.

20 Refit the carburettor as described in Section 6 and then adjust it as described in Section 5.

8   Fuel pump – servicing and testing

1   The fuel pump is a non-repairable item and if found to be faulty should be renewed.

2   Regular maintenance of the fuel pump entails cleaning the gauge filter screen and sediment cap at 10 000 mile (16 000 km) intervals.

3   To clean the fuel pump remove the sediment cap retaining screw and withdraw the gauze filter and sealing ring. Clean the filter, sealing ring and sediment cap in fuel or paraffin and then refit them. Finally after starting the engine check for any signs of fuel leakage (photo).

4   If the fuel pump is suspected of being faulty it can be tested without removing it from the engine.

5   To test the pump, open the bonnet and disconnect the fuel pipe from the carburettor. Place the open end of the pipe in a container.

6   Pull the centre HT lead from the distributor cap to prevent the engine firing when the starter is operated.

7   Operate the starter/ignition key and observe the fuel ejected from the open end of the fuel pipe. This should come out in regular well defined spurts if the pump is operating correctly.

Warning: *Make sure that the disconnected end of the HT lead is not allowed near the fuel pipe or container as if the lead is close to any*

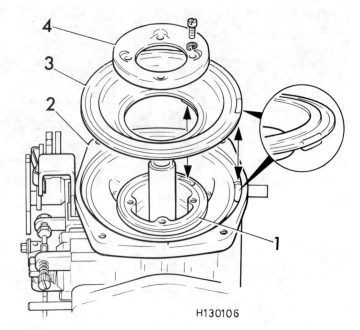

Fig. 3.6 Carburettor diaphragm and associated components (Sec. 7)

1   Air valve piston
2   Carburettor body
3   Diaphragm
4   Retaining ring

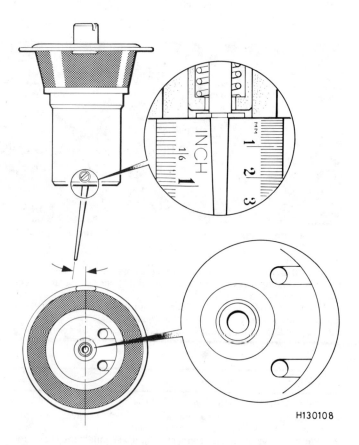

Fig. 3.7 Correct fitting of needle assembly (inset diagrams show the Delrin washer flush with the base of the piston and the needle bias) (Sec. 7)

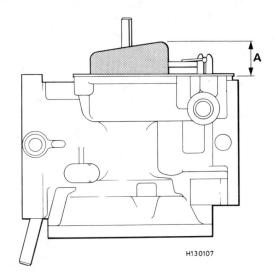

Fig. 3.8 Float setting dimension (Sec. 7)
A equals 16 to 17 mm (0.624 to 0.663 in)

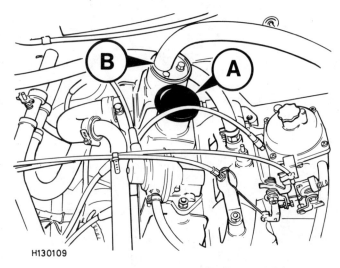

H130109

Fig. 3.9 Location of flame trap (930 cc models)
A Oil filler B Flame trap (Sec. 10)

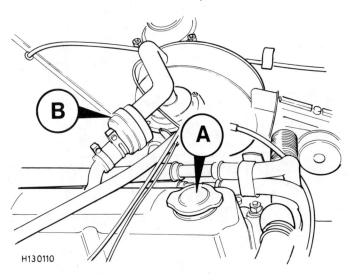

H130110

Fig. 3.10 Location of flame trap (1300/1600 cc models)
A Oil filler B Flame trap (Sec. 10)

metal component, a strong spark may bridge the gap when the ignition key is turned.
8   On completion of the test, reconnect the fuel pipe and the HT lead to the distributor.

9 Fuel pump – removal and refitting

1   Disconnect the fuel inlet and outlet pipes at the fuel pump. Plug the inlet pipe to prevent fuel leakage due to the syphoning reaction and to prevent the possible ingress of dirt.
2   Remove either the fuel pump securing nuts (930 cc engine) or the securing bolts (1300/1600 cc engines) and withdraw the pump and heat insulator block (photo).
3   Before refitting the fuel pump ensure that both the faces of the fuel pump and the cylinder block or cambox are clean. The heat insulator can be re-used if it is not damaged.
4   When refitting the fuel pump, tilt the top of the pump body away from the engine to ensure that the operating arm engages correctly with the eccentric formed on the camshaft. Failure to take this precaution may cause the operating arm to locate under the camshaft.
5   Tighten the pump fixings evenly to the correct torque setting and connect the inlet and outlet fuel pipes.
6   Finally start the engine and check for fuel or oil leaks.

10 Crankcase emission control system – servicing

The engine crankcase is ventilated by means of a rubber tube connection between the rocker/camshaft cover and the air cleaner assembly. A flame trap is interposed between the two components which requires regular servicing at 5000 mile (3000 km) intervals.
1   To carry out this servicing operation on 1300/1600 engine models, simply disconnect the rubber hoses at the flame trap canister, immerse the canister in paraffin (never fuel) and agitate it. After draining, apply a tyre pump to dry the interior.
2   The flame trap on 930 cc engine models is fitted into the top of the camshaft cover. To remove the flame trap pull off the rubber hose and undo the three retaining screws. Lift away the connection stub plate and withdraw the flame trap mesh. Clean the mesh as detailed in Paragraph 1.
3   Refitting of both forms of flame trap is the reverse of the removal procedure.
4   Finally check the condition and cleanliness of the rubber interconnecting hose(s). Renew any that show signs of deterioration.

11 Inlet and exhaust manifolds – removal and refitting

The inlet and exhaust manifolds are bolted together and it is for this reason that they should always be removed as one unit.
1   Remove the air cleaner and carburettor assemblies as described in Section 2 and 6 of this Chapter.
2   Loosen the vacuum servo hose connection at the inlet manifold and pull the hose off.
3   Remove the bolts that retain the throttle cable support bracket. On automatic transmission models also disconnect the downshift cable bracket.
4   Disconnect the exhaust system at the manifold flange connection (photo).
5   Remove the nuts and bolts that retain the manifolds to the cylinder head. In the case of 930 cc models there are clamp brackets fitted at either end of the manifolds (photos).
6   Slide the manifolds off and if necessary separate them by removing the retaining bolts. Note that a gasket will be found fitted between the two items.
7   Refitting of the manifolds is the reverse of the removal procedure but remember to ensure that all joint faces are clean and to fit a new gasket. Tighten the retaining nuts and bolts to the recommended torque setting.

12 Exhaust system – general

1   The exhaust system is of a conventional design and consists of a resonator and a silencer box. The resonator unit absorbs high fre-

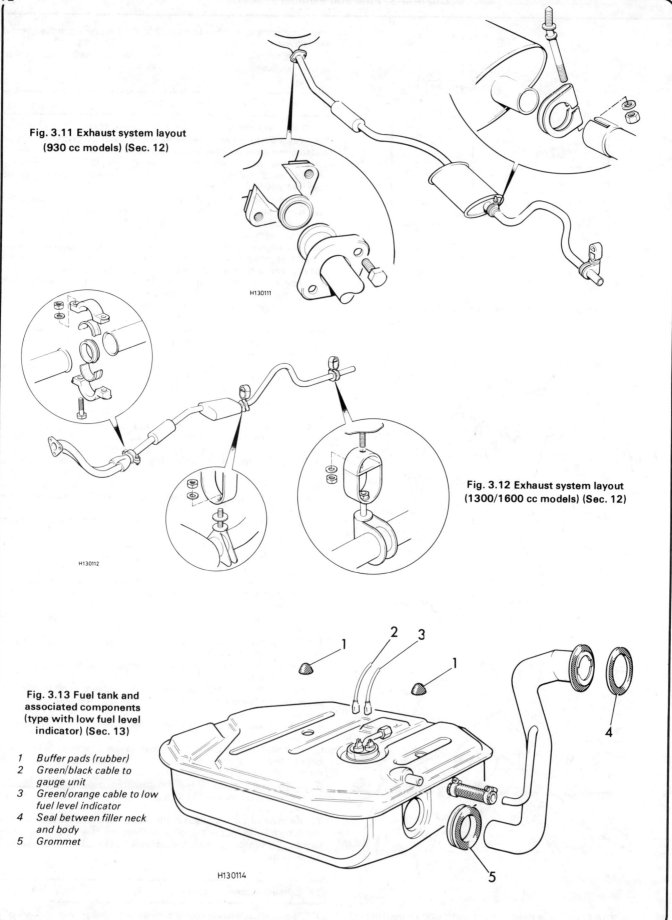

Fig. 3.11 Exhaust system layout
(930 cc models) (Sec. 12)

H130111

H130112

Fig. 3.12 Exhaust system layout
(1300/1600 cc models) (Sec. 12)

Fig. 3.13 Fuel tank and
associated components
(type with low fuel level
indicator) (Sec. 13)

1   Buffer pads (rubber)
2   Green/black cable to
    gauge unit
3   Green/orange cable to low
    fuel level indicator
4   Seal between filler neck
    and body
5   Grommet

H130114

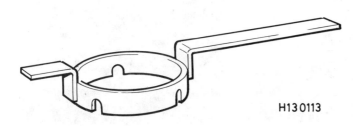

Fig. 3.14 Talbot Service tool (cc 0026/20279000) used for releasing the fuel gauge transmitter lock ring (Sec.13)

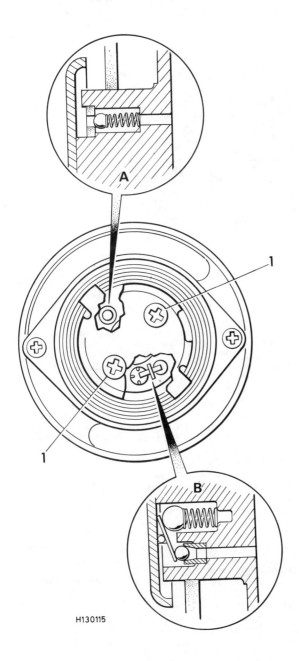

Fig. 3.15 Fuel tank filler cap detail (Sec. 14)

1 Shutter retaining screws
A Pressure valve
B Vacuum valve

quency sounds while the silencer absorbs the low frequency sound and also provides a controlled expansion of the exhaust gases. Figs. 3.11 and 3.12 show the layouts fitted to the Talbot Sunbeam range and it will be noted that the silencer and tail pipe assemblies are common to all models. The front pipe and resonator however, vary in both fixing and size between the 930 and 1300/1600 models.

2 The exhaust system should be inspected at 10 000 mile (16 000 km) intervals for signs of deterioration and security. Gas leakage at joints will appear as sooty marks and may sometimes be rectified simply by tightening the securing clamp. The support mountings tend to deteriorate with age and if allowed to break will cause unnecessary strain on the joints and coupling flanges (photo).

3 It is important when fitting exhaust systems that the twists and contours are correctly positioned and that each connecting pipe overlaps the correct distance. Any stresses imparted in order to force the system to fit the hangers rubbers will result in early fractures or failures.

4 When fitting a new part or a complete system, it is well worth removing the whole system from the car and cleaning up all the joints so that they will fit together easily. The time spent struggling with obstinate joints whilst lying flat on your back under the car is less and likelihood of distorting or even breaking a section is greatly reduced. Do not waste time trying to undo rusted clamps and bolts. Cut them off. New ones will be required anyway if the original ones are badly rusted or corroded.

13 Fuel tank and transmitter unit — removal, servicing and refitting

1 The pressed steel fuel tank is located at the rear of the car beneath the load floor.

2 A pipe connects the top of the fuel tank to the main filler pipe and its purpose is to reduce the possibility of fuel blowback if the tank is filled too quickly.

3 The fuel gauge transmitter unit is fitted to the top of the tank and can be detached without having to remove the fuel tank from the car (photo).

4 To remove the fuel tank assembly first disconnect the battery and remove the luggage compartment mats, spare wheel cover and spare wheel.

5 Remove the self-tapping screws that secure the spare wheel bracket and lift the bracket away to reveal the transmitter unit.

6 Remove the transmitter wire(s) and disconnect the fuel pipe.

7 Where the fuel tank contains a large volume of fuel it will be necessary to drain some out to reduce its effective weight. A drain plug is not provided and a syphoning hose cannot be inserted down the filler tank neck. Talbot recommend that the fuel gauge transmitter unit must be removed and the fuel syphoned or pumped out through this aperture.

8 A special service tool is available (CC0026/20279000), as shown in Fig. 3.14 for removing the fuel tank transmitter unit. A similar, less elaborate, tool can be manufactured from pieces of scrap metal to perform the same function. After turning the transmitter unit locking ring, withdraw the transmitter unit.

9 Syphon or pump the fuel from the fuel tank into a suitable container.

10 Remove the fuel tank filler cap and the screws that secure the filler neck to the body.

11 Chock the front wheels and raise the rear of the car to gain access to the clip that secures the flexible breather hose to the breather pipe on the filler neck.

12 Pull the filler pipe away from the fuel tank and grommet.

13 Place a support jack under the fuel tank and interpose a piece of wood between the jack and tank to spread the load.

14 With the tank adequately supported remove the nuts and bolts that secure the tank. Lower the support jack and remove the tank from beneath the car.

15 If the tank is dirty or contains sediment, use two or three lots of clean paraffin to wash it out and then let it dry thoroughly.

16 Warning: *Do not try to solder a leak in the fuel tank or apply any form of flame to it, as an explosion will result due to pockets of fuel vapour still present within the tank.* In some instances if the leak is small and the area around cleaned thoroughly, a cold setting compound (ie body filler) can make an effective repair. For a more permanent repair entrust the work to a specialist repairer (most radiator

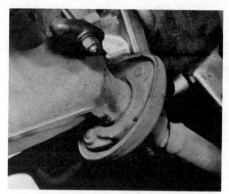
11.4 Exhaust manifold to downpipe flange (930 engine)

11.5A Manifold clamp (930 engine)

11.5B Inlet and exhaust manifold in position on cylinder head (930 engine)

12.2 Typical exhaust pipe clamp and flexible mounting

13.3 Fuel tank transmitter showing fuel outlet pipe

repair specialists will undertake fuel tank repairs). Where there are several isolated leaks or the fuel tank is very corroded, then a new fuel tank is the only satisfactory solution.

17 Refitting of the fuel tank is basically a reversal of the removal procedure but the following points should be noted:

(a) Use a suitable adhesive tape to secure temporarily the fuel pipe and tank wire(s) to the edge of the floor aperture while the tank is being refitted
(b) Apply a small trace of suitable lubricant to the tank grommet and the lower end of the filler neck, to ease assembly
(c) When refitting the tank securing bolts, make sure that the large toothed washers are refitted against the tank and the shakeproof washers fitted against each nut and bolt
(d) Where a low fuel level warning light is fitted, the warning light wire (green/orange) is fitted to the right hand terminal and the gauge connection (green/black wire) is fitted to the terminal next to the fuel pipe

18 The fuel tank gauge transmitter unit, as mentioned previously, can be unscrewed without removing the fuel tank. The unit is not repairable and, if faulty, must be renewed. After renewal, ensure that the wires are connected to the correct terminals (only applicable to models fitted with a low fuel level warning light).

14 Fuel filler cap – description and servicing

1 The fuel filler cap is fitted with pressure and vacuum valves. The filler cap is designed to seal the fuel system in the event of the vehicle overturning, thus preventing the escape of fuel. The rubber sealing ring of the cap is spring loaded and this provides the positive seal but if the

pressure within the fuel tank reaches 4 lbf/in^2 (275 m bar) the ring is lifted off its seat to release the excess pressure. The vacuum operated valve maintains the necessary balance within the tank and prevents the tank from collapsing which theoretically could result, if air were not permitted to enter the tank to replace the fuel drawn out by the fuel pump in response to the engine's demands.

2 The filler cap cannot be serviced in the true sense of the word but it is possible to dismantle it and clean the various components. However, where any parts are found to be faulty a complete fuel filler cap will have to be obtained.

3 Refer to Fig. 3.15 and remove the two screws (1) that retain the shutter to the base.

4 Carefully lever the shutter from the locating bosses.

5 Invert the cap into the palm of your hand and withdraw the rocker, glass ball valve, steel ball and spring (not fitted to later models) of the vacuum valve assembly.

6 Immerse the base in clean fuel and agitate it to remove any deposits. Do not apply any form of compressed air to the unit as this will damage the pressure valve spring.

7 Very carefully probe the pressure valve aperture with a soft instrument, to check that the ball valve is free and not stuck fast to its seating.

8 Clean the component parts of the vacuum valve by wiping them in a lint-free cloth and check that the sealing ring flange is free to move on its spigot.

9 Having cleaned the components and carefully inspected them, reassembly can commence by inserting the spring (if fitted) into the blind hole, followed by the steel ball.

10 Refit the glass ball in the vent hole and refit the rocker with the plain surface towards the balls.

11 Refit the shutter and secure it in position with the retaining screws.

15 Fault diagnosis – fuel and exhaust systems

Symptom	Reason(s)
Fuel consumption excessive	
Carburation and ignition faults	Air cleaner choked and dirty causing rich mixture
	Air temperature control device faulty
	Fuel leaking from carburettor, fuel pump or fuel lines
	Float chamber flooding or air vent blocked
	Generally worn carburettor or damaged diaphragm
	Balance weights or vacuum advance mechanism in distributor faulty
Incorrect adjustment	Carburettor incorrectly adjusted; mixture too rich
	Idling speed too high
	Valve clearances incorrect
	Spark plug electrode gap incorrect
	Tyres under-inflated
	Incorrect type of spark plug fitted
	Brakes dragging
Insufficient fuel delivery	
Dirt in system	Filler cap valves restricted
	Partially clogged filter in fuel pump
	Dirt lodged in float chamber needle housing
Fuel pump faults	Incorrectly seating valves in fuel pump
	Fuel pump diaphragm leaking or damaged
	Sealing ring in fuel pump damaged
	Fuel pump valves sticking, due to petrol gumming
Air leaks	Too little fuel in fuel tank (prevalent when climbing steep hills)
	Hose clips at pipe unions slack
	Split or perforation in fuel pipe on suction side of fuel pump
	Inlet manifold to cylinder head leaking at joint
	Inlet manifold to carburettor gasket leaking
Faulty slow running	Sticking air valve piston
	Fast idle cam not returning fully
	Float chamber flooding
Insufficient top speed	Throttle not opening fully
	Damaged diaphragm
	Weak mixture
Flat spot at small throttle openings	Weak mixture
	Leak in distributor vacuum pipe
Poor acceleration	Dirty damper piston
	Lack of oil in damper or incorrect viscosity
Difficult cold starting	Choke control cable incorrectly adjusted
	Fast idle speed screw nut set to specification
	Starter device travel stop not correctly set for ambient climatic conditions

Chapter 4 Ignition system

For modifications, and information applicable to later models, see Supplement at end of manual

Contents

Specifications

Type . . . . Electronic

Distributor
Make and model . . . . Lucas 45 DM4 or Bosch JG FU-4
Direction of rotation . . . . Anti-clockwise
Firing order . . . . 1–3–4–2 (No 1 cylinder at timing cover end of engine)
Pick-up coil resistance (Lucas) . . . . 250 to 380 ohms
Reluctor to pick-up air-gap (Lucas) . . . . 0.006 to 0.008 in (0.15 to 0.20 mm)

Ignition coil
Primary resistance . . . . 1.4 to 1.6 ohms
Secondary resistance . . . . 8000 to 10 000 ohms

Resistor block
Ballast resistor (coil) . . . . 0.50 to 0.60 ohms
Auxiliary resistor (control unit) . . . . 4.75 to 5.75 ohms

Spark plugs
Type:
  930 cc engine . . . . Champion RN9Y
  1300 and 1600 cc engines (with 1.50 carburettor):
    Normal operation . . . . Champion RN9Y
    Mainly high speed operations . . . . Champion RN7Y
  1300 and 1600 cc engines (with 1.75 carburettor)
    Normal operation . . . . Champion RN7Y
    Mainly low speed (city) operations . . . . Champion RN9Y
Electrode gap:
  930 cc engine . . . . 0.025 in (0.63 mm)
  1300 and 1600 cc engines . . . . 0.030 in (0.75 mm)

Ignition timing (dynamic)

At idling speed* . . . .

Engine	BTDC	Idling speed (rpm)
930	2° to 4°	820 to 880
1300 (with 1.50 carburettor)**	9° to 11°	770 to 830
1300 (with 1.75 carburettor)**	9° to 11°	870 to 930
1600 (with 1.50 carburettor)**	9° to 11°	770 to 830
1600 (with 1.75 carburettor)**	9° to 11°	870 to 930

At 3000 engine rpm* . . . .

Engine	BTDC
930	23° to 25°
1300 (with 1.50 carburettor)**	29° to 31°
1300 (with 1.75 carburettor)**	31° to 33°
1600 (with 1.50 carburettor)**	25° to 27°
1600 (with 1.75 carburettor)**	29° to 31°

* Vacuum pipe disconnected
**Automatic transmission in N (neutral)

Torque wrench settings

	lbf ft	Nm
Spark plugs	12	16
Distributor bracket to cylinder block	7	9.5
Distributor clamp	4	5.5

1 General description

In order that the engine can run correctly, it is necessary for an electrical spark to ignite the fuel/air mixture in the combustion chamber at exactly the right moment in relation to engine speed and load. The ignition system is based on feeding low tension voltage from the battery to the coil where it is converted to high tension voltage. The high tension voltage is powerful enough to jump the spark plug gap in the cylinders many times a second under high compression pressures, providing that the system is in good condition and that all adjustments are correct.

The Sunbeam models are fitted with an electronic ignition system. Very early Sunbeams were produced with a conventional contact breaker system (due to a supply problem); these, however, were replaced by the electronic system at the first free service. The electronic ignition system provides a high degree of reliability with virtually no servicing requirements, apart from lubricating the felt pad in the top of the spindle (Lucas type only) and periodically checking the HT (high tension) and LT (low tension) lead connections.

On the 930 cc engine the driven end of the distributor spindle is spigotted and driven by an offset dog on the oil pump spindle. The oil pump driven gear takes its drive from a similar skew gear on the front of the crankshaft. The distributor and oil pump are both fitted to the timing cover casing (photos). On 1300 and 1600 cc engines the distributor is of the spigotted type, fitted to the right-hand side of the crankcase and driven by an offset dog on the oil pump spindle in a similar manner to that of the 930 cc engine.

The electronic ignition system uses a coil similar to, but not interchangeable with, a conventional ignition coil, a distributor advance mechanism and distributor cap, but replaces the conventional contact breakers and condenser with a reluctor and pick-up unit operating in conjunction with a control unit. The reluctor unit is a four-toothed wheel, (one tooth for each cylinder) that is fitted to the distributor shaft in place of the conventional contact breaker operating cam. The pick-up unit is located in the distributor, and consists basically of a coil and permanent magnet. The control unit is a transistorised amplifier that is used to boost the voltage induced by the pick-up coil.

A simplified circuit diagram is shown in Fig. 4.2. When the ignition is switched on, the ignition primary circuit is energised. When the distributor reluctor 'teeth' or 'spokes' approach the magnetic coil assembly, a voltage is induced which signals the amplifier to turn off the coil primary current. A timing circuit in the amplifier module turns

on the coil current after the coil field has collapsed.

When switched on, current flows from the battery through the ignition switch, through the coil primary winding, through the amplifer module and then to earth. When the current is off, the magnetic field in the ignition coil collapses, inducing a high voltage in the coil secondary winding. This is conducted to the distributor cap where the rotor directs it to the appropriate spark plug. This process is repeated for each power stroke of the car engine.

The distributor is fitted with devices to control the actual point of ignition according to the engine speed and load. As the engine speed increases, two centrifugal weights move outwards and alter the position of the armature in relation to the distributor shaft to advance the spark slightly. As engine load increases (for example when climbing hills or accelerating), a reduction in intake manifold depression causes the baseplate assembly to move slightly in the opposite direction (anti-clockwise) under the action of the spring in the vacuum unit, thus retarding the spark slightly and tending to counteract the centrifugal advance. Under light load conditions (for example at moderate steady speeds), the comparatively high intake manifold depression on the vacuum advance diaphragm causes the baseplate assembly to move in a clockwise direction to give a large amount of spark advance.

Warning: *As the HT circuit on this type of ignition operates at very high voltage, avoid handling HT leads or other components when the engine is running. This can be particularly dangerous for people with a heart condition or those with 'pacemakers'.*

2 Distributor – servicing

1 Periodically check the condition of the distributor cap and rotor.
2 Release the two spring clips and lift off the distributor cap.
3 Clean the inside and outside of the distributor cap with a clean cloth and check the central spring-loaded carbon contact and four segments on the inside of the cap for excessive wear or burning. If excessive wear or burning is evident the cap should be renewed.
4 Pull off the rotor arm and check the end of the brass segment for burning. Renew if necessary (photo).
5 Where a Lucas distributor is used, a felt pad will be found fitted to the centre of the central spindle. Apply three drops of clean engine oil to this pad before refitting the rotor arm (photo).
6 The air gap between the reluctor rotor tips and the magnetic pick-up point is adjustable on the Lucas distributor only. The air gap has

1.0A Distributor drive gear on oil pump driveshaft (930 engine)

1.0B Distributor drive dog viewed from above (930 engine)

1.0C Distributor driven shaft (930 engine)

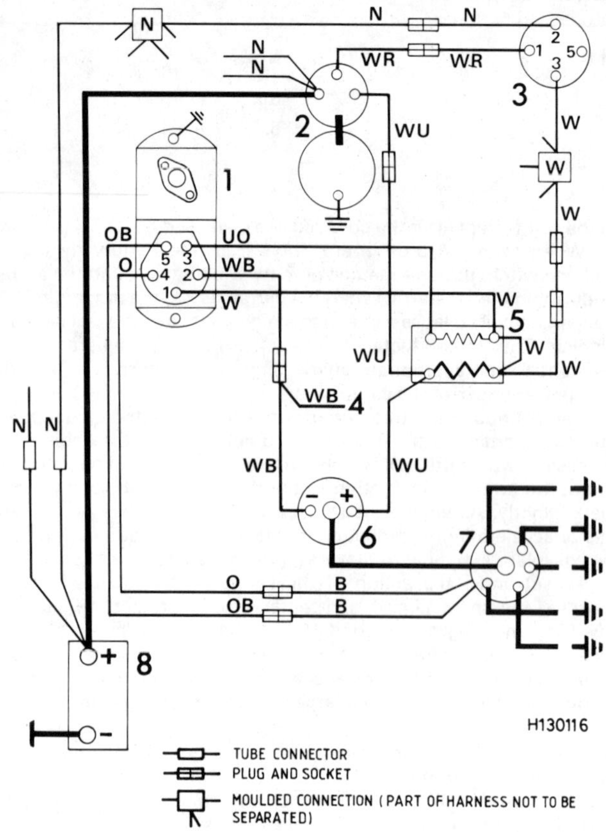

H130116

Fig. 4.1 Ignition system wiring circuit, colour code and symbols (Sec. 1)

1	Control/amplifier unit	5	Resistor block
2	Starter motor and solenoid	6	Ignition coil
3	Ignition switch	7	Distributor with pick-up
4	Tachometer connection (where applicable)	8	Battery

TUBE CONNECTOR
PLUG AND SOCKET
MOULDED CONNECTION (PART OF HARNESS NOT TO BE SEPARATED)

Cable colour code

B	BLACK	R	RED
N	BROWN	U	BLUE
O	ORANGE	W	WHITE

H130117

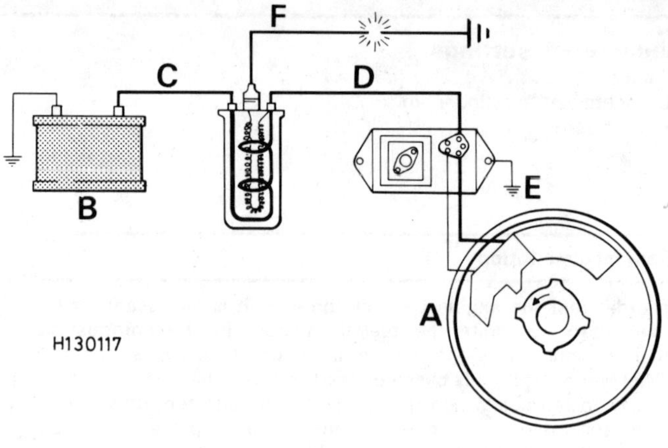

Fig. 4.2 Simplified diagram of ignition system (Sec. 1)

A Pick-up coil inducing negative voltage
B Battery
C Supply to ignition coil
D Coil LT to control unit
E LT open circuit in control unit
F HT induced in coil secondary

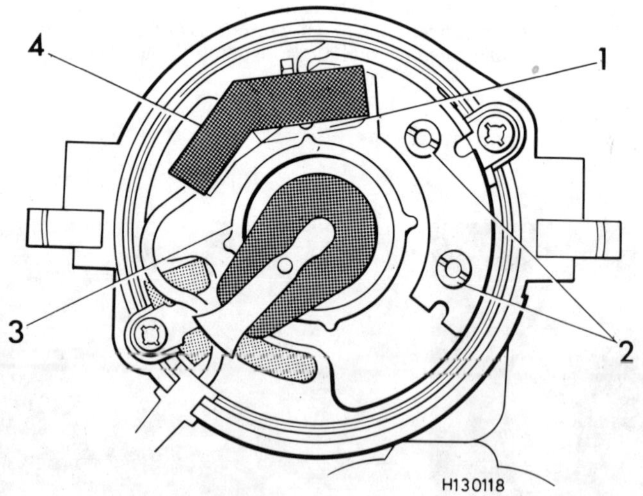

15° BTDC
10° BTDC
5° BTDC
T.D.C.

H130119

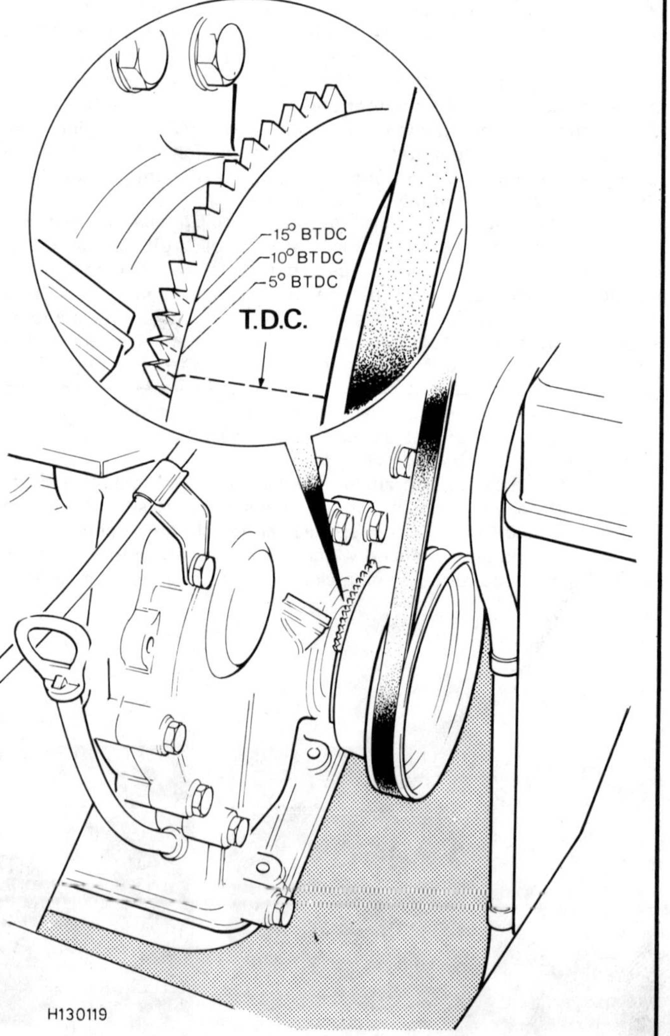

Fig. 4.4 Ignition timing marks (1300/1600 models shown) (Sec. 4)

H130118

Fig. 4.3 Reluctor alignment when checking air gap (Lucas distributor) (Sec. 2)

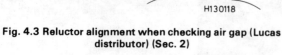

1	Air gap	3	Reluctor
2	Barrel nuts	4	Pick-up unit

2.4 Rotor arm on 930 engine distributor

2.5 Distributor with rotor removed (930 engine)

3.4 Removing distributor (930 engine)

4.3 Ignition timing marks

5.2 Distributor vacuum pipe attachment (930 engine)

8.1 Location of ignition coil

been set during manufacture with precision instruments and will only need resetting if it has been interfered with.

7   If such adjustment must be made, a non-magnetic feeler blade (brass) must be used. Turn the crankshaft (by applying a spanner to the crankshaft pulley nut) until a reluctor tooth is in alignment with the pick-up link.

8   Set the gap to the tolerance given in 'Specifications', by slackening the barrel nuts (2) and moving the pick-up assembly in or out as necessary.

9   Refit the plastic arc shield, the rotor arm and cap.

3   Distributor – removal and refitting

1   Remove the distributor cap as described in the previous Section and disconnect the vacuum pipe.

2   Disconnect the wires from the distributor to the control unit at the twin plug.

3   Using a small sharp screwdriver, or a similar instrument, carefully scribe an alignment mark between the distributor body and the clamp plate.

4   Loosen the distributor clamp screw and withdraw the distributor. Do **not** rotate the engine after the distributor has been removed unless absolutely necessary (photo).

5   The distributor can be dismantled, but if excessive wear is found then it is strongly advisable to obtain a service exchange replacement as some parts are not readily available. Refer to Sections 6 or 7 for dismantling and reassembly procedures.

6   To refit the distributor, insert it into the crankcase or timing cover aperture and ensure that the tongue or spigot on the end of the distributor driveshaft engages with the offset slot in the driveshaft.

7   Rotate the distributor body to line up the scribe marks and retighten the clamp screw.

8   Refit the remaining distributor components using the reverse procedure to that of removal.

9   Provided the engine was not rotated while the distributor was removed and the scribe marks are correctly aligned, it should not be

necessary to re-time the ignition. However, if any doubt exists, re-time the ignition using the procedure described in Section 5.

10   If the engine was rotated while the distributor was removed, it will be necessary to re-time it to the engine as described in the following Section.

4   Distributor – timing to the engine

1   To time the distributor to the engine, first remove No 1 spark plug (nearest the timing cover end of the engine).

2   Place a finger over the spark plug hole and rotate the engine until pressure is felt, this indicates the piston is on the compression stroke.

3   Continue to turn the engine until the notch on the crankshaft pulley which represents the correct number of degrees BTDC (before top dead centre) is opposite the pointer on the timing cover case. The required number of degrees BTDC is listed in the Specifications section and varies according to the engine capacity and type. Note that each one of the serrated teeth on the crankshaft pulley wheel represents five crankshaft degrees (photo).

4   On Bosch type distributors, with the distributor removed from the engine, turn the rotor until it is aligned with the groove in the body. In the case of the Lucas distributor, align the rotor arm with the No 1 segment in the distributor cap. To set the Lucas distributor properly, remove the rotor arm and plastic arc shield. Refit the rotor, aligning it with the No 1 segment in the distributor cap and check that the pick-up link is opposite the reluctor tooth.

5   Maintain the rotor arm in the timed position and refit the distributor to the engine as described in Section 3, ensuring that the driveshaft is correctly engaged. Check that the timing marks are still in alignment (rotate the distributor body if necessary) and lightly tighten the distributor clamp screw.

6   Finally, check the ignition timing using a stroboscopic timing light as described in the following Section.

5   Ignition timing

Note: *the auxiliary tachometer referred to in this Section must not* *be of the type which is triggered by the coil LT (low tension). This type is not suitable for electronic ignition systems.*

1   Because the distributor only gives a timing signal when the shaft is rotating, a stroboscopic timing light must be used with the engine running at idling speed.

2   Disconnect the vacuum advance pipe from the distributor. Connect the stroboscopic timing light between No 1 spark plug and its associated HT lead. To ensure that the engine is idling at the correct speed, connect an auxiliary type tachometer (photo).

3   Clean the crankshaft pulley and the timing cover in the region of the timing marks and mark them with a small spot of white paint. For the correct degree mark, refer to the Specifications at the beginning of this Chapter.

4   Start the engine and set the idling speed,using the tachometer to indicate the correct idling speed given in the Specifications. Refer to Chapter 3 for details on adjusting the carburettor, if necessary. Where automatic transmission is fitted, the speed selector lever should be in the N (neutral) position.

5   Aim the stoboscopic timing light at the crankshaft pulley. The flashing light will 'freeze' the white marks and it is when these marks are in exact alignment that the ignition timing is correct.

6   Loosen the distributor clamp screw and turn the body of the distributor clockwise to advance the ignition and anti-clockwise to retard it. When the timing marks are aligned, tighten the distributor clamp screw.

7   Re-check the timing and then disconnect the stroboscopic timing light and reconnect the vacuum advance pipe.

6   Distributor (Lucas type) – dismantling and reassembly

1   Remove the distributor as described in Section 3.

2   Remove the distributor cap, rotor arm and plastic arc shield.

3   Using a pair of external circlip pliers, remove the circlip (item 9 in Fig. 4.5) which retains the reluctor.

4   After having removed the circlip, lift out the washer (10) followed by an O-ring (11) and the reluctor (2).

5   Using a cross-head type screwdriver, remove the screws retaining the vacuum capsule (6) to the distributor body. Tilt the vacuum capsule to separate the pull rod from the lower side of the pick-up mounting plate. Fig. 4.6 shows the detailed fixing arrangement of the vacuum capsule pull rod and the pick-up mounting plate pin.

6   Remove the screws and the guide bracket which hold the baseplate in position. Withdraw the assembly, complete with the pick-up and leads, after disengaging the pick-up lead grommet from the body of the distributor.

7   The coupling ring (item 12) can now be withdrawn from the shaft.

8   In practice this is generally the normal limit of dismantling,as the distributor shaft and plate, centrifugal weights and cam are an assembly and renewal of these components due to wear would not be an economical proposition.

9   However, if for any reason further dismantling must be carried out, mark the relationship of the driving dog and the rotor, which should be as shown in Fig. 4.7. If the relationship of these two components is not as shown in the illustration, make scribed marks to ensure accurate realignment.

10 Support the shank part of the distributor and using a suitable pin punch drive out the roll pin.

11 Withdraw the drive dog and the thrust washer.

12 Examine the end of the drive spindle for burrs and if any are present remove them using a fine file. Withdraw the shaft assembly from the distributor body, noting the thrust washer located below the centrifugal weight assembly.

13 Remove the rubber O-ring from the shank part of the distributor body.

14 Having fully dismantled the distributor, examine each component for wear or deterioration.

15 The centrifugal weight and spring assembly cannot be dismantled, apart from removing the springs. When examining this assembly check that the weights move freely on their pivots and that, with the springs fitted, the cam and weights return to the full retard position. If the springs are suspect then they should be renewed.

16 Slide the shaft into the distributor body and check if there is any discernible side play. If wear is evident then it is advisable to obtain a new or service exchange distributor, as there is no provision for renewing the shaft bearings.

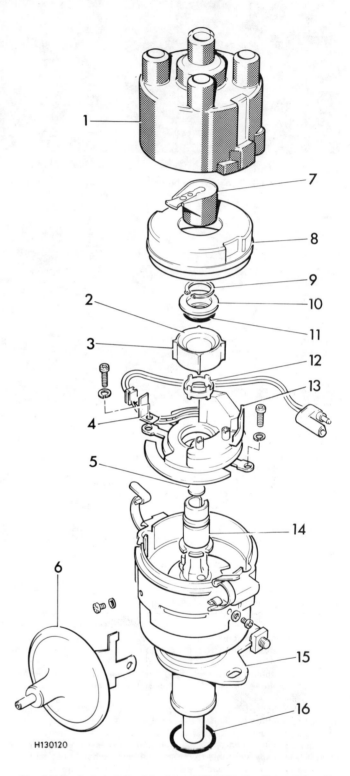

H130120

Fig. 4.5 Exploded view of the Lucas 45 DM4 distributor (Sec. 6)

1	Cap	9	Circlip
2	Reluctor	10	Washer
3	Reluctor tooth	11	O-ring
4	Guide bracket	12	Coupling ring
5	Felt lubrication pad	13	Pick-up and baseplate
6	Vacuum capsule	14	Shaft
7	Rotor	15	Clamp plate
8	Plastic arc shield	16	O-ring

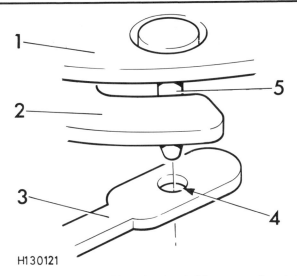

Fig. 4.6 Vacuum capsule pull rod and pick-up mounting plate pin fixing detail (Lucas distributor) (Sec. 6)

1 Pick-up unit mounting plate
2 Baseplate
3 Vacuum unit pull rod
4 Hole in pull rod
5 Pin

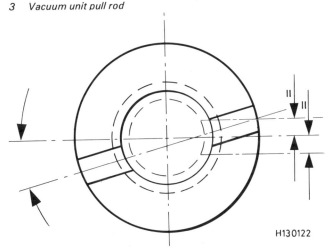

Fig. 4.7 Relationship of the drive dog and the rotor (Lucas distributor) (Sec. 6)

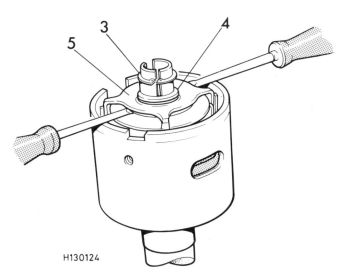

Fig. 4.8 Levering off the reluctor (Bosch distributor) (Sec. 7)

3 Circlip 4 Belville washer 5 Reluctor

17 Examine the pick-up mounting plate. The uppper portion must rotate smoothly without the tendency to tilt on the lower part.
18 Having examined the various components and renewed those which have worn or deteriorated, reassembly can commence.
19 Lubricate the bearing part of the shaft and body with a heavy duty molybdenum oil, together with the pivots and moving parts of the centrifugal advance mechanism and the pin which engages with the vacuum capsule pullrod. The contact surfaces of the baseplate and the pick-up mounting plate should be lubricated with Shell Retinax 'A' grease, or an equivalent grease if a different brand is used.
20 Place the thrust washer on the shaft and slide the assembly into the distributor body.
21 Refit the lower thrust washer and the drive dog. Align the drive dog and rotor slot as described in paragraph 9 and as shown in Fig. 4.6.
22 Having aligned the drive dog and rotor slot, refit a new roll pin and check that the shaft turns freely. Check that the shaft has an endfloat not in excess of 0·004 in (0·10 mm), by placing selective feeler blades between the thrust washer and drive dog. If all is well, the metal round the ends of the roll pin can be lightly staked to prevent the pin from sliding out in use.
23 Refit the pick-up and baseplate assembly, so that the guide bracket is under the screw and away from the pick-up. The retaining screws should be tightened evenly.
24 Move the pick-up plate in a clockwise direction (fully advance position) and refit the vacuum capsule, ensuring that the pull rod engages with the pin in the pick-up mounting plate. Secure the vacuum capsule with its retaining screws.
25 Slide the pick-up lead grommet into the slot provided and tuck the leads behind the guide bracket.
26 Refit the coupling ring over the shaft, noting that its design will allow it to be fitted in one position only.
27 Refit the reluctor which will similarly locate in one position only.
28 Fit the O-ring, washer and circlip, above the reluctor in that order. When fitting the circlip, ensure that it is correctly seated in the groove provided.
29 Set the air gap as described in Section 2.
30 Apply a few drops of clean engine oil to the felt lubricator pad located in the centre of the distributor shaft.
31 Fit a new rubber O-ring to the distributor shank.
32 Refit the plastic arc shield, rotor arm and distributor cap.
33 The distributor can now be refitted and tuned as described in Sections 3, 4 and 5.

7 Distributor (Bosch type) – dismantling and reassembly

1 Remove the distributor from the engine as described in Section 3.
2 Remove the distributor cap, rotor arm and plastic arc shield.
3 Undo the screws that secure the vacuum capsule to the distributor body. Tip the vacuum capsule to disengage the pull rod from the pick-up plate. The vacuum capsule can now be withdrawn.
4 Remove the securing screws and lift away the distributor cap clips.
5 Remove the single securing screw which retains the terminal block and pick-up harness and slide the terminal block and harness away from the distributor body.
6 Using a pair of external circlip pliers, remove the circlip which retains the Belleville washer and the reluctor.
7 Withdraw the Belleville washer and lever off the reluctor unit as shown in the accompanying illustration (Fig. 4.9). Two flat-bladed screwdrivers are ideal, but whatever form of leverage is used to withdraw the reluctor, it is essential that the two levers are positioned diametrically opposite to one another and even pressure is exerted on each.
8 Using the circlip pliers remove a further circlip.
9 Remove the second pick-up retaining screw and withdraw the pick-up assembly.
10 This is the practical limit of dismantling, apart from that necessary to renew the springs of the centrifugal advance mechanism.
11 Where further dismantling must be done, the procedure is similar to that described in the previous Section.
12 Examine the dismantled components and renew any that show signs of wear or deterioration.
13 Commence reassembly by inserting the pick-up assembly, taking care to align the securing holes.
14 Slide the vacuum capsule into position, ensuring that the vacuum

pull rod fits over the pin on the advance plate. Refit the securing screws but do not tighten them fully.

15 Refit the insulator on top of the pick-up connector blades and fit the securing screw loosely.

16 Refit the remaining pick-up securing screw but do not fully tighten it.

17 Using the circlip pliers refit the circlip, ensuring that it seats correctly in its locating groove.

18 Slide the reluctor onto the distributor shaft, ensuring that the keyways are aligned and then insert the lockpin.

19 Refit the Belleville washer followed by the second circlip.

20 Rotate the shaft so that the reluctor teeth are directly opposite the pole pieces. Ensure that the air gaps are approximately equal. Where it is found that the air gaps are unequal, move the pick-up assembly within the limits of the screw holes.

21 Finally tighten the three securing screws and recheck the air gaps. The remaining vacuum capsule retaining screw can now be tightened.

22 The remaining assembly details are the reverse of the dismantling procedures.

8 Coil – general

1 The two LT wire connections on top of the coil should be periodically checked for security. Remove the rubber sleeve from the centre HT lead and make sure that the end of the wire is clean and making good contact with the coil (photo).

2 A possible source of arcing is between the top of the coil or sleeve and the LT terminals. To avoid this, keep the top of the coil clean and renew the rubber sleeve if cracked or perished.

3 The coil cannot be repaired and if it is thought to be faulty, it should be taken to an auto electrical specialist for testing or renewal.

4 As the coil operates in conjunction with two ballast resistors, it must always be replaced with one of the same specifications.

9 Resistor block – general description

The resistor block consists of the ballast resistor, which is rated at 0·5 ohms, and an auxiliary resistor which is rated at 5 ohms.

The function of the ballast resistor is to maintain a constant primary current in the ignition coil, which tends to vary according to engine speed. At low engine speeds the primary current would be excessive without the ballast resistor being fitted in the circuit. For starting purposes the ballast resistor is bypassed, thus permitting full battery voltage to be supplied to the ignition coil.

The auxiliary resistor is fitted in series with the feed to the control unit and its function is to protect the control unit by limiting the current flow in the electronic part of the circuit.

10 Resistor block – removal and refitting

Note: *It is most important that the wires on the output terminals of the resistors are not interchanged. Interchanging these wires will result in possible damage to the control unit due to excessive current. The engine will start with the wires interchanged but will stop as soon as the ignition key is released from the 'start' position because the primary current is insufficient.*

1 Disconnect the battery earth terminal connection.

2 Take careful note of the wire cable colours and their positions at the resistor terminals before disconnecting them.

3 Note the fitted position of the resistor block and if necessary mark it and the bodywork to ensure accurate replacement.

4 Remove the single retaining screw and remove the terminal block.

5 Refitting is a direct reversal of the removal procedure. Do not over-tighten the retaining screw as the resistor block is made of porcelain and is easily cracked.

6 When connecting the wires, it is most important that the blue /white wire is fitted to one of the ballast resistor terminals. The

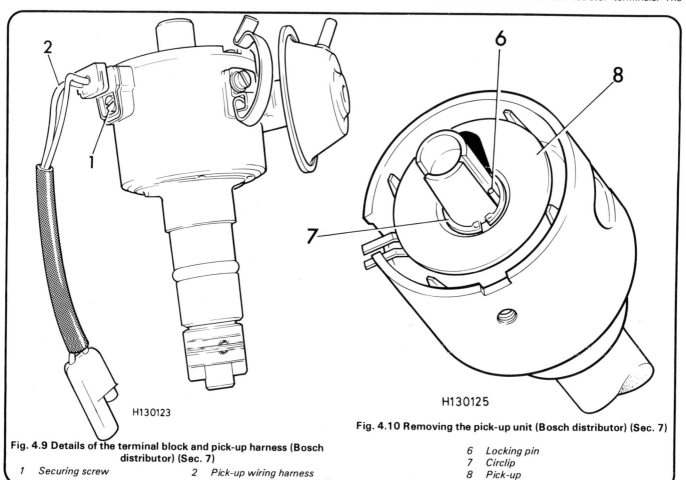

Fig. 4.9 Details of the terminal block and pick-up harness (Bosch distributor) (Sec. 7)

1   *Securing screw*   2   *Pick-up wiring harness*

Fig. 4.10 Removing the pick-up unit (Bosch distributor) (Sec. 7)

6   *Locking pin*
7   *Circlip*
8   *Pick-up*

Measuring plug gap. A feeler gauge of the correct size (see ignition system specifications) should have a slight 'drag' when slid between the electrodes. Adjust gap if necessary

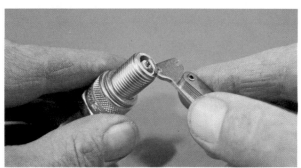

Adjusting plug gap. The plug gap is adjusted by bending the earth electrode inwards, or outwards, as necessary until the correct clearance is obtained. Note the use of the correct tool

Normal. Grey-brown deposits, lightly coated core nose. Gap increasing by around 0.001 in (0.025 mm) per 1000 miles (1600 km). Plugs ideally suited to engine, and engine in good condition

Carbon fouling. Dry, black, sooty deposits. Will cause weak spark and eventually misfire. Fault: over-rich fuel mixture. Check: carburettor mixture settings, float level and jet sizes; choke operation and cleanliness of air filter. Plugs can be re-used after cleaning

Oil fouling. Wet, oily deposits. Will cause weak spark and eventually misfire. Fault: worn bores/piston rings or valve guides; sometimes occurs (temporarily) during running-in period. Plugs can be re-used after thorough cleaning

Overheating. Electrodes have glazed appearance, core nose very white – few deposits. Fault: plug overheating. Check: plug value, ignition timing, fuel octane rating (too low) and fuel mixture (too weak). Discard plugs and cure fault immediately

Electrode damage. Electrodes burned away; core nose has burned, glazed appearance. Fault: pre-ignition. Check: as for 'Overheating' but may be more severe. Discard plugs and remedy fault before piston or valve damage occurs

Split core nose (may appear initially as a crack). Damage is self-evident, but cracks will only show after cleaning. Fault: pre-ignition or wrong gap-setting technique. Check: ignition timing, cooling system, fuel octane rating (too low) and fuel mixture (too weak). Discard plugs, rectify fault immediately

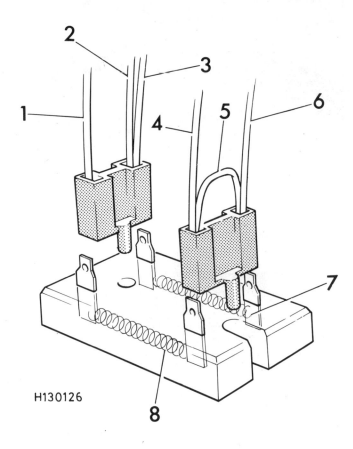

H130126

Fig. 4.11 Resistor block and wiring connection details (Sec. 9)

1	Blue/orange wire to control unit No 3 cavity	5	White link wire to auxiliary resistor
2	White/blue from starter solenoid	6	White wire from ignition switch
3	White/blue wire to coil positive terminal	7	Ballast resistor 0.5 ohm
4	White wire to control unit No 1 cavity	8	Auxiliary resistor 5 ohm

blue/orange wire must be fitted to one of the auxiliary resistor terminals. The ballast resistor can be identified as it is exposed, whereas the auxiliary resistor is hidden in the block.

7   Finally refit the battery earth terminal connection.

11 Spark plugs

1   The correct functioning of the spark plugs is vital for the correct running and efficiency of the engine.

2   At intervals of 6000 miles (9500 km) the plugs should be removed, examined, cleaned, and if worn excessively, renewed. The condition of the spark plugs will also tell much about the overall condition of the engine.

3   If the insulator nose of the spark plug is clean and white, with no deposits, this is indicative of a weak mixture, or too hot a plug (a hot plug transfers heat away from the electrode slowly — a cold plug transfers it away quickly).

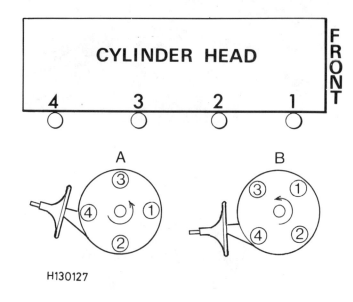

H130127

Fig. 4.12 Spark plug lead connecting diagram (Sec. 11)

A 930 models   B 1300/1600 models

4   The plugs fitted as standard are listed in the Specifications at the beginning of this Chapter. If the tip and insulator nose is covered with hard, black looking deposits,then this is indicative that the mixture is too rich. Should the plug be black and oily, then it is likely that the engine is fairly worn, as well as the mixture being too rich.

5   If the insulator nose is covered with light tan to greyish brown deposits, then the mixture is correct and it is likely that the engine is in good condition.

6   If there are any traces of long brown tapering stains on the outside of the white portion of the plug, then the plug will have to be renewed, as this shows that there is a faulty joint between the plug body and the insulator, and compression is being leaked away.

7   Plugs should be cleaned by a sand blasting machine, which will free them from carbon more thoroughly than cleaning by hand. The machine will also test the condition of the plugs under compression. Any plug that fails to spark at the recommended pressure should be renewed.

8   The spark plug gap is of considerable importance, as, if it is too large or too small, the size of the spark will be seriously impaired. The spark plug gap should be set to the figure given in the Specifications at the beginning of this Chapter.

9   To set it, measure the gap with a feeler gauge, and then bend open, or close, the outer plug (earth) electrode until the gap is achieved. The centre electrode should never be bent as this may crack the insulation and cause plug failure if nothing worse.

10   When refitting the plugs, remember to use new plug washers and refit the leads from the distributor in the correct firing order. The correct firing order is 1–3–4–2, No 1 cylinder being at the timing cover end of the engine.

11   The plug leads require no routine attention other than being wiped over regularly and kept clean. At intervals of 6000 miles (9500 km) however, pull the leads off the plugs and distributor one at a time and make sure no water has found its way onto the connections. Remove any corrosion from the brass ends, wipe the collars on top of the distributor, and refit the leads.

12 Fault diagnosis – ignition system

Symptom	Reason(s)
Engine turns over on starter but will not fire	Damp leads or moisture inside distributor cap Disconnected or insecure lead in circuit especially earth and battery terminals Faulty coil Faulty ballast resistor
Engine runs but misfires	Faulty spark plug Faulty HT lead or poor connections Crack in distributor cap Crack in rotor arm Pick-up leads between distributor and control unit touching metal parts of engine Poor earth connection at control unit Faulty ballast resistor
Engine overheats, loss of power	Seized centrifugal weights or cam on distributor shaft Leaking vacuum hose Incorrectly timed ignition
Engine 'pinks' under load	Ignition timing too advanced Centrifugal advance mechanism stuck in advanced position Broken counterweight spring Octane rating of fuel too low

Chapter 5 Clutch

Contents

Specifications

Type . . . . Single dry plate, diaphragm spring

Make
930 cc models . . . . Borg and Beck DST 190
1300 and 1600 cc models . . . . Laycock DS

Actuation . . . . Mechanical (cable)

Diameter of friction plate . . . . 7.5 in (190 mm)

Identification of drive plate
930 cc models . . . . Exposed damper springs
1300 and 1600 cc models with 1.50 carburettor . . . . Brown spot on hub, enclosed springs
1300 and 1600 cc models with 1.75 carburettor . . . . Lining material is near white in colour, enclosed springs

Release bearing type . . . . Self aligning ball

Release lever pivot post length
930 cc models . . . . 3.3 in (85 mm)
1300 and 1600 cc models . . . . 2.6 in (66 mm)

Clutch pedal height (basic setting) . . . . 7 in (177 mm)

Torque wrench settings

	lbf ft	Nm
Cover assembly attachment nuts (930 cc models)	16	22
Cover assembly attachment bolts (1300 and 1600 cc models)	15	20
Lever pivot post	10	14
Cable adjuster locknut	3	4
Clutch bellhousing to engine	34	46

---

1 General description

All models with manual transmission are fitted with a 7½ in (190 mm) single dry plate diaphragm spring clutch, of either Borg and Beck or Laycock manufacture. Basically the unit comprises a steel cover which is dowelled and either retained to the rear face of the flywheel by nuts (Borg and Beck), or bolts (Laycock), and contains the pressure plate, diaphragm spring and fulcrum rings.

The clutch disc is free to slide along the splined gearbox primary shaft and is held in position between the flywheel and the pressure plate by the pressure plate spring. The friction lining material is riveted

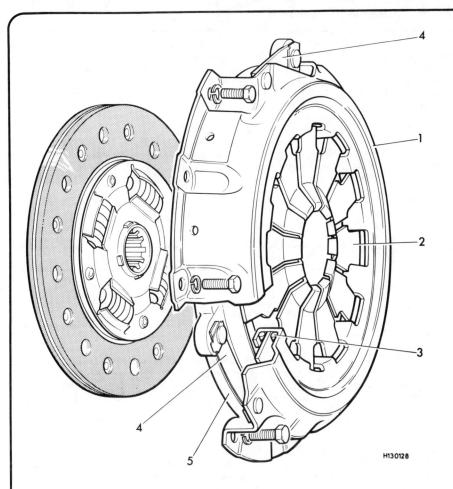

Fig. 5.1 Clutch assembly (Borg
and Beck type) (Sec. 1)

1   Cover
2   Diaphragm spring
3   Fulcrum rings
4   Spring straps
5   Pressure plate

H130128

Fig. 5.2 Clutch assembly
(Laycock type)

1   Cover
2   Pressure plate
3   Diaphragm spring
4   Fulcrum rings
5   Support ring
6   Spring straps
7   Rivets

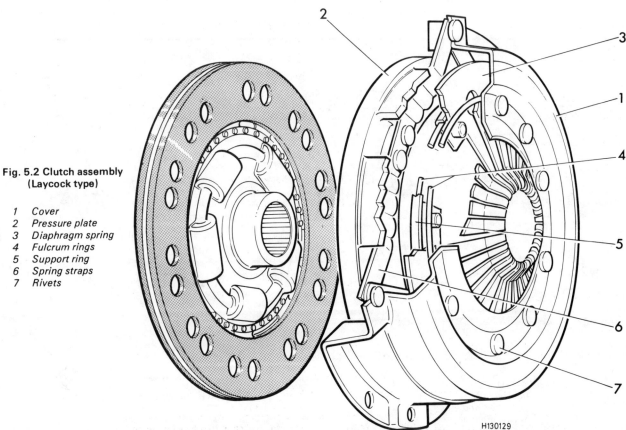

H130129

to the clutch disc and it has a spring cushioned hub to absorb transmission shocks and to help ensure a smooth take-up of drive.

The circular diaphragm spring is mounted on shoulder pins and is held in place in the cover by two fulcrum rings. The spring is also held to the pressure plate by three spring steel straps which are riveted in position. On the Borg and Beck type clutch these springs are arranged tangentially, whereas with the Laycock type they are longer and riveted together to form a triangle.

The clutch is actuated by a cable, controlled by the clutch pedal. The clutch release mechanism consists of a release fork and bearing which are in permanent contact with the release fingers on the pressure plate. There should therefore never be any free play at the release fork. Wear of the friction material in the clutch is adjusted out by means of a cable adjuster nut on the outer end of the clutch release fork. Depressing the clutch pedal actuates the clutch release arm by means of the cable.

The release arm pushes the release bearing forwards to bear against the release fingers, so moving the centre of the diaphragm spring inwards. The spring is sandwiched between two annular rings which act as fulcrum points. As the centre of the spring is pushed in the outside of the spring is pushed out, so moving the pressure plate backwards and disengaging it from the clutch disc.

When the clutch pedal is released the diaphragm spring forces the pressure plate into contact with the high friction linings on the clutch disc; at the same time it pushes the clutch disc a fraction of an inch forwards on its splines so engaging the clutch disc with the flywheel. The clutch disc is now firmly sandwiched between the pressure plate and the flywheel so the drive is taken up.

2   Clutch – adjustment

1   Depress the clutch pedal fully several times to seat the cable.
2   Using a straight edge, measure the distance required to raise or lower the clutch pedal to bring it to the same level as the brake pedal.
3   Where it is found that the clutch pedal height is not equal to that of the footbrake pedal, it will be necessary to adjust the clutch cable.
4   Refer to Fig. 5.3 and loosen the locknut (1) at the adjuster.
5   Prevent the inner cable from twisting by fitting a spanner on the cable end fitting (3).

6   Turn the adjuster nut (2) to raise or lower the clutch pedal. If it is desired to lower the clutch pedal unscrew the adjuster nut and vice versa. Seven complete turns of the adjuster nut will move the pedal by approximately 1 in (25 mm).
7   After making the necessary adjustment tighten the adjuster locknut, but ensure that when doing so neither the adjuster nut or cable turn.
8   Finally make sure that the clutch frees itself fully when the clutch pedal is depressed, by starting the engine and engaging reverse gear. Having engaged reverse gear, slowly release the clutch pedal and note the amount of pedal travel before the clutch fully engages.
9   If repeated attempts to adjust the clutch fail, then it is reasonable to assume that the clutch centre plate is worn or faulty.
10 Excessive slackness in the clutch operating cable can cause the cable to jump out of engagement with the notch in the pedal arm. Avoid this with regular adjustment.

3   Clutch pedal – removal, overhaul and refitting

Refer to Chapter 9, Section 21 for details.

4   Clutch – removal

1   Remove the gearbox as described in Chapter 6.
2   Scribe a mating line from the clutch cover to the flywheel to ensure identical positioning on replacement. Remove the nuts or bolts retaining the cover to the rear face of the flywheel. Unscrew the nuts or bolts diagonally half a turn at a time to prevent distortion to the cover flange and relieve the pressure of the diaphragm spring.
3   With all the nuts or bolts and spring washers removed lift the clutch assembly off the locating dowels. The driven plate or clutch disc may fall out at this stage, as it is not attached to either the clutch cover assembly or the flywheel, so be prepared to catch it (photo).

5   Clutch – dismantling and refitting

1   It is not practicable to dismantle the pressure plate assembly. The term 'clutch' dismantling and refitting, is the term usually used for

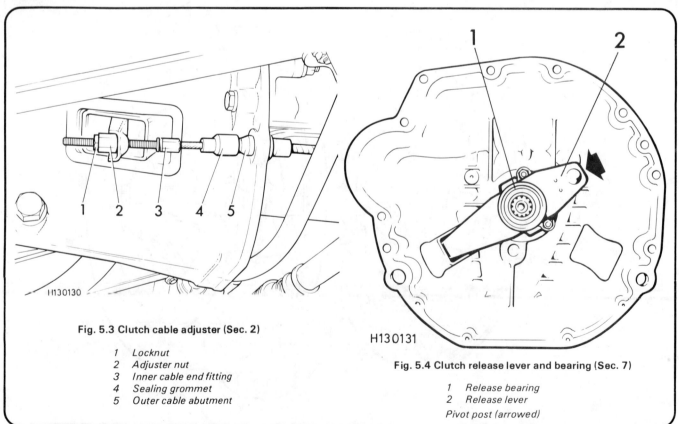

Fig. 5.3 Clutch cable adjuster (Sec. 2)

1   Locknut
2   Adjuster nut
3   Inner cable end fitting
4   Sealing grommet
5   Outer cable abutment

H130131

Fig. 5.4 Clutch release lever and bearing (Sec. 7)

1   Release bearing
2   Release lever
Pivot post (arrowed)

4.3 Removing clutch components

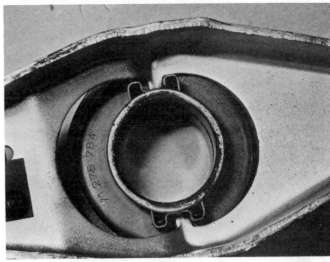

7.3 Rear view of clutch release lever and bearing

7.5 Clutch release ballstud clip

7.6 Clutch release lever and bearing assembled

simply fitting a new clutch friction plate.

2   If a new clutch disc is being fitted it is a false economy not to renew the release bearing at the same time. This will prevent having to renew it at a later date when wear on the clutch linings will still be minimal.

3   If the pressure plate assembly requires renewal (see Section 6, paragraphs 3 and 4) an exchange unit must be purchased. This will have been accurately set up and balanced to very fine limits.

6   Clutch – inspection

1   Examine the clutch disc friction linings for wear and loose rivets and the disc for rim distortion, cracks, broken hub springs and worn splines. The surface of the friction linings may be highly glazed, but as long as the clutch material pattern can be clearly seen this is satisfactory. If you are in doubt at all about the serviceability of your clutch disc then it is advisable to take it to your local Talbot dealer for examination.

2   It is always sound practice to renew the clutch driven plate as an assembly to preclude further trouble. At one time it was possible to obtain new linings and fit them to the driven plate after drilling out the rivets and removing the worn linings. The manufacturers do not advise

that only the linings are renewed and personal experience dictates that it is far more satisfactory to renew the driven plate complete, than to try to economise by only fitting new friction linings.

3   Check the machined faces of the flywheel and the pressure plate; if either are grooved they may be machined until smooth or renewed.

4   If the pressure plate is cracked or split, or the pressure of the diaphragm spring is suspect, it is essential that an exchange unit is fitted.

5   Check the release bearing for smoothness of operation. There should be no harshness and no slackness in it. It should rotate reasonably freely bearing in mind it has been prepacked with grease. Avoid cleaning the bearing with any solvent, as this will degrease the bearing.

7   Clutch release bearing – removal and refitting

1   With the engine and gearbox separated to provide access to the clutch, attention can be given to the release bearing located in the bellhousing on the input shaft bearing retainer.

2   The release bearing is a relatively inexpensive but important item and unless it is nearly new it is a mistake not to renew it during an overhaul of the clutch.

3   Remove the release bearing simply by grasping it and pulling it

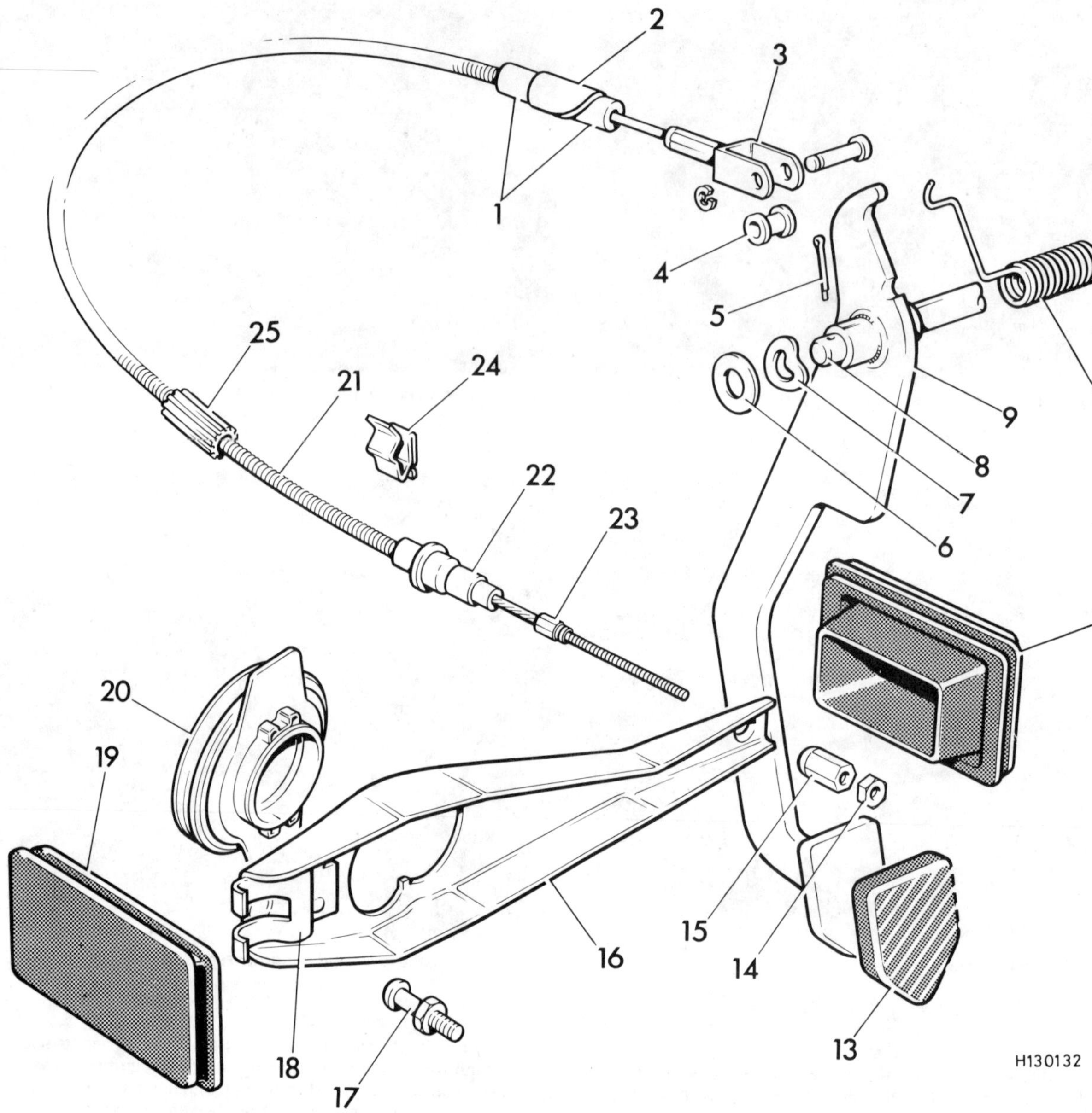

Fig. 5.5 Clutch operating mechanism (right-hand drive) (Sec. 9)

1   Outer cable sleeve
2   Nylon abutment
3   Cable clevis
4   Roller
5   Split pin
6   Washer
7   Belleville washer
8   Cross shaft
9   Pedal arm
10   Pedal return spring
11   Belleville washer
12   Grommet
13   Pedal pad

14   Locking nut
15   Adjuster nut
16   Release lever
17   Pivot post
18   Spring retainer
19   Blanking grommet
20   Release bearing
21   Outer cable
22   Seal
23   Inner cable
24   Cable retaining clip
25   Insulator

H130132

away from the release lever lugs (photo).

4   Should difficulty be found then it is advisable to remove the release lever aperture grommet on the side opposite the cable adjuster, insert a lever through the aperture and ease the bearing from its locating lugs.

5   The release lever can be removed from the pivot post by pulling it sideways in order to clear the clips from the domed head of the post (photo).

6   Refitting of the components is the reverse of the removal procedure. It is advisable to apply a small amount of high melting point grease to the pivot post ball, the two bearing lugs on the release lever and the gearbox front cover bearing retainer (photo).

8   Clutch – refitting

1   It is important that no oil or grease gets on the clutch disc friction linings, or the pressure plate and flywheel faces. It is advisable to refit the clutch with clean hands and to wipe down the pressure plate and flywheel faces with a petrol moistened rag before assembly begins.

2   Place the clutch disc against the flywheel, ensuring that it is the correct way round. The flywheel side of the clutch disc is clearly marked near the centre. If the disc is fitted the wrong way round it will be quite impossible to operate the clutch.

3   Refit the clutch cover loosely on the dowels aligning the mating marks. Refit the spring washers and nuts or bolts and tighten them finger tight so that the clutch disc is gripped but can still be moved.

4   The clutch disc must now be centralised, so that when the engine and gearbox are mated the gearbox primary shaft splines will pass through the splined hub of the clutch disc.

5   Centralisation can be carried out quite easily by inserting a round bar or long screwdriver through the hole in the centre of the clutch, so that the end of the bar rests in the small hole in the end of the crankshaft containing the input shaft bearing bush. Ideally an old Sunbeam primary shaft should be used.

6   Using the input shaft bearing bush as a fulcrum, moving the bar sideways, or up and down, will move the clutch disc in whichever direction is necessary to achieve centralisation.

7   Centralisation is easily judged by removing the bar and viewing the driven plate hub in relation to the hole in the centre of the clutch cover diaphragm spring. When the hub appears exactly in the centre of the hole all is correct. Alternatively, the primary gearbox shaft will fit the bush and centre of the clutch hub exactly, obviating the need for visual alignment.

8   Tighten the clutch bolts or nuts firmly in a diagonal sequence to ensure that the cover plate is pulled down evenly and without distortion of the flange. Finally tighten the nuts or bolts down to the recommended torque setting. The flywheel may need jamming to prevent it rotating while the nuts are being tightened.

9   Clutch cable – removal and refitting

1   Place chocks behind the rear wheels, jack up the front of the car, and place stands under the front crossmember. Alternatively, place the car over an inspection pit.

2   Remove the locknut and the cable adjuster nut from the clutch cable.

3   Pull out the threaded end of the clutch inner cable from the release arm.

4   Unclip the cable, withdrawing it from the bellhousing aperture and through the engine mounting.

5   From inside the car pull the end of the clutch pedal spring away from the inner cable roller, then lift the pedal slowly and release the roller from the clutch pedal hook.

6   Pull back the outer cable from the nylon bulkhead abutment and remove from the bulkhead abutment by squeezing it together and pulling it into the engine compartment. The cable can now be lifted out of the car.

7   Refitting commences by inserting the inner cable through the aperture in the bulkhead. Push the nylon bulkhead abutment off the end of the outer cables and squeeze the ends of the abutment together. Push it into place in the bulkhead, sandwiching it with the abutment slot.

8   Refit the outer cable to the nylon bulkhead abutment, gently pushing the outer cable fully home ensuring that its key is in line with the slot in the abutment.

9   The remainder of the refitting process is now a simple reversal of the removal instructions.

10 Finally refer to Section 2 and adjust the clutch.

10 Fault diagnosis – clutch

Symptom	Reason(s)
Judder when taking up drive	Loose engine or gearbox mountings Badly worn friction surfaces or contaminated with oil Worn splines on gearbox input shaft or driven plate hub Worn input shaft spigot bush in crankshaft rear flange
Clutch spin (failure to disengage) so that gears cannot be meshed	Incorrect release bearing to diaphragm spring finger clearance Driven plate sticking on input shaft splines due to rust. May occur after vehicle standing idle for long period Damaged or misaligned pressure plate assembly
Clutch slip (increase in engine speed does not result in increase in vehicle road speed – particularly on gradients)	Incorrect release bearing in diaphragm spring finger clearance Friction surfaces worn out or oil contaminated
Noise evident on depressing clutch pedal	Dry, worn or damaged release bearing Weak or broken pedal return spring Weak or broken clutch release lever return spring Excessive play between driven plate hub splines and input shaft splines
Noise evident as clutch pedal released	Distorted driven plate Broken or weak driven plate cushion coil springs Weak or broken clutch pedal return spring Weak or broken release lever return spring Distorted or worn input shaft Release bearing loose on retainer hub

Chapter 6 Part A Manual gearbox

Contents

Specifications

Gearbox type . . . . Four forward speeds (all synchromesh) and reverse

Oil capacity . . . . 3 pints (1.7 litres)

Gear ratios

	Standard	Wide
Top	1.000 : 1	1.000 : 1
3rd	1.387 : 1	1.527 : 1
2nd	2.165 : 1	2.382 : 1
1st	3.538 : 1	3.894 : 1
Reverse	3.680 : 1	4.050 : 1

Speedometer drive pinion

Rear axle ratio	No of teeth	Colour
3.545 : 1	16	Blue
3.700 : 1	16	Blue
3.889 : 1	17	White
4.111 : 1	18	Red
4.375:1	19	Light green

Primary shaft selection washers
Availability . . . . 0.051 to 0.053 in (1.30 to 1.35 mm)
0.056 to 0.058 in (1.42 to 1.47 mm)
0.060 to 0.062 in (1.52 to 1.57 mm)

Primary shaft endfloat (circlip to washer) . . . . 0.001 to 0.007 in (0.30 to 0.18 mm)

Mainshaft gear endfloat
1st speed . . . . 0.005 to 0.0085 in (0.12 to 0.21 mm)
2nd and 3rd speeds . . . . 0.004 to 0.0075 in (0.10 to 0.19 mm)

Layshaft endfloat . . . . 0.006 to 0.010 in (0.15 to 0.25 mm)

Layshaft thrust washer availability
Rear washer . . . . 0.058 to 0.060 in (1.47 to 1.52 mm)
0.061 to 0.063 in (1.55 to 1.60 mm)
0.064 to 0.066 in (1.63 to 1.68 mm)

Front washer . . . . 0.070 to 0.072 in (1.78 to 1.83 mm)

Torque wrench settings

	lbf ft	Nm
Front bearing retainer nuts	6	8
Top cover bolts	4	6
Reverse plunger bolts	4	6
Speedometer drive bolts	4	6
Extension housing bolts	14	19
Detent plunger cover plate	4	6
Reverse lever pivot screw	25	34
Mainshaft front nut	70	95
Mainshaft rear nut*	80	109
Clutch bellhousing bolts to engine	34	46
Drain and filler plugs	30	41
Gearbox to rear mounting	26	35
Gearbox mounting crossmember to body	12	16
Rear bearing retainer bolts	12	16
Sump stiffener bolts	16	22

*Torque to 69 lbf ft (94 Nm) only if special nut tightening tool (part No RG 544) is used

1 General description

The gearbox fitted to all models contains four constant mesh helically cut forward gears and one sheer cut reverse gear. Synchromesh is fitted between 1st and 2nd, 2nd and 3rd and 3rd and top. The bellhousing cannot be separated from the gearbox.

Attached to the rear of the gearbox casing is an aluminium alloy extension which supports the rear of the mainshaft and the gearchange rod.

The gearbox casing is also cast in aluminium and is fitted with a removable top cover.

Viewed from the rear, the drain plug is at the bottom of the right-hand side of the gearbox casing and the filler plug is half way up the same side.

All the mainshaft gears are bushed internally and wear therefore normally takes place in these bushes and not on the mainshaft itself.

The gearbox is 'filled for life' and no changing of lubricant is nor-mally required. However, a drain plug is fitted for owners who believe that an occasional renewal of oil (eg 20 000 mile intervals) is beneficial (photo).

The operations described in Sections 2 to 9 can be carried out without removing the gearbox from the car, although where stated, the rear mounting may have to be disconnected.

2 Gearshift lever – removal and refitting

1   Remove the knob and gaiter and extract the dust pad. On models where the gaiter is secured by the centre console moulding, extract the five self-tapping screws from the points indicated.
2   Withdraw the rubber boot and slide it up the control lever. Check that the gear lever is in neutral.
3   Unscrew and remove the three screws that retain the gear lever cap (photo).

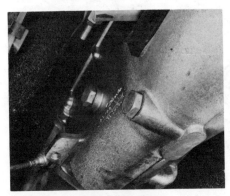
1.6 Gearbox drain and filler plugs

2.3 Extracting a gear lever cap screw

2.4 Gear lever removed

3.2A Reverse lamp switch

3.2B Reverse lamp switch removed

4.2 Speedometer cable disconnected from gearbox

4   Withdraw the gear lever together with cap, disc and spring (photo).
5   Refitting is a reversal of removal, eut apply grease liberally to the contact surfaces of the ball and turret.

3   Reverse lamp switch – removal, refitting and adjustment

1   Disconnect the battery.
2   Disconnect the leads from the switch and then unscrew the switch from the rear extension housing. Retain any shims fitted below the switch (photos).
3   Refitting is a reversal of removal. Do not use excessive force when tightening the switch.
4   If the reverse lamp switch does not operate correctly, adjust it in the following way. If the reverse lamps illuminate with 3rd or top gear engaged, increase the number of shims under the switch. If the lamps do not come on when reverse gear is selected, reduce the number of shims. Should the reverse lamps flicker as the gearchange lever is moved across the gate, add one shim and recheck the operation.

4   Speedometer pinion and oil seal – removal and refitting

1   Two types of pinion are used. It is important that if the type fitted to your vehicle is identified as (B), it must be installed with the arrow, tongue and slot facing upward.
2   To remove the pinion, disconnect the speedometer drive cable by unscrewing the knurled ring (photo).
3   Unscrew and remove the two set-bolts that secure the pinion assembly.
4   Withdraw the pinion components (photo). To renew the oil seal, separate the pinion and housing and prise out the seal.
5   Refitting is a reversal of removal, after the components have been smeared with oil. Refer to paragraph 1 before refitting.

5   Extension housing oil seal – renewal

1   Raise the rear of the car and support securely.
2   Place a container under the rear end of the gearbox to catch any oil as the propeller shaft is withdrawn.
3   Remove the propeller shaft as described in Chapter 7.
4   Prise out the old oil seal taking great care not to damage the splines on the end of the gearbox output shaft. If the seal cannot be extracted using a lever, try a small two-legged puller with outward facing claws.
5   Tap the new seal fully to the bottom of its recess then pack the groove between the seal lips with grease.
6   Refit the propeller shaft. When the car is again lowered to the ground, check the gearbox oil level.

6   Rear extension housing – removal and refitting

1   With the car over an inspection pit or raised on ramps, drain the gearbox.
2   Disconnect the battery. Remove the gear lever as described in Section 2.
3   Remove the propeller shaft guard and the propeller shaft itself, as described in Chapter 7.
4   Disconnect the speedometer cable from the gearbox.
5   Disconnect the leads from the reverse lamp switch.
6   Support the rear end of the main gear case on a jack.
7   Unscrew and remove the rear mounting from the bodyframe (photo).
8   Unscrew and remove the five bolts that hold the rear extension housing to the main gearcase. Note the locations (arrowed in Fig. 6.6) of the longer bolts.
9   With the gearbox having been set in neutral at the time of removal of the gear lever, rotate the gearshift remote control rod in an anti-clockwise direction to its stop and then move it to the rear, to disengage it from the selector shaft.
10 Pull the extension housing from the main gearcase in a straight line, to prevent damage to the oil transfer tube. An initial resistance

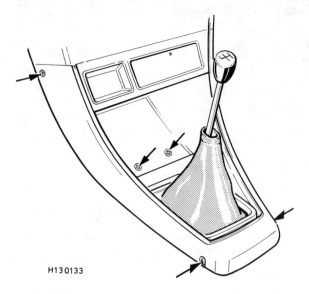

Fig. 6.1 Centre console mounting screws (Sec. 2)

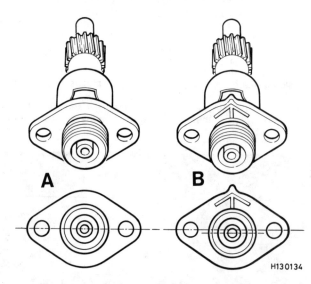

Fig. 6.2 Two types of speedometer pinion (Sec. 4)

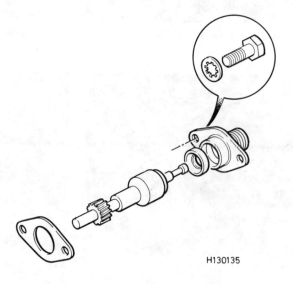

Fig. 6.3 Exploded view of the speedometer pinion (Sec. 4)

will be felt during withdrawal caused by the locating dowels at the push fit oil transfer tube.

11 Peel away the joint gasket and clean the mating faces.

12 Before fitting the rear extension housing, make sure that the oil transfer tube is positioned correctly in the cover, with its double bend facing forward and angled upward towards the top of the gearbox (photo).

13 Fit a new joint gasket, smeared both sides with jointing compound.

14 Move the gearshift remote rod fully to the rear and rotate it anti-clockwise (viewed from the rear) as far as it will go.

15 Refit the extension housing, locating the oil transfer pipe in the hole at the rear of the gearbox.

16 Refit the extension to gearcase bolts, making sure that the two longer ones are correctly located.

17 Refit and connect all the remaining components and refill the gearbox with oil.

7 Reverse bias assembly – removal and refitting

1 Raise the rear of the car or place it over an inspection pit.

2 Unscrew the two cap set-bolts evenly and withdraw the cap, plunger, spring sheath and spring (photo).

3 Refitting is a reversal of removal.

8 Gearshift remote control rod – removal and refitting

1 Withdraw the rear extension housing as described in Section 6.

2 With the extension housing on the bench, extract the seven screws that secure the remote control rod cover plate.

3 Using a small punch, drive out the roll pin that attaches the swing lever to the rod. Align the projecting end of the pin with the forward bolt hole for the reverse bias cap and drive the pin right out of its hole.

4 Remove the control rod from the swing lever by jerking the rod forward from the rear cover (photo).

5 To refit the components, insert the rod and swing lever and push a temporary pin through the forward bolt hole of the reverse bias assembly.

6 Drive the new roll pin in flush from the extension housing side, so that the temporary pin is displaced.

7 Apply grease to the swing lever socket and then fit the control rod cover plate.

8 Refit the extension housing.

9 Detent plungers and springs – removal and refitting

1 Set the gearshift lever in neutral.

2 Raise the car on ramps or place it over an inspection pit.

3 Release the two set-bolts evenly at the detent plunger side plate.

4 Extract the set-bolts, withdraw the plate, springs and plungers (photos).

5 Peel away the gasket.

6 Renew the plungers if they are pitted, worn or show flat spots.

7 Refitting is a reversal of removal. Lubricate the plunger holes and insert them, radiused ends first. Insert the springs and then position a new gasket, smeared both sides with gasket cement.

8 Fit the side plate and tighten the bolts to the specified torque.

10 Gearbox – removal and refitting

1 Disconnect the battery and then remove the starter motor upper bolt and push aside the earth strap. Place the car over an inspection pit, or raise the rear of the car on ramps sufficiently high to be able to withdraw the gearbox from under the car.

930 models

2 Disconnect the exhaust downpipe from the manifold.

1300/1600

3 Drain the cooling system. Disconnect the radiator upper hose and the heater hoses from their rear clip.

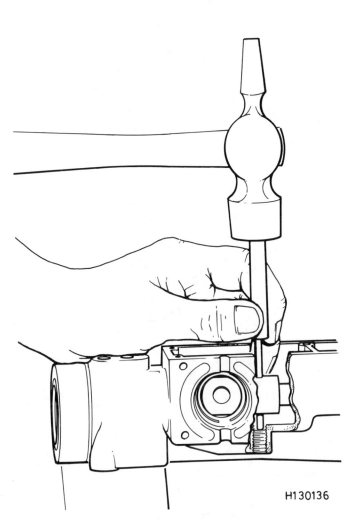

H130136

Fig. 6.4 Removing remote control swing lever roll pin (Sec. 8)

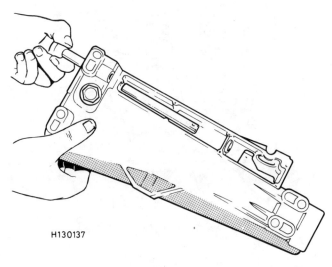

H130137

Fig. 6.5 Withdrawing gearshift remote control rod (Sec. 8)

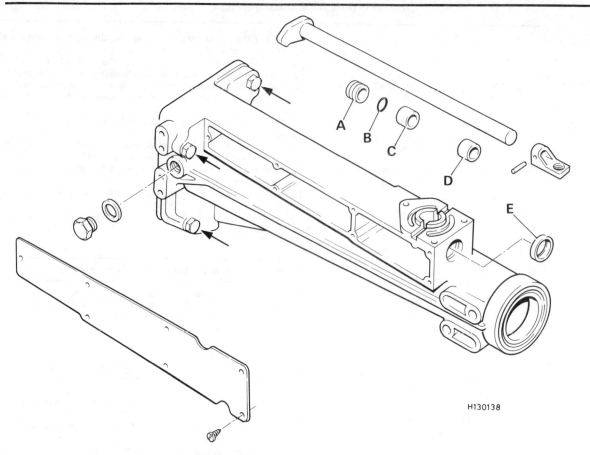

H130138

Fig. 6.6 Gearshift remote control rod and bushes (Sec. 8)

A Seal retainer and bush   C Front bush   E Plug
B Oil seal   D Rear bush

Arrows indicate positions of longer bolts for attachment to gearbox

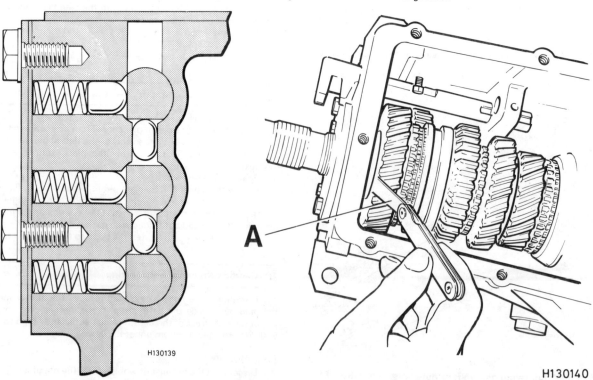

H130139

**Fig. 6.7 Sectional view of detent plunger/spring arrangement
(Sec. 9)**

H130140

Fig. 6.8 Checking gear endfloat (A) Feeler gauge (Sec. 11)

4.4 Withdrawing speedometer pinion from gearbox

6.7 Gearbox rear mounting

6.12 Gearbox oil transfer tube

7.2 Reverse bias assembly (cap unbolted)

8.4 Gearshift remote control rod, viewed from front end of extension housing

9.4A Detent cover plate removed

9.4B Detent plunger

10.12 Clutch bellhousing cover plate

11.29 Mainshaft with all components removed

4   Disconnect the exhaust pipe joint adjacent to the propeller shaft guard.

5   Release the sump to clutch housing stiffeners by loosening the securing screws to the sump and then removing the nuts and bolts that pass through the stiffener and flywheel dust cover. Retrieve any shims located between the stiffeners and the dust covers, noting carefully their positions.

All models

6   Remove the gearshift lever assembly as described in Section 2.

7   Drain the oil from the gearbox.

8   Remove the propeller shaft as described in Chapter 7; also the propeller shaft guard.

9   Disconnect the speedometer cable from the gearbox.

10 Release the clutch cable from the clip on the engine front bearer.

11 Note the approximate setting of the threaded adjuster at the bellhousing and then release the locknut. Detach the clutch cable from the release lever arm and pull the cable assembly from the bellhousing.

12 Unbolt and remove the cover plate from the front cover face of the clutch bellhousing (photo).

13 Release the stabiliser bar brackets to give a clearance between them and the side members of approximately $\frac{3}{8}$ in (10.0 mm).

14 Disconnect the reverse lamp wires at the gearbox.

15 Support the gearbox rear extension housing on a jack, unbolt the rear mounting crossmember from the side members.

16 Lower the jack slowly until the rear edge of the cylinder head almost contacts the engine rear bulkhead. Insert a piece of 3 ply wood between the engine and the bulkhead and then let the engine rest fully rearward.

17 Release the reverse lamp wires from the clips at the upper right hand bolt that connects the clutch bellhousing to the engine.

18 Remove the two uppermost bolts connecting the bellhousing to the engine.

19 Unscrew and remove the starter motor lower bolt nut and push the bolt forward to clear the bellhousing.

20 Place a piece of packing wood between the sump and crossmem-

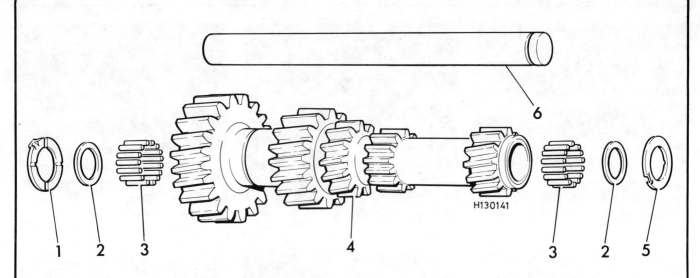

Fig. 6.9 Layshaft and gear components (Sec 11)

1 Front thrust washer
2 Abutment rings
3 Needle rollers
4 Layshaft cluster

5 Rear (selective) thrust
   washer
6 Layshaft

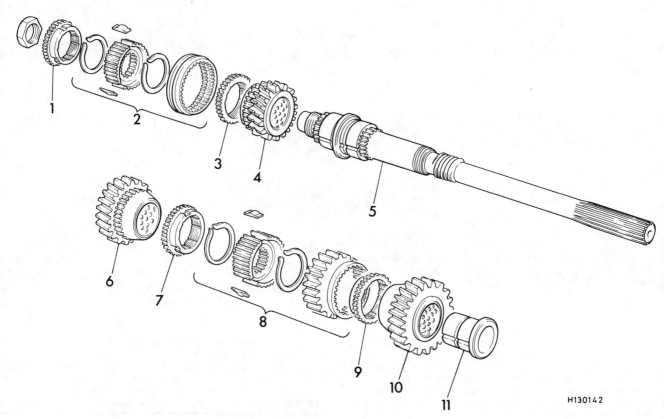

Fig. 6.10 Mainshaft components

1 4th speed baulk ring
2 3rd/4th synchro hub
3 3rd speed baulk ring
4 3rd speed gear
5 Mainshaft
6 2nd speed gear

7 2nd speed baulk ring
8 1st/2nd synchro hub and
   reverse gear
9 1st speed baulk ring
10 1st speed gear
11 Spacer

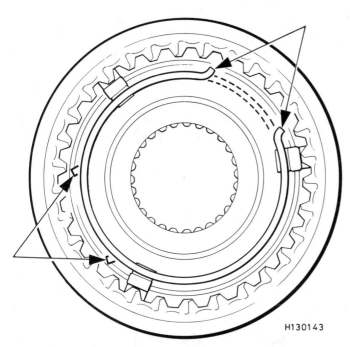

Fig. 6.11 Location of synchro unit circlips (Sec. 11)
Note open ends of clips must be 180° apart on opposite sides of synchro

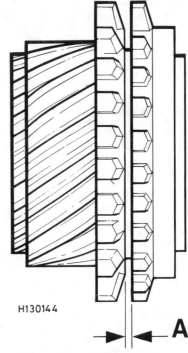

Fig. 6.12 Synchro baulk ring to dog teeth minimum clearance
A = 0.03 in (0.75 mm) (Sec 11)

ber, to prevent the engine tilting forward once the gearbox has been withdrawn.

21 Extract the remaining bellhousing to engine bolts. Draw the gearbox to the rear in a straight line and remove it from under the car.

22 Refitting is a reversal of removal but observe the following points.

23 If the clutch has been dismantled, make sure that it is centralised before offering up the gearbox (see Chapter 5).

24 Smear the input shaft lightly with high melting point grease.

25 With the help of an assistant, hold the gearbox in line with the engine and push it into position. It may assist the refitting if the output shaft is turned at the same time (gear engaged). Do not allow the weight of the gearbox to hang upon the input shaft while the shaft is only engaged in the clutch driven plate hub.

26 Engage the bellhousing dowels and push the gearbox fully home. Insert the two upper securing bolts first and then the remainder.

27 On 1300/1600 models, once the sump screws are tight and the stiffener to dust cover bolts not yet inserted, measure the clearance between the stiffener and gearbox. Pack out this clearance as necessary.

28 Adjust the clutch cable (Chapter 5).

29 Refill the gearbox.

30 On 1300/1600 models, refill the cooling system.

11 Gearbox – overhaul

1 With the gearbox removed from the car, wash the exterior clean with paraffin or water soluble solvent.

2 Disengage the clutch release arm from its ball stud pivot by pushing the arm towards the aperture in the bellhousing.

3 Remove the release bearing.

4 Remove the setscrews and washers from the top cover and lift the cover, with its gasket, off the gearbox.

5 Stand the gearbox on the bellhousing flange. Remove the reverse gear stop plate spring and plunger by undoing the two retaining bolts and washers. Undo the five bolts that hold the rear extension to the back of the gearbox.

6 Remove the rear extension housing as described in Section 6.

7 Undo the bolt from the centre of the keep plate between the layshaft and the reverse idler gear shaft. The keep plate can now be slid out from the slots in the layshaft and reverse idler shaft. If the keep plate is stiff drift it out with a screwdriver.

8 Undo the two bolts that hold the selector spring cover plate in position on the rear top corner of the gearbox casing on the left hand side. Lift off the selector spring cover plate and take out the three springs. Remove the plungers if they will slip out easily, otherwise leave them in place. Use a container to keep these parts together.

9 To drive out the roll pins that hold the selector forks in place use a $\frac{1}{8}$ inch (3.2 mm) pin punch. If one is not available cut the sharp end off a round headed $1\frac{1}{2}$ inch nail.

10 The nail makes an excellent punch. Drive out the roll pin that secures the 3rd/4th gear selector fork to its selector rod and also the pin that secures the 1st/2nd gear selector fork to its rod. Remove the forks and pins.

11 The selector rods can now be removed from the rear of the gearbox. To avoid confusion later stick a piece of masking tape to each rod indicating from which hole it was taken.

12 With the aid of a piece of wire slide out the interlock plungers from their drillings in the rear face of the gearbox. Plungers are fitted between the 3rd/4th and 1st/2nd selector rod holes and also between 1st/2nd and reverse.

13 Before the reverse gear selector rod can be removed it is necessary to undo the pivot bolt (see Fig. 6.14). To start it use a pair of mole grips. A Phillips screwdriver will only slip. Drive the layshaft out rearwards with a long drift.

14 Before removing either the primary or mainshafts check the end-float of 1st, 2nd and 3rd gears with a feeler gauge placed between the gear and its flange. Undo the nuts and washers holding the front cover in place.

15 Remove the cover. When the layshaft was removed the laygear will have fallen to the bottom of the gearbox. Drift out the primary shaft bearing very carefully from inside the gearbox.

16 The primary shaft bearing can then be removed complete with the primary shaft. Ensure the primary gear does not foul the laygear as it is removed.

17 At the rear of the gearbox undo the two bolts and washers that secure the rear bearing clamp plate in position.

18 Clamp the long exposed portion of the mainshaft between the soft jaws in a vice. In the absence of a large enough spanner ($1\frac{5}{8}$ AF) start the self-locking nut by holding a drift to the lower or left hand side of one of the nuts six faces, hitting the drift smartly until the nut starts to turn.

19 Release the mainshaft from the vice and drive it forward with a heavy mallet or hammer with a block of wood interposed, until the

shoulder on the shaft is free from the rear bearing.

20 The bearing must now be removed from the casing. Although free from the shaft it can usually be started from the casing by drifting the front of the shaft rearwards. The shaft will tend to push the bearing out rather than enter the bore in the bearing it has just left.

21 Once the bearing has started to move it can be levered out of the rear of the casing with the aid of two open ended spanners.

22 When free from the gearbox lift the bearing off the tail end of the mainshaft.

23 The mainshaft assembly can now be lifted out, front end first, through the hole in the top of the gearbox casing.

24 Lift out the layshaft and thrust washers from the bottom of the gearbox. To remove the reverse idler gear and shaft, remove the reverse selector shaft guide peg and pull out the shaft, with a pair of mole grips, from the rear of the gearbox.

Mainshaft – dismantling and reassembly

25 The mainshaft has to be dismantled before some of the synchroniser rings can be inspected. With a soft faced hammer tap the splined end of the shaft holding onto second gear.

26 Slide off from the splined end of the shaft 1st gear and then the 1st/2nd gear synchroniser hub (reverse is on its periphery) and 2nd gear. Ensure all the parts are kept in their relative positions.

27 Mount the plain portion of the shaft between two pieces of wood in a vice and undo the nut that retains the 3rd/4th gear synchroniser assembly.

28 Slide off the synchroniser hub followed by 3rd gear. Note that on the 3rd/4th gear synchro sliding sleeve the selector fork groove is fitted opposite the hub wide face boss.

29 If during the removal of one of the synchroniser hubs the outer sleeve slips off the inner hub do not worry as reassembly is straightforward. Fit the sleeve to the hub and then the three sliding keys (photo).

30 Retain the sliding keys to the outer sleeve by fitting the two internal circlips with their ends evenly spaced between two sliding keys. Note that the 1st/2nd gear synchro hub can be fitted either way round (photo).

31 Renew all worn or damaged components. Check the synchro baulk ring to dog teeth clearance as shown Fig. 6.15.

32 Throughout reassembly lightly lubricate all the components as they are fitted together. Slide 3rd gear onto the short end of the mainshaft until it abuts the flange. Fit a new synchro ring (photo).

33 Fit the 3rd/4th gear synchro hub so the wide face hub boss is adjacent to 3rd gear and the selector fork groove, which is offset, is towards the nose of the shaft (photo).

34 Note that when the synchro hub is fitted, it is essential that the cut-outs in the periphery of the synchroniser ring mate with the sliding keys on the inside of the synchroniser sleeve.

35 Place the mainshaft between two blocks of wood in a vice and replace the self-locking nut with its plain side against the synchro hub. Tighten the nut to the specified torque (photo).

36 Moving to the longer end of the mainshaft, fit second gear with its flat side towards the flange on the shaft. Follow with a new synchro ring and the 1st/2nd gear synchroniser hub (photo).

37 Note when fitting the 1st/2nd gear synchro hub, that the end of the hub with the groove on its periphery is fitted facing the tail end of the shaft.

38 Ensure that the sliding key on the inside of the synchroniser sleeve fits onto the cut-out on the synchro ring.

39 With a drift, gently tap alternate sides of the synchro hub until the hub is on as far as possible (photo).

40 Fit a further synchro ring, 1st gear with the cone side facing the 1st/2nd gear synchroniser hub and finally the distance piece. The mainshaft is now reassembled (photo).

Primary shaft – dismantling and reassembly

41 The only reason for dismantling the primary shaft is to fit a new ball bearing assembly. If the gear on the shaft is badly worn the bearing will be worn too. With circlip pliers remove the circlip from the primary shaft (photo).

42 Place the input shaft vertically in a vice so the gear faces down and is free of the vice jaws. The sides of the bearing will now lie across the top of the vice. Carefully drift the shaft out of the bearing with a mallet.

43 Fit the oil thrower and then the bearing with the groove for the circlip away from the gear. Using the jaws of a vice as a support

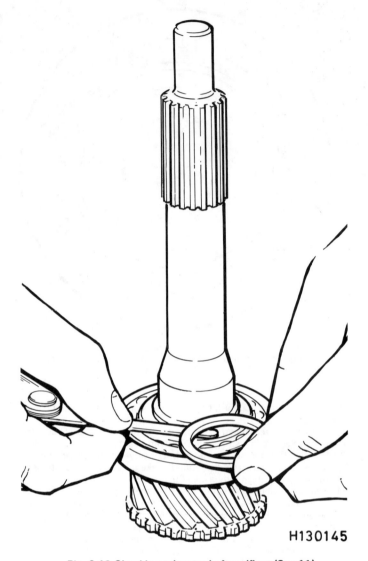

H130145

Fig. 6.13 Checking primary shaft endfloat (Sec 11)

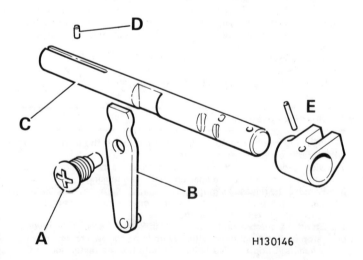

H130146

Fig. 6.14 Reverse selector components (Sec. 11)

A Pivot bolt   D Guide peg
B Relay lever   E Dog
C Reverse selector rod

11.30 Synchroniser

11.32 Refitting 3rd speed gear and synchro ring to the front end of the mainshaft

11.33 Refitting 3rd/4th synchro hub to mainshaft

11.35 Mainshaft front end nut

11.36 2nd speed gear and synchro ring refitted to mainshaft

11.39 Refitting 1st/2nd synchro to mainshaft

11.40 Refitting 1st gear and distance piece to mainshaft

11.41 Primary shaft inner and outer circlips

11.45A Reverse gear idler shaft

11.45B Reverse idler gear and shaft refitted

11.47 Inserting laygear needle rollers

11.48 Fitting laygear needle roller abutment ring

11.50A Laygear thrust washer

11.50B Laygear thrust washer in position in casing

11.51 Laygear and shaft refitted

11.52 Refitting the mainshaft assembly

11.53 Refitting mainshaft rear bearing

11.55 Mainshaft rear bearing nut

11.57 Mainshaft rear bearing retainer plate

11.60 Primary shaft needle rollers in position

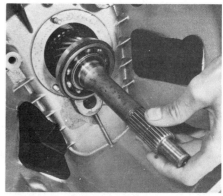
11.61 Refitting the primary shaft

11.62 Primary shaft and bearing refitted

11.66 Reverse idler and layshaft retainer plate in position

11.68 Front retainer and oil seal

11.70A Front retainer gasket in position

11.70B Front retainer plate refitted

11.73 Reverse gear selector rod

11.75 Reverse selector pivot screw

11.76 Reverse selector fulcrum lever (reverse selector rod removed for clarity)

11.77 Detent interlock plunger (Reverse to 1st/2nd)

11.78 1st/2nd selector rod and fork

11.79 Shift fork roll pin

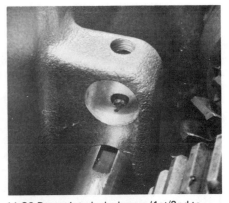

11.80 Detent interlock plunger (1st/2nd to 3rd/4th)

11.81 3rd/4th selector rod and shift fork

11.83 Refitting rear extension housing

11.86 Refitting gearbox top cover

behind the bearing, drift the input shaft into place.

44 Fit the selective washer and with the edge of the circlip in the groove measure the clearance with a feeler gauge to achieve the correct endfloat (see Specifications for details). Fit the washer and then a new circlip.

Gearbox — reassembly

45 Ensure the interior of the gearbox is spotlessly clean. Hold the reverse gear idler in place with the groove for the selector fork towards the rear of the gearbox. Drift in the reverse gear idler shaft until the slot is adjacent to the gearbox outer end face (photos).

46 It is now necessary to assemble the needle roller bearings at either end of the laygear. Spread grease round the orifice at each end.

47 Fit 26 needle rollers to each end of the shaft. Press them well into the grease so they will not drop out (photo).

48 With the rollers assembled, fit a steel abutment ring at each end of the laygear (photo).

49 Slide in a dummy layshaft so the needle rollers will not drop out of place. The shaft can be cut from a length of mild steel and must be a fraction under the length of the laygear and of the same diameter, or

very slightly under, that of the layshaft.

50 Grease the backs of the laygear thrust washers and fit the thicker washer to the rear with its tag in the cut-outs in the casing. Fit the thinner washer similarly to the front of the casing. Fit the laygear, larger end to the front (photos).

51 Temporarily refit the layshaft from the rear of the gearbox and drive out the dummy shaft. Measure the endfloat between the front of the laygear and the thrust washer (0.006 to 0.010 in). Fit a different washer if necessary and refit the dummy layshaft (photo).

52 Fit the mainshaft assembly to the gearbox through the top cover, holding onto 1st gear and the distance piece to prevent them slipping down the mainshaft (photo).

53 Fit the rear bearing to the gearbox casing from the tail end of the mainshaft, with the retainer circlip to the rear of the bearing (photo).

54 With a broad drift, tap the bearing into place in the gearbox until the retainer ring is fully home and in contact with the casing. Support the underside of the bearing and with a soft faced hammer tap the mainshaft fully into the bearing. Make sure that the gears do not foul the laygear and that the blocker bars and synchro cut-outs are all in line.

55 Fit a new self-locking nut to the rear of the mainshaft bearing. This

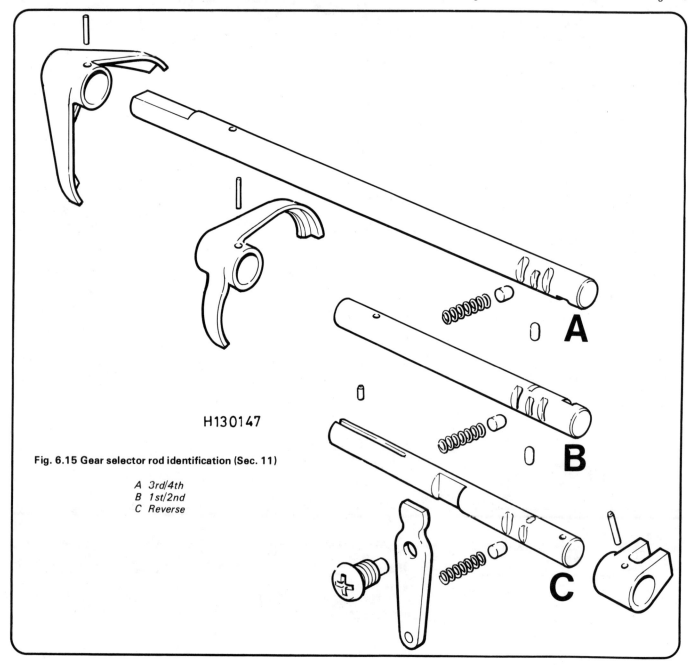

H130147

Fig. 6.15 Gear selector rod identification (Sec. 11)

A *3rd/4th*
B *1st/2nd*
C *Reverse*

nut must be tightened to the specific torque (photo).

56 If a suitable torque wrench is not available use a ring or open ended spanner, or a pipe wrench, and tighten very firmly. To prevent the shaft from turning grip it between soft jaws in a vice.

57 Refit the rear bearing retainer plate and tighten down the two bolts and washers firmly (photo).

58 With a feeler gauge, recheck the endfloat of 1st, 2nd and 3rd gears between the gears and their abutment flanges.

59 Slide the abutment ring over the nose of the mainshaft, as if fitted to the bore in the rear of the primary shaft after the needle roller bearings have been fitted.The ring tends to drop out when fitting the primary shaft in place.

60 Grease the annulus in the end of the primary shaft and fit the 23 needle rollers, pressing them firmly into the grease so they will not fall out when the primary gear is refitted (photo).

61 Very carefully offer up the primary shaft to the mainshaft, so the nose of the latter seats squarely in the needle rollers. Do not forget the remaining synchro ring which lies between 3rd and 4th gears (photo).

62 With a broad faced drift, tap the bearing evenly and lightly on its outer track into position in the gearbox casing. Ensure it enters the casing squarely (photo).

63 Turn the gearbox upside down, so the laygear falls into mesh with the mainshaft and primary gears. Insert the layshaft from the rear of the gearbox. Keep the forward end of the layshaft up against the dummy shaft as the latter is driven out.

64 Coat the front end of the layshaft, where it enters the bellhousing, with a sealing compound. Turn the layshaft and reverse idler shafts until the slots are vertical and facing each other.

65 Slip the retainer plate into the slots in the layshaft and reverse gear idler shaft.

66 Refit and tighten up the bolt and washer that secures the retainer plate to the gearbox end face (photo).

67 To avoid oil leaks from the front of the gearbox, always fit a new oil seal to the front cover. With a broad bladed screwdriver lever the old seal out.

68 Select a socket the same diameter as the new oil seal and with the jaws of the vice extended and the front cover and socket placed between them press the seal firmly into place (photo).

69 Grease the new seal with multi-purpose grease and spread a non-setting jointing compound on the front cover and gearbox casing face.

70 Fit a new gasket and position the front cover in place over the studs. Tighten down the three securing nuts and washers (photos).

71 Slide the reverse gear selector rod into place in the bottom hole in the rear of the casing, ensuring that the cut-out in the front of the rod faces upwards.

72 Carefully insert the guide peg for the reverse gear selector rod through the hole in the top of the lug.

73 With a piece of thin wire manipulate the guide peg, so that it enters the narrower bore in the bottom of the larger hole and seats in the reverse gear selector rod cut-out (photo).

74 Coat the underside of the head of the reverse gear selector pivot bolt and the adjacent area on the gearbox casing with non-setting jointing compound.

75 Screw the reverse gear selector pivot bolt into the side of the gearbox, holding the fulcrum lever so that the nose of the pivot enters the hole in the lever (photo).

76 As the bolt is tightened, make sure that the lower end of the fulcrum lever enters the groove on the periphery of the reverse idler gear and the broader upper end locates in the cut-out in the reverse gear selector rod (photo).

77 Carefully insert an interlock plunger into the hole in the end of the casing between the reverse gear selector rod and the 1st/2nd gear selector rod (photo).

78 Slide the 1st/2nd gear selector rod into the middle hole and at the same time fit the 1st/2nd gear selector fork with its boss to the rear, so its forks enter the groove in the 1st/2nd gear synchro hub (photo).

79 Line up the small hole in the 1st/2nd gear selector rod with the hole in the boss of the fork and drift the roll pin into place (photo).

80 Place an interlock plunger in the small hole between the 1st/2nd gear selector rod and the 3rd/4th gear selector hole (photo).

81 Slide the 3rd/4th gear selector rod into the top hole and at the same time fit the remaining selector fork, with its boss towards the rear of the gearbox. Secure the fork to the rod with a roll pin (photo). Check that the primary shaft, mainshaft and layshaft all turn freely and, if not, check that two gears have not been engaged simultaneously.

82 Ensure that the slots in the end of the three selector rods face inwards, are in line and are in neutral. Make sure the gearbox and extension mating faces are clean and smooth an with non-setting jointing compound.

83 Refit the rear extension housing as described in Section 6 (photo).

84 Refit the detent plungers, springs and plate as described in Section 9.

85 Refit the reverse gear plunger, spring and cover and tighten the two bolts and washers that hold the cover in place. Fit a new gasket to the gearbox top cover face and lubricate all the gears well.

86 Check that the oil feed pipe is 1 in (25.4 mm) below the level of the gearbox top cover face and bend it carefully up or down as necessary. Refit the top cover (photo).

87 Refit the bolts and washers holding the top cover in position and tighten the bolts to the specified torque. Do not overtighten.

88 The source of an annoying squeak whenever the clutch pedal is pressed, can be a dry release arm pivot post. Smear the head of the pivot post well with multi-purpose grease.

89 Slide the clutch release arm into the bellhousing so the narrower portion of the arm enters the bellhousing cut-out. Fit the groove in the release bearing to the two pivot points in the release arm.

90 Finally push the clutch release arm into place on the release arm pivot post, so that the spring clip rests behind the head of the post. Gearbox reassembly is now complete.

12 Fault diagnosis – gearbox

Symptom	Reason(s)
Ineffective synchromesh	Worn baulk rings or synchro hubs
Jumps out of one or more gears (on drive or over-run)	Weak detent springs or worn selector forks or worn gears
Noisy, rough, whining and vibration	Worn bearings and/or laygear thrust washers (initially) resulting in extended wear generally due to play and backlash
Noisy and difficult engagement of gears	Clutch fault

Note: *It is sometimes difficult to decide whether it is worthwhile removing and dismantling the gearbox for a fault which may be nothing more than a minor irritant. Gearboxes which howl, or where the synchromesh can be 'beaten' by a quick gear change, may continue to perform for a long time in this state. A worn gearbox usually needs a complete rebuild to eliminate noises because the various gears, if re-aligned on new bearings, will continue to howl when different wearing surfaces are presented to each other.*

The decision to overhaul, therefore, must be considered with regard to time and money available, relative to the degree of noise or malfunction that the driver has to suffer.

Chapter 6 Part B Automatic transmission

Contents

Specifications

Type . . . . Borg-Warner Type 45 4 speed, epicyclic with 3 element hydrokinetic torque converter

Fluid capacity (including converter) . . . . 10.5 pints (6 litres)

Speed ratios:
1st . . . . 3.00 : 1
2nd . . . . 1.94 : 1
3rd . . . . 1.35 : 1
4th . . . . 1.00 : 1
Reverse . . . . 4.69 : 1

Torque converter diameter . . . . 9.5 in (241.3 mm)

Approximate shift speeds (final drive ratio 3.89 : 1)

Speed shift	Light throttle: mph (km/h)	Full throttle: mph (km/h)	Kick-down: mph (km/h)
1 to 2	6 to 9 (9 to 14)	23 to 27 (37 to 43)	–
2 to 3	8 to 13 (13 to 21)	40 to 47 (65 to 76)	–
3 to 4	13 to 20 (21 to 32)	58 to 68 (94 to 110)	–
4 to 3	–	–	66 to 51 (107 to 82)
3 to 2, 4 to 2	–	–	37 to 30 (60 to 49)
2 to 1, 4 to 1	–	–	22 to 16 (35 to 26)

Approximate shift speeds (final drive ratio 4.11 : 1)

Speed shift	Light throttle: mph (km/h)	Full throttle: mph (km/h)	Kick-down: mph (km/h)
1 to 2	6 to 9 (9 to 14)	22 to 27 (35 to 43)	–
2 to 3	8 to 13 (13 to 21)	38 to 45 (61 to 73)	–
3 to 4	13 to 20 (21 to 32)	54 to 65 (87 to 105)	–
4 to 3	–	–	62 to 48 (100 to 77)
3 to 2, 4 to 2	–	–	36 to 28 (58 to 45)
2 to 1, 4 to 1	–	–	20 to 16 (32 to 25)

Torque wrench settings

	lbf ft	Nm
Oil pan to transmission bolts	6	8
Inhibitor switch	4	6
Torque converter to driveplate bolts	32	44
Driveplate to crankshaft	40	54
Converter housing to transmission case	25	34
Torque converter housing to engine	34	46

1 General description

Automatic transmission may be specified on 1300 and 1600 engine models.
The transmission is the Borg-Warner 4-speed type 45.
The system comprises two main components:

(a) *A three element hydrokinetic torque converter coupling, capable of torque multiplication at an infinitely variable ratio between approximately 2.4:1 and 1:1*
(b) *A torque/speed responsive and hydraulically operated epicyclic gearbox, comprising a planetary gearset providing four (type 45) forward ratios and one reverse ratio*

Due to the complexity of the automatic transmission unit, if performance is not up to standard, or overhaul is necessary, it is imperative that this be left to the local main agents who will have the special equipment for fault diagnosis and rectification. The content of the following Sections is therefore confined to supplying general information and any service information and instructions that can be used by the owner.

2 Fluid level – checking and maintenance

1   It is important that transmission fluid manufactured only to the correct specification is used. Refer to the Specifications Section for details of the capacity of the complete unit. Drain and refill capacity will be less, as the torque converter cannot be completely drained, but this operation should not be necessary except for repairs.
2   Every 10 000 miles (16 000 km) or more frequently, check the fluid level in the automatic transmission. To do this, it is recommended that the transmission fluid is at normal operating temperature. This will only be attained after a minimum of 6 miles (9.6 km) operation on the road. (Check on the 'HOT' side of the dipstick).
3   The transmission fluid level can be checked from a cold start if the engine is run at a fast idle for five minutes at the selector lever moved through all positions. (Check on the 'WARM' side of the dipstick).
4   With the car on level ground, move the speed selector lever slowly through all positions and then select 'P'. Switch off the engine. Withdraw the dipstick, wipe it, re-insert it, and then withdraw it again after 30 seconds and read off the level.

5   The fluid level should be between the 'LOW' and 'FULL' marks, but check that the correct side (marked 'WARM' or 'HOT') of the dipstick is being read according to the transmission fluid temperature. The distance between the 'LOW' and 'FULL' marks represents a quantity of fluid of approximately 1 Imp pint (0.56 litres). Top-up as necessary, using a Dexron type fluid poured through the filler tube.
6   If the unit has been drained, it is recommended that only new fluid is used. Fill up to the correct 'HIGH' level by gradually refilling the unit. The exact amount will depend on how much was left in the converter after draining.
7   Ensure that the exterior of the converter housing and gearbox is always kept clean of dust or mud, otherwise overheating will occur.

3 Downshift cable – adjustment

1   The correct position of the production-set crimped sleeve on the downshift cable is when a 0.010 to 0.020 in (0.25 to 0.50 mm) feeler gauge will pass between its lower face and the end face of the threaded outer cable conduit.
2   Before checking this gap, ensure that the idling speed is correctly set (refer to Specifications).
3   Where adjustment of the downshift cable is required, slacken the locknut on the outer cable conduit and rotate as necessary. Retighten the locknut.
4   When the downshift cable adjustment has been correctly set, check that the throttle pedal linkage and cable are operating correctly, particularly that with the throttle pedal fully depressed, the carburettor butterfly is fully open. If adjustment is required, refer to Chapter 3 of this manual.
5   Incorrect adjustment of the downshift cable can cause very rapid wear to the internal clutch components of the transmission, with consequent loss of traction.

4 Speed selector linkage – adjustment

1   Push the hand lever into the 'P' position.
2   Working underneath the vehicle, loosen the self-locking nut securing the transmission lever to the selector rod.
3   Check that the transmission lever is in its rearmost detent by moving the lever as far backward as possible, then rocking it to

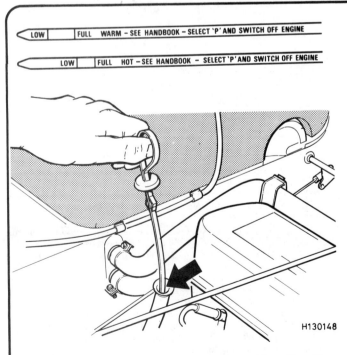

Fig. 6.16 Checking fluid level and dipstick markings (Sec. 2)

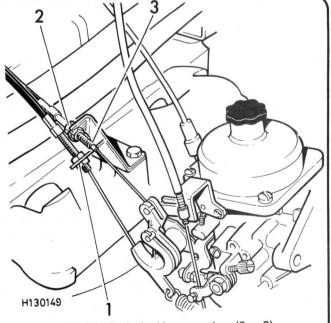

Fig. 6.17 Typical cable connections (Sec. 3)

1   Throttle cable adjustment
2   Downshift cable adjustment
3   Clearance (see Specifications) at crimped stop

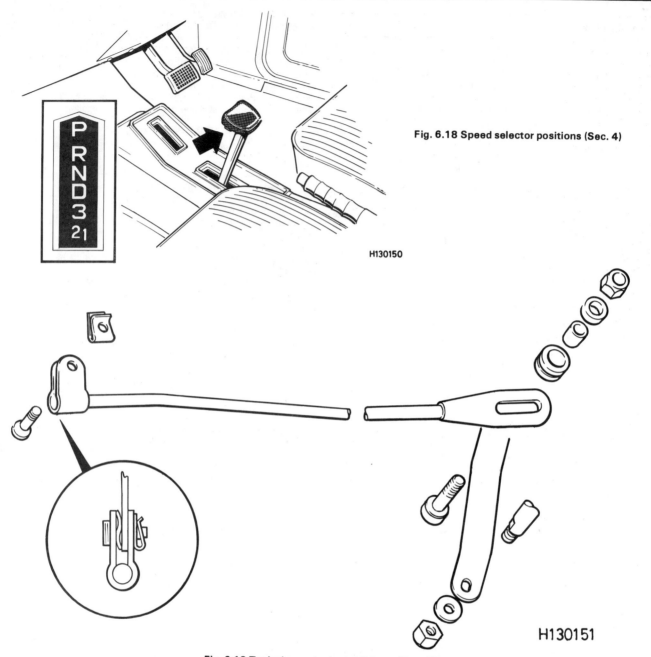

Fig. 6.18 Speed selector positions (Sec. 4)

H130150

H130151

Fig. 6.19 Typical speed selector linkage (Sec. 4)

confirm that the roller is firmly in the detent.
4   With the hand lever still in the 'P' position, tighten the self-locking nut without moving the operating rod or transmission lever.
5   Move the hand lever to all positions, and check that a distinct click can be heard at each position as the detents engage. Check that the key start only operates with the hand lever in 'N' or 'P'.

5   Performance testing

The procedure in the following Section is given to enable the owner to satisfy himself that the automatic transmission is operating correctly. It is not intended that he should diagnose or rectify any faults, but a detailed report of the exact nature of the malfunction will enable your Talbot dealer to quickly ascertain the trouble with reduced cost to the owner. Before carrying out the tests, ensure that the transmission fluid level is correct, and also all adjustments, as previously described in this Section.

6   Stall test procedure

The function of a stall test is to determine that the torque converter and transmission are operating satisfactorily.
1   Check the condition of the engine. An engine which is not developing full power will affect the stall test readings.
2   Allow the engine and transmission to reach correct working temperatures.
3   Connect a tachometer to the vehicle.
4   Chock the wheels and apply the handbrake and footbrake.
5   Select 'D' or 'R' and depress the throttle to the kick-down position. Note the reading on the tachometer which should be between 2300 and 2650 rpm. If the reading is below 1800 rpm suspect the converter for stator sprag clutch slip. If the reading is below 2100 rpm, the engine is not developing full power. If the reading is in excess of 2800 rpm the transmission or converter is slipping. **Note:** *Do not carry out a stall test for a longer period than 10 seconds, otherwise the transmission will become overheated. Consecutive tests must be separated by*

an interval of at least 30 minutes.

6   Inability to start on steep gradients, combined with poor acceleration from the rest and low stall speed (1000 rpm), indicate that the converter stator uni-directional clutch is slipping. This condition permits the stator to rotate in an opposite direction to the impeller and turbine, and torque multiplication cannot occur.

7   Poor acceleration in third speed above 30 mph (48 kph) and reduced maximum speed, indicates that the stator uni-directional clutch has seized. The stator will not rotate with the turbine and impeller and the 'fluid flywheel' phase cannot occur. This condition will also be indicated by excessive overheating of the transmission although the stall speed will be correct.

19 Automatic transmission – removal and refitting

1   Position the car over a service pit or on suitable car ramps. Considerable clearance is required beneath the car, as the transmission must be lowered enough to allow the torque converter to clear the body.

2   Disconnect the battery negative terminal.

3   Drain the radiator and disconnect the top hose.

4   Disconnect the downshift cable from its connection at the carburettor.

5   Mark the propeller shaft rear flange in relation to the rear axle input flange, unscrew and remove the securing bolts and withdraw the propeller shaft from the transmission output shaft splines.

6   Drain the transmission fluid into a container of adequate size by loosening the oil filler tube union nut. Detach the oil filler tube from the transmission and support bracket and withdraw it.

7   Disconnect the oil cooler pipe unions at the transmission and plug the pipe ends to prevent entry of dirt.

8   Unscrew and remove the exhaust manifold flange nuts and disconnect the exhaust downpipe to eexhaust pipe joint. Lower the front section of the exhaust pipe away from the manifold.

9   Disconnect the throttle linkage at the carburettor and bulkhead.

10   Unbolt and remove the transmission guard plate, and remove the sump stiffener brackets and dirt shield.

11   Note the location of the selector rod on the transmission lever, mark its position in the elongated adjustment slot, and then disconnect the rod from the lever.

12   Identify, and then disconnect, the leads from the starter inhibitor/reversing light switch and then release them from the retaining clip.

13   Disconnect the speedometer cable and tie it out of the way.

14   Unscrew and remove the bolts that secure the torque converter to the crankshaft drive plate. These bolts are accessible, one at a time, by rotating the crankshaft with a socket spanner applied to the crankshaft pulley bolt. If necessary jam the starter ring gear with a screwdriver.

15   Support the rear of the engine sump on a jack and then place a trolley jack under the base of the transmission oil pan. Use a piece of wood as an insulator between the jack and the oil pan to prevent damage to the pan.

16   Remove the rear crossmember mounting bolts, insulating rubber and sleeves.

17   Unscrew and remove the remaining torque converter housing to engine securing bolts but leave the starter motor bolts in position. Note the location of the engine earthing strap.

18   Lower both jacks in unison until the weight of the transmission is just supported. A further jack placed under the front of the engine sump will prevent the engine tilting forward when the transmission is removed.

19   Withdraw the transmission unit, making sure that the torque converter disengages from the driveplate and stays fully engaged with the transmission oil pump, otherwise there will be considerable loss of fluid and possible damage to the torque converter oil seal. The use of a cranked lever or length of wood will help during this operation.

20   Refitting is a reversal of the removal procedure but, if the torque converter has been removed, then, before refitting can be carried out, it will be necessary to align the front drive tangs with the slots in the inner gear and then slide the torque converter into position. Make sure that the oil seal is not damaged. Use new bolts to connect the driveplate to the torque converter.

21   Refill the unit with the correct quantity of fluid.

8   Fault diagnosis – automatic transmission

Most minor faults or malfunctions occurring in the operation of the automatic transmission can be attributed to one of the following:

(a) Low fluid level
(b) Incorrect selector linkage adjustment
(c) Incorrect downshift cable adjustment

More detailed diagnosis should be left to your Talbot dealer who has the necessary gauges and equipment to carry out this work.

Chapter 7 Propeller shaft

Contents

Specifications

Type .... Single piece tubular steel with two universal joints, damper and sliding sleeve at front end (930 cc and automatic transmission models have undamped propeller shafts)

Tube outer diameter
930 models .... 2.75 in (70 mm)
1300/1600 models .... 3.00 in (76 mm)

Universal joints .... Sealed, needle roller bearing type

Torque wrench setting

	lbf ft	Nm
Propeller shaft flange bolts	17	23

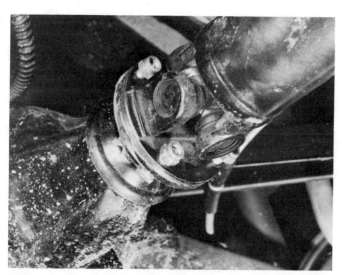

3.9 Location of propeller shaft rear flange bolts

---

1 General description

The drive from the gearbox to the rear axle is via the propeller shaft, which is in fact a tube. Due to the variety of angles caused by the up and down movement of the rear axle in relation to the gearbox, universal joints are fitted to each end of the shaft to convey the drive through the constantly varying angles. As the movement also increases and decreases the distance between the rear axle and the gearbox, the forward end of the propeller shaft is a splined sleeve which is a sliding fit over the rear of the gearbox mainshaft. The splined sleeve runs in an oil seal in the gearbox mainshaft rear cover and is supported with the mainshaft on the gearbox rear bearing. The splines are lubricated by oil in the rear cover coming from the gearbox.

The universal joints each comprise a four-way trunnion or 'spider', each leg of which runs in a needle roller bearing race, pre-packed with grease and fitted into the bearing journal yokes of the sliding sleeve and propeller shaft and flange. The universal joints at either end of the one-piece shaft are renewable as a kit. All universal joints are of the lubricant sealed type and require no maintenance.

On certain models (see Specifications), the propeller shaft incorporates an outer sleeve with a rubber 'sandwich' to act as a damper.

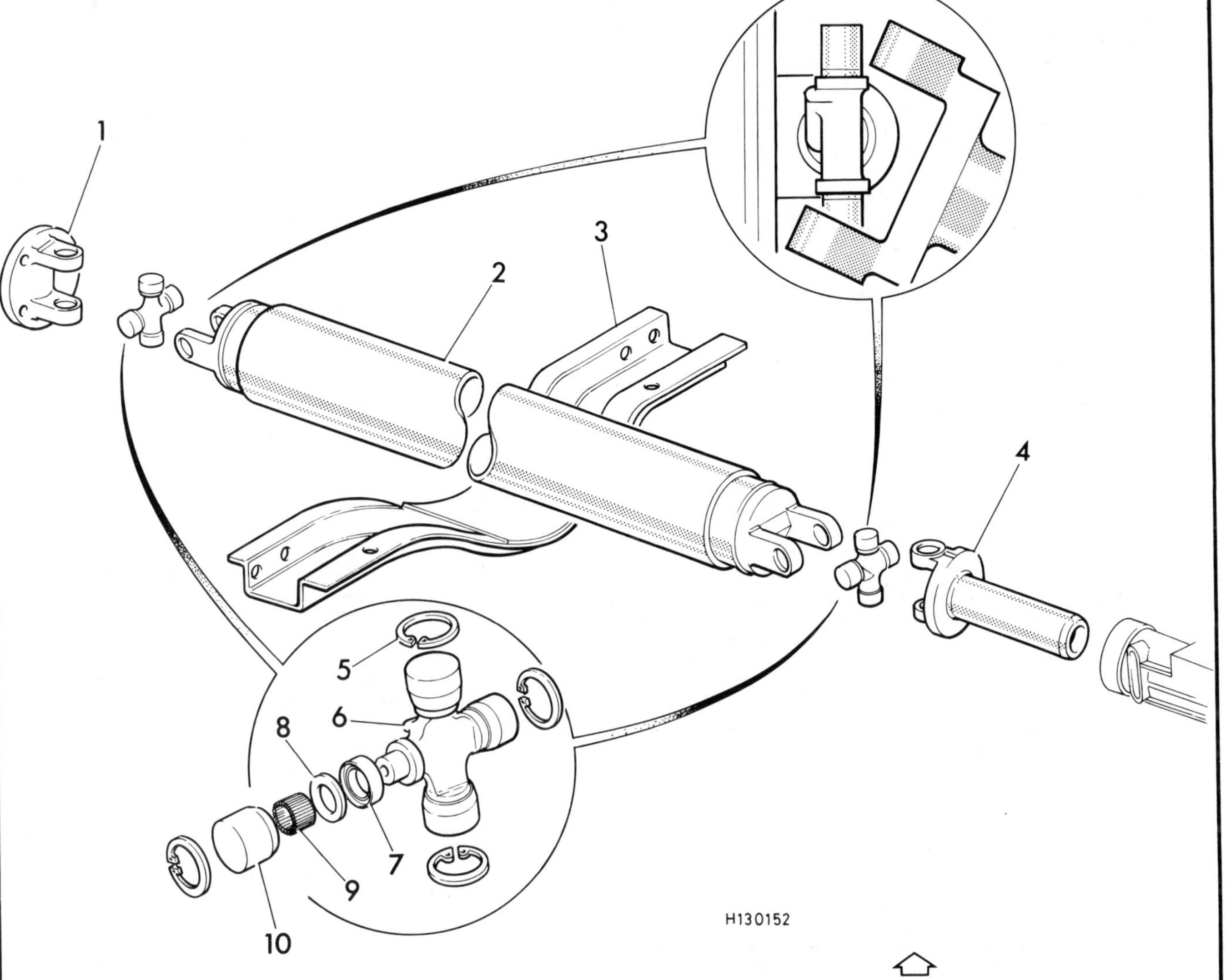

H130152

Fig. 7.1 Component parts of the propeller shaft (damped type shown) (Sec. 1)

1   Rear flange yoke
2   Propeller shaft
3   Guard (crossmember)
4   Front yoke sliding sleeve
5   Circlip
6   Spider
7   Seal
8   Bearing washer
9   Needle roller
10   Bearing cup

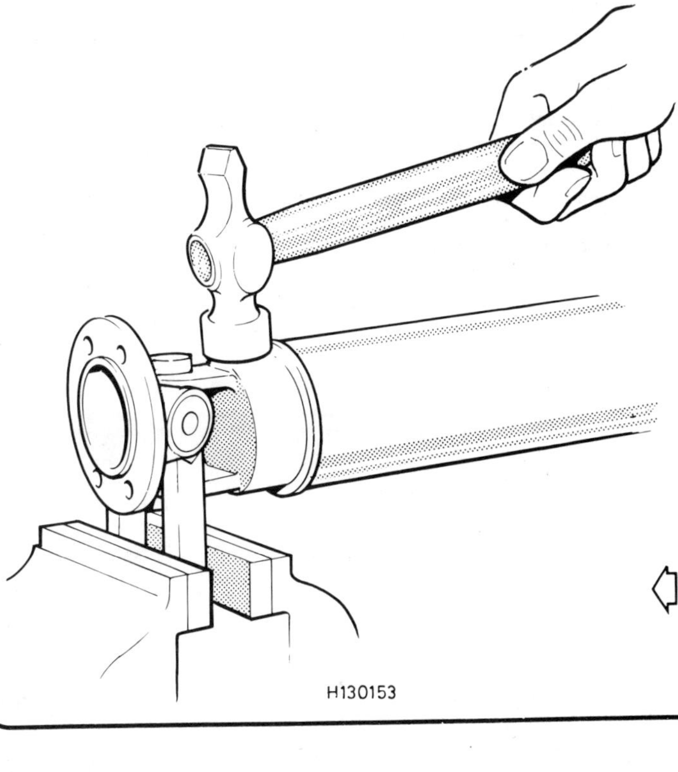

Fig. 7.2 Using shock treatment to eject universal joint bearing cups (Sec. 4)

H130153

2   Routine maintenance

No lubrication of the universal joints is required as they are pre-packed with grease on assembly. The sliding sleeve of the forward end of the propeller shaft is lubricated from the gearbox. It is recommended that periodic inspection is carried out, however, whenever the car may be undergoing service, to check for any slackness in the universal bearings or at the flange bolts at the rear.

3   Propeller shaft – removal, inspection and refitting

1   Jack up the rear of the car and support it on stands, or place the car over a pit.
2   The rear of the shaft is connected to the rear axle pinion by a flange held by four nuts and bolts. Mark the position of both flanges relative to each other and then undo the bolts.
3   Move the propeller shaft forward to disengage it from the pinion flange and then lower it to the ground.
4   Draw the other end of the propeller shaft, that is the splined sleeve, out of the rear of the gearbox extension cover. The shaft is then clear for removal.
5   Place a receptacle under the gearbox rear cover opening to catch any oil, which will certainly come out if the gearbox is tilted.
6   If the propeller shaft is removed for inspection, first examine the bore and counterbore of the two flanges which mate at the rear. If they are damaged in any way, or a slack fit, it could mean that the propeller shaft is running off centre at the flange and causing vibration in the drive. If nothing obvious is wrong and the universal joints are in good order, it is permissible to reconnect the flanges with one turned through 180° relative to the other. This may stop or reduce any vibration.
7   Refitting of the shaft is a reversal of the removal procedure. Ensure that the sliding sleeve is inserted into the gearbox end cover with care, and is perfectly clean, so as not to cause damage to, or failure of, the oil seal in the cover.
8   The flanges should be mated according to the position marks (unless a 180° turn is being carried out as mentioned in paragraph 6).
9   The four bolts should be fitted with the heads towards the rear axle (photo).

4   Universal joints – inspection, removal and refitting

1   Preliminary inspection of the universal joints can be carried out with the propeller shaft on the car.
2   Grasp each side of the universal joint, and with a twisting action, determine whether there is any play or slackness in the joint. Also try an up and down rocking motion for the same purpose. If there is any sign whatsoever of play, the joints need to be renewed.
3   Remove the propeller shaft as described in the previous Section. Mark the relative position of the yokes to each other.
4   Clean away all dirt from the ends of the bearings on the yokes, so that the circlips may be removed using a pair of contracting circlip pliers. If they are very tight, tap the end of the bearing race (inside the circlip) with a drift and hammer to relieve the pressure.
5   Once the circlips are removed, tap the universal joints at the yoke with a soft hammer. The bearings and races will come out of the housing and can be removed easily.
6   If they are obstinate they can be gripped in a self-locking wrench (once they have protruded far enough) for final removal, provided they are to be renewed.
7   Once the bearings are removed from each opposite journal the trunnion can be easily disengaged.
8   Refitting of the new trunnions and needle rollers and races is a reversal of the removal procedure.
9   Keep the grease seals on the inner ends of each trunnion as dry as possible. Ensure the journal is located in the yoke as shown in the inset to Fig. 7.1.
10   Place the needles in each race. Fill the race one-third full with grease prior to placing it over the trunnion and tap each one home with a brass drift. Any grease exuding from the fourth bearing journal, after three have been fitted, should be removed before fitting the fourth race. Where a vice is available with jaws that open sufficiently wide, sockets may be used (held between the end of the bearing cup and the vice jaw) to press the cup into position. Alternatively, an old bearing cup is useful. Take care not to trap any of the needles as pressure is applied. If they become displaced, release the vice, re-position the needles and re-commence the reassembly.
11   Replace the circlips, ensuring they seat neatly in the retaining grooves.
12   In cases of extreme wear or neglect, it is conceivable that the bearing housings in the propeller shaft, sliding sleeve or rear flange, have worn so much that the bearing races are a slack fit in them. In such cases it will be necessary to replace the item affected as well. Check also that the sliding sleeve splines are in good condition and not a sloppy fit in the gearbox mainshaft.
13   Refit the propeller shaft as described in Section 3.

5   Fault diagnosis – propeller shaft

Symptom	Reason(s)
Vibration when vehicle is running on road	Out of balance or distorted propeller shaft Backlash in splined shaft Loose flange securing bolts Worn universal joints

Chapter 8 Rear axle

Contents

Specifications

Type	Semi-floating, hypoid bevel gears

Axle code and ratio*

Code No 1	4.375 : 1
Code No 3 or 4	4.111 : 1
Code No 5 or 6	3.889 : 1
Code No 7 or 8	3.700 : 1
Code No 9 or 0	3.545 : 1

Axle code is shown as sixth character from end of vehicle service number

Road speed (in top gear, per 1000 rpm of the engine)

4.375 : 1 axle ratio	15.5 mph (25 kmh)
4.111 : 1 axle ratio	16 mph (26 kmh)
3.889 : 1 axle ratio	17 mph (27 kmh)
3.700 : 1 axle ratio	17.5 mph (28 kmh)
3.545 : 1 axle ratio	18.5 mph (30 kmh)

For overall ratio, multiply axle ratio by gearbox ratio shown in Specifications, Chapter 6

Bearings

Pinion and differential	Taper roller
Rear wheel hub	Ball with combined oil seal

Adjustment

Crownwheel to pinion backlash	0.005 to 0.009 in (0.13 to 0.23 mm)

Number of teeth

	Crownwheel	Pinion
4.375 : 1 ratio	35	8
4.111 : 1 ratio	37	9
3.889 : 1 ratio	35	9
3.700 : 1 ratio	37	10
3.545 : 1 ratio	39	11

Lubricant capacity	1.5 pints (0.85 litres)

Torque wrench settings

	lbf ft	Nm
Axle shaft retaining plate	18	24.5
Rear cover securing bolt	14	19

114

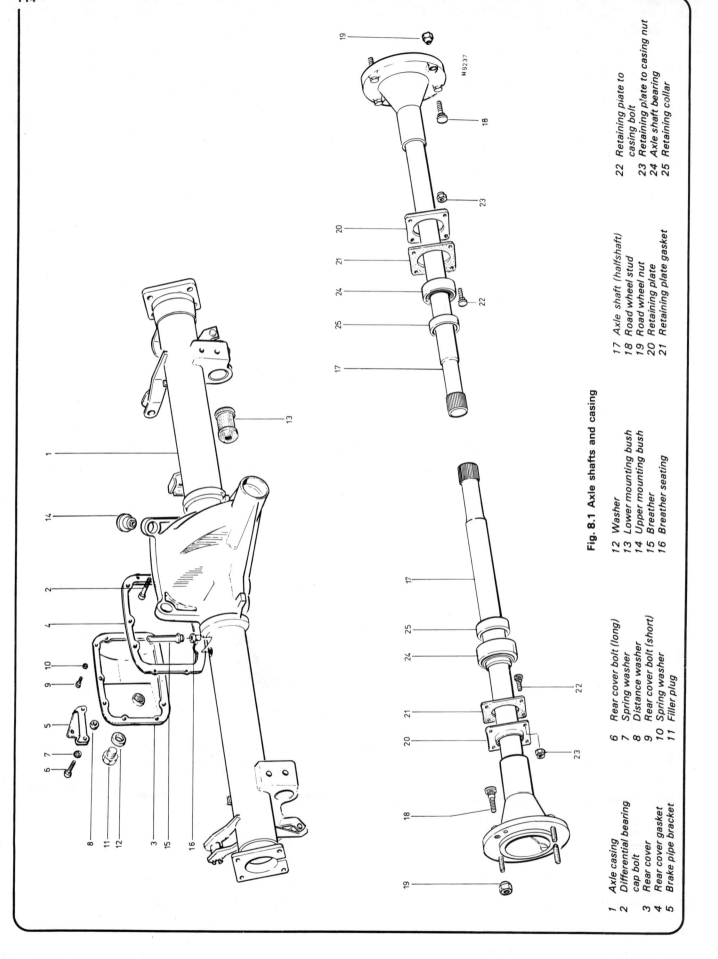

Fig. 8.1 Axle shafts and casing

1 Axle casing
2 Differential bearing
cap bolt
3 Rear cover
4 Rear cover gasket
5 Brake pipe bracket

6 Rear cover bolt (long)
7 Spring washer
8 Distance washer
9 Rear cover bolt (short)
10 Spring washer
11 Filler plug

12 Washer
13 Lower mounting bush
14 Upper mounting bush
15 Breather
16 Breather seating

17 Axle shaft (halfshaft)
18 Road wheel stud
19 Road wheel nut
20 Retaining plate
21 Retaining plate gasket

22 Retaining plate to
casing bolt
23 Retaining plate to casing nut
24 Axle shaft bearing
25 Retaining collar

H9237

1 General description

The semi-floating axle incorporates a hypoid gear final drive. The unit construction axle casing embodies a differential carrier and welded-in axle tubes. The casing has four rubber bushed mounting points to which the suspension links are attached. The pinion is carried on two taper roller bearings adjusted to a specified preload by the incorporation of a compressible spacer.

A single, cast, differential unit with hypoid gear assembly is carried in the axle casing by adjustable taper roller bearings. Crownwheel to pinion meshing is accurately attained by the use of lockable screwed adjusters.Steel thrust washers are fitted between the differential gears and casing.

The halfshafts are one piece flanged type forgings and each is carried on sealed, combined ballbearings and oil seals. No provision is made for regular draining. A plastic breather unit is located on the top of the right-hand axle tube.

2 Routine maintenance

1   Every 5000 miles (8000 km) clean the area round the rear axle filler plug. Ensure that the car is standing on level ground and remove the plug. If necessary, add sufficient gear oil of the correct grade to bring the level to the filler plug threads. Although draining the rear axle oil is not specified at regular intervals, it should be carried out every 25 000 miles due to the accumulation of metal particles due to normal wear. Draining should be carried out when the oil is warm after a run by removing the cover bolts (6 and 9) and pulling away the rear cover (3) (Fig. 8.1). A certain amount of oil will remain in the base and this should be mopped from the casing. Refit the rear cover, using a new gasket (4) and noting carefully the correct location of the longer retaining bolts used for the hydraulic pipe bracket. Tighten the bolts to the recommended torque setting and refill the unit with approximately 1½ pints (0·85 litres) of 90EP oil. Refit the filler/level plug on completion.

3 Rear axle – removal and refitting

1   Jack up the rear of the car, having chocked the front wheels and placed axle stands under the car jacking points. Place another jack under the axle differential.

2   Remove the roadwheels.

3   Mark the edges of the pinion and propeller shaft joint flanges to ensure exact replacement.

4   Unscrew and remove the four flange coupling bolts and remove the propeller shaft by sliding it rearwards out of the gearbox extension housing.

5   Release the handbrake and disconnect the cables at the backplate operating levers. Remove the cables from their abutments by drawing the outer cable through the abutments and passing the exposed inner cables through the slots in the abutments, as shown in Fig. 8.2.

6   Disconnect the brake hydraulic flexible hose connection (see Chapter 9) at the bracket mounted to the under floor panel to the rear of the differential housing. Cap the ends of the pipes to prevent the loss of brake fluid and the possible ingress of dirt. A bleed nipple dust cap is useful for this.

7   Disconnect the shock absorbers at their lower mounting and remove the bushes. Push the lower section of the shock absorber up into the upper section.

8   Lower the axle jack sufficiently to permit the removal of the coil springs.

9   Slacken the upper front suspension arm pivot nuts and bolts.

10 Remove the four nuts and bolts that connect the suspension links to the axle pivot points.

11 Push the upper links off the axle, then lower the axle carefully and draw it rearwards off the lower links.

12 Refitting is largely a reversal of the removal procedure. The method of refitting the coil springs is described in Chapter 11. When reconnecting the propeller shaft ensure that the flange mating marks are aligned (not applicable if refitting a new axle). Tighten the pivot nuts and bolts to the figures given in the Specifications section of Chapter 11 with the car standing under its own weight on the roadwheels on level ground. Bleed the brakes as detailed in Chapter 9 and fill the rear axle to the level of the filler plug hole with EP 90 oil.

4 Halfshafts – removal and refitting

1   Chock the front wheels of the car and jack up the rear of the car under the differential unit. Take care that the jack does not impinge

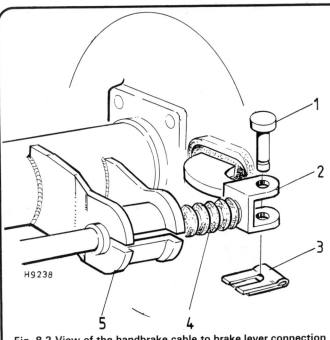

Fig. 8.2 View of the handbrake cable to brake lever connection (Sec. 3)

1   Pin
2   Trunnion
3   Clip
4   Rubber boot
5   Abutment

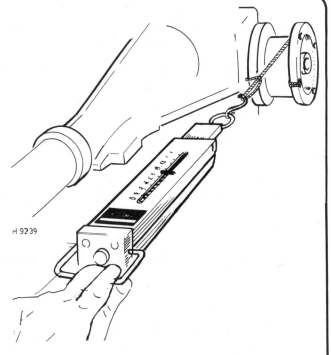

Fig. 8.3 Checking pinion bearing pre-load (Sec. 6)

upon the lower lip of the axle rear cover, or it may be distorted during jacking with subsequent oil leakage.

2 Remove the roadwheel and brush the dirt and mud from the brake backing plate and axle flange. Remove the brake drum.

3 Refer to Fig. 8.1 and remove the four self-locking nuts (23) that secure the axleshaft plate (20).

4 A slide hammer attached to the roadwheel studs will now normally be required. However, refitting a roadwheel and tapping the inner side with a wooden or rubber faced hammer may remove the axleshaft from its housing without damaging the wheel. Place a short plank of wood across the rim and tap firmly but equally along its length.

5 *Never lever the shaft out against the brake backing plate or the plate will be distorted. Never pull the axleshaft; you will only succeed in pulling the car off the jacks and axle stands.*

6 Refitting is carried out by first ensuring that the shaft is clean and the splines lightly lubricated.

7 Check the condition of the brake backplate gasket and renew if necessary.

8 Clean the periphery of the bearing thoroughly then apply a suitable sealant to it. Talbot recommend that 'Loctite 242 Superfast Nut Lock' is used.

9 Pass the axleshaft into the casing, keeping it level and rotating it slightly until the splines on the shaft engage with the differential gearwheel.

10 Push the axleshaft inwards and engage the bearing (24) in its recess in the axle casing.

11 Position the retaining plate (20) over the four securing studs (22), so that the drain hole pressing is in alignment with the backplate cut-out and the drain hole in the axle end. Gently drive the axleshaft fully home.

12 Fit the four self-locking nuts and tighten them to the recommended torque setting. *Do not use the retaining plate as a means of drawing in the axleshaft, otherwise excessive endfloat will be apparent on final assembly.*

13 Fit the brake drum and roadwheel and lower the car. The loss of oil during halfshaft removal and refitting is normally very slight, but a check of the oil level should be carried out when the refitting is complete.

5 Halfshaft outer bearings and oil seals – renewal

These are of combined type and must be renewed as an assembly when failure occurs. The combined bearings/oil seals are a press fit on the axleshaft and removal and fitting should be left to a garage having the appropriate press and gauge. The security of the halfshaft is solely dependent upon the interference fit of the bearing on the axleshaft. The importance of correct fitting within the specified tolerances cannot be over-emphasised.

6 Pinion oil seal – renewal

The pinion oil seal can be renewed with the axle in position in the car, provided the following operations are carefully followed:

1 Jack up the rear of the car and support the axle on stands.

2 Mark the edges of the propeller shaft and pinion coupling flanges to ensure exact replacement.

3 Remove the four coupling bolts, detach the propeller shaft at the axle pinion flange and tie the propeller shaft to one side.

4 Remove both rear roadwheels and brake drums to eliminate any drag.

5 Wind a cord round the pinion flange coupling and exerting a steady pull, note the reading on a spring balance as shown in Fig. 8.3. The spring balance reading indicates the pinion bearing pre-load.

6 Mark the coupling in relation to the pinion splines for exact replacement.

7 Hold the pinion coupling flange quite still with a length of flat steel bolted to it and then unscrew and remove the self-locking nut. Using a suitable two or three legged puller, withdraw the coupling flange from the pinion shaft splines.

8 Remove the defective oil seal by driving in one side of the seal as far as it will go to force the opposite side of the seal from the housing.

9 Refit the new oil seal, first having greased the mating surfaces of the seal and the axle housing. The flanges of the oil seal must face inwards. Using a piece of brass or copper tubing of suitable diameter, carefully drive the new oil seal into the axle housing recess until the face of the seal is flush with the housing. Make sure that the end of the pinion is not knocked during this operation.

10 Refit the coupling to its original position on the pinion splines, after first having located the dust cover.

11 Fit a new pinion nut and holding the coupling still with the length of flat steel used as a lever, tighten the nut until the pinion endfloat only just disappears. Do not overtighten, otherwise the collapsible spacer will be overcompressed and unscrewing the nut will not remedy the situation. The axle will have to be dismantled and the spacer renewed.

12 Rotate the pinion to settle the bearings and then check the pre-load using the cord and spring balance method previously described. By slight fractional adjustment of the nut and rotation of the pinion, obtain a spring balance pre-load figure to match that which applied before dismantling.

13 Remove the two holding bolts and refit the propeller shaft, making sure to align the mating marks. Refit the brake drums and roadwheels and lower the car.

7 Differential unit

It is not within the scope of the home mechanic to service the differential unit, owing to the need for special tools and gauges. It is therefore recommended that the complete axle assembly is removed as described in Section 3 and is taken to a specialist repairer or exchanged for a factory replacement unit.

8 Fault diagnosis – rear axle

Symptom	Reason(s)
Oil leakage	Faulty pinion oil seal*
	Faulty axleshaft seals*
	Defective cover or gasket
*Oil leakage can sometimes occur because the breather pipe is blocked	
Noise	Lack of oil
	Worn bearings
	General wear
'Clonk' on taking up drive; also excessive backlash	Incorrectly tightened pinion nut
	Worn components
	Worn axleshaft splines
	Elongated roadwheel stud holes

Chapter 9 Braking system

For modifications, and information applicable to later models, see Supplement at end of manual

Contents

Specifications

System type . . . .   Girling hydraulic, servo-assisted

Front brake

Type . . . .   Disc (twin piston calipers)
Disc diameter . . . .   9.5 in (241 mm)
Minimum disc thickness after machining . . . .   0.33 in (8.46 mm)
Piston diameter . . . .   1.890 in (48 mm)

Rear brake

Type . . . .   Drum with automatic adjustment
Drum internal diameter . . . .   8.0 in (203 mm)

Master cylinder

Type . . . .   Tandem, split circuit incorporating either a pressure differential
warning actuator or combination valve Mk 2
Piston diameter . . . .   0.75 in (19.05 mm)

Brake servo

Type . . . .   Girling Supervac type 38, direct acting
Diameter (extreme outer) . . . .   8 in (203 mm)
Boost ratio . . . .   2.2 : 1

Torque wrench settings	lbf ft	Nm
Disc to hub	33	44.5
Caliper to stub axle carrier	60	81.5
Splashguard to stub axle carrier	6	8
Bleed screws (valves)	9	12
Backplate to axle casing	18	24.5

Hydraulic pipe unions	8	11
Master cylinder to servo	18	24.5
Servo to bulkhead:		
Phosphated nuts	9	12
Zinc plated nuts	13	17.5
Handbrake lever to body	18	24.5
Pressure conscious valve to valance	7	9.5
Pressure differential warning actuator to valance	7	9.5
Brakelight switch to bracket	Hand-tight only	

1 General description

The braking system is hydraulically operated, with servo-assisted disc brakes on the front wheels and drum brakes on the rear. The handbrake operates mechanically, via cables, on the rear wheels only. Both front and rear brakes are self-adjusting. The master cylinder is of the dual circuit tandem type. The primary cylinder supplies the rear brakes and the secondary cylinder supplies the front brakes. Both circuits are independent so that in the event of a hydraulic leak occurring in one system, the other circuit will remain fully operative, although the brake pedal travel will increase.

A pressure differential warning actuator (PDWA) switch is incorporated in the fluid supply line between the master cylinder and brakes. The switch in turn is connected to a warning light on the instrument panel. During normal braking operation, the fluid pressure between the primary and secondary circuits is equal and the PDWA switch piston is thus held in a state of balance. Should a pressure difference occur in either circuit, due to a leakage, then the switch piston will be displaced and the warning light will be illuminated.

In certain instances the PDWA unit is integral with a pressure conscious reducing valve (PCRV), which has the function of regulating the fluid in the primary circuit and thus preventing rear wheel locking due to excessive brake pressure. In the event of a fluid pressure loss in the secondary circuit, the PCRV is by-passed automatically by an extended part of the PDWA unit in order to utilise the full braking effort from the rear brakes.

2 Disc brake pads – inspection, removal and refitting

1   Although the disc brakes are self-adjusting, pad wear should be checked every 5000 miles or at 6 month intervals, whichever occurs first.
2   Jack up the vehicle, support it with axle stands or strong packing blocks and remove the front roadwheels.
3   Inspect the caliper unit for signs of oil or grease contamination. Where these are evident, then the source must be found and the leak cured. Almost certainly it will be due to a defective hub oil seal or leaking caliper piston seals.
4   Renew the pads when their thickness (friction material only) has been reduced to $\frac{1}{8}$ in (3 mm). Refer to Fig. 9.2 and withdraw the spring clips and pad retaining pins (photos).
5   Withdraw the friction pads together with the anti-squeal shims. Note the position and directional arrow stamped on the shim for exact refitment (photos).
6   Clean the surfaces of the exposed caliper pistons. Ensure that the rubber dust covers are in good condition or renew as described in Section 4.
7   Before fitting the new pads, release the caliper bleed screw half a turn. Press in the caliper pistons squarely to the bottom of their bores in order to accommodate the new thicker pads.
8   Retighten the bleed screw and fit the new pads together with the anti-squeal shims, noting carefully their position is exactly as originally located.

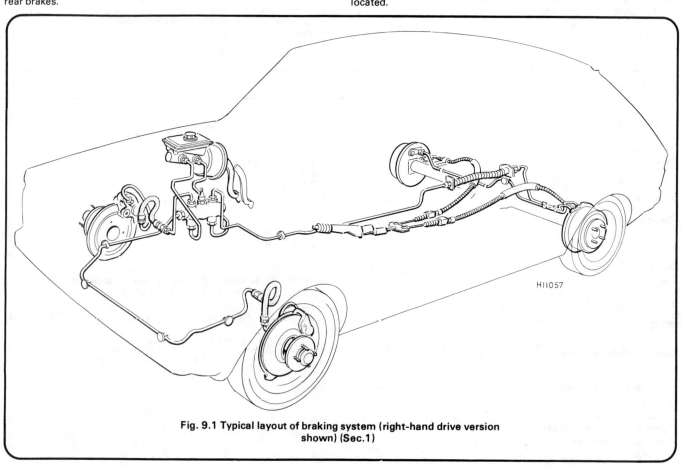

H11057

Fig. 9.1 Typical layout of braking system (right-hand drive version shown) (Sec.1)

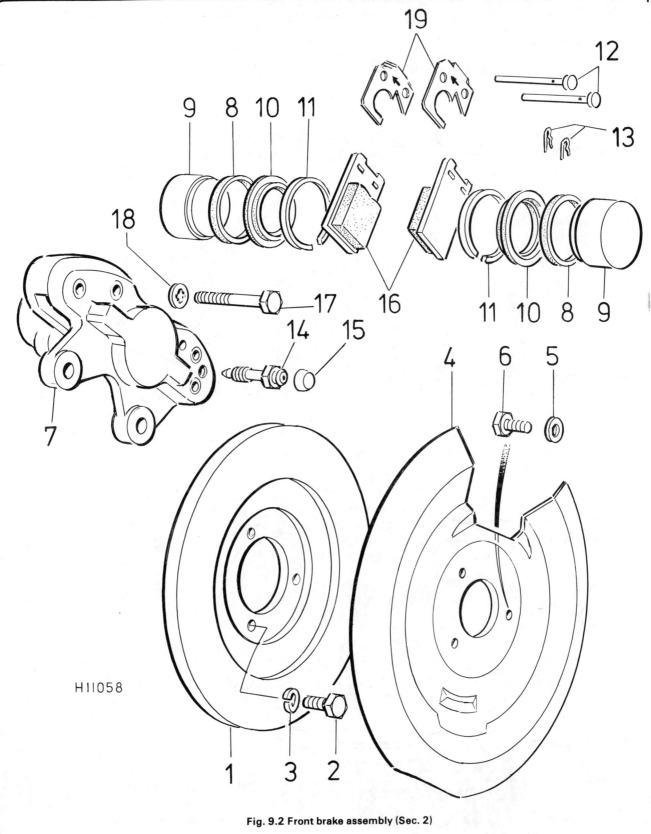

H11058

Fig. 9.2 Front brake assembly (Sec. 2)

1	Disc	6	Guard plate screw	11	Dust cover securing ring	16 Friction pad
2	Disc-to-hub bolt	7	Caliper unit	12	Pad retaining pin	17 Caliper mounting bolt
3	Spring washer	8	Seal	13	Spring clip	18 Lockwasher
4	Guard plate	9	Piston	14	Bleed screw	19 Anti-squeal shims
5	Washer	10	Dust cover	15	Dust cap	

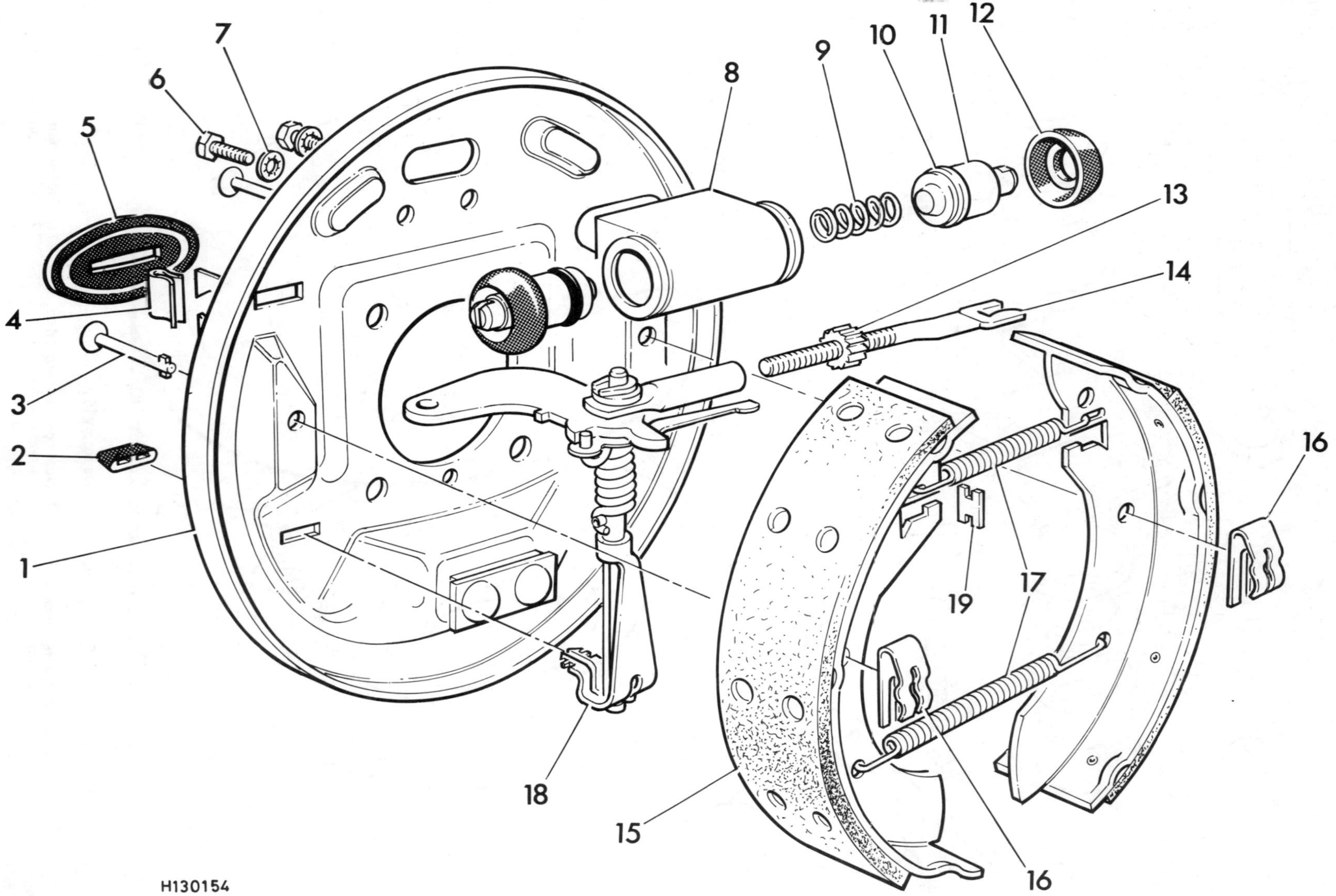

Fig. 9.3 Rear brake assembly (Sec. 3)

H130154

1 Backplate
2 Dirt excluder
3 Shoe steady pin
4 Handbrake lever support
5 Dirt excluder

6 Backplate-to-hub bolt
7 Lockwasher
8 Wheel cylinder body
9 Centring spring
10 Seal

11 Piston
12 Dust cover (boot)
13 Adjuster nut
14 Pushrod
15 Brake shoe

16 Shoe steady spring
17 Shoe return spring
18 Automatic (self) adjuster assembly
19 Support plate

2.4A Spring clip used on disc pad retaining pin

2.4B Extracting disc pad retaining pin

2.5A Removing a disc pad

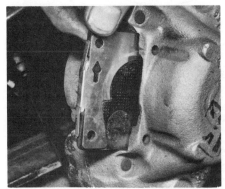

2.5B Disc pad and anti-squeal shim

3.3 Brake shoe steady spring and pin

3.4A A rear drum brake assembly

3.4B Lower shoe return spring

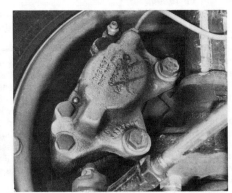

4.3 Caliper mounting bolts

5.6 Rear wheel cylinder

9   Refit the retaining pins and spring clips.

10   Bleeding is not required after this operation, but pump the foot brake pedal until solid resistance indicates that the caliper pistons are repositioned against the pads.

11   Top up the fluid reservoir if required, replace the roadwheel and lower the car to the ground.

3   Drum brakes – removal, inspection and refitting of shoes

1   Chock the front wheels, release the handbrake, jack up the rear of the car and remove the brake drum (countersunk screw). Do not operate the brake pedal.

2   The linings must be renewed if they have worn level with their securing rivets. It is strongly recommended that reconditioned shoes should be obtained rather than attempt to reline the original shoes. Factory lined shoes will have their linings ground to contour to facilitate immediate operating efficiency with quicker bedding-in.

3   Refer to Fig. 9.3 and remove the shoe steady springs (16) and pins (3).

4   Carefully note the position of the shoes with regard to leading and trailing edges of the friction material and which return spring (17) holes are used. Make sketches, if necessary, to ensure exact replacement of the new shoes (photos).

5   Prise the leading shoe away from the fixed abutment on the brake backplate and extract the trailing shoe from the handbrake lever mechanism.

6   By pulling outwards against the return springs, remove both brake shoes and return springs together with the threaded pushrod (14).

7   Before fitting the new shoes, clean the handbrake lever mechanism and backplate. Check the wheel cylinders for leakage and service them if required as described later in this Chapter.

8   Examine the tip of the lever which rotates the adjuster nut and the spindle roller which bears against the backplate. If the roller shows

signs of wear on its outer surface it may be rotated 90° to present a new wearing surface. Should the tip of the lever be worn, then a complete new lever assembly should be fitted.

9   Lightly smear the moving parts of the lever mechanism with high melting point grease (not the tip of the lever nor the adjuster nut serrations), also the shoe bearing surfaces of the backplate and the engagement slots in the backplate fixed abutment and the wheel cylinder piston slots. Take extreme care that grease is not applied too liberally and does not contaminate the friction lining surfaces.

10 Carefully position the replacement shoes on a flat surface and engage the shoe return springs. Take particular care that the shoes are in the correct position with respect to leading and trailing edges and that the return springs are engaged in the correct holes as originally fitted.

11 Exerting slight outward pressure against the return springs, offer up the brake shoes to the backplate and first engage the ends of both shoes in the fixed abutment slots. With the screwed adjuster rod engaged in its tube, prise the brake shoes outwards to engage the upper ends with the wheel cylinder unit piston slots.

12 Refit the shoe steady pins and springs.

13 Thoroughly clean the interior of the brake drum and refit it, finally inserting the countersunk securing screw. Should the brake drum be difficult to slide over the shoes, screw the adjuster nut (13) as far as it will go towards the forked end of the threaded rod (14).

14 Repeatedly operate the handbrake lever to bring the brake shoes to full adjustment. Test the foot pedal and finally rotate the roadwheel to check for binding. Slight drag should be ignored.

15 Lower the car.

Note: *If service has been neglected, it is possible for the shoes to have worn down to the lining rivets and in consequence, the internal surface of the drum may have become grooved, causing the shoes to become 'pocketed'. If this happens, it will be found impossible to withdraw the drum unless the shoes can be unlocked from the grooves.*

Initially, try and release the shoes by extracting the handbrake lever stop clip on the brake backplate and pulling the lever towards the backplate as far as it will go, at the same time try withdrawing the drum. If this method fails, then the drum will have to be drilled in accordance with the diagram and the drum rotated until, using a small screwdriver, the automatic adjuster start wheel can be rotated to release the shoe adjustment.

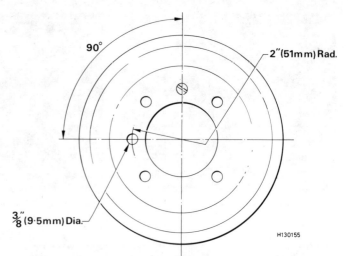

Fig. 9.4 Brake drum drilling diagram for release of grooved drum (Sec. 3)

hydraulic fluid and fit the new seals (8) in their grooves. Use the fingers only to manipulate the seals as the use of tools or probes is liable to diamage their sealing edges and surfaces.

11 Insert each piston fully into its cylinder and fit the dust covers and retaining rings. Assembly of these components will be facilitated if they are fitted dry.

12 Refit the caliper unit to the stub axle carrier, refit the friction pads, the anti-squeal shims, the retaining pins and springs.

13 Reconnect the pipeline, remove the tape and bleed the system. Provided the fluid in the master cylinder reservoir has not fallen very far, only one circuit need be bleed (refer to Section 11).

14 Refit the roadwheel, lower the car and top up the master cylinder reservoir.

4   Disc brake calipers – removal, overhaul and refitting

1   Apply the handbrake, raise the front of the car and remove the roadwheels.

2   Tape over the vent hole in the master cylinder fluid reservoir cap. This creates a vacuum and will reduce the loss of hydraulic fluid when the brake pipeline is disconnected. This should now be done by disconnecting the flexible and rigid pipes at the front suspension strut.

3   Unscrew and remove the two mounting bolts and lockwashers that retain the caliper unit to the stub axle. Withdraw the caliper unit complete with short rigid fluid pipe. The caliper can be withdrawn complete with disc pads for subsequent removal, but they may be removed at an earlier stage if required (photo).

4   Carefully clean off all dust and dirt from the exterior surfaces of the unit. **Do not split the caliper in two.**

5   Refer to Fig. 9.2 and remove the piston dust covers (10) and retaining rings (11).

6   All dismantling operations must be undertaken with extreme conditions of cleanliness prevailing. The internal components and rubber items must only be cleaned in clean hydraulic fluid or methylated spirit. The use of any other cleaning medium will cause corrosion and swelling and deterioration of the system's seals.

7   Pack a piece of clean rag between the opposing surfaces of the caliper pistons and eject them carefully by applying a tyre pump to the inlet connection of the caliper body.

8   Extract the piston sealing ring (8) from the cylinder bore, using a non-metallic probe to avoid scratching the operating surfaces.

9   Discard the original seals and dust covers and thoroughly examine the surfaces of pistons and cylinders for scoring or wear. The pistons may be renewed as separate items, but where scoring has occurred in the cylinder bores, then the caliper unit must be renewed as an assembly.

10 Obtain the correct service kit which will include the appropriate new seals and components. Lubricate the cylinder interiors with clean

5   Drum brake hydraulic wheel cylinder – inspection, servicing and removal

1   The rear brake wheel cylinders should be inspected periodically for leaks and seizure. The latter will be detectable if the brake pedal is applied and then released with the rear wheel jacked up. If the brake drum is extremely stiff to turn or will not rotate at all, then almost certainly the wheel cylinder is seized and its piston cannot be returned by the shoe return springs. A similar condition but much less severe, can be experienced where air is present in the wheel cylinder and bleeding will be necessary.

2   Jack up the rear of the car, remove the roadwheel and brake drum.

3   Remove the brake shoes as described in Section 3.

4   Disconnect the hydraulic pipe at its union with the wheel cylinder and plug the pipe to avoid fluid loss. A rubber bleed nipple cap is useful for this. Tape over the vent hole in the fluid reservoir cap (see previous Section).

5   Unscrew the wheel cylinder to backplate securing bolts.

6   Carefully clean the exterior of the wheel cylinder and withdraw the dust covers (1) (Fig. 9.5), the pistons (2) (applying a tyre pump if necessary to the fluid connection to eject the piston), seals (3) and spring (4) (photo).

7   Carefully examine the surfaces of the pistons and cylinder bores. If scoring is apparent, then the wheel cylinder should be renewed as an assembly.

8   Obtain a service kit which will contain the appropriate seals and dust covers. It should be noted that wheel cylinders are left and right-handed and in the event of renewal, the correct replacement unit must be obtained. Lubricate the cylinder bores with clean brake fluid.

9   Fit the new seals to the pistons with the wider end of the seal furthest from the slotted end of the piston. Dip the assembled piston in clean brake fluid and carefully insert it into the cylinder (seal end first), ensuring that the seal is not nipped or damaged during the operation.

10 Fit the new rubber boots in position. Refit the wheel cylinder to the backplate, which is largely a reversal of removal procedure, but check the correct location of the seal which is fitted between the wheel

cylinder and the backplate. Refit the shoes and drum.
11 Bleed the cylinder as described in Section 11 of this Chapter, top up the reservoir, refit the roadwheel and lower the jack.

6 Master cylinder – removal and refitting

Caution: *Brake fluid is a solvent and will react as a paint stripper if spilt on any bodywork.*
1   Disconnect the battery earth lead.
2   Tape over the reservoir fluid filler cap vent. This will create a vacuum and reduce the loss of fluid when the pipe lines are disconnected.
3   Place a suitable container under the master cylinder then unscrew the fluid pipe union nuts. Plug the ends of the pipes to prevent dirt ingress and fluid loss.
4   Remove the two nuts and spring washers that secure the master cylinder to the servo unit (photo).
5   Withdraw the master cylinder after wrapping a piece of lint free cloth around it to prevent fluid dripping onto the paintwork.
6   Refitting is the reverse of the removal procedure. Remember to remove the tape from the vent and to bleed the system as described in Section 11. The master cylinder retaining nuts should be tightened to the recommended torque setting.

7 Master cylinder – dismantling, examination and reassembly

1   Remove the reservoir cap and drain the fluid into a suitable container.
2   Refit the reservoir cap and clean the exterior of the master cylinder of all road dirt.
3   Remove the two clips and pins from the side of the cylinder and remove the fluid reservoir.
4   Depress the primary piston fully and withdraw the secondary piston stop pin from the fluid inlet port using a pair of pliers.
5   Extract the piston retaining circlip from the master cylinder bore and remove the primary and secondary pistons and springs by tapping the end of the master cylinder with a block of wood.
6   Lay the components on a clean bench in exactly the same order as they are removed. Identify the primary and secondary return springs with adhesive tape as they have different characteristics.
7   Dismantle the springs, retainers, seals and washers, if necessary using a wooden or plastic lever to avoid damaging the plunger surfaces.
8   Examine the surfaces of the pistons and cylinder bores. If these are found to be scored or worn, renew the unit as a complete assembly.
9   Where the pistons and cylinder bores are found to be serviceable, obtain the correct service kit and renew all the seals. All items should be cleaned with fresh hydraulic fluid or methylated spirit and all parts should be lubricated with unused brake fluid immediately prior to assembly. Take the opportunity to renew the fluid reservoir filler cap washer.
10 Refer to Fig. 9.7 and assemble the seals to the pistons using the fingers only to manipulate them into position. Make sure the sealing lips are fitted the correct way round, otherwise the operation of the master cylinder will be impaired.
11 Check that the springs are fitted with the small coil abutting the piston and that each spring locates with the correct piston as previously identified.
12 Insert the assembly into the master cylinder bore, being careful not to damage the leading edges of the seals. Fit the circlip to the end of the bore.
13 Depress the primary plunger fully and fit the secondary piston stop pin into the fluid inlet aperture.
14 Refit the fluid reservoir and secure with the two pins and clips. Refit the master cylinder to the servo unit using the spring washers and nuts. Tighten the nuts to the recommended torque setting.
15 Reconnect the fluid pipes, taking care not to overtighten the union nuts.
16 Bleed the brakes as described in Section 11.

8 Pressure differential warning actuator (PDWA) – description and renewal

1   The unit is fitted in the brake hydraulic fluid lines, between the

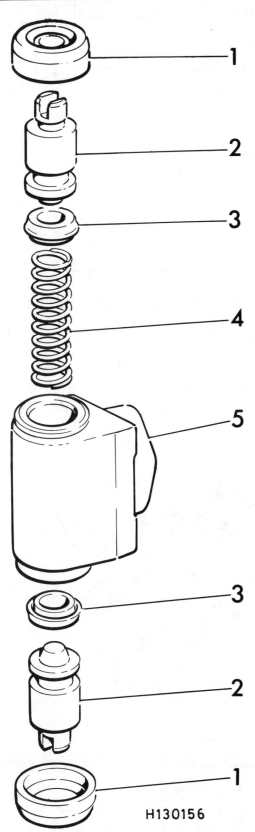

H130156

Fig. 9.5 Exploded view of a rear wheel cylinder (Sec. 5)

1 Dust excluder
2 Piston
3 Seal
4 Spring
5 Cylinder body

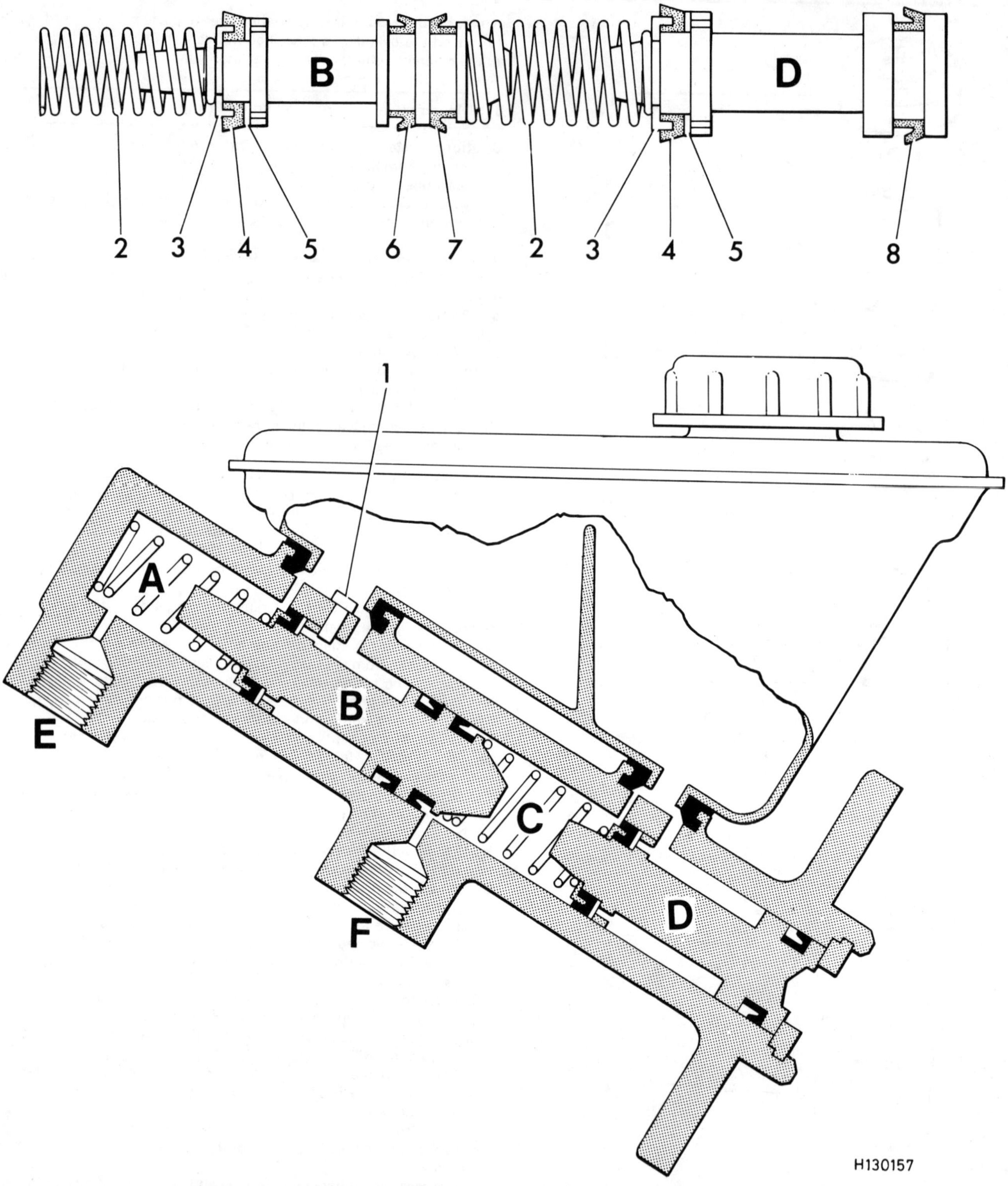

Fig. 9.6 Sectional view of master cylinder (Sec. 7)

H130157

1	Stop pin	A	Secondary chamber
2	Piston return springs	B	Secondary piston
3	Seal retainers	C	Primary chamber
4	Seals	D	Primary piston
5	Seal backing washer	E	Front circuit fluid outlet
6	Seal	F	Rear circuit fluid outlet
7	Seal		
8	Primary seal		

master cylinder and the wheel cylinders. It consists of a floating double acting piston unit which is only displaced if there are unequal pressures in the front and rear brake lines. Should a brake fault develop, resulting in loss of fluid from one circuit, the piston will move and cause the switch contacts to close which will illuminate a warning light on the car instrument panel (photo).

2 When the fault has been rectified and the brakes bled, the plunger will return to its central position.

3 It is not possible to dismantle the unit for the renewal of seals. The following operations are confined to renewing the unit as an assembly and renewing the actuator switch.

Separate renewal of switch section

4 Disconnect the battery negative terminal and pull the lead from the actuator switch.

5 With a box spanner unscrew the switch from the actuator body, being careful not to damage the switch terminal or body.

6 Before refitting the switch, check that the floating piston in the actuator is in its central position. If not, the movable sleeves will prevent the switch from being fully entered.

7 Tighten the switch to the specified torque only and reconnect the supply lead and battery negative terminal earth lead. There is no need to bleed the system, as the hydraulic lines will not have been broken by removal of the switch only.

Renewal of complete actuator assembly

8 Disconnect the battery and disconnect the lead from the actuator switch.

9 Tape over the vent hole in the master cylinder fluid reservoir cap. This will create a vacuum and reduce the loss of fluid when the pipelines are disconnected.

10 Place a suitable container under the actuator and disconnect the pipelines from it.

11 Extract the single securing bolt and detach the actuator from the wheel valance. Take care not to spill fluid onto the paintwork.

12 Refitting is a reversal of removal, but bleed the system as described in Section 11 once the work is completed.

9 Pressure conscious reducing valve (PCRV) – description, removal and refitting

1 To comply with legislation in certain countries, a pressure differential warning actuator, which embodies a pressure conscious reducing valve (PCRV), is fitted in the brake hydraulic system.

2 The PDWA section of the unit operates as described in Section 8.

3 The PCRV section of the unit effectively governs the maximum pressure which can be applied to the rear brakes, by means of a spring-tensioned shuttle valve. Refer to Fig. 9.8 and observe that in the square inset 1, the shuttle valve, under spring tension, allows hydraulic

fluid to pass the rubber valve face and hydraulic fluid pressure to the rear brakes is normal.

4 Once the predetermined hydraulic fluid pressure has been reached, a condition which could occur in an emergency stop, the shuttle valve overcomes the spring tension and moves the valve head against the rubber seal (inset 2). The pressure in the rear hydraulic brake line remains constant although the brake pedal may be depressed further, any further effort being directed to the front brakes.

5 The action of the PCRV prevents the rear wheels from locking under excessive braking conditions and, by directing hydraulic pressure to the front wheels, improves the all round braking efficiency under these conditions.

6 Should a fault occur in the brake hydraulic system, the PDWA piston will be displaced and the end seal (inset 3C) will allow full hydraulic pressure to be applied to the rear wheel brakes, the PCRV being by-passed.

7 Removal and refitting are as described in Section 8, paragraphs 8 to 12, except that two mounting bolts are used.

10 Hydraulic pipes (rigid and flexible) – inspection, removal and refitting

1 Periodically carefully examine all brake pipes, both rigid and flexible, for rusting, chafing and deterioration. Check the security of unions and connections.

2 First examine for signs of leakage where the pipe union occur. Then examine the flexible hoses for signs of chafing and fraying and, of course, leakage. This is only a preliminary part of the flexible hose inspection, as exterior condition does not necessarily indicate their interior condition which will be considered later in the Section.

3 The steel pipes must be examined equally carefully. They must be cleaned off and examined for any signs of dents, or other percussive damage and rust and corrosion. Rust and corrosion should be scraped off and if the depth of pitting in the pipes is significant, they will need renewal. This is particularly likely in those areas underneath the car body and along the rear axle, where the pipes are exposed to the full force of road and weather conditions.

4 If any section of pipe is to be taken off, first of all tape over the vent in the fluid reservoir cap. This will minimise the amount of fluid dripping out of the system, when pipes are removed, by creating a vacuum.

5 Rigid pipe removal is usually quite straightforward. The unions at each end are undone, the pipe and union pulled out and the centre sections of the pipe removed from the body clips where necessary. Underneath the car, exposed unions can sometimes be very tight. As one can use only an open ended spanner and the unions are not large, burring of the flats is not uncommon when attempting to undo them. For this reason, a self-locking grip wrench (mole) is often the only way to remove a stubborn union.

6.4 Brake master cylinder and vacuum servo unit

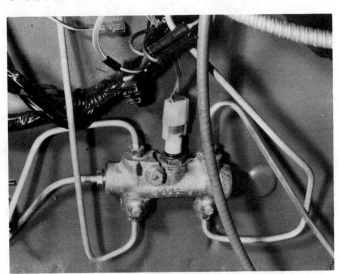

8.1 Pressure differential warning actuator

6   Flexible hoses are always mounted at both ends in a rigid bracket attached to the body or a sub-assembly. To remove them it is necessary first of all to unscrew the pipe unions of the rigid pipes which go into them. Then, with a spanner on the hexagonal end of the flexible pipe union, the locknut and washer on the other side of the mounting bracket need to be removed. Here again exposure to the elements often tends to seize the locknut and in this case the use of penetrating oil or freeing fluid is necessary. The mounting brackets, particularly on the bodyframe, are not very heavy gauge and care must be taken not to wrench them off. A self-grip wrench is often of use here as well. Use it on the pipe union, in this instance, as one is unable to get a ring spanner on the locknut.

7   With the flexible hose removed, examine the internal bore. If it is blown through first, it should be possible to see through it. Any specks of rubber which come out, or signs of restriction in the bore, mean that the inner lining is breaking up and the pipe must be renewed.

8   Rigid pipes which need replacement can usually be purchased at any local garage, where they have the pipe, unions and special tools to make them up. All they need to know is the total length of the pipe and the type of flare used at each end with the union. This is very important as one can have a flare and a mushroom on the same pipe.

9   Flexible and rigid fluid pipes are available in both unified and metric patterns with differing union nuts, pipe flares and threads. If renewing any parts, check which type is fitted to your car by comparison with the parts shown in Fig. 9.9. Under no circumstances attempt to mix the components.

10   Screw in a fitting by hand initially to make sure that the threads are compatible.

11   The attachment of a flexible hose to a hydraulic assembly differs fundamentally between UNF and metric types. On UNF types, the end fitting seats tightly at the shoulder and a copper sealing washer is used. On metric types, the end fitting seats at the bottom of the threaded socket and a gap exists at the shoulder. No washer is fitted and one should never be used. Do not attempt to overtighten the fitting in order to reduce or remove the gap.

12   Refitting of pipes is straightforward reversal of the removal procedure. If the rigid pipes have been made up, it is best to get all the sets (or bends) in them before trying to refit them. Also if there are any acute bends, ask your supplier to put these in for you on a tube bender. Otherwise you may kink the pipe and thereby restrict the bore area and fluid flow.

13   With the pipes refitted, remove the tape from the vent in the reservoir cap (paragraph 4) and bleed the system as described in Section 20. It is not necessary always to bleed at all four wheels. It depends which pipe has been removed. Obviously if the main one from the master cylinder is removed, air could have reached any line from the later distribution of pipes. If, however, a flexible hose at a front wheel is replaced, only that wheel needs to be bled.

11 Bleeding the hydraulic system

1   Whenever the brake hydraulic system has been dismantled to renew a pipe, flexible hose or other major part, air will have inevitably been introduced into the circuit. The system will therefore require bleeding in order to remove this air and restore its efficiency. Fluid cannot be compressed but air can and its inclusion in the system will make the brakes feel spongy.

2   During the bleeding operation the level of the hydraulic fluid in the reservoir must be maintained at least half full, to prevent more air from being taken into the system via the reservoir and master cylinder.

3   Obtain a clean glass jar and some plastic tube (15 in long and of a suitable diameter to fit tightly over the bleed valves). A can of unused brake fluid will also be required. This should have been stored in an air-tight tin.

4   Clean dirt from unions and bleed valves. Check that all connections are tight and the bleed valves closed.

5   It will be easier to gain access to the bleed valve and the rear of the assemblies if the appropriate roadwheel is removed. Chock the other wheels while the system is being bled. Release the handbrake and destroy the vacuum in the servo by pumping the footbrake pedal several times.

6   Fill the master cylinder reservoir, and the bottom inch or so of the jar, with hydraulic fluid. Take extreme care that no fluid is allowed to come into contact with the paintwork, it is corrosive and will react like a paint stripper.

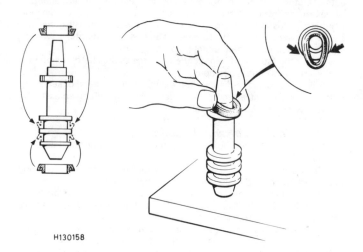

H130158

Fig. 9.7 Refitting master cylinder piston seals (Sec. 7)

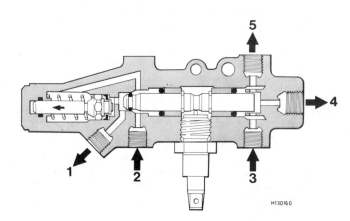

H130160

Fig. 9.8 Pressure conscious reducing valve (Sec. 9)

1   Fluid outlet to rear circuit
2   Fluid inlet from master cylinder primary circuit
3   Fluid inlet from master cylinder secondary circuit
4   Fluid outlet to front left-hand caliper
5   Fluid outlet to front right-hand caliper

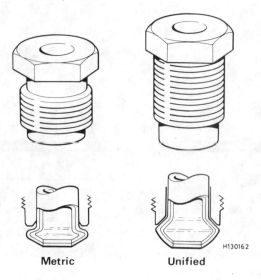

Metric   Unified

H130162

Fig. 9.9 Brakeline union nuts and pipe flares (Sec. 10)

7 Remove the dust cap (if fitted) from the end of the bleed valve on the front disc caliper which is furthest away from the master cylinder. Insert the other end of the bleed tube in the jar, keeping its open end below the surface of the fluid.
8 Use a suitable spanner and unscrew the bleed valve about half a turn.
9 An assistant should now pump the brake pedal by first depressing it one full stroke slowly and then releasing it, so that the pedal returns rapidly against its stop. Pause for a period of 3 to 4 seconds and repeat the operation. Keep a constant check on the fluid level in the reservoir and carefully watch the flow of fluid into the glass jar. When the flow of hydraulic fluid into the jar is seen to be completely free from air bubbles, tighten the bleed valve at the end of the next downward pedal stroke. Remove the plastic bleed tube and refit the dust cap.
10 Repeat the operations detailed in paragraphs 4 to 9 for the opposite front brake.
11 The rear brake circuit can be bled in the self same manner as the front brakes but there is only one bleed nipple and this is fitted on the right-hand wheel cylinder.
12 Sometimes it may be found that the bleeding operation for one or more cylinders is taking a considerable time. The cause is probably due to air being drawn past the bleed valve threads when the valve is loose. To counteract this condition it is recommended that, at the end of each downward stroke, the bleed valve be tightened to stop air being drawn past the threads.
13 Should the brake failure warning light come on during bleeding; close the bleed valve which is open at the time and open the one at the opposite end of the car. Apply a steady pressure at the foot pedal until the light goes out. Release the pedal and close the bleed valve. When the brake failure warning light goes out a click will be felt through the brake pedal, indicating that the piston in PDWA unit has moved to its point of balance.
14 If, after the bleed operation has been completed, the brake pedal operation still feels spongy, this is an indication that there is still air in the system, or that the master cylinder is faulty.
15 Check and top up the reservoir fluid level with fresh hydraulic fluid. Never re-use the old brake fluid.

12 Disc run-out – checking, removal and refitting

The condition of the front brake discs is a vital factor in braking efficiency. The disc should run true to within 0.004 in (0.1 mm) between the brake pads.
1 The disc must run equidistant between the caliper cylinders. Checking should be done with feeler gauges placed between the pad abutments and the disc face while the disc is being rotated. The gap on opposite sides of the disc may differ by 0.010 in (0.25 mm) but on the same side of the disc there should be no difference between the gaps at the two abutments. This check ensures that the caliper is in line and that the pads and the pistons are square with the discs. Any discrepancy should be corrected by the addition of shims behind the caliper mounting bolts.
2 Where the discs are found not to be running true and in line, they should be renewed. It is not recommended that regrinding should be undertaken. Light scratching or scoring is normal.
3 Should it be found impossible to obtain a replacement disc, then the disc can be rotary ground but under no circumstances should its thickness be reduced below 0.33 in (8.46 mm). Both sides of the disc must be ground equally and the rubbing faces should be maintained flat and parallel to the mating face to within 0.001 in (0.025 mm).
4 Remove the disc and hub assembly as described in Chapter 11 and then separate the disc from the hub by removing the four securing bolts and washers.
5 Refitting is a reversal of removal and dismantling procedure but ensure that the new disc is free from dirt, burrs and any protective coating has been removed.
6 Tighten the securing bolts to the torque specified in the Specifications Section.

13 Brake drum – inspection and reconditioning

1 Whenever the rear drums are removed for lining inspection, take the opportunity to inspect the inside surface of the drum for grooves and cracks.

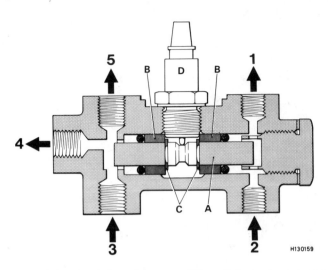

Fig. 9.10 Sectional view of pressure differential warning actuator (Sec. 8)

1 Fluid outlet to rear circuit
2 Fluid inlet from master cylinder primary circuit
3 Fluid inlet from master cylinder secondary circuit
4 Fluid outlet to left-hand front caliper
5 Fluid outlet to right-hand front caliper
A Floating piston
B Sleeves
C Circlips
D Switch assembly

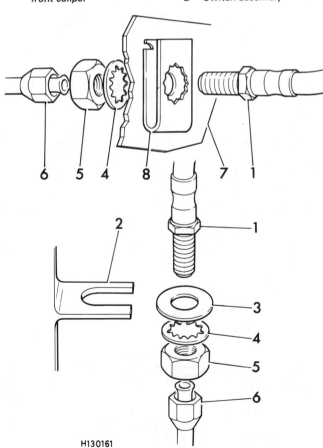

Fig. 9.11 Typical brake line connections (Sec. 10)

1 Flexible hose end fitting
2 Support bracket
3 Washer
4 Lockwasher
5 Locknut
6 Union nut
7 Panel or bracket
8 Location plate

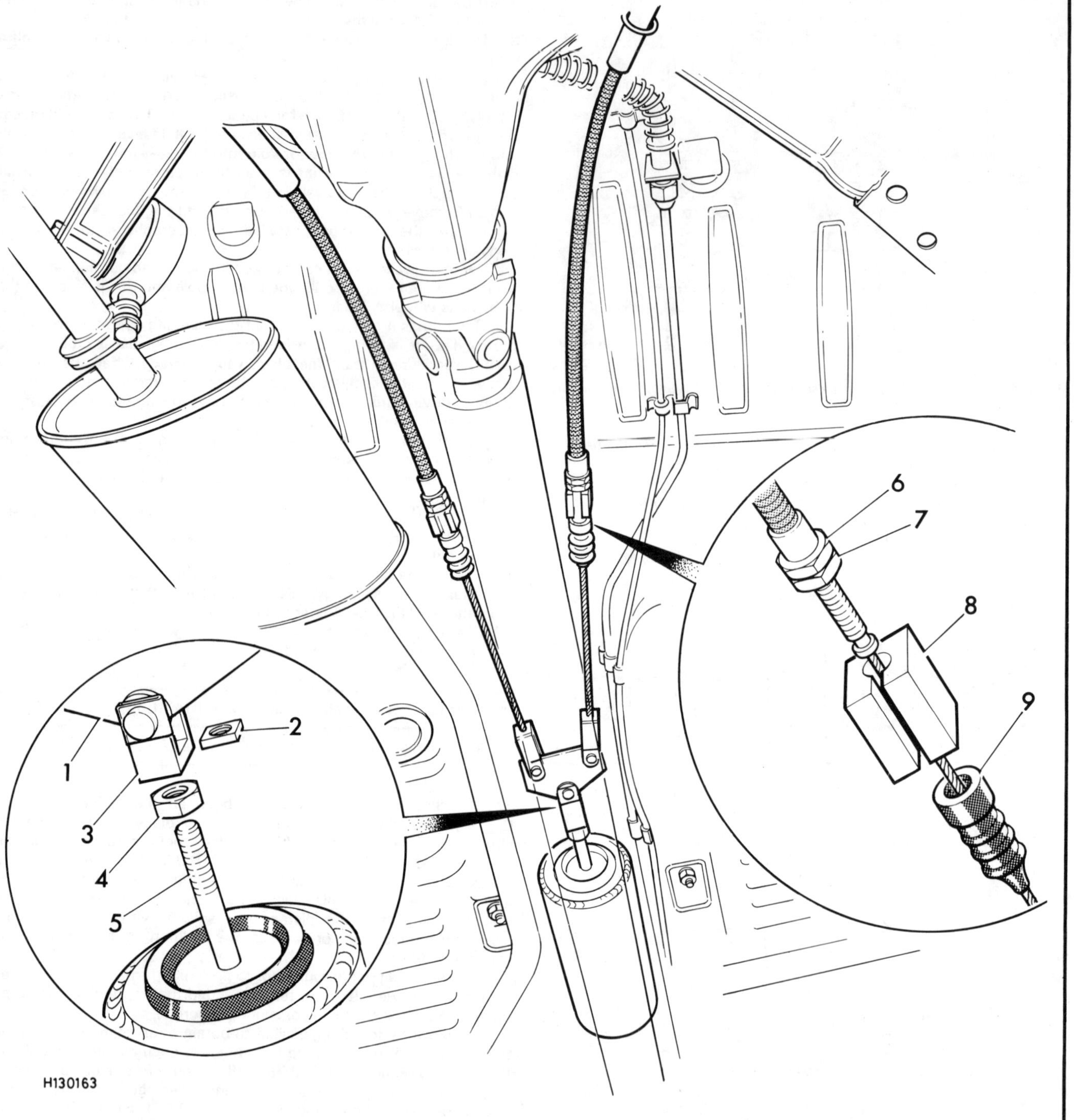

H130163

Fig. 9.12 Handbrake cable detail (Sec. 14)

1	Compensator	4	Locknut	7	Adjuster nut
2	Yoke nut	5	Actuator rod	8	Adjuster block
3	Yoke	6	Locknut	9	Boot

2   All internal dust should be cleaned away. *Take great care not to inhale it as it is injurious to health.*

3   It may be possible to have the drums refinished internally provided that the amount of metal to be removed is very small, otherwise new drums must be refitted.

4   After a very high mileage, brake drums sometimes wear oval in shape internally. This can give rise to judder during brake applications and make automatic adjustment impossible without causing binding.

5   This condition should be rectified by fitting new drums.

14 Handbrake – adjustment

1   The handbrake is normally self-adjusting due to the actuation of the automatic rear brake shoe adjusters.

2   However, after a considerable mileage, cable stretch may cause the handbrake lever to pass over an excessive number of notches on the lever ratchet before the handbrake is fully applied. When correctly adjusted, the handbrake lever should be fully on after passing over between three and five notches.

3   To commence adjustment release the handbrake lever, loosen the adjuster locknuts (item 6 in Fig. 9.12) at both adjusters and release the rubber boot or wiper seal from the adjuster thread.

4   Turn each of the adjuster nuts by an equal amount, ensuring that the flat edge of the compensator arm is always maintained at 90° to the actuator rod. During the adjusting operation make checks to ensure that the brake operating levers remain in contact with their backplate stops. Over adjustment of the cables will prevent the automatic brake shoe adjusters from working.

5   Having removed all the slackness from the cables, retighten the adjuster locknuts.

6   If during the foregoing adjustment, the boots (9) or wiper seals contact the blocks, then additional clearance must be provided by screwing in the compensator yoke (3) to the actuator rod (5). To be able to carry out this operation, the rear end of the propeller shaft will first have to be disconnected (refer to Chapter 7). Release the adjusters (7) from their blocks. Release the locknut (4). Extract the clip and clevis pin that secure the yoke to the compensator arm (1). Screw in the yoke, making sure that the actuator rod will not foul the compensator arm. Refit the yoke and locknut.

7   Readjust the handbrake cables and tighten the locknuts.

8   Operate the handbrake lever to settle the linkage and release it. Spin the rear roadwheels to ensure that the brakes are not binding.

15 Handbrake cables – removal and refitting

1   Chock the front roadwheels, release the handbrake, raise and support the rear of the car.

2   Disconnect the handbrake cable yokes at the rear brake backplate levers after removing the spring retainer clips and withdrawing the clevis pins (photo).

3   Remove the two hairpin clips that support the cables around the protective sleeves at the upper link arms by squeezing the clip sides.

4   Disconnect the handbrake cables at their forward ends by removing the single clevis pin which attaches the compensator arm to the front yoke.

5   Pull the rear end of each handbrake cable through the axle tube abutment brackets.

6   Slide the rubber boots or wiper seals forward, away from the adjusters.

7   Draw the cables rearward and pass the inner cables down through the slots in the adjuster blocks (photo).

8   Where new cables are to be fitted, carry out the instructions detailed in paragraphs 9 to 11 below.

9   Remove the two spring clips that secure the cables to the compensator arm (photo).

10   Disconnect the rear end of the propeller shaft and swing the shaft to one side to gain access to the actuator rod and yoke. Before removing the bolts mark the flanges to ensure accurate refitment.

11   Loosen the actuator rod/yoke locknut. Turn the yoke in an anti-clockwise direction until the end of the actuator rod is level with the yoke nut and then retighten the locknut.

12   Before refitting the handbrake cables examine all the components for wear, paying particular attention to the clevis pins, yokes and other fixing holes.

13   Refitting is the reverse of the dismantling and removal procedure.

14   After fitting the cables, lubricate the attachment points and adjust the cables as described in Section 14.

16 Handbrake lever – removal and refitting

1   Chock the front roadwheels, raise the rear of the car and support it on axle stands.

2   Disconnect the battery earth lead.

3   Remove the driver's seat as described in Chapter 12.

4   Remove the nuts, spring and plain washers that secure the inner seat runner of the front passenger's seat.

5   Fold the section of the front carpet in front of the handbrake lever forwards, at the same time withdraw the gear lever gaiter and stiffener through the aperture in the carpet.

6   If a handbrake warning light switch is fitted, separate the wiring connector at the switch and remove the single screw retaining the switch.

7   Withdraw the spring clip retainer, plain washer and clevis pin that attach the lever assembly to the actuator rod.

8   Undo the three handbrake retaining bolts and withdraw the handbrake lever assembly.

9   Refitting of the handbrake lever assembly is the reverse of the removal procedure. Remember to tighten the three retaining bolts to the recommended torque setting.

17 Vacuum servo unit – general description

The servo unit is designed to reduce the effort required by the driver's foot when applied to the brake pedal. The unit is an independent mechanism, so that in the event of its failure the normal braking effort of the master cylinder is retained. A vacuum is created in the servo unit by its connection to the engine inlet manifold. With this condition applying on one side of a diaphragm, atmospheric pressure applied on the other side of the diaphragm is harnessed to assist the foot pressure on the master cylinder.

Refer to Fig. 9.14. With the brake pedal released the diaphragm (2) is fully recuperated and is held against the rear shell by the return spring (19). The valve rod assembly (8) is also fully recuperated by the brake pedal return spring (20). With the valve rod in this position, the vacuum port is fully open and there is a vacuum each side of the diaphragm.

With the brake applied, the valve rod assembly moves forward

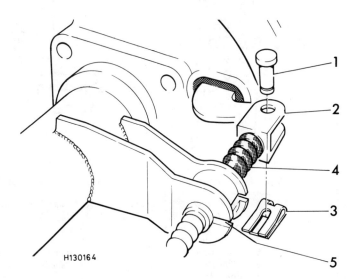

Fig. 9.13 Handbrake cable connection at brake backplate (Sec. 15)

1   Clevis pin   4   Boot
2   Yoke   5   Slot in abutment bracket
3   Clip

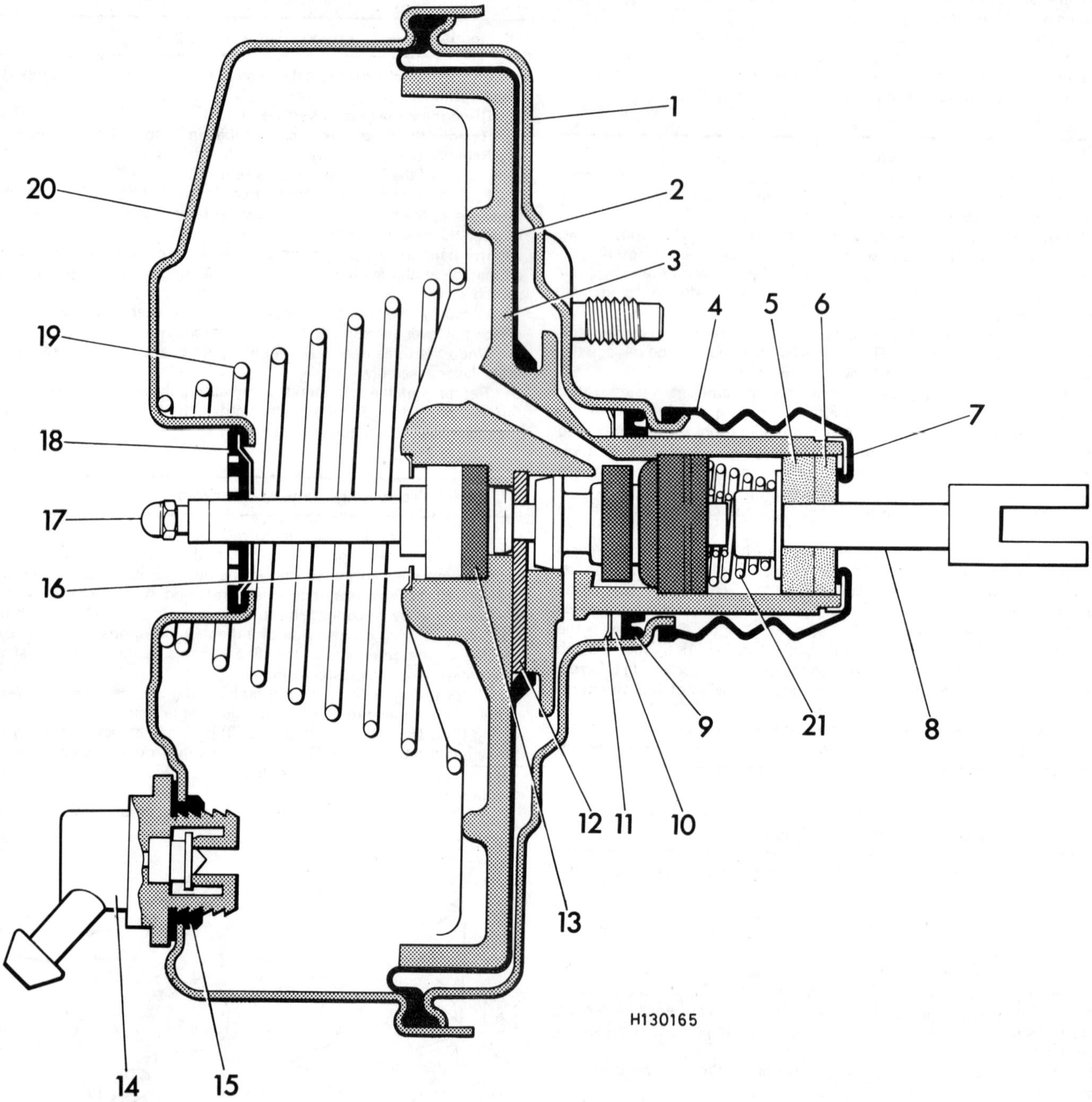

Fig. 9.14 Sectional view of the vacuum servo unit (Sec. 17)

1	Rear shell	8	Valve operating rod assembly	15	Grommet
2	Diaphragm	9	Seal	16	Sprag washer
3	Diaphragm plate	10	Bearing	17	Pushrod
4	Dust cover	11	Retainer	18	Seal and plate assembly
5	Filter (foam)	12	Valve retaining plate	19	Diaphragm return spring
6	Filter (felt)	13	Reaction disc	20	Front shell
7	End cap	14	Non-return valve	21	Brake pedal return spring

H130165

until the control valve closes the vacuum port. Atmospheric pressure then enters behind the diaphragm and is assisted by the valve rod to push the diaphragm plate (3) forward. This enables the pushrod (17) to actuate the master cylinder plunger.

With the pressure on the brake pedal released, the vacuum port is opened and the atmospheric pressure in the rear chamber is extracted to the front chamber and thence to the inlet manifold via the non-return valve (14). The atmospheric pressure port remains closed whilst the valve rod assembly returns to its original position, assisted by the diaphragm return spring. The diaphragm then remains suspended in vacuum until the next occasion on which the brake pedal is depressed, when the operating cycle is repeated.

18 Vacuum servo unit – removal and refitting

The brake master cylinder can be disconnected from the vacuum servo unit with the hydraulic pipes still attached, by following the instructions below:

1 Disconnect the operating rod from the brake pedal by removing the locating plate and clevis pin.
2 Unscrew the four nuts and washers from the servo unit mounting studs.
3 Disconnect the vacuum pipe at the servo non-return valve connection.
4 Remove the single bolt retaining the PDWA unit (or two bolts retaining the combined PDWA/PCRV unit) to the wing valance.
5 Remove the two nuts and spring washers that secure the brake master cylinder to the servo unit.
6 Ease the master cylinder away from the servo unit. Withdraw the servo unit away from the bulkhead until the mounting studs are clear. Tilt the servo unit to remove it.
7 Extract the foam dust pad and four distance pieces as shown in Fig. 9.15.
8 Refitting is the reverse of the removal procedure. Ensure that the foam dust pad is fitted with the large cut-out hole in the upper position and all nuts and bolts are tightened to the recommended torque setting.

19 Vacuum servo unit – maintenance and servicing

Major servicing of the servo unit is not recommended and a new or service exchange unit should be obtained if damage or severe deterioration has occurred. Service kits are available, however, to permit renewal of the filter elements, non-return valve and the seal and plate assembly.

Filter renewal

1 The only regular maintenance required is to change the filter elements every 30 000 miles (48 000 km) or every 30 months, whichever comes first.

15.2 Handbrake attachment at backplate

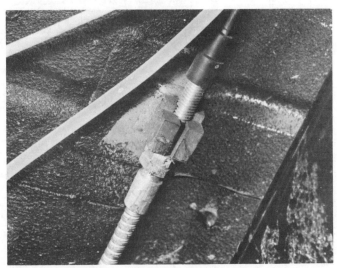

15.7 Handbrake cable adjuster block

15.9 Handbrake compensator

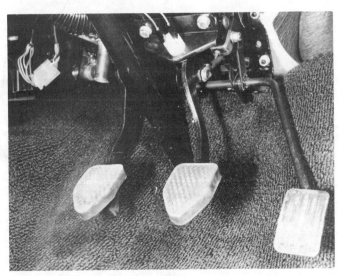

20.0 Control pedal arrangement (RHD)

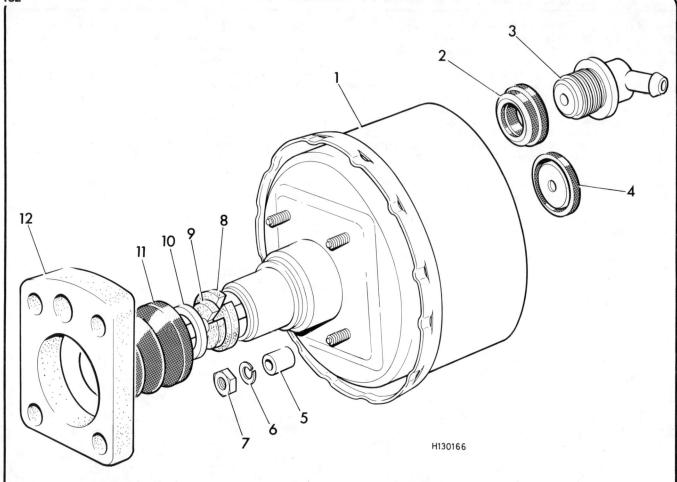

H130166

Fig. 9.15 Components of the vacuum servo unit (Sec. 18)

1 Servo unit body	4 Seal and plate assembly	7 Nut	10 End cap
2 Rubber grommet	5 Spacer	8 Foam filter	11 Dust cover
3 Non-return valve	6 Spring washer	9 Felt filter	12 Dust pad (foam)

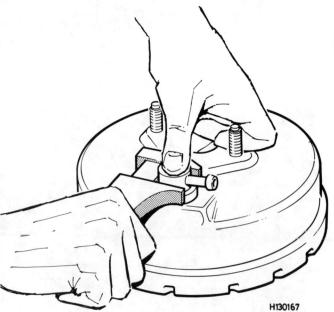

H130167

Fig. 9.16 Removing the non-return valve (early bayonet fixing type) (Sec. 19)

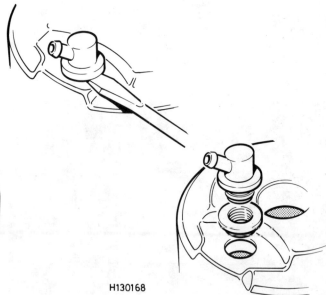

H130168

Fig. 9.17 Removing the non-return valve (later push-fit type) (Sec. 19)

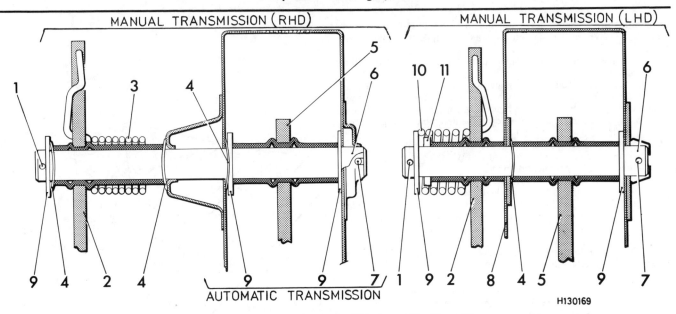

Fig. 9.18 Sectional view of typical pedal assemblies (Sec. 20)

1	Split pin	5	Brake pedal	9	Plain washers
2	Clutch pedal	6	Cross shaft	10	Return spring (LHD)
3	Return spring (RHD)	7	Roll pin	11	Washer (LHD only)
4	Belville washer	8	Mounting bracket		

2   Remove the servo unit as described in Section 20.

3   Withdraw the rubber dust cover and the filter retainer ring.

4   Hook out the filters and cut them as shown in Fig. 9.16, in order to remove them from the valve operating rod assembly.

5   Cut the new filters in a similar fashion and fit them into the neck of the diaphragm plate.

6   Fit a new filter retaining ring and rubber dust cover.

7   The remainder of the reassembly is the reverse of the dismantling procedure.

Non-return valve renewal

Two different types of non-return valve will be found. On early models the valve is of the bayonet fixing type, whereas on later models the valve is of the push fit type. It is not possible to interchange an early type valve with a later type.

8   Note the exact position of the non-return valve in relation to the front shell of the servo unit.

9   Pump the footbrake pedal several times to exhaust the vacuum supply in the servo unit.

10   Disconnect the vacuum hose from the non-return valve connection.

11   In order to give sufficient clearance for removal of the valve, it will be found necessary to undo the master cylinder retaining nuts and draw the master cylinder away from the servo unit.

12   To remove the (early) bayonet fixing type of valve. Use an adjustable spanner and while pressing down on the valve turn it through 120° in an anti-clockwise direction to release the fixing rings. Withdraw the valve and O-ring.

13   Fit a new O-ring (from the service kit) to the new non-return valve and refit them dry (unlubricated) by reversing the removal procedure.

14   To remove the later, push-fit, type valve, simply insert a flat blade screwdriver between the rubber grommet and valve flange and carefully lever the valve from the shell as shown in Fig. 9.17.

15   Remove the grommet, ensuring that it does not fall into the vacuum chamber.

16   Lubricate the new grommet sparingly with grease and fit it into the front shell. Likewise lubricate the ribs of the new non-return valve and push it fully into the grommet, making certain that the pipe connection is pointing in the correct direction.

17   Reassembly for both early and later types is now the reverse of the dismantling procedure.

Seal and plate assembly

18   To renew the seal and plate assembly, remove the complete servo assembly from the car as described in Section 18.

19   Having removed the servo unit, the seal and plate assembly can be removed from the front recess of the servo unit shell by gripping the centre rib with pliers.

20   Using only grease supplied in the service kit, lubricate the new seal and plate assembly and press into the servo unit recess.

21   Refitting the unit is now the reverse of the removal procedure.

20 Brake (and clutch) operating pedal – removal, overhaul and refitting

The clutch and brake pedals are fitted to a common cross-shaft which is mounted to a support bracket, which in turn is bolted to the bulkhead and the facia. This mounting also carries the throttle pedal assembly (photo).

The instructions given below are primarily for right-hand drive cars with manual transmission. Differences applicable to left-hand drive cars with manual transmission or cars fitted with automatic transmission, are shown in Fig. 9.18.

1   Disconnect the battery earth lead.

2   Mark a line around the brake stop warning light switch bracket, to ensure correct location on refitting.

3   Pull off the switch wires, remove the two bracket retaining bolts and lift away the switch bracket.

4   Remove the throttle stop bracket.

5   Disconnect the servo pushrod yoke from the brake pedal by removing first the split pin and then withdrawing the clevis pin.

6   Refer to Fig. 9.18 and the appropriate illustration for right-hand or left-hand drive arrangement. Pull the spring (item 3 or 10) from the clutch pedal to release the cable roller.

7   Disconnect the clutch cable from the hooked end of the pedal.

8   Extract the split pin, plain washer and belville washer from the end of the cross-shaft. Slide the clutch pedal and spring from the cross-shaft. Note that on right-hand drive cars there is a small spring anchor hole drilled in the side of the mounting bracket behind the cross-shaft.

9   Remove a further Belville washer, lift the throttle pedal upwards and slide the pedal shaft to the right from the mounting bracket. Note that the special spiral pin engages with a cut out in the mounting bracket. This prevents the cross-shaft from rotating when assembled.

10   Remove the brake pedal, noting the positions of the washers.

11   Examine all the dismantled components for wear and renew as found necessary. The pedal bushes, cross-shaft and spacing washers are all suspect items which tend to wear.

12   Reassembly is the reverse of the dismantling procedure, but can be simplified if a dummy shaft is used to hold the brake pedal com-

ponents together. The dummy shaft should be 4.5 in (115 mm) long and 0.6 in (15.75 mm) in diameter with a 0.125 in (3 mm) chamfer at one end.

13 Before reassembly apply a smear of multi-purpose grease to the cross-shaft, spring and washer.

14 Insert the assembled cross-shaft from the right-hand side just enough to support the right-hand washers. The dummy shaft can now be slid through the pedal support bracket, left-hand washer and brake pedal bush. Slide the cross-shaft through the assembly to displace the dummy shaft.

15 Reconnect the servo pushrod yoke and refit a new split pin.

16 Refit the stop light switch, bracket and wiring connections; aligning the bracket to the scribed datum mark.

17 Reconnect the clutch inner cable to the hooked end of the pedal.

18 After refitting the battery terminal, switch on the ignition and check that there is $\frac{1}{8}$ in (3 mm) of free movement at the brake pedal pad before the brake stop lights illuminate. If this free movement is not evident then the switch will require adjustment as described in Section 22.

19 Refit the throttle stop bracket and adjust it as described in Chapter 3 before fully tightening the securing nut.

21 Brake light switch – renewal and adjustment

1   Disconnect the battery earth lead terminal.

2   Scribe a line around the brake stop light switch bracket for correct location on refitting.

3   Remove the two bolts securing the bracket, lift the bracket away and pull off the switch wires.

4   Release the switch from the bracket and fit the new replacement.

5   Refit the switch bracket, taking care to re-adjust it with the scribed datum mark.

6   Reconnect the battery and switch on the ignition. Depress the brake pedal pad and check that there is $\frac{1}{8}$ in (3 mm) of free movement before the brake stop lights illuminate.

7   Where adjustments are necessary, disconnect the battery earth terminal and pull off the stop light switch wires.

8   Loosen the bracket retaining bolts and slide the bracket upwards away from the pedal. Ensure that the switch plunger is free to move.

9   Connect the switch in series with a test lamp and battery. When the components have been connected the test lamp bulb should illuminate.

10 Move the switch bracket squarely towards the pedal to compress the plunger. Note the position at which the test lamp goes out. When this position has been reached, move the switch bracket a further 0.040 in (1 mm) towards the pedal and nip the bracket retaining bolts.

11 Depress the pedal pad by $\frac{1}{8}$ in (3 mm), the test lamp should come on. If necessary make small adjustments at the bracket to achieve this condition before fully tightening the bracket retaining bolts.

12 Note that excessive switch movement towards the brake pedal can take up the specified servo rod free play. This may cause a condition of brake pressure build-up. Make sure that this condition is not allowed to occur.

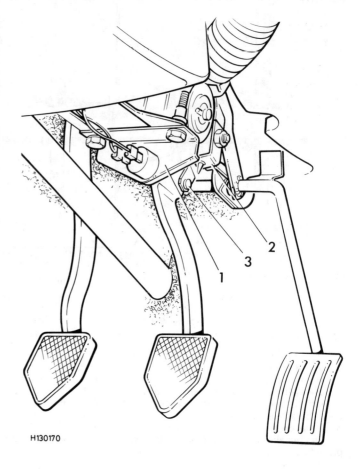

H130170

Fig. 9.19 Clutch and brake pedal assembly (right-hand drive) (Sec. 20)

1   Stop light switch bracket
2   Accelerator pedal stop
3   Servo rod yoke and clevis pin

22 Fault diagnosis – braking system

Symptom	Reason(s)
Pedal travels almost to floor before brakes operate	Brake fluid level too low Caliper leaking Master cylinder leaking (bubbles in master cylinder fluid) Brake flexible hose leaking Brake line fractured Brake system unions loose Pad or shoe linings over 75% worn Rear brake badly out of adjustment (automatic adjusters seized)
Brake pedal feels springy	New linings not yet bedded-in Brake discs or drums badly worn or cracked Master cylinder securing nuts loose

Symptom	Reason(s)
Brake pedal feels spongy and soggy	Caliper or wheel cylinder leaking Master cylinder leaking (bubbles in master cylinder fluid) Brake pipe line or flexible hose leaking Unions in brake system loose
Excessive effort required to brake car	Faulty vacuum servo unit Pad or shoe linings badly worn New pads or shoes recently fitted – not yet bedded-in Harder linings fitted than standard causing increase in pedal pressure Linings and brake drums contaminated with oil, grease or hydraulic fluid
Brake uneven and pulling to one side	Linings and discs or drums contaminated with oil, grease or hydraulic fluid Tyre pressures unequal Brake caliper loose Brake pads or shoes fitted incorrectly Different type of linings fitted at each wheel Anchorage for front suspension or rear suspension loose Brake discs or drums badly worn, cracked or distorted
Brakes tend to bind, drag or lock-on	Rear brakes over adjusted Air in system Handbrake cables over-tightened Wheel cylinder or caliper pistons seized
Brake warning light comes on and stays on	Leak in front or rear hydraulic circuit Check master cylinder reservoirs

Chapter 10 Electrical system

For modifications, and information applicable to later models, see Supplement at end of manual

Contents

Specifications

System type . . . . 12 volt negative earth

Battery . . . . 40 amp hour

Alternator
Type . . . . Mitsubishi AH-2040C-4
Rated output at 13.5 volts . . . . 38 Amps

Regulated voltage . . . . 14.3 ± 0.3 volts
Slip ring brush wear limit . . . . $\frac{5}{16}$ in (8.0 mm)
Capacitor . . . . 2 microfarad

Starter motor
Type . . . . Pre-engaged Lucas M35 J-PE or Mitsubishi MEA-16-0
Minimum brush length . . . . Lucas $\frac{3}{8}$ in (9.5 mm); Mitsubishi $\frac{7}{16}$ in (11.4 mm)

Fuses

Number	Fuse rating	Circuit protected
1	Red 16A	Heated tailgate (ignition controlled)
2	White 8A	Horns (ignition controlled)
3	White 8A	Heater blower (ignition controlled)
4	White 8A	Brake pressure warning light, door pillar switches, interior lamps, clock and cigar lighter.

5	White 8A	Flasher unit, warning light and lamps. Hazard warning switch illumination
6	White 8A	Brake stop lamps, reversing lamps, windscreen wipers, rear wipe/wash, heated tailgate switch and relay coil and automatic transmission indicator light (ignition controlled)
7	White 8A	Right-hand headlamp (main beam)
8	White 8A	Right-hand headlamp (dip beam)
9	White 8A	Right-hand side and tail lamps, heater panel illumination – rheostat dimmer control, facia panel illumination and rear fog lamps
10	White 8A	Left-hand side and tail lamps, rear number plate lamps, under-bonnet lamp, switch panel and clock illumination
11	White 8A	Left-hand headlamp (dip beam)
12	White 8A	Left-hand headlamp (main beam)

Bulbs

Lamp	Bulb number	Wattage
Headlamps:		
Right-hand drive (standard)	410	45/40
Right-hand drive (Quartz Halogen H4)	472	60/55
Left-hand drive (standard)	410 or 411	45/40
Left-hand drive (Quartz Halogen H4)	472	60/55
Sidelamps	949	4
Stop/tail lamp	380	21/5
Reversing lamp	382	21
Rear fog lamp	382	21
Direction indicator lamp	382	21
Side repeater flasher lamp	254	6
Number plate lamp	254	5
Underbonnet lamp	989	5
Interior lamp	254	6
Instrument illumination	504	3
Instrument warning (except 'no charge')	504	3
Instrument warning 'no charge'	505*	3
Automatic transmission indicator light	505*	3
*24 volts		

Torque wrench settings

	lbf ft	Nm
Alternator mounting nuts and bolts	16	22
Alternator pulley nut	40	54
Starter motor mounting bolts	34	46
Wiper motor bracket mounting bolts	6	8
Motor crank to spindle nut	15	20

1 General description

The electrical system is of a 12 volt negative earth type and comprises a battery, a belt-driven alternator, a pre-engaged starter motor and the usual range of conventional electrical items.

2 Battery – maintenance and care

1 The battery is located within the engine compartment on the right-hand side (photo).
2 At weekly intervals, the electrolyte level should be checked and topped up if required.
3 One of three types of battery may be encountered. On a battery with a non-removable cover, raise the cover as far as it will go. If the electrolyte level is below the bottom of the filling tubes, top up using distilled water only.
4 On a battery with a removable cover or screw plugs, lift off the cover and inspect the electrolyte level. This should be just above the perforated splash gaurd. If it is below this, top it up with distilled water (photo).
5 It should be noted that with the non-removable cover, battery,

distilled water is poured into the trough on top of the cells and will not actually enter them until the cover is partially refitted.
6 On modern cars, the addition of distilled water is required very infrequently. If the need for it becomes excessive, suspect overcharging caused by a fault in the alternator control section.
7 Periodically inspect the battery tray and mounting bolts for corrosion. This will appear as a white deposit and must be neutralised before permanent damage to the metalwork occurs.
8 Disconnect the battery leads, release the battery mountings and remove the battery from the car.
9 Sponge any deposits with ammonia, dry the surface and protect with anti-corrosive paint such as underseal.
10 Refit the battery, clean the terminals and clamps if necessary by careful scraping. Connect the leads, making quite sure that they are fitted to the correct polarity terminals by having the battery the right way round.
11 Smear the battery terminals and clamps with petroleum jelly (never grease) and wipe away any moisture or dirt from the top of the battery.
12 The foregoing operations are all that should be required to keep a battery in first class condition.
13 The addition of acid or so called rejuvinators will never be required throughout the life of the battery.

2.1 Battery with screw type vent plugs

2.4 Filling a battery cell

5.2 Rear view of Mitsubishi alternator

3   Battery – charging

1   As a result of the efficiency of the alternator, the battery will be kept in a good state of charge even if only short journeys are undertaken.
2   Only in a case where electrical equipment has been left on by mistake, should mains charging be necessary.
3   On cars with a battery charge indicator, the battery charge condition will be visually apparent whenever the ignition is on or the engine running.
4   On cars without this instrument, the state of charge can be ascertained using a hydrometer. The specific gravity of the electrolyte for fully charged conditions at the electrolyte temperature indicated, is listed in **Table A**. The specific gravity of a fully discharged battery at different temperatures of the electrolyte is given in **Table B**:

Table A
Specific gravity – battery fully charged
1.268 at 100°F or 38°C electrolyte temperature
1.272 at 90°F or 32°F electrolyte temperature
1.276 at 80°F or 27°F electrolyte temperature
1.280 at 70°F or 21°F electrolyte temperature
1.284 at 60°F or 16°F electrolyte temperature
1.288 at 50°F or 10°C electrolyte temperature
1.292 at 40°F or 4°F electrolyte temperature
1.296 at 30°F or –1.5°C electrolyte temperature

Table B
Specific gravity – battery fully discharged
1.098 at 100°F or 30°C electrolyte temperature
1.102 at 90°F or 32°C electrolyte temperature
1.106 at 80°F or 27°C electrolyte temperature
1.110 at 70°F or 21°C electrolyte temperature
1.114 at 60°F or 16°C electrolyte temperature
1.118 at 50°F or 10°C electrolyte temperature
1.122 at 40°F or 4°C electrolyte temperature
1.126 at 30°F or –1.5°C electrolyte temperature

5   When the time comes that regular battery charging from a mains charger is required to give the battery enough life to start the car in the mornings and it is known that the alternator is working correctly and reasonable mileages are being run, then the battery should be checked for failure by your dealer and if found to be at the end of its useful life, renewed.

4   Alternator – general description and maintenance

1   The belt-driven alternator incorporates a sealed voltage regulator assembly.
2   Maintenance operations consist of checking the drivebelt tension at the intervals specified in 'Routine maintenance', wiping away grease and dirt from the outside of the alternator and checking the security of the wiring connecting plugs.
3   The method of checking and adjusting the drivebelt tension is described in Chapter 2, Section 11.

4   No lubrication is required as the bearings are grease sealed for life.
5   Take extreme care when making circuit connections to a vehicle fitted with an alternator. When making connections to the alternator from a battery always match correct polarity. Before using electric-arc welding equipment to repair any part of the vehicle, disconnect the battery leads from their terminals. Never start the car with a battery charger connected. Always disconnect both battery leads before using a mains charger. If boosting from another battery, always connect in parallel using heavy cable. It is not recommended that testing of an alternator should be undertaken at home, due to the testing equipment required and the possibility of damage occurring during testing. It is best left to automotive electrical specialists.

5   Alternator – removal and refitting

1   Loosen the alternator mounting bracket bolts and strap, push the unit towards the engine block sufficiently far to enable the fan belt to be slipped off the alternator pulley.
2   Remove the cable connectors from the alternator and withdraw the mounting bracket bolts. Lift away the alternator (photo).
3   Refitting is a reversal of removal procedure, but ensure that the connections are correctly made and that the fan belt is adjusted as described in Chapter 2.

1300/1600 engines only

4   Where the alternator is to be removed with the engine hot, then remove the radiator cap to depressurise the system in order to prevent a water leak when loosening the timing cover strap bolt.

6   Alternator – dismantling and reassembly

1   The alternator has a long service life and when it does eventually develop a fault or a component wears out, it is recommended that a new or reconditioned unit is fitted.
2   However where only a small item requires renewal and provided the spare parts are available (check first), the following work can be undertaken.

Regulator – removal
3   Extract the screw which secures the capacitor, withdraw the capacitor and field terminal plug.
4   Extract the three screws and the regulator.

Stator/heat sink – removal
5   Remove the regulator as just described.
6   Mark the relationship of the drive end bracket stator and slip ring end bracket to assist when reassembling.
7   Remove the three end bracket screws. An impact driver may be required to extract these screws.
8   Separate the drive end bracket and rotor assembly from the stator and slip ring end brackets by careful levering at the slots provided.
9   Extract the four screws that hold the heat sink and brush box assembly to the slip ring end brackets. Take care not to completely

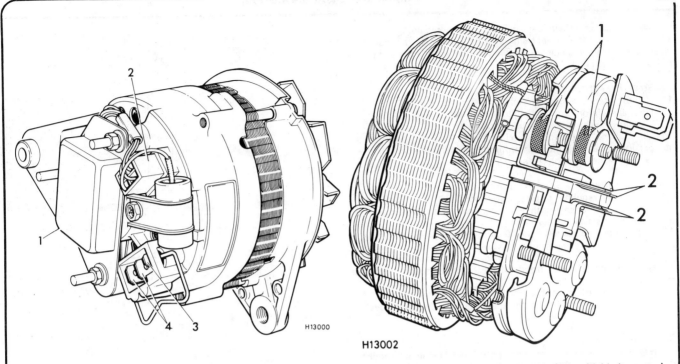

Fig. 10.1 Rear view of Mitsubishi alternator (Sec. 6)

H13000

Fig. 10.2 Stator and heat sink assembly (Mitsubishi alternator) (Sec. 6)

H13002

1   Voltage reglator
2   Field terminal plug
3   Ind (5 amp) terminal
4   Main output terminals

Fig. 10.3 Exploded view of Mitsubishi alternator (Sec. 6)

H13001

1	Pulley nut and washer	10	Slip ring end bracket
2	Pulley flanges	11	Voltage regulator
3	Fan	12	Securing bolt
4	Tie bolts	13	Field terminal plug
5	Drive end bracket	14	Capacitor
6	Bearing inner shield	15	Insulator
7	Rotor/slip ring assembly	16	Brush box
8	Stator	17	Heat sink
9	Field terminal	18	Fan and bearing spacer

remove any screws if their heads will foul the stator winding.

10 Withdraw the stator/heat sink assembly. Retrieve the insulating washers and plain and star washers located between the positive heat sink and the end bracket.

Brush box – removal

11 Remove the stator/heat sink as just described.
12 Lift the insulator from the field terminal block.
13 Withdraw the brush box securing screws.
14 Lift out the earth and capacitor blades and then extract the stepped insulators from the heat sink and the brush box.
15 Withdraw the brush box from the heat sink.

Rotor – removal

16 Remove the regulator as previously described.
17 Mark the relationship of the drive end bracket, stator and slip ring end bracket to assist in reassembly.
18 Extract the three screws that secure the end brackets. Separate the drive end bracket and rotor assembly from the stator and slip ring end bracket by levering at the slots provided.
19 Grip the rotor in a vice fitted with jaw protectors and loosen the pulley nut.
20 Remove the nut, and pull off the pulley components. Withdraw the drive end bracket from the stator shaft. Retrieve the inner bearing shield.

Bearings – removal

21 It is unlikely that the sealed bearings will need renewal throughout the life of the alternator unless the belt has been too tightly tensioned or the pulley has been running out of alignment, in which case carry out the following operations.
22 With the drive end bracket removed as previously described, extract the three bearing retainer screws and press out the bearing.
23 To remove the slip ring end bearing, a forked plate will have to be positioned under the bearing while the rotor shaft is pressed through it. A two or three legged extractor may prove a useful alternative.

Reassembly

24 This is generally a reversal of dismantling. A piece of wire may be used to retain the brushes in the raised position in the brush box while the rotor/drive end bracket is refitted.

---

7   Starter motor – description and maintenance

1   The starter motor is of the pre-engaged type and may be one of two makes – Lucas or Mitsubishi.
2   Both starters are interchangeable but only as complete units, not individual components.
3   Periodically check the tightness of the terminal nuts and the starter motor mounting bolts.
4   Keep the outside of the motor and solenoid clean.

---

8   Starter motor – removal and refitting

1   Disconnect the battery.
2   Disconnect the leads from the starter motor solenoid, making sure that the position of the connections is recorded beforehand.
3   Unscrew the mounting bolts and withdraw the starter motor.
4   When refitting the starter motor to 1300 and 1600 models, make sure that the dust shield is in position.
5   Refit the earth strap under the starter motor upper mounting bolt.
6   Reconnect all disconnected leads.

---

9   Starter motor (Lucas) – overhaul

The pre-engaged type of starter motor uses a face commutator on which the brushes make end-on contact. A certain amount of thrust is therefore created along the armature shaft and a thrust washer (17) is incorporated as shown.

1   Separate the solenoid plunger and drive return spring from the engagement lever (5).
2   Remove the grommet (4) from between the drive end bracket (6) and the motor yoke.

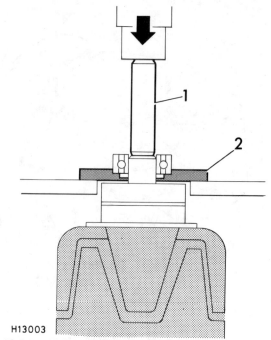

H13003

Fig. 10.4 Pressing rotor shaft out of slip ring and bearing (Sec. 6)

1   *Distance piece*
2   *Support plate*

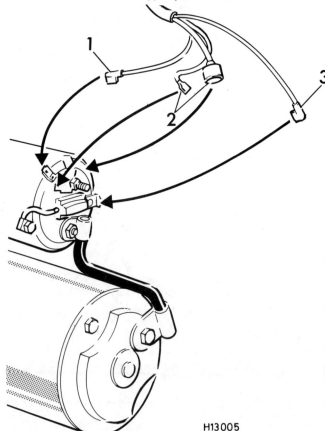

H13005

Fig. 10.5 Wiring connections to starter motor solenoid (Lucas type) (Sec. 8)

1   *White/blue to ballast resistor*
2   *Brown from alternator*
3   *White/red from ignition switch*

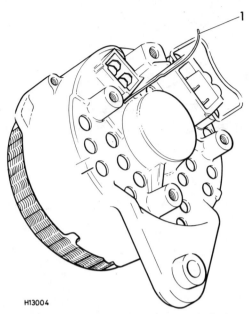

Fig. 10.6 Retaining brushes in raised position during reassembly of alternator (Sec. 6)

1 Wire

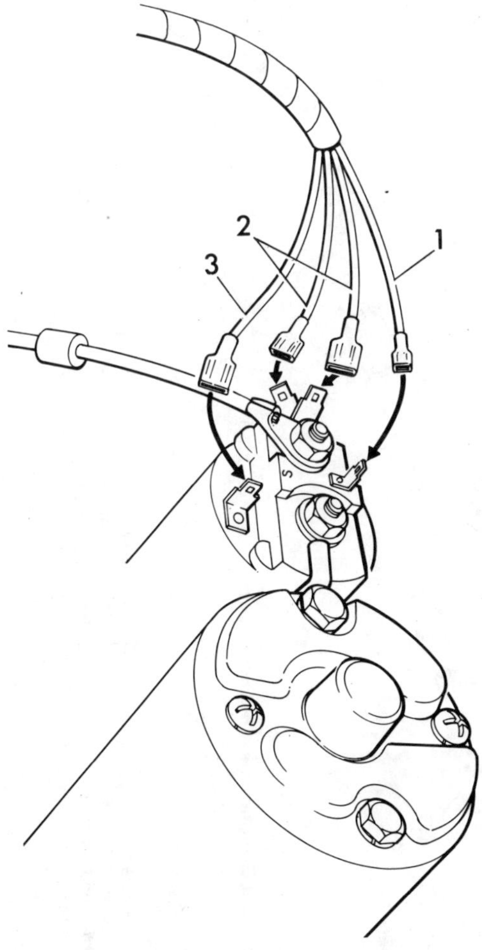

Fig. 10.7 Wiring connections to starter motor solenoid (Mitsubishi type) (Sec. 8)

Key as for Fig. 10.5

3 Remove the engagement lever pivot pin by first removing the retaining ring.
4 Remove the drive end bracket securing bolts and withdraw the bracket from the yoke.
5 Lift the drive engagement lever off the drive operating plate.
6 Remove the split pin, shim washers and thrust washer (17) from the armature shaft.
7 Withdraw the armature complete with internal thrust washer and drive assembly from the drive end of the yoke. Remove the thrust washer from the commutator end of the armature shaft.
8 Remove the two commutator end bracket screws. Lift it from the yoke, at the same time disengaging the brushes from the brush box.
9 Remove the drive assembly (14) complete, from the armature. Dismantle into separate parts by using a tube to sufficiently compress the coil spring to enable the jump ring (11) to be removed from its groove.
10 Reassembly is essentially a reversal of dismantling procedure, but note that the plunger attached to the top of the engagement lever (5) is matched to the main part of the solenoid and is therefore not interchangeable.

10 Starter motor (Mitsubishi) – overhaul

1 Remove the nut and washer from the solenoid terminal and then disconnect the field lead (photo).
2 Remove the two securing screws and withdraw the solenoid.
3 Retain the fibre adjustment packings and withdraw the solenoid plunger and spring.
4 Extract the tie bolts and withdraw the commutator end bracket and yoke from the armature and drive end bracket.
5 Remove the spring plate and bearing retaining spring, withdraw the armature engagement lever and the half bearings.
6 Extract the two screws and the commutator end bracket from the yoke, disengaging it carefully from the grommet of the field lead.
7 Retrieve any washers from the end bracket.
8 Raise the brush springs and remove the insulated brushes from their boxes, so that the brush mounting plate can be withdrawn.
9 Support the armature shaft in a vice fitted with jaw protectors and with a suitable piece of tubing, drive the stop collar down to expose the stop ring. Remove the stop ring and the starter drive components.
10 Wipe components with a rag moistened in white spirit. Never immerse insulated assemblies in a cleaning tank, nor the lubricant-sealed clutch assembly.
11 Check that the brushes slide freely in their boxes. Clean them with a petrol moistened cloth if they do not.
12 Check the brush length for wear, if they are less than the minimum specified (see Specifications) renew them as a set.
13 To renew the earth brush, prise back the clip that secures the brush lead and cut the lead about $\frac{1}{4}$ in (6.0 mm) from the joint. Solder the new brush lead to the old lead. Do not allow the solder to flow back along the lead more than $\frac{1}{4}$ in (6.0 mm). Bend back the clip.
14 To renew the insulated brushes, cut each brush lead from its joint with the field winding, leaving a stub $\frac{1}{4}$ in (6.0 mm) long and solder the new leads as described for the earth brush. Make sure that the insulating sleeve is correctly positioned to insulate against a short circuit when the starter motor is reassembled.
15 If the commutator is burned or discoloured, try cleaning it with a non-fluffy rag moistened in petrol. If necessary, use fine grade glass-paper and undercut the slots slightly using a hacksaw blade suitably ground down. The drivegear should rotate smoothly and the teeth should be free from burrs. The clutch should rotate in one direction only and be locked in the other.
16 Check the field coil insulation visually. If any breakdown of the insulation is suspected, test with a lamp and battery.
17 Commence reassembly by smearing engine oil to the armature shaft and splines. Refit the clutch and drivegear. Refit the stop collar.
18 Refit the stop ring and then using a small two legged puller, draw the stop collar into position over the jump ring.
19 Apply engine oil to the drive end of the armature shaft and fit the thrust washer.
20 Fit the engagement lever and bearings, engage the forked end of the lever with the over running clutch and insert the armature and engagement lever into the drive end bracket. Do not displace the thrust washer.
21 Fit the spring and the spring plate in their recess to retain the

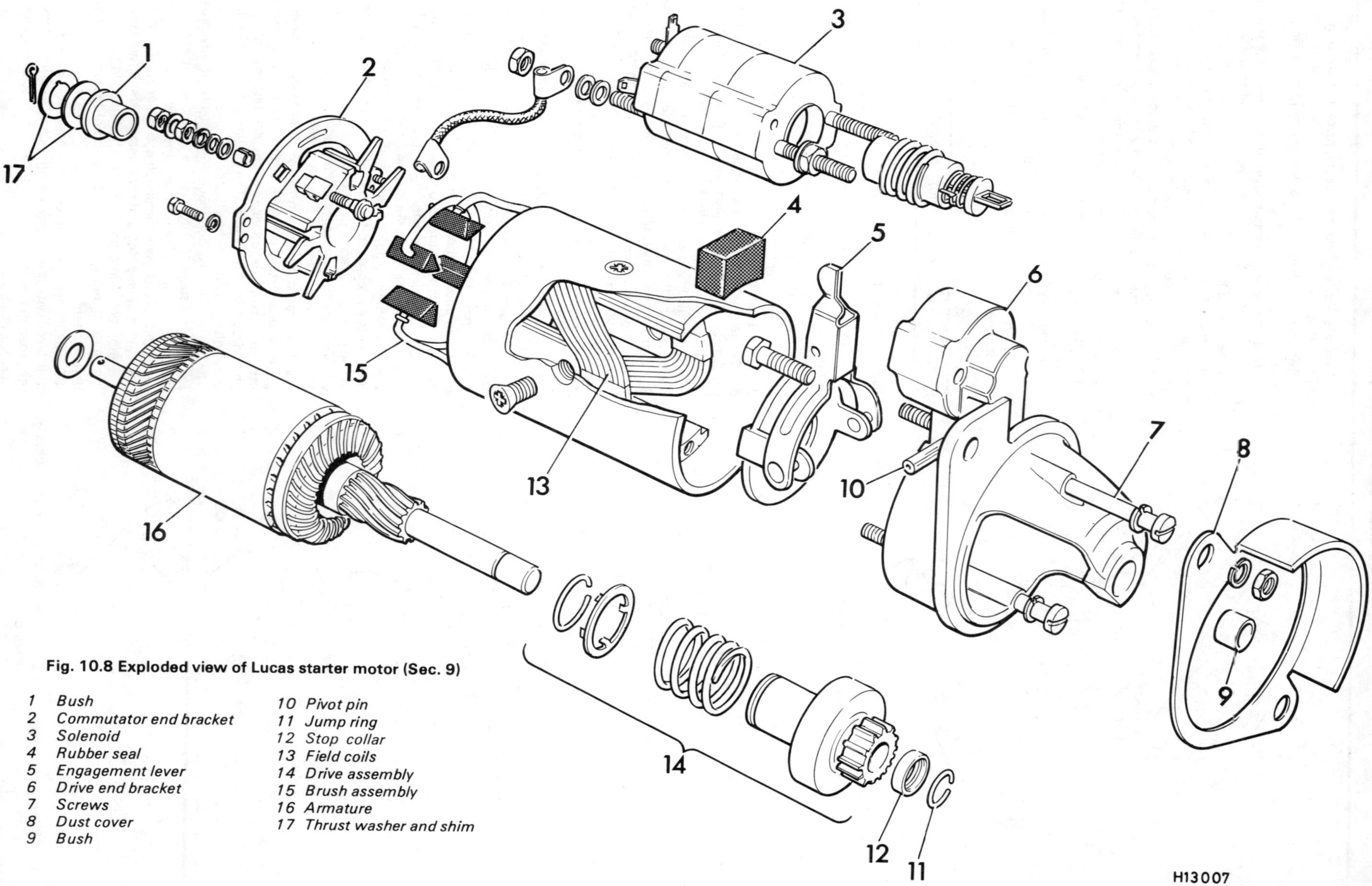

Fig. 10.8 Exploded view of Lucas starter motor (Sec. 9)

1 Bush	10 Pivot pin
2 Commutator end bracket	11 Jump ring
3 Solenoid	12 Stop collar
4 Rubber seal	13 Field coils
5 Engagement lever	14 Drive assembly
6 Drive end bracket	15 Brush assembly
7 Screws	16 Armature
8 Dust cover	17 Thrust washer and shim
9 Bush	

H13007

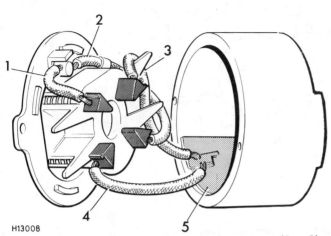

Fig. 10.9 Lucas starter motor brush gear arrangement (Sec. 9)

1   Short brush (end bracket)
2   Long brush (end bracket)
3   Long brush (field winding)
4   Short brush (field winding)
5   Yoke insulation

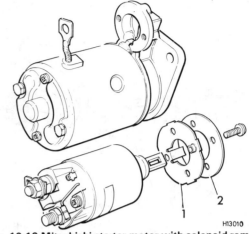

Fig. 10.10 Mitsubishi starter motor with solenoid removed (Sec. 10)

1   Securing washer
2   Packing washer

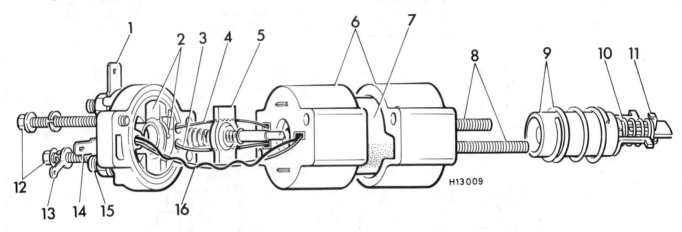

Fig. 10.11 Exploded view of Lucas starter motor solenoid (Sec. 9)

1   Main terminal (unmarked)
2   Baseplate
3   Closing coil connection to STA terminal
4   Holding coil connection to earth strip
5   Moving spindle and contact assembly
6   Solenoid body
7   Coil
8   Studs
9   Plunger and drive return spring
10 Lost motion spring
11 Spring retaining plate
12 Tie bolts
13 Earth strip
14 Small terminal (unmarked)
15 Main STA terminal
16 Closing and holding coil connections to small unmarked Lucar terminal

engagement lever bearing.

22 Refit the yoke over the armature, aligning the slot with the spring plate.

23 Fit the brush mounting plate over the commutator. Insert the brushes in their boxes. Make sure that the springs are central on the brushes.

24 Apply engine oil to the end of the armature shaft and fit the thrust washers so that the fibre washer is between the steel washer and the end cover. Refit the end cover, aligning the slot with the grommet at the field lead.

25 Refit the tie bolts, fingertight at this stage, then fit and tighten the brush mounting plate screws. Now tighten the tie bolts and check that the armature turns freely.

26 Insert the plunger return spring in the solenoid, making sure that it passes over the operating pin in the base of the recess. Engage the plunger and press it into position under its clip. Refit any fibre packings (retained at dismantling) over the solenoid flange.

27 Slide the drive gear to the outer end of the armature shaft and engage the solenoid plunger with the engagement lever. Refit the solenoid and connect the field lead to the solenoid terminal.

28 The starter motor pinion setting must now be checked. To do this, measure the distance (A) between the front edge of the pinion to the face of the mounting flange. This should be between $1\frac{1}{16}$ and $1\frac{9}{64}$ in (27.0 to 29.0 mm).

29 Now connect the positive terminal of a 12 volt battery to the S terminal on the starter motor solenoid and the negative lead to the starter motor body. The solenoid will be energised and the pinion will be moved to the engaged position. Measure the distance (B) from the front of the pinion to the face of the mounting flange. This dimension should be $1\frac{37}{64}$ to $1\frac{21}{32}$ in (40.0 to 42.0 mm).

30 If either of these dimensions differ from those specified, remove the solenoid and add or remove packing washers (C) as necessary.

11 Fuses

1   The fuse box is located under the bonnet on the right-hand wing valance (photo).

2   The circuits protected are given in the Specifications Section at the beginning of this Chapter.

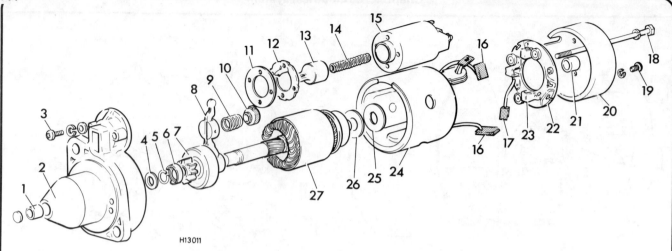

H13011

Fig. 10.12 Exploded view of Mitsubishi starter motor (Sec. 10)

1	Drive end bush	8	Engagement lever	15	Solenoid	22	Brush holder
2	Drive end bracket	9	Spring	16	Field brush	23	Brush box
3	Solenoid mounting screw	10	Rubber end cap	17	Earth brush	24	Yoke
4	Thrust washer	11	Packing washer	18	Tie bolt	25	Plain washer
5	Stop ring	12	Securing washer	19	Brush holder screw	26	Thrust washer
6	Stop collar	13	Solenoid plunger	20	Commutator end bracket	27	Armature
7	Drive gear/clutch	14	Plunger return spring	21	Bush		

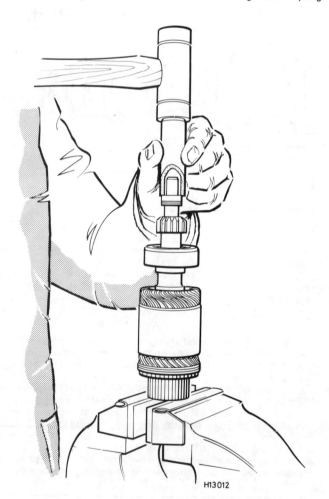

H13012

Fig. 10.13 Driving starter shaft stop collar downward to expose stop ring (Sec. 10)

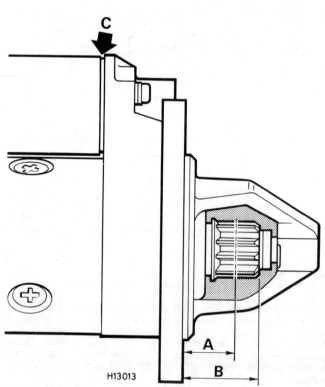

H13013

Fig. 10.14 Drive pinion adjustment diagram (Mitsubishi starter motor) (Sec. 10)

For key see text

3   Always renew a fuse with one of similar rating. If it blows for the second time, immediately trace and rectify the fault which is very often due to a short circuit caused by damaged wiring insulation.

12 Flasher unit – testing and renewal

1   The flasher unit is located under the instrument panel to the left of the left-hand steering column support (photo).
2   The unit operates the direction indicator and the hazard warning system.
3   In the event of failure of the systems to operate correctly, first check all the lamp bulbs and fuses.
4   Check the multi-plug connections at the bulkhead and the steering column.
5   Operate the hazard warning switch. If the hazard warning system operates but not the direction indicators, then the fault must be in the direction indicator switch or its multi-plug connector.
6   If neither system will operate, then the fault will be between the moulded harness connection (brown wires) and the steering column switch multi-plug.
7   If the fault still persists, detach the flasher unit and remove its connector. Bridge the purple/green and light green/brown wire terminals and depress the hazard warning switch. If the lamps operate, the fault must lie in the flasher unit. Disconnect the battery before renewing the unit.

13 Headlamp unit – removal and refitting

1   Remove the radiator grille (Chapter 12).
2   Using the wheel hub cap removal tool or similar, place it behind the lamp upper ball socket bracket.
3   Support the headlamp lens and pull the lamp sharply forward to disengage the ball sockets and studs.
4   Repeat on the two remaining lamp ball sockets, disengaging the outer one first.
5   Draw the lamp unit forward and disconnect the green wire at the connector (photo). Refitting is a reversal of removal.

14 Bulbs – renewal

Headlamp
1   The headlamp bulbs are accessible from within the engine compartment.
2   Pull off the bulb socket connector and remove the rubber water seal. Unhook the bulb retainer spring (photos).
3   Renew the bulb. It can only be refitted one way as it has a key cutout on its bore.
4   Refit the spring, seal, connector and wire. Press the lamp unit firmly back onto the ball studs. Refit the grille.
5   If quartz halogen bulbs are fitted, never finger them as this will reduce their life. Should these bulbs be handled in error, clean the glass thoroughly with methylated spirit and allow to dry.
6   Renewal of the pre-set type of headlamp bulb used on these cars will not alter the original beam setting.

Side lamp
7   This bulb is accessible from within the engine compartment. It is simply pulled with its holder from the base of the headlamp unit (photo).

Rear number plate lamp
8   Extract the two lens securing screws and withdraw the lamp. Pull the festoon type bulb from its spring contacts (photo).

Front flasher lamp
9   Extract the lens securing screws and remove the lens (photo).
10 The bulb is of normal bayonet fixing type (photo).

Side repeater lamp
11 The bulb is accessible after removal of the lens (two screws).

Rear lamp cluster
12 Access to the stop, tail, reverse, flasher and rear fog lamps is obtained after removing the three lens securing screws (photos).
13 Do not overtighten the lens screws when refitting.

10.1 Mitsubishi starter motor and solenoid on 930 engine

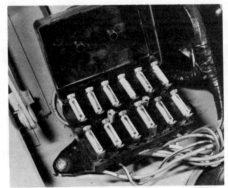
11.1 Fuse box with lid raised

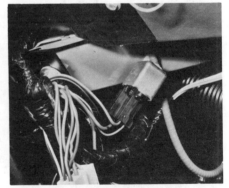
12.1 Flasher unit and connecting plug

13.5 Withdrawing a headlamp unit

14.2A Headlamp connecting plug and rubber cover

14.2B Headlamp bulb holder

14.2C Headlamp bulb removed

14.7 Sidelamp bulb withdrawn from head-lamp

14.8 Rear number plate lamp withdrawn

14.9 Extracting a front lens screw

14.10 Front flasher lamp with lens removed

14.12A Removing a rear cluster lamp lens

14.12B Rear lamp bulbs

14.14 Interior lamp withdrawn

15.3A Horn location and headlamp adjuster (arrowed)

15.3B Headlamp horizontal adjuster

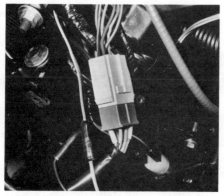
19.8 Steering column multi-connector plug

20.2 View of horn (grille removed)

Interior lamp
14 Extract the lamp screw and pull the lamp downwards (photo).
15 Pull the festoon type bulb from its spring contacts.

Instrument panel bulbs
16 The bulbs which are located between the steering column and the driver's door can be renewed by reaching up under the instrument panel.
17 The remaining bulbs located on the other side of the steering column can only be renewed if the instrument panel is partially withdrawn. See Section 17, this Chapter.

15 Headlamp – beam adjustment

1 It is recommended that this work is carried out by a service station but the following procedure will give a reasonably accurate result:
2 Set the car on level ground so that the front is 25 ft (7.5 m) from, and square to, a wall or screen. Check that the tyres are correctly inflated.
3 Cover one headlamp and then switch the headlamps to dipped beam. The light pattern should be as shown, otherwise turn the adjusting screws to achieve it. The top adjuster controls the vertical movement while the two lower screws move it horizontally (photos).
4 When the light pattern is correct, change over the lamp masking cover and repeat the operations on the other lamp.

16 Facia panel switches – removal and refitting

1 The push and rocker type switches mounted just below the instrument panel are a press fit in their panel cutouts. They can be withdrawn individually complete with wiring, simply by pulling them from the panel.
2 The complete switch panel can be removed in the following way.
3 Disconnect the battery, extract the screws that secure the lower half of the steering column cowl and lower the cowl complete with choke control.
4 Unscrew and remove the two nuts that secure the outer legs of the steering column upper mounting bracket.
5 Remove one nut and one bolt that secure the steering column lower mounting. Lower the column and rest the steering wheel on the driver's seat.
6 Extract the five screws (A) that hold the switch panel to the facia rail and instrument panel. Remove the finisher and lower the complete switch panel assembly.
7 Refitting is a reversal of removal.

17 Instrument panel – removal and refitting

1 Removal of the complete facia panel including the instrument panel, is described in Chapter 12, Section 12. Where the instrument panel alone is to be removed, carry out the following operations:
2 Repeat the work described in paragraphs 3 to 6 of the preceding Section.
3 Extract the two screws that secure the bottom of the instrument panel to the steering column plate.
4 Extract the four screws (B) that secure the mounting plate to the crash roll.
5 Reach up behind the instrument panel and disconnect the speedometer cable.
6 Remove the outer printed circuit multi-socket connector.
7 Extract the two screws (C) that secure the upper part of the instrument panel to the crash roll.
8 Partially withdraw the instrument panel and disconnect the inner printed circuit multi-socket connector and the choke warning lamp bulb holder.
9 Withdraw the instrument panel.
10 Refitting is a reversal of removal.

18 Instruments – removal and refitting

1 Several different makes of instruments are used in the Sunbeam instrument panel assembly.
2 The instruments are removed from the panel by extracting screws or clips. Take great care not to damage the printed circuits during removal.
3 Only the Smiths instrument panel has a voltage stabiliser plugged into its rear face.
4 Refitting is a reversal of removal.

19 Steering column switch – removal and refitting

1 Disconnect the battery.
2 Insert the ignition key and release the steering column lock.
3 Extract the screws that secure the lower half of the steering column cowl and lower the cowl complete with choke control.
4 Carefully prise the motif from the centre of the steering wheel and remove the steering wheel as described in Chapter 11, Section 20.
5 Remove the two nuts that secure the outer legs of the steering column upper mounting bracket, also the single nut and bolt that hold the steering column lower mounting.
6 Lower the steering column to expose the two screws that secure the upper half of the cowl.

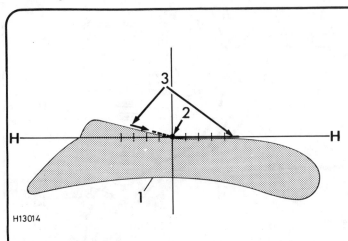

Fig. 10.15 Headlamp beam adjustment diagram (Sec.15)

1 Concentrated area of light	*H Horizontal line 4 in (102 mm)*
2 Centre of V-pattern	*below headlamp centres*
3 Light to dark cut off	

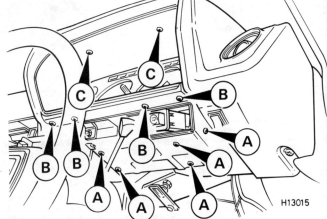

Fig. 10.16 Panel fixing screws (Sec.16)

A Switch panel screws   *C Instrument panel mounting*
B Hexagonal headed screws   *screws*

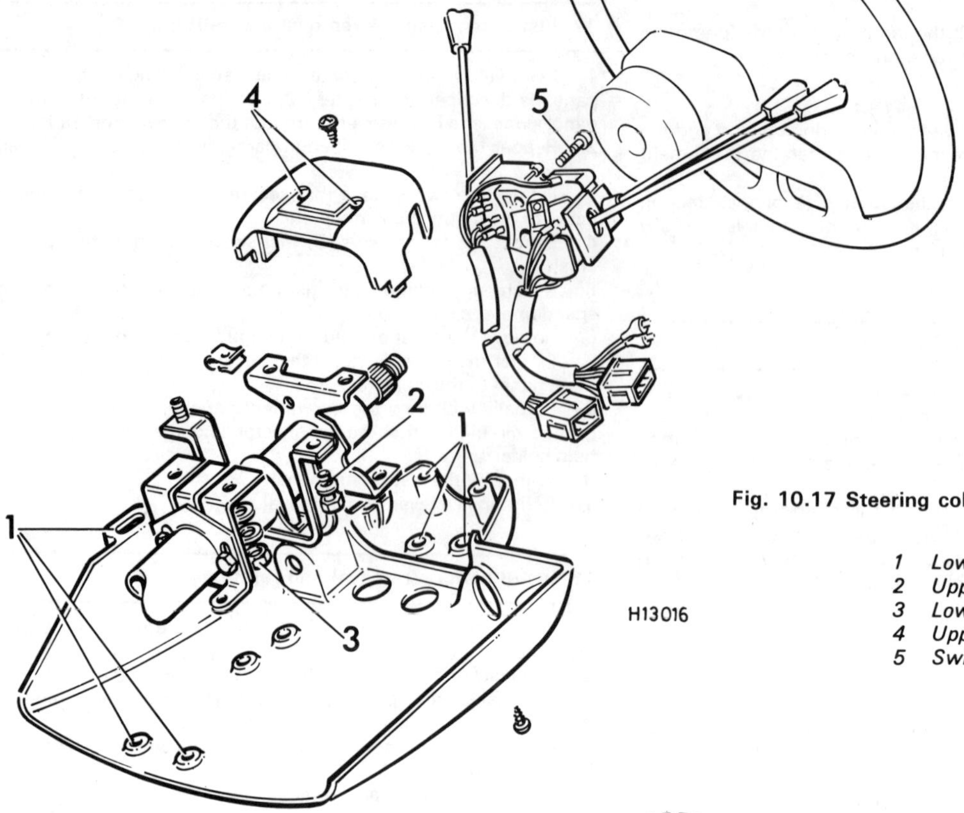

Fig. 10.17 Steering column switch details (Sec. 19)

H13016

1   Lower cowl screw holes
2   Upper support bracket bolts
3   Lower support bracket nut
4   Upper cowl screw holes
5   Switch mounting screw

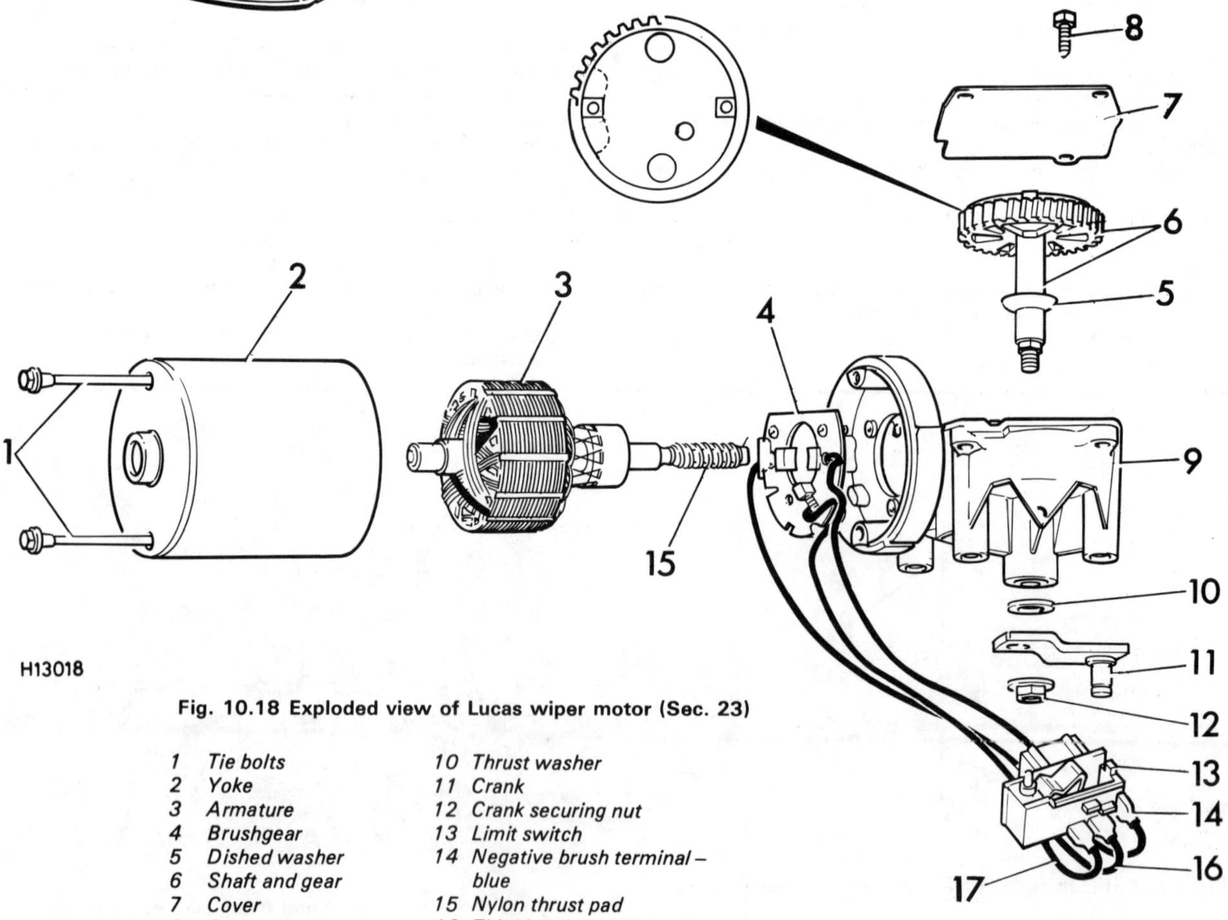

H13018

Fig. 10.18 Exploded view of Lucas wiper motor (Sec. 23)

1   Tie bolts
2   Yoke
3   Armature
4   Brushgear
5   Dished washer
6   Shaft and gear
7   Cover
8   Cover screws
9   Gear casing
10 Thrust washer
11 Crank
12 Crank securing nut
13 Limit switch
14 Negative brush terminal – blue
15 Nylon thrust pad
16 Third brush terminal yellow
17 Positive brush terminal – red

7 Extract the screws and the cowl.
8 Release the strap which secures the column switch harness. Separate all the multi-plugs and in-line connectors, marking them is necessary for ease of reconnection (photo).
9 Extract the three screws that secure the column switch to the column and withdraw the switch.
10 Refitting of the multi-function steering column switch is a reversal of removal.

20 Horns

1 Single or dual horns may be fitted according to the model.
2 The only maintenance required is to occasionally check the security of the connecting leads and the tightness of the mounting bracket screws (photo).

21 Windscreen wiper blades and arms – removal and refitting

1 To remove a wiper blade, depress the small spring tab with the thumb nail and pull the blade from the arm (photo).
2 To remove a wiper arm, swivel the covering cap upwards and unscrew and remove the nut which holds the arm to the driving spindle (photo).
3 Pull the arm from the spindle.
4 The arm should be refitted parallel to the lower edge of the screen, making sure that the wiper motor has been switched off in the 'parked' position by means of the wiper switch, not the ignition key.

22 Windscreen wiper motor and linkage – removal and refitting

1 A two speed wiper mechanism is fitted and the complete motor, linkage and wheel boxes are all mounted as a unit and removed and refitted as one assembly.
2 Disconnect the battery. Remove the wiper arm assemblies from their spindles.
3 Remove the complete facia/instrument panel as described in Chapter 12, Section 12.
4 Remove the demister ducts, the face level vent hoses and the centre duct.
5 Disconnect the multi-plug at the wiper motor.
6 Unscrew and remove the two mounting bolts and screw. Withdraw the complete wiper motor and linkage assembly from the car.
7 Extract the spring clips that secure the link rods to the motor crank and remove the washer and the rods. Retrieve the nylon bushes if they are loose, also the Belleville washer.
8 Extract the three securing bolts and separate the motor from the linkage.
9 Refitting is a reversal of removal.

23 Windscreen wiper assembly – overhaul

1 Extract the three securing screws and remove the gearbox cover.
2 Wipe away the grease from the gear and note the relative positions of the crank and gear to each other. If assembled incorrectly, the wiper arms will not park correctly.
3 Grip the crank securely and unscrew and remove the shaft nut and washer.
4 Remove the crank and then lift out the gear and shaft assembly. Remove the dished washer(5).
5 If the motor is also to be dismantled, check the mating marks on the yoke (2) and the body (9). This is most important as any transposing of the permanent magnets would result in the armature reversing its direction of rotation.
6 Unscrew and remove the tie bolts and withdraw the yoke and armature. Remove the armature from the yoke.
7 Insert a thin screwdriver blade under the retaining post end of the limit switch, prise up the switch, slide it until it clears the retaining clip and lift it out. Note the wiring colours and disconnect them.
8 Examine the dismantled components for wear or damage. The operating plunger on the limit switch should project by $\frac{9}{32}$ in (7.0 mm). If it does not, renew the switch.

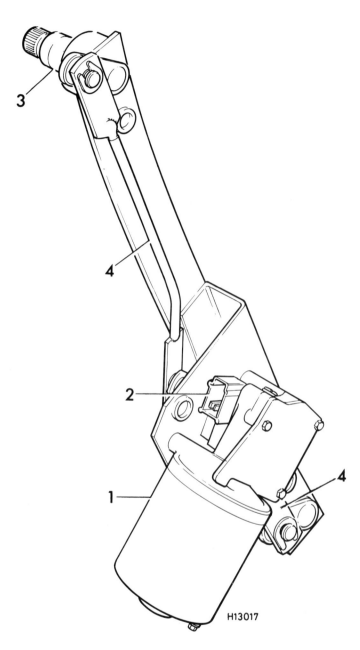

Fig. 10.19 Wiper motor/linkage assembly (Sec. 22)

1 *Motor*
2 *Multi-connector*
3 *Wheel box*
4 *Link rods*

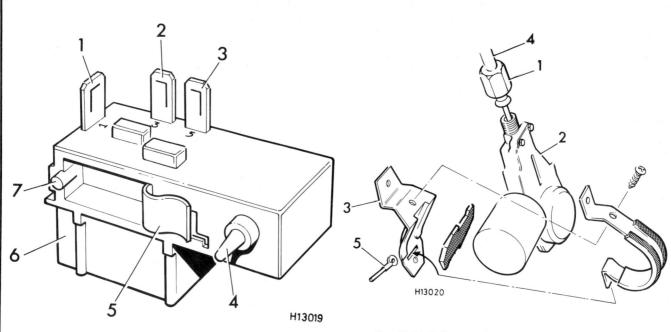

H13019

Fig. 10.20 Wiper motor limit switch (Sec. 23)

1 Negative brush terminal (blue)
2 Third brush terminal (yellow)
3 Positive brush terminal (red)
4 Operating plunger
5 Clip
6 Multi-connector
7 Locating post

H13020

Fig. 10.21 Tailgate wiper mounting detail (Sec. 24)

1 Union nut
2 Wiper motor
3 Bracket
4 Rack
5 Earth lead from tail lamps

Fig. 10.22 Exploded view of tailgate wiper motor (Sec. 25)

1 Cover
2 Screws
3 Circlip
4 Washer
5 Spring
6 Friction plate
7 Connecting rod/cam
8 Gearwheel
9 Dished washer
10 Cable rack
11 Slider block
12 Casing
13 Limit switch
14 Screws
15 Bush
16 Brushgear mounting plate
17 Armature
18 Yoke
19 Tie bolts

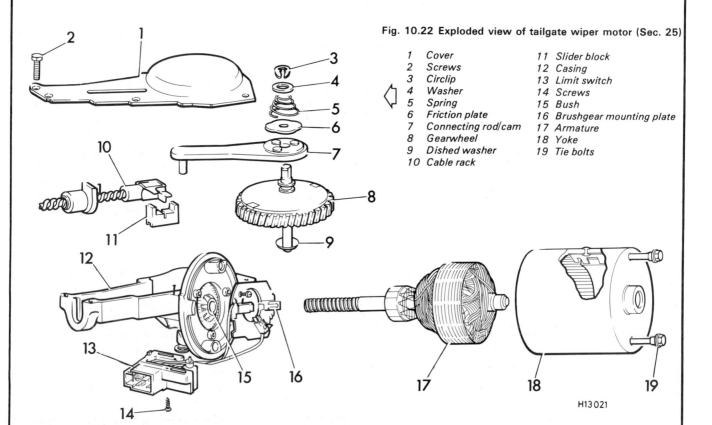

H13021

9 Check the brushes for freedom of movement in the mounting plate. If the main (diametrically opposite) brushes are worn down to $\frac{3}{16}$ in (4.8 mm) or the narrow section of the third brush is worn away to leave only the wider section, then the brush gear must be renewed. A kit is supplied complete with self-tapping screws to replace the rivets, which will have to be drilled out to remove the original assembly.
10 If the gear teeth are worn, a new gear is supplied complete with shaft.
11 Commence reassembly of the wiper motor by connecting the brush wires to the limit switch. Slide the switch into position.
12 Lubricate the gear and bearing surfaces of the armature shaft with multi-purpose grease and insert the shaft into the bushes. Make sure that the grease does not spread onto the brushes. Ease the brushes outward and onto the commutator.
13 Check that the yoke magnets are clean and the thrust disc is flat against the bearing. Check the lubricator felt pad has a hole punched on its centre, so that the armature shaft thrust ball will be able to make contact with the thrust disc. Soak the felt pad in clean engine oil and squeeze it out.
14 Refit the yoke over the armature and align the mating marks on the yoke and the motor body. Fit the tie bolts and tighten to the specified torque.
15 Fill the gearbox two thirds full with grease and smear some on the teeth and shaft. Fit the dished washer so that the concave side is towards the gearwheel. Refit the gearwheel into the gearbox.
16 Place the thrust washer bracket (10) over the shaft and fit the crank in the same relative position as it was in before removal.
17 Grip the crank and tighten the shaft nut to the specified torque.
18 Apply some more grease to the gear and refit the cover.
19 The armature endfloat should now be adjusted. To do this, hold the assembly so that the thrust screw is uppermost. Turn the screw in until it just contacts the end of the armature shaft. Now unscrew it one $\frac{1}{4}$ turn and tighten the locknut.

24 Tailgate wiper motor and linkage – removal and refitting

1 The tailgate wiper is a single speed, self-parking assembly which drives a wheelbox through a flexible rack contained in a rigid tube.
2 The motor is located in the left-hand rear quarter and accessible when the trim panel is partially removed. The wheelbox is mounted directly on the tailgate glass (see Chapter 12).
3 Remove the wiper arm/blade assembly just as described for a windscreen wiper in Section 21.
4 Open and raise the tailgate and release the rear quarter trim panel (rear edge). Wedge it outward to give access to the motor.
5 Release the hexagon nut which holds the rack tube to the wiper motor. Remove the wiper motor bracket screws from the inner panel, noting the earth wire under the lower screw.
6 Partially withdraw the wiper motor through the aperture. Disconnect the wiring and withdraw the motor complete with rack nut leaving the rack tube in position.
7 Mark the position of the bracket on the motor and remove the two halves of the bracket.
8 If necessary, the cover can be removed and the rack lifted and disengaged from the pin and slider block.
9 Refitting is a reversal of removal. It will facilitate entry of the rack into the tube if the wheelbox spindle is turned with the fingers at the same time. Remember to connect the earth wire under the lower mounting screw.
10 Operate the motor and switch if off using the tailgate wiper switch, not the ignition key. This will ensure that the motor is in the parked position before refitting the arm/blade to the wheelbox spindle.

25 Tailgate wiper and linkage – overhaul

1 With the motor removed from the car, withdraw the gearbox cover.
2 Extract the circlip (3) from its groove in the gearwheel crankpin. Remove the flat washer, conical spring, friction plate, connecting rod and second flat washer.
3 Extract the circlip and washer from the other end of the shaft. Use a fine cut file to remove any burrs from the circlip groove, so that no damage will occur to the bearing on the gearwheel and shaft as they

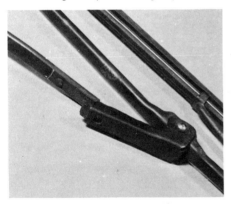
21.1.Wiper blade to arm connection

21.2 Removing a wiper arm nut

27.3 Washer fluid reservoir (viewed from under wing)

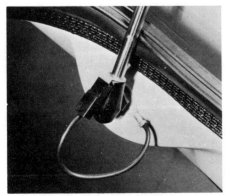
28.1A Heated tailgate connection (lower)

28.1B Heated tailgate connection (upper)

29.1 Radio and heater control panel

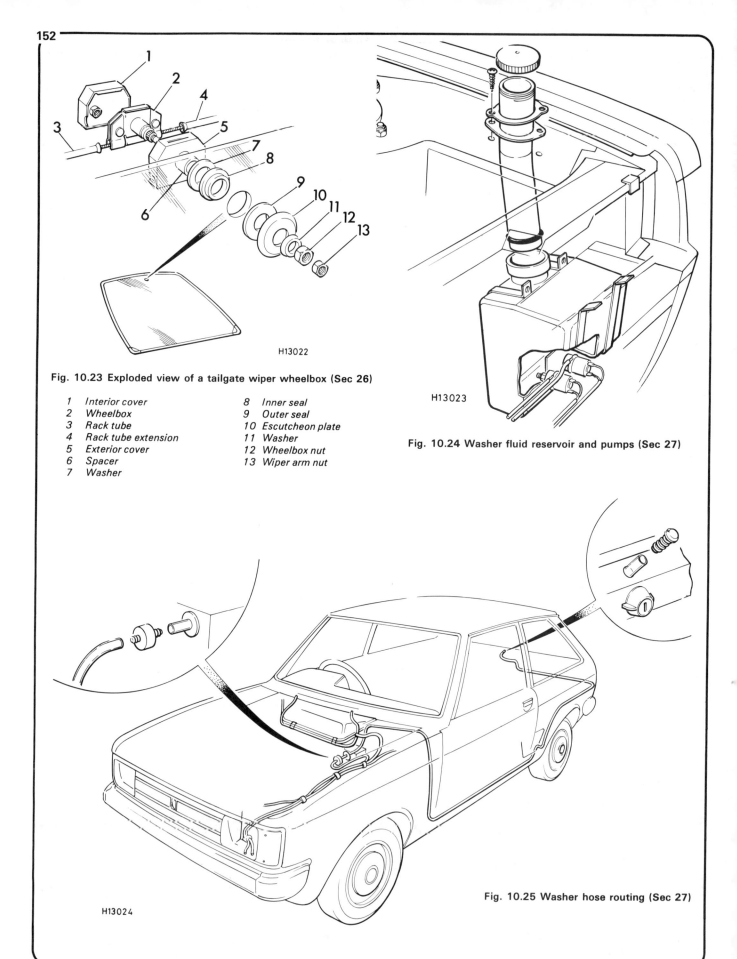

H13022

Fig. 10.23 Exploded view of a tailgate wiper wheelbox (Sec 26)

1 Interior cover	8 Inner seal
2 Wheelbox	9 Outer seal
3 Rack tube	10 Escutcheon plate
4 Rack tube extension	11 Washer
5 Exterior cover	12 Wheelbox nut
6 Spacer	13 Wiper arm nut
7 Washer	

H13023

Fig. 10.24 Washer fluid reservoir and pumps (Sec 27)

Fig. 10.25 Washer hose routing (Sec 27)

H13024

are withdrawn. Remove the dished washer (9) from below the gear.
4 Check the mating marks on the yoke (18) and on the gearbox casing (12). It is essential that the components are reassembled correctly otherwise the armature will rotate in the reverse direction.
5 Unscrew the tie-bolts and withdraw the yoke and the armature. Remove the armature from the yoke.
6 Where necessary, extract the screws that secure the brushgear and the terminal/switch unit. Withdraw both assemblies with their connecting wires.
7 Check all components for wear or damage. If the brushes are worn down to $\frac{3}{16}$ in (4.8 mm) the brushgear must be renewed.
8 Reassembly is a reversal of dismantling but observe the following points: Smear the bearing bushes with clean engine oil. Soak the felt lubricating pad at the yoke bearing with clean engine oil and squeeze out the surplus. Lubricate all other moving parts with a smear of high melting point grease.
9 Make sure that the nylon slider block is fitted correctly into its channel. The slider must be fitted so that the deeper end of the slot on its underside is towards the switch plunger.
10 Make sure that the dished washer is fitted to the gearshaft with its concave side towards the gearwheel. Also make sure that the smaller of the two flat washers is under the connecting rod.

26 Tailgate wiper wheelbox – removal and refitting

1 Remove the wiper arm/blade assembly as previously described.
2 Unscrew and remove the wheelbox spindle nut (photo).
3 Raise the tailgate and remove the wheelbox cover. Slacken the nuts at the back of the wheelbox, then separate the clamp and disengage it from the rack tube.
4 Withdraw the wheelbox from the glass and slide it off the rack.
5 Refitting is a reversal of removal, but turn the wheelbox spindle with the fingers to facilitate engagement of the rack with the wheelbox.
6 Make sure that all the glass seals and washers are refitted in their correct order. Do not overtighten the wheelbox nut.

27 Windscreen and tailgate washers – general

1 The washer fluid container is mounted under the left-hand wing with the filler cap within the engine compartment.
2 The electrically operated washer pumps are mounted on the front of the fluid container. One pump is for the screen, the second pump is for the headlamp washers. It depends on the specification of the particular car how many washer pumps are fitted.
3 To remove the fluid container, extract the screws that hold the filler neck flange in position and withdraw the filler tube (photo).
4 Raise the front of the car and remove the left-hand front wheel.
5 Mark the positions of the washer tubes and electrical connections before detaching them. If the washer tubes will not pull off with reasonable force, pour a little boiling water on the end of the tube to make it pliable. Using excessive force to remove a tube may snap the nozzle from the pump body.
6 To remove a pump from the fluid container, insert a long screwdriver into the filler aperture and jam the blade into one of the slots in the plastic retaining nut. Hold the nut still and unscrew the pump.
7 When refitting a pump, position the nut inside the container by wrapping a piece of wire round it. Hold the nut still for tightening, again using the long screwdriver.
8 Washer jets are adjustable by inserting a pin into the jet and moving the jet ball. Do not insert the pin too deeply when adjusting.

28 Heated tailgate

1 The tailgate heater element is connected to terminals at the top and bottom of the gas support struts (photos).
2 Never stick labels over a heater element or clean the glass with a wet leather or cloth in the direction which the filaments run.
3 Take care not to scratch the heater element with untidily packed articles in the luggage area.
4 Repair of a damaged element can be carried out, but this is a specialist job and small quantities of repair material are not generally available.

29 Radio and tape player – general fitting

1 The radio fitted during production of the car is fitted in the facia panel below the heater controls (photo).
2 If a radio is being fitted at a later date, it is recommended that this position is used after prising out the blanking plate.
3 A radio or tape player is an expensive item to buy and will only give its best performance if fitted properly. It is useless to expect concert hall performance from a unit that is suspended from the dash panel on string with its speaker resting on the back seat or parcel shelf! If you do not wish to do the fitting yourself there are many in-car entertainment specialists who can do the fitting for you.
4 Make sure the unit purchased is of the same polarity as the vehicle. Ensure that units with adjustable polarity are correctly set before the commencement of fitting.
5 It is difficult to give specific information with regard to fiting, as final positioning of the radio/tape player, speakers and aerial is entirely a matter of personal preference. However, the following paragraphs give guidelines to follow, which are relevant to all installations.

Radios

Most radios are a standardised size of 7 inches wide, by 2 inches deep; this ensures that they will fit into the radio aperture provided in most cars. Alternatively, a special console can be purchased which will fit between the dashpanel and the floor, or on the transmission tunnel. These consoles can also be used for additional switches and instrumentation if required.

Some radios will have mounting brackets provided with instructions, others will need to be fitted using drilled and slotted metal strips, bent to form mounting brackets; these strips are available from most accessory shops. The unit must be properly earthed, by fitting a separate earth lead between the casing of the radio and the vehicle frame.

Use the radio manufacturers' instructions when wiring the radio into the vehicle's electrical system. If no instructions are available, refer to the relevant wiring diagram to find the location of the radio 'feed' connection in the vehicle's wiring circuit. A 1–2 amp 'in-line' fuse must be fitted in the radio's feed wire; a choke may also be necessary (see next Section).

The type of aerial used, and its fitted position, is a matter of personal preference. In general the taller the aerial, the better the reception. It is best to fit a fully retractable aerial, especially if a mechanical car-wash is used or if you live in an area where cars tend to be vandalised. In this respect electric aerials which are raised and lowered automatically when switching the radio on or off are convenient, but are more likely to give trouble than the manual type.

When choosing a site for the aerial the following points should be considered:

(a) The aerial lead should be as short as possible; this means that the aerial should be mounted at the front of the vehicle
(b) The aerial must be mounted as far away from the distributor and HT leads as possible
(c) The part of the aerial which protrudes beneath the mounting point must not foul the roadwheels, or anything else
(d) If possible, the aerial should be positioned so that the coaxial lead does not have to be routed through the engine compartment
(e) The plane of the panel on which the aerial is mounted should not be so steeply angled that the aerial cannot be mounted vertically (in relation to the 'end-on' aspect of the car). Most aerials have a small amount of adjustment available

Having decided on a mounting position, a relatively large hole will have to be made in the panel. The exact size of the hole will depend upon the specific aerial being fitted, although generally, the hole required is of $\frac{3}{4}$ inch diameter. A 'tank-cutter' of the relevant diameter is the best tool to use for making the hole. This tool needs a small diameter pilot hole drilled through the panel, through which the tool clamping bolt is inserted. When the hole has been made, the raw edges should be de-burred with a file and then painted, to prevent corrosion.

Fit the aerial according to the manufacturer's instructions. If the aerial is very tall, or if it protrudes beneath the mounting panel for a considerable distance, it is a good idea to fit a stay between the aerial and the vehicle frame. This stay can be manufactured from the slotted and drilled metal strips previously mentioned. The stay should be securely screwed or bolted in place. For best reception it is advisable

LARGE TERMINAL

BOLT DOWN TO EARTH
(CLEAN WELL FIRST)

1.0uf–3.0uf

HEAVY WIRE

THIN WIRE

LOOM

GENERATOR

H 5353.

SMALL
TERMINAL

Generator capacitor

TO IGNITION
SWITCH

TO DISTRIBUTOR

TO CONTACT BREAKER

H 5354

COIL

Ignition coil suppressor

TO COIL

DISTRIBUTOR

INTERNAL RESISTOR

SCREW IN
FOR HT LEAD

Resistive spark plug caps

COIL

H 5356

DISTRIBUTOR

INTERNAL
RESISTOR

TWIN SCREW–IN

'In-line' suppressors

Typical HT lead suppressors

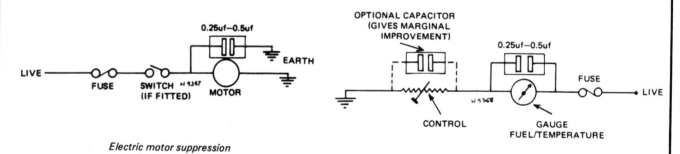

0.25uf–0.5uf

LIVE

FUSE

SWITCH
(IF FITTED)

H 5367

MOTOR

EARTH

Electric motor suppression

OPTIONAL CAPACITOR
(GIVES MARGINAL
IMPROVEMENT)

0.25uf–0.5uf

FUSE

H 5368

CONTROL

GAUGE
FUEL/TEMPERATURE

LIVE

Suppression of gauges and control units

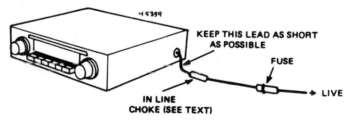

H 5359

KEEP THIS LEAD AS SHORT
AS POSSIBLE

FUSE

IN LINE
CHOKE (SEE TEXT)

LIVE

Location of in-line choke

Fig. 10.26 Typical radio interference suppressors and connections (Sec. 30)

to fit an earth lead between the aerial and the vehicle frame.

It will probably be necessary to drill one or two holes through bodywork panels in order to feed the aerial leads into the interior of the car. Where this is the case ensure that the holes are fitted with rubber grommets to protect the cable, and to stop possible entry of water.

Positioning and fitting of the speaker depends mainly on its type. Generally, the speaker is designed to fit directly into the aperture already provided in the car. Where this is the case, fitting the speaker is just a matter of removing the protective grille from the aperture and screwing or bolting the speaker in place. Take great care not to damage the speaker diaphragm whilst doing this. It is a good idea to fit a 'gasket' between the speaker frame and the mounting panel, in order to prevent vibration; some speakers will already have such a gasket fitted.

When connecting a rear mounted speaker to the radio, the wires should be routed through the vehicle beneath the carpets or floor mats, preferably through the middle, or along the side of the floorpan, where they will not be trodden on by passengers. Make the relevant connections as directed by the radio manufacturer.

By now you will have several yards of additional wiring in the car; use PVC tape to secure this wiring out of harm's way. Do not leave electrical leads dangling. Ensure that all new electrical connections are properly made (wires twisted together will not do) and completely secure.

The radio should now be working, but before you pack away your tools it will be necessary to 'trim' the radio to the aerial. Follow the radio manufacturer's instructions regarding this adjustment.

Tape players

Fitting instructions for both cartridge and cassette stereo players are the same and in general the same rules apply as when fitting a radio. Tape players are not usually prone to electrical interference like radio, although it can occur, so positioning is not so critical. If possible the player should be mounted on an 'even-keel'. Also, it must be possible for a driver wearing a seat belt to reach the unit in order to change, or turn over, tapes.

For the best results from speakers designed to be recessed into a panel, mount them so that the back of the speaker protrudes into an enclosed chamber within the car (eg door interiors or the rear quarter panels).

To fit recessed type speakers in the front doors, first check that there is sufficient room to mount a speaker in each door without it fouling the latch or window winding mechanism. Hold the speaker against the skin of the door, and draw a line around the periphery of the speaker. With the speaker removed, draw a second 'cutting-line', within the first, to allow enough room for the entry of the speaker back, but at the same time providing a broad seat for the speaker flange. When you are sure that the 'cutting-line' is correct, drill a series of holes around its periphery. Pass a hacksaw blade through one of the holes and then cut through the metal between the holes until the centre section of the panel falls out.

De-burr the edges of the hole and then paint the raw metal to prevent corrosion. Cut a corresponding hole in the door trim panel, ensuring that it will be completely covered by the speaker grille. Now drill a hole in the door edge and a corresponding hole in the door surround. These holes are to feed the speaker leads through, so fit grommets. Pass the speaker leads through the door trim, door skin and out through the holes in the side of the door and door surround. Refit the door trim panel and then secure the speaker to the door using self-tapping screws. **Note**: *If the speaker is fitted with a shield to prevent water dripping on it, ensure that this shield is at the top.*

30 Radio and tape player – suppression of interference

To eliminate buzzes and other unwanted noises, costs very little and is not as difficult as sometimes thought. With a modicum of common sense and patience, and following the instructions in these paragraphs, interference can be virtually eliminated.

The first cause for concern is the generator. The noise this makes over the radio is like an electric mixer and the noise speeds up when you rev up (if you wish to prove the point, you can remove the drivebelt and try it). The remedy for this is simple: connect a 1.0 mfd/3.0 mfd capacitor between earth, probably the bolt that holds down the generator base, and the *large* terminal on the alternator. This is most important, for if you connect it to the small terminal, you will probably damage the generator permanently.

A second common cause of electrical interference is the ignition system. Here a 1.0 mfd capacitor must be connected between earth and the + terminal on the coil. This may stop the 'tick, tick, tick' sound that comes over the speaker. Next comes the spark itself.

There are several ways of curing interference from the ignition HT system. One is to use carbon film HT leads (fitted as original equipment on the Sunbeam) and the more successful method is to use resistive spark plug caps of about 10 000 ohm to 15 000 ohm resistance. If, due to lack of room, these cannot be used, an alternative is to use in-line suppressors. If the interference is not too bad, you can get away with only one suppressor in the coil to distributor line. If the interference does continue (a 'clacking' noise) then service all HT leads.

At this stage, it is advisable to check that the radio and the aerial are well earthed, and to see that the aerial plug is pushed well into the seat and that the radio is properly trimmed (see preceding Section). In addition, check that the wire which supplied the power to the set is as short as possible and does not wander all over the car. At this stage, it is a good idea to check that the fuse is of the correct rating. For most sets this will be about 1 to 2 amps.

At this point, the more usual causes of interference have been suppressed. If the problem still exists, a look at the cause of interference may help to pinpoint the component generating the stray electrical discharges.

The radio picks up electromagnetic waves in the air; some are made by radio stations and other broadcasters and some, not wanted, are made by the car. The home made signals are produced by stray electrical discharges floating around the car. Common producers of these signals are electric motors; ie, the windscreen wipers, electric screen washers, electric window winders, heater fan or an electric aerial if fitted. Other sources of interference are electric fuel pumps, flashing turn signal and instruments. The remedy for these cases is shown for an electric motor whose interference is not too bad and for instrument suppression. Turn signals are not normally suppressed. In recent years, radio manufacturers have included in the live line of the radio, in addition to the fuse, an 'in-line' choke.

All the foregoing components are available from radio stores or accessory shops. If you have an electric clock fitted, this should be suppressed by connecting a 0.5 mfd capacitor directly across it.

If after all this, you are still experiencing radio interference, first assess how bad it is. The human ear can filter out unobtrusive unwanted noises quite easily, but if you are still adamant about eradicating the noise, then continue.

As a first step, a few experts seem to favour a screen between the radio and the engine. This is OK as far as it goes, literally! The whole set is screened and if interference can get past that, then a small piece of aluminium is not going to stop it.

A more sensible way of screening is to discover if interference is coming down the wires. First, take the live lead; interference can get between the set and the choke (hence the reason for keeping the wires short). One remedy here is to screen the wire and this is done by buying screened wire and fitting that. The loudspeaker lead could be screened also to prevent 'pick-up' getting back to the radio, although this is unlikely.

Without doubt, the worst source of radio interference comes from the ignition HT leads, even if they have been suppressed. The ideal way of suppressing these is to slide screening tubes over the leads themselves. As this is impractical, we can place an aluminium shield over the majority of the lead areas. In a vee or twin-cam engine, this is relatively easy but for a straight engine the results are not particularly good.

Now for the really impossible cases, here are a few tips to try out. Where metal comes into contact with metal, an electrical disturbance is caused, which is why good clean connections are essential. To remove interference due to overlapping or butting panels, you must bridge the join with a wide braided earth strap (like that from the frame to the engine/transmission). The most common moving parts that could create noise and should be strapped are, in order of importance.

(a) Silencer to frame
(b) Exhaust pipe to engine block and frame
(c) Air cleaner to frame
(d) Front and rear bumpers to frame
(e) Steering column to frame
(f) Bonnet and boot lids to frame

These faults are most pronounced when the engine is idling or labouring under load. Although the moving parts are already connected with nuts, bolts, ets, these do tend to rust and corrode, thus creating a high resistance interference source.

If you have a ragged sounding pulse when mobile, this could be wheel or tyre static. This can be cured by buying some anti-static powder and sprinkling it liberally inside the tyres.

If the interference takes the shape of a high pitched screeching noise that changes its note when the car is in motion and only comes now and then, this could be related to the aerial, especially if it is of the telescopic or whip type. This source can be cured quite simply by pushing a small rubber ball on top of the aerial as this breaks the electric field before it can form; but it would be much better to buy yourself a new aerial of a reputable brand. If, on the other hand, you are getting a loud rushing sound every time you brake, then this is brake static. The effect is most prominent on hot dry days and is cured only by fitting a special kit, which is quite expensive.

In conclusion, it is pointed out that it is relatively easy, and therefore cheap, to eliminate 95 per cent of all noises, but to eliminate the final 5 per cent is time and money consuming. It is up to the individual to decide if it is worth it. Please remember also, that you will not get concert hall performance out of a cheap radio.

31 Fault diagnosis – electrical system

Symptom	Reason/s
Starter fails to turn engine	Battery discharged Battery defective internally Battery terminal leads loose or earth lead not securely attached to body Loose or broken connections in starter motor circuit Starter motor switch or solenoid faulty Starter brushes badly worn, sticking, or brush wires loose Commutator dirty, worn or burnt Starter motor armature faulty Field coils earthed
Starter turns engine very slowly	Battery in discharged condition Starter brushes badly worn, sticking or brush wires loose Loose wires in starter motor circut
Starter spins but does not turn engine	Pinion or flywheel gear teeth broken or worn Battery discharged
Starter motor noisy or excessively rough engagement	Pinion or flywheel gear teeth broken or worn Starter motor retaining bolts loose
Battery will not hold charge for more than a few days	Battery defective internally Electrolyte level too low Plate separators no longer fully effective Battery plates severely sulphated Drive belt slipping Battery terminal connections loose or corroded Alternator not charging Short in lighting circuit causing continual battery drain Regulator unit not working correctly
Ignition light fails to go out, battery runs flat in a few days	Drive belt loose and slipping or broken Alternator brushes worn, sticking, broken or dirty Alternator brush springs weak or broken Internal fault in alternator
Horn operates all the time	Horn push either earthed or stuck down Horn cable to horn push earthed
Horn fails to operate	Blown fuse Cable or cable connection loose, broken or disconnected Horn has an internal fault
Horn emits intermittent or unsatisfactory noise	Cable connections loose
Lights do not come on	If engine not running, battery discharged Wire connections loose, disconnected or broken Light switch shorting or otherwise faulty
Lights come on but fade out	If engine not running battery discharged Light bulb filament burnt out Wire connections loose, disconnected or broken Light switch shorting or otherwise faulty
Lights give very poor illumination	Lamp glasses dirty Lamps badly out of adjustment

Lights work erratically – flashing on and off, especially over bumps	Battery terminals or earth connection loose Lights not earthing properly Contacts in light switch faulty
Wiper motor fails to work	Blown fuse Wire connections loose, disconnected or broken Brushes badly worn Armature worn or faulty Field coils faulty
Wiper motor works very slowly and takes excessive current	Commutator dirty, grease or burnt Armature bearings dirty or unaligned Armature badly worn or faulty
Wiper motor works slowly and take little current	Brushes badly worn Commutator dirty, greasy or burnt Armature badly worn or faulty
Wiper motor works but wiper blades remain static	Wiper motor gearbox parts badly worn

Location of snap connectors and multiplugs. The location of the multiplug connectors are shown individually on the wiring diagram, but on the vehicle they are as detailed below.

Qty	Type	Location
1	2 way multiplug	Front of left-hand wing valance
1	2 way multiplug	Front of right-hand wing valance
1	2 way multiplug	Adjacent to battery
1	3 way multiplug	Below battery tray
1	Tube connector, double	Adjacent to fuse unit, engine side
1	Tube connector, single	Adjacent to fuse unit, engine side
3	Tube connectors, single	On centre-line of car, below centre panel
1	Tube connector, double	On centre-line of car, below centre panel
3	Tube connectors, double	At bottom of left-hand. 'A' post
2	Tube connectors, single	Behind left-hand quarter panel
1	2 way multiplug	Adjacent to left-hand rear lamp cluster

Colour code

B	Black	P	Purple
G	Green	R	Red
K	Pink	S	Slate
L/G	Light green	U	Blue
N	Brown	W	White
O	Orange	Y	Yellow

Key to symbols

- Tube connector
- Plug and socket
- Moulded cable connection (part of harness, not to be separated)
- Earth by cable
- Earth through unit
- When fitted

Key to wiring diagrams

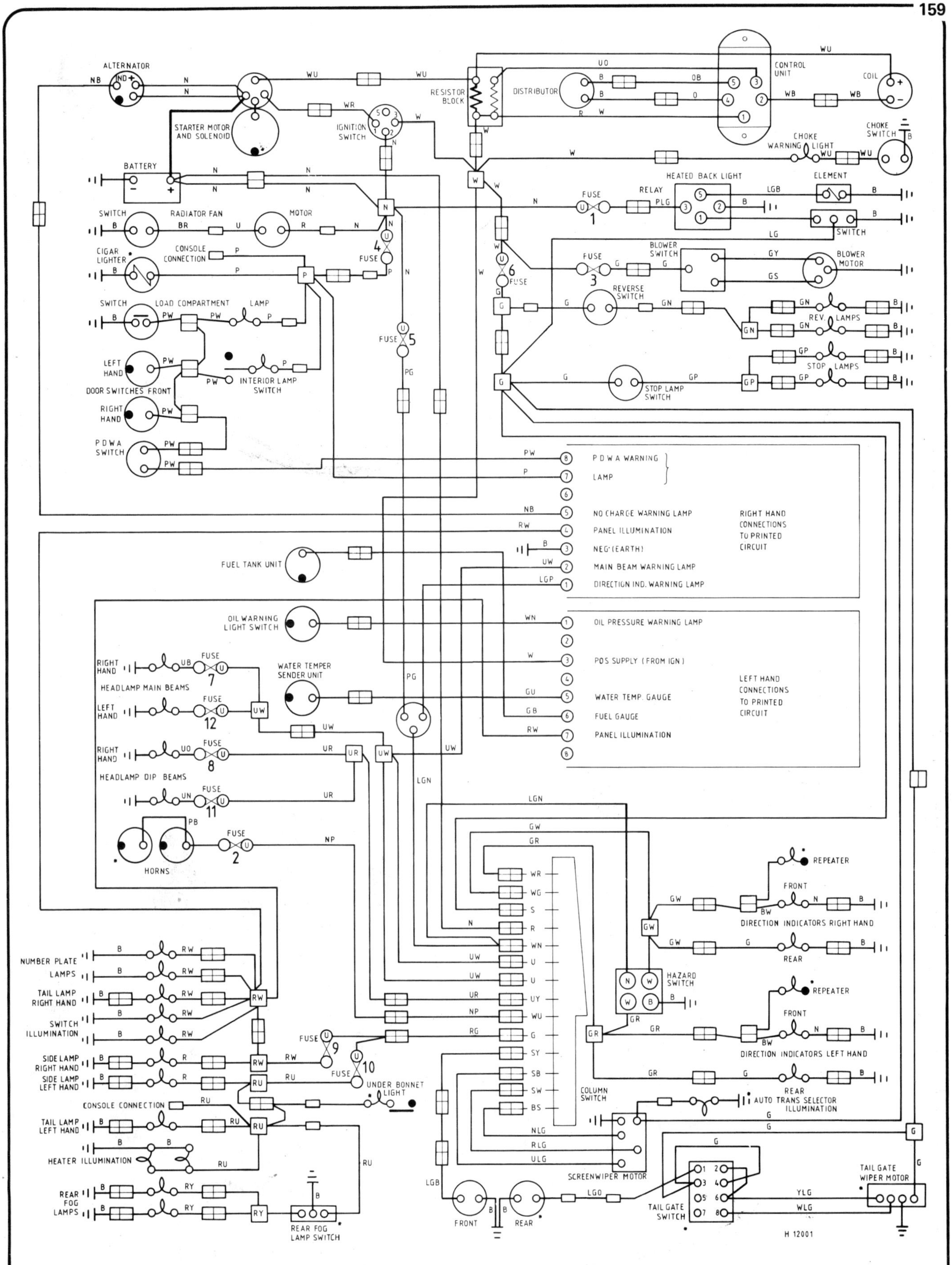

Fig. 10.27 Wiring diagram. Right-hand drive models with two-dial instrument panel

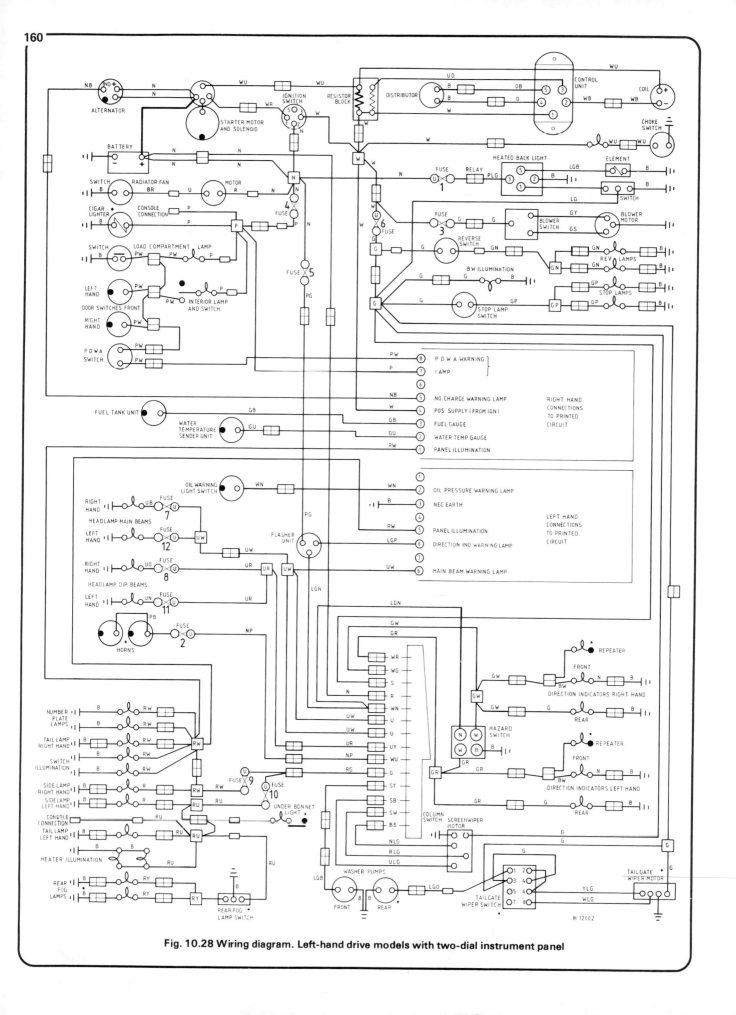

Fig. 10.28 Wiring diagram. Left-hand drive models with two-dial instrument panel

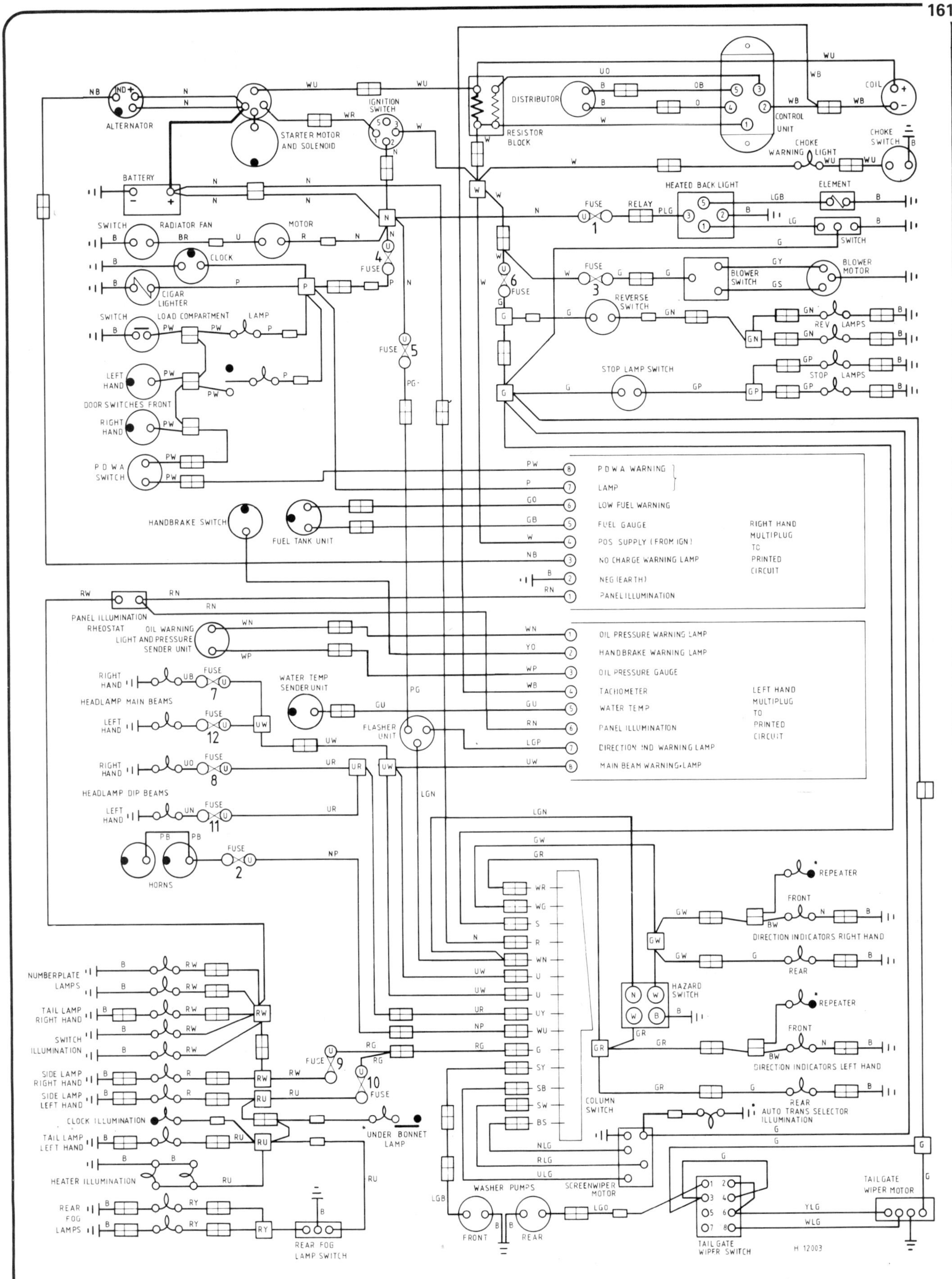

ALTERNATOR
NB IND+
N
N
WU
IGNITION SWITCH
WU
U0
DISTRIBUTOR
B
0B
5 3
WB
WB
COIL
+ −
WR
STARTER MOTOR AND SOLENOID
W
W
B
CONTROL UNIT
4 2 1
CHOKE WARNING LIGHT
WU
WU
CHOKE SWITCH
BATTERY − +
RESISTOR BLOCK
W
HEATED BACK LIGHT
LGB
ELEMENT
B
N
N
W W
FUSE 1
RELAY
PLG
3 5
1 2
B
LG
SWITCH
G
SWITCH
RADIATOR FAN
BR
MOTOR
U R
N
N
N
U
FUSE 4
WU
FUSE 6
W
FUSE 3
G
BLOWER SWITCH
GY
GS
BLOWER MOTOR
CLOCK
B
CIGAR LIGHTER
P
P
P
G
REVERSE SWITCH
GN
GN
GN
REV LAMPS
SWITCH
LOAD COMPARTMENT
PW PW
LAMP
P
FUSE 5
PG
G
STOP LAMP SWITCH
GP
GP GP
STOP LAMPS
LEFT HAND
PW
PW
DOOR SWITCHES FRONT
RIGHT HAND
PW
PDWA SWITCH
PW
PW
PW
8
PDWA WARNING
P
7
LAMP
GO
6
LOW FUEL WARNING
GB
5
FUEL GAUGE
RIGHT HAND MULTIPLUG TO PRINTED CIRCUIT
W
4
POS SUPPLY (FROM IGN)
HANDBRAKE SWITCH
NB
3
NO CHARGE WARNING LAMP
FUEL TANK UNIT
B
RN
2
NEG (EARTH)
1
PANEL ILLUMINATION
RW
RN
RN
PANEL ILLUMINATION RHEOSTAT
OIL WARNING LIGHT AND PRESSURE SENDER UNIT
WN
WP
WN
1
OIL PRESSURE WARNING LAMP
YO
2
HANDBRAKE WARNING LAMP
WP
3
OIL PRESSURE GAUGE
WB
4
TACHOMETER
LEFT HAND MULTIPLUG TO PRINTED CIRCUIT
RIGHT HAND
UB
FUSE 7
WATER TEMP SENDER UNIT
GU
GU
5
WATER TEMP
HEADLAMP MAIN BEAMS
LEFT HAND
FUSE 12
UW
RN
6
PANEL ILLUMINATION
LGP
7
DIRECTION IND WARNING LAMP
FLASHER UNIT
UW
8
MAIN BEAM WARNING LAMP
RIGHT HAND
U0
FUSE 8
UR
UR
UW
PG
HEADLAMP DIP BEAMS
LEFT HAND
UN
FUSE 11
UR
LGN
LGN
PB PB
GW
HORNS
FUSE 2
NP
GR
REPEATER
WR
WG
S
R
WN
GW
GW
FRONT
BW
DIRECTION INDICATORS RIGHT HAND
NUMBERPLATE LAMPS
B RW
RW
UW
U
U
GW
G
REAR
TAIL LAMP RIGHT HAND
B RW
GW
HAZARD SWITCH
N W
W B
SWITCH ILLUMINATION
B RW
UR
UY
NP
WU
GR
REPEATER
SIDE LAMP RIGHT HAND
R RW
RW
RG
RG
FUSE 9
SY
GR
GR
FRONT
BW
N
B
SIDE LAMP LEFT HAND
R RU
RU
SB
SW
FUSE 10
DIRECTION INDICATORS LEFT HAND
CLOCK ILLUMINATION
RU
BS
COLUMN SWITCH
GR
REAR
TAIL LAMP LEFT HAND
B RU
RU
UNDER BONNET LAMP
NLG
AUTO TRANS SELECTOR ILLUMINATION
G
G
HEATER ILLUMINATION
RU
RU
RLG
ULG
TAILGATE WIPER MOTOR
REAR FOG LAMPS
B RY
RY
RY
REAR FOG LAMP SWITCH
LGB
WASHER PUMPS
FRONT REAR
LGO
SCREENWIPER MOTOR
G
TAILGATE WIPER SWITCH
1 2 3 4 5 6 7 8
YLG
WLG
H 12003

Fig. 10.29 Wiring diagram. Right-hand drive models with six-dial instrument panel

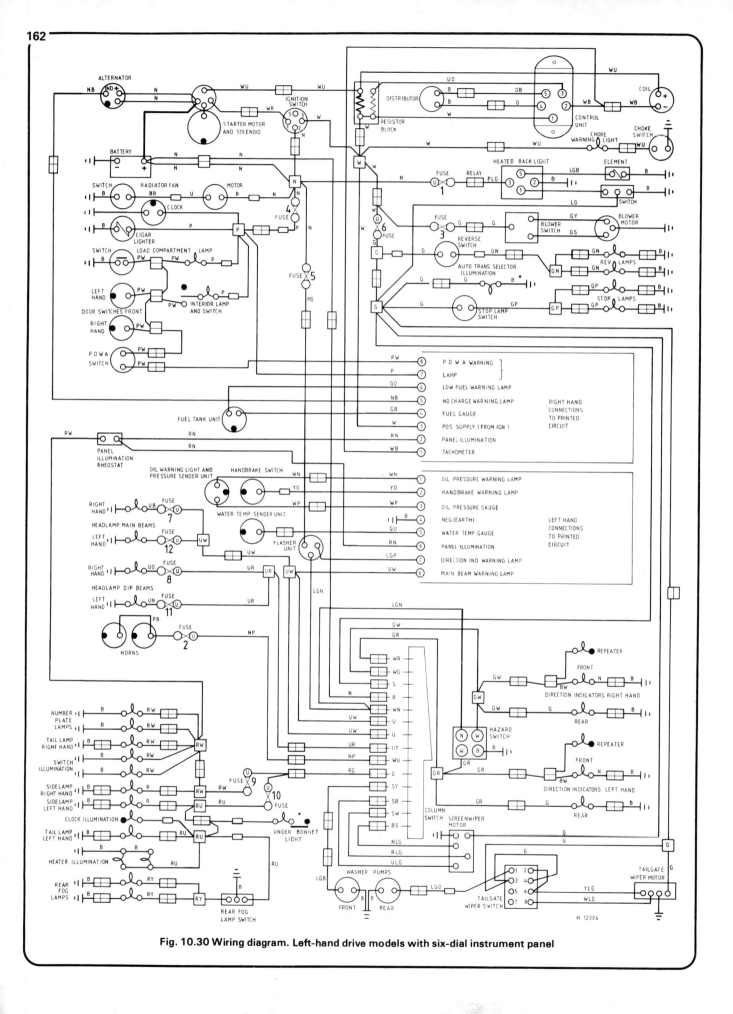

Fig. 10.30 Wiring diagram. Left-hand drive models with six-dial instrument panel

Chapter 11 Suspension and steering

Contents

Specifications

Front suspension

Type .... Independent, MacPherson strut, coil springs and stabiliser bar
Front hub endfloat .... 0.0015 to 0.004 in (0.04 to 0.010 mm)
Track .... 51.80 in (1316 mm)

Rear suspension

Type .... Four link with coil springs and telescopic hydraulic shock absorbers
Track .... 51.30 in (1303 mm)

Steering

Type .... Rack and pinion (Burman)
Overall ratio .... 17.65 : 1
Number of turns lock-to-lock of steering wheel 3.66
Turning circle (between kerbs) .... $31\frac{1}{2}$ ft (9.6 m)
Toe-in .... $\frac{1}{32}$ to $\frac{1}{8}$ in (1.0 to 3.0 mm)
Wheel angles (at full lock):
    Inner .... 38° 10'
    Outer .... 36° 30'
Camber .... 0° ± 45'
Castor .... 1° ± 30'
Steering axis inclination .... 12° 43'

Roadwheels

Type and size .... Pressed steel $4\frac{1}{2}$J x 13
Wheel stud thread .... 12 mm

Tyres

Radial ply size:
    930 model . . . .   145 x 13
    1300/1600 models . . . .   155 x 13

Pressures (cold):	Front	Rear
930 model	21 lbf/in² (1.45 bar)	25 lbf/in² (1.75 bar)
1300/1600 models	22 lbf/in² (1.5 bar)	22 lbf/in² (1.5 bar)
If full luggage load carried in addition to four occupants, increase pressures to:		
930 model	22 lbf/in² (1.5 bar)	32 lbf/in² (2.2 bar)
1300/1600 models	22 lbf/in² (1.5 bar)	28 lbf/in² (1.9 bar)

For continuous high speed driving, the pressures on 1300/1600 models may be increased by 2 lbf in² (0.14 bar)

Torque wrench settings

	lbf ft	Nm
Front suspension		
Steering arm to stub axle carrier	58	78.5
Strut top mounting to valance	15	20.5
Strut damper rod nut	35	47.5
Anti-roll bar bracket screws	28	38
Tie-rod to body bracket	40	54
Tie-rod to track control arm	36	49
Tie-rod bracket to body	28	38
Track control arm ball-stud nut	44	59.6
Track control arm to crossmember	30	41
Track-rod end ball-stud nut	28	38
Track-rod end locknut	30	41
Crossmember to body bolts	54	73
Engine mounting brackets to crossmember	27	36.5
Rack and pinion mounting brackets	18	24.5
Rear suspension		
Shock absorber upper mounting nuts	13	17.6
Shock absorber lower mounting bolt	12	16.3
Upper and lower link pivot bolts	44	59.6
Steering		
Rack and pinion mounting brackets	18	24.5
Steering wheel nut	32	43.5
Intermediate shaft to column	18	24.5
Flexible coupling to intermediate shaft	15	20.5
Flexible coupling to pinion flange	15	20.5
Pinion flange pinch bolt	15	20.5
Column upper mounting bracket to fascia	29	40
Column U-bolts	5	3.5
Column support to pedal mounting bracket	17	23
Column to support bracket	17	23
Roadwheel nuts	55	75

1 General description

Front suspension

The front suspension is of the MacPherson strut type, incorporating a hydraulic damper unit and coil spring. An anti-roll bar is fitted to reduce rolling on corners.

Rear suspension

The rear suspension is of the four link and two coil spring type, connected between the body and the rigid rear axle. Telescopic, hydraulic shock absorbers are used.

Steering

Rack and pinion steering gear is fitted. The steering column incorporates a flexible coupling and a universal joint.

2 Maintenance and inspection

1   Inspect the condition of all rubber gaiters, balljoint covers and particularly the convoluted rubber protectors at each end of the steering gear, for splits or deterioration. Renew as necessary after reference to the appropriate section of this Chapter.
2   Check the security of the locknuts on the outer track rod ends, also the ball-pin nuts.
3   Check the security of the front strut securing nuts and examine the condition of the drag strut and stabiliser bar rubber bushes. Renew as necessary.
4   At the intervals specified in 'Routine maintenance' dismantle, clean, repack and adjust the front hub bearings and check the front wheel alignment as described in this Chapter, Section 29.
5   No maintenance is required for the rear suspension, other than periodically checking the security of the link and shock absorber mounting bolts and nuts in accordance with the torque wrench settings given in the Specifications.
6   The top and bottom anchorage points of the hydraulic rear shock absorber should be firm. If there are signs of oil on the outside of the lower cylinder section it indicates that the seals have gone and the shock absorber must be renewed. The shock absorber may also have failed internally and this is more difficult to detect. It is usually indicated by excessive bounce at the rear end and axle patter or 'tramp' on even surfaces. When this occurs remove the shock absorber in order to check its damping power in both directions.
7   The front suspension should be checked by first jacking the car up so that the wheel is clear of the ground. Then place another jack under the track control arm near the outer end. When the arm is raised by the jack any movement in the suspension strut ball stud will be apparent. So also will any wear in the inner track control arm bush. The balljoint endfloat should not exceed 0.060 in (1.5 mm). However, it is not possible to gauge this movement very accurately without removing the joint, so if there is some doubt it is better to be on the safe side and dismantle it. There should be no play of any sort in the track control arm bush.

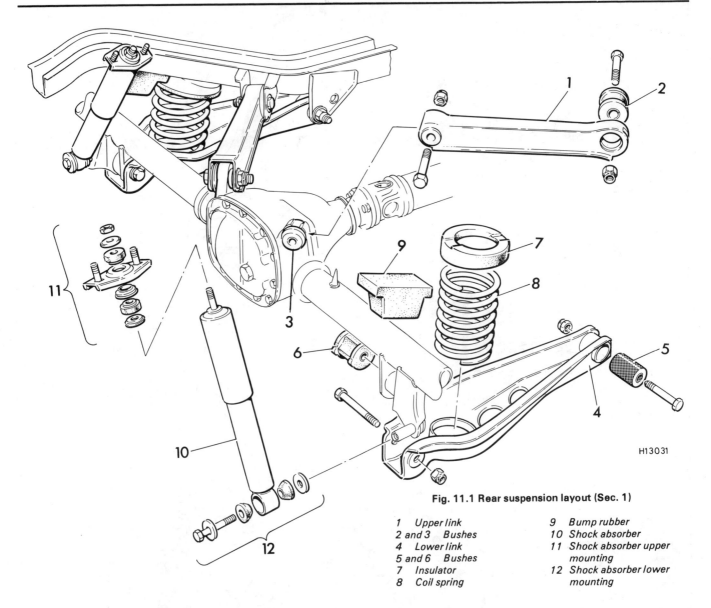

Fig. 11.1 Rear suspension layout (Sec. 1)

1 Upper link	9 Bump rubber
2 and 3 Bushes	10 Shock absorber
4 Lower link	11 Shock absorber upper
5 and 6 Bushes	mounting
7 Insulator	12 Shock absorber lower
8 Coil spring	mounting

8   The top end of the suspension unit should have no discernible movement and to check it, grip the strut at the lower spring seat and try pushing it from side to side. There should be no detectable movement, either between the outer cylinder and the inner piston rod at the top of the piston rod near the upper mounting.

9   With the help of an assistant, have him gently turn the steering wheel while you observe the movement of the front roadwheels. Any lost motion will indicate wear in the track-rod end balljoints, the steering gear itself, or wheel bearings.

3   Front hub bearings – adjustment

1   Front hub endfloat is essential to prevent brake pad or wheel bearing efficiency being reduced (photo).

2   To carry out the adjustment it is recommended that the disc pads are removed, the car jacked up and the road wheel removed from each front hub in turn.

3   Prise off the hub dust cap. This is normally quite simply achieved by tapping the rounded part of the cap in an outward direction.

4   Withdraw the split pin now exposed and remove the castellated lock cap (photo).

5   Using a torque wrench (setting 15 to 20 lbf ft) on the hub nut, tighten to the indicated torque at the same time rotating the hub.

6   Back off the nut 1 to 1½ flats and check the endfloat by using either a dial gauge or feelers between the hub nut and the thrust

washer. The correct adjustment is obtained when the endfloat is as listed in the Specifications section.

7   Fit a new split pin to the castellated lock cap. Do not fill the dust cap with grease.

4   Front hub bearings – removal, lubrication and refitting

1   Raise the front of the car, support securely and remove the roadwheel.

2   Loosen the locknut which secures the brake flexible hose to the suspension strut bracket.

3   Unscrew and remove the caliper mounting bolts, taking care to extract and retain any mounting shims which may be fitted.

4   Withdraw the caliper rearwards and upwards from the disc, sliding the hose out of its slot in the suspension strut bracket. Tie the caliper up out of the way with a piece of wire, making sure not to strain the flexible hose. Place a pad of clean rag or other packing between the two pads to keep them apart.

5   Remove the dust cap, split pin and lock cap as described in the preceding Section.

6   Unscrew the nut from the end of the stub axle and extract the thrust washer (photo).

7   Withdraw the hub/disc assembly, catching the outer bearing as it is displaced.

8   Check that the distance piece at the inner end of the stub axle

166

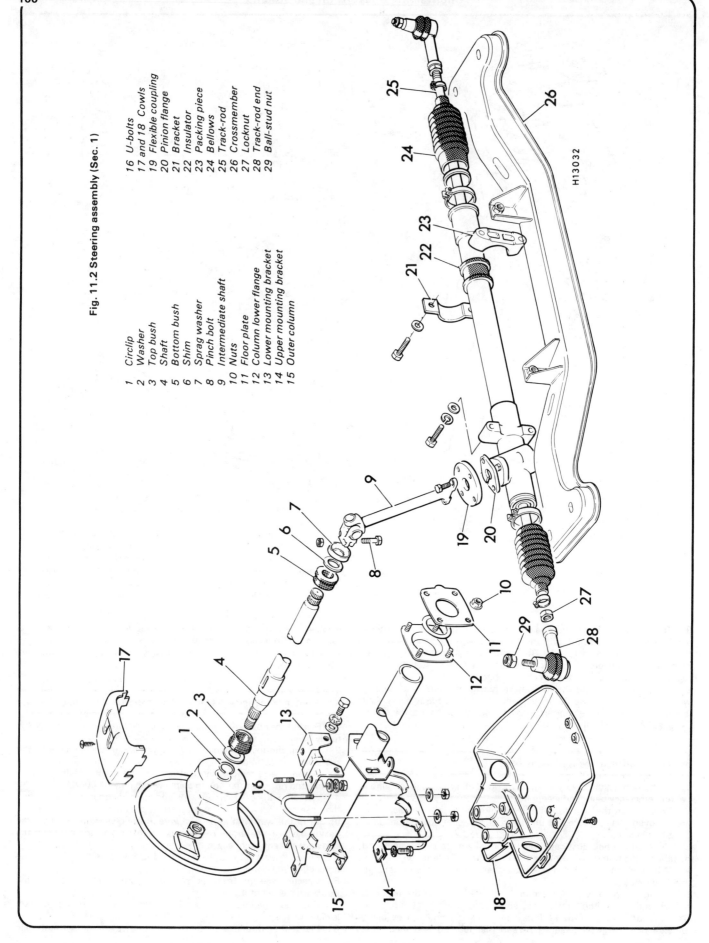

Fig. 11.2 Steering assembly (Sec. 1)

1 Circlip
2 Washer
3 Top bush
4 Shaft
5 Bottom bush
6 Shim
7 Sprag washer
8 Pinch bolt
9 Intermediate shaft
10 Nuts
11 Floor plate
12 Column lower flange
13 Lower mounting bracket
14 Upper mounting bracket
15 Outer column
16 U-bolts
17 and 18 Cowls
19 Flexible coupling
20 Pinion flange
21 Bracket
22 Insulator
23 Packing piece
24 Bellows
25 Track-rod
26 Crossmember
27 Locknut
28 Track-rod end
29 Ball-stud nut

H13032

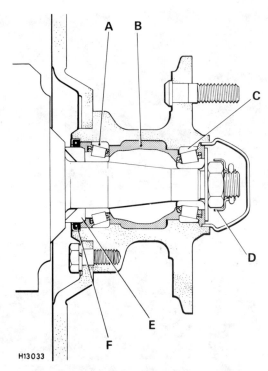

Fig. 11.3 Sectional view of a front hub (Sec. 4)

A	Inboard bearing track	D	Nut locking cap
B	Grease packing area	E	Distance piece
C	Outboard bearing track	F	Oil seal

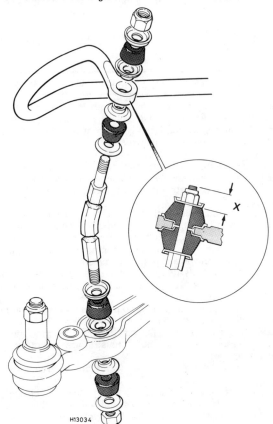

Fig. 11.4 Stabiliser bar drop link arrangement (Sec. 5)

X is $\frac{9}{16}$ to $\frac{5}{8}$ in (14.29 to 15.88 mm)

came out with the hub assembly, if not, slide it off now.

9   If the bearings, races and oil seal are in good condition, then wipe out all the old lubricant and pack new grease between the inner and outer bearings as indicated. Do not over-lubricate.

10   If the oil seal is worn and grease has obviously been escaping, prise out the old seal, discard it and tap in a new one.

11   If the bearings are worn, the inner and outer bearing tracks must be drifted out of the hub using a brass drift. Drive the new tracks into position using a suitable piece of tubing as a drift. If both front hubs are being overhauled at the same time, do not mix up the bearing components by opening two bearing packs at the same time, as the bearing components are manufactured in matched sets.

12   Fit a new oil seal and pack the hub with grease as described in paragraph 9.

13   Refit the distance piece into the oil seal so that the bevel on the inner diameter is visible when fitted. Lightly smear the lips of the oil seal with grease and push the hub assembly onto the stub axle, taking care not to damage the oil seal lips with the axle threads.

14   Push the outer bearing into position, fit the thrust washer and nut, finger tight.

15   Adjust the hub endfloat as described in Section 3.

16   Refit the caliper, tightening the mounting bolts to the specified torque.

17   Refit the roadwheels and lower the car.

5   Stabiliser bar – removal and refitting

1   Do not jack up the front of the car but allow the weight of the car to remain on the wheels, by running the car over a pit or up on ramps.

2   Remove the nuts, washers and rubber bushes that secure the lower ends of the drop links to the track control arms.

3   Remove the rubber insulated brackets that hold the stabiliser bar to the body side members. The stabiliser bar can now be withdrawn complete with drop links for later removal if required.

4   Renew any rubber bushes which have deteriorated.

5   Refitting is largely a reversal of removal procedure but be sure of the following: The rubber bushes are compressed into the insulated brackets to facilitate the entry of their retaining bolts; the drop links are fitted with the shorter leg, from the bend, downwards.

6   Ensure that bushes, nuts and washers are fitted in the sequence shown. Tighten each nut until the rubber bush has sufficiently compressed to provide a measurement of between $\frac{9}{16}$ and $\frac{5}{8}$ in (14.29 and 15.88 mm) from the nut-facing side of the washer to the tip of the drop link threads.

6   Track control arm and balljoint – removal and refitting

1   Jack the car and support securely on stands under the body frame.

2   Disconnect the track-rod from the steering arm (2 in Fig. 11.5). To do this, first remove the retaining nut and then use an extractor or suitable wedges. Two club hammers of equal weight may be used to jar the ball-pin taper from its locating eye. They should be used to strike the diametrically opposite edges of the eye simultaneously when the pin will drop out.

3   Remove the nuts that secure the steering arm to the suspension strut.

4   Remove the lower nut, washers and rubber bushes from the stabiliser bar drop link as described in the preceding section.

5   Remove the tie-rod (4) by detaching the two nuts and bolts from the mounting bracket on the body underframe.

6   Remove the nut and bolt which secures the tie-rod to the track control arm.

7   Pull the front mounting forward and downward to withdraw the tie-rod.

8   Withdraw the pivot nut and bolt which locate the track control arm to the crossmember. This operation will necessitate full lock of the steering in order to gain access to the nut.

9   Prise out the track control arm from the crossmember and remove the rubber bushes from the inner pivot pin.

10   Remove the nut which secures the steering arm to the track control rod balljoint and using a suitable extractor (balljoint remover), detach the two components.

11   Refitting of the track control arm and its balljoint is made as a complete assembly and is largely a reversal of removal, but take

3.1 Checking for excessive front hub endfloat

3.4 Front hub with dust cap removed

4.6 Removing front hub bearing thrust washer

7.4 Tie-rod front end attachment

8.9 Front suspension strut upper mounting nuts

11.5 Engine mounting bracket nut viewed from beneath crossmember

special care with the following: Always use the new nut supplied with the new track control arm and tighten it to the specified torque given in the Specifications. Engage the locating dowels and fit the steering arm squarely to the bottom of the suspension strut.

12 Reassemble the track control arm to crossmember pivot bolts with their heads to the rear, otherwise, if reversed, the nuts will damage the steering gear convolute rubber covers.

13 Adjust the drop link nuts as described in Section 5 and tighten all nuts to the torques specified in the Specifications.

14 Check the front wheel alignment, see Section 29.

7 Tie-rod – removal and refitting

1 The tie-rod is located between the track control arm and the body underframe. Its purpose is to stabilise the lower end of the suspension strut during braking torque.

2 The tie-rod may be removed with the car placed over an inspection pit or standing on its roadwheels on the floor.

3 To remove the tie-rod, turn the steering to full lock as necessary to gain access to the tie-rod being removed.

4 Refer to Fig. 11.7. Remove the nut (7) washer (6) and bush (5) from the tie-rod (photo).

5 Unscrew the nut from the bolt (8).

6 Pull down on the car body. This will have the effect of tilting the suspension strut slightly so that the bolt connecting the tie-rod to the track control arm can be withdrawn.

7 Remove the tie-rod and pull off the rear bush (3) and washer (2).

8 If both tie-rods are being removed at the same time, make sure that the cast bush mounting brackets are not mixed up. These brackets are handed to ensure that each tie-rod inclines rearward, downward and outward.

9 Identification of the left-hand and right-hand brackets is shown in Fig. 11.9.

10 Refitting is a reversal of removal. Assemble the tie-rod completely but loosely initially and then tighten all nuts and bolts to the specified

torque. Use new self-locking nuts. Check the front wheel alignment – see Section 29.

8 Front suspension strut – removal, overhaul and refitting

1 The strut assembly may be removed complete with hub, coil road spring and top. Removal for left and right-hand assemblies is identical.

2 Apply the handbrake and jack up the front of the car, supporting adequately under the body sidemembers.

3 Remove the roadwheel from the side to be dismantled.

4 Unbolt and remove the brake caliper unit, disengage the hydraulic fluid line from its bracket, and tie the caliper to the stabiliser bar.

5 From the top of the strut, disengage the throttle and choke cables from the clip.

6 If the strut is to be dismantled after removal or the top mounting removed, then hold the rebound stop plate quite still while the damper rod nut is unscrewed one complete turn. Do not remove the nut completely at this stage. This operation is not necessary if the strut assembly is being removed and refitted complete.

7 Remove the two nuts that secure the steering arm to the foot of the strut and withdraw the arm, allowing it still to be connected to the track-rod and track control arm.

8 Remove the lower nut, rubber bushes and washers from the stabiliser bar drop link, through the track control arm.

9 Support the strut at its base and remove the three nuts and washers that secure the upper end of the strut assembly to the inner wing valance (photo).

10 Prise the track control arm downwards and then withdraw the strut complete with hub assembly from below the front wing.

11 A faulty, 'soft' or leaking suspension strut should be replaced with a new unit. An alternative method of renewal is to obtain a repair cartridge kit. Full instructions are usually supplied with these kits but the saving over a new or factory reconditioned strut is marginal.

12 If the strut is being exchanged or a new one purchased, the coil spring, the upper mounting, the hub/disc assembly and steering arm components must all be removed and fitted on the new unit.

13 To refit the strut, offer it up under the wing and engage the studs

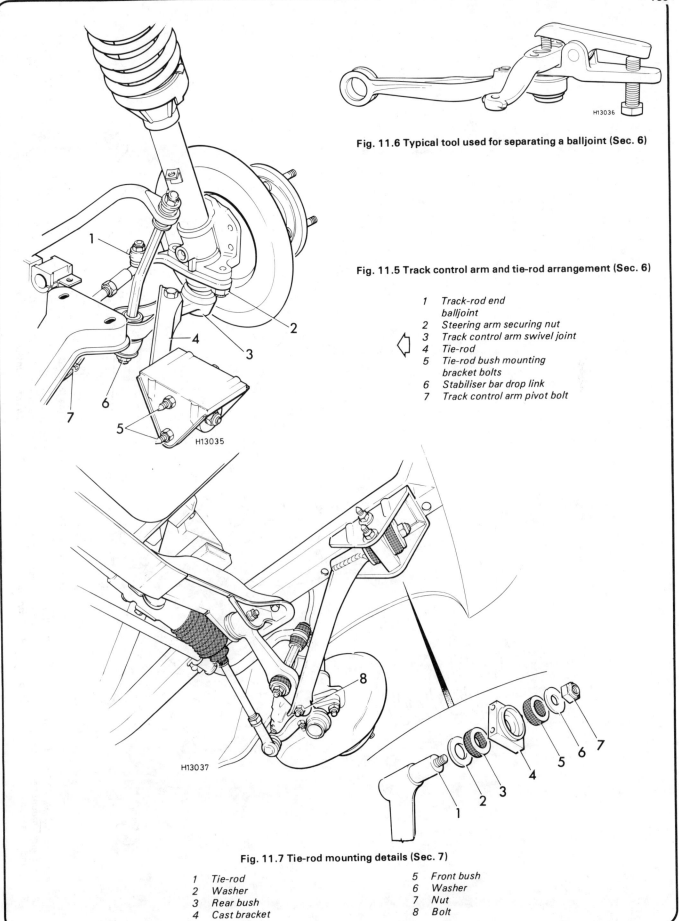

Fig. 11.6 Typical tool used for separating a balljoint (Sec. 6)

Fig. 11.5 Track control arm and tie-rod arrangement (Sec. 6)

1 Track-rod end
   balljoint
2 Steering arm securing nut
3 Track control arm swivel joint
4 Tie-rod
5 Tie-rod bush mounting
   bracket bolts
6 Stabiliser bar drop link
7 Track control arm pivot bolt

Fig. 11.7 Tie-rod mounting details (Sec. 7)

1 Tie-rod
2 Washer
3 Rear bush
4 Cast bracket
5 Front bush
6 Washer
7 Nut
8 Bolt

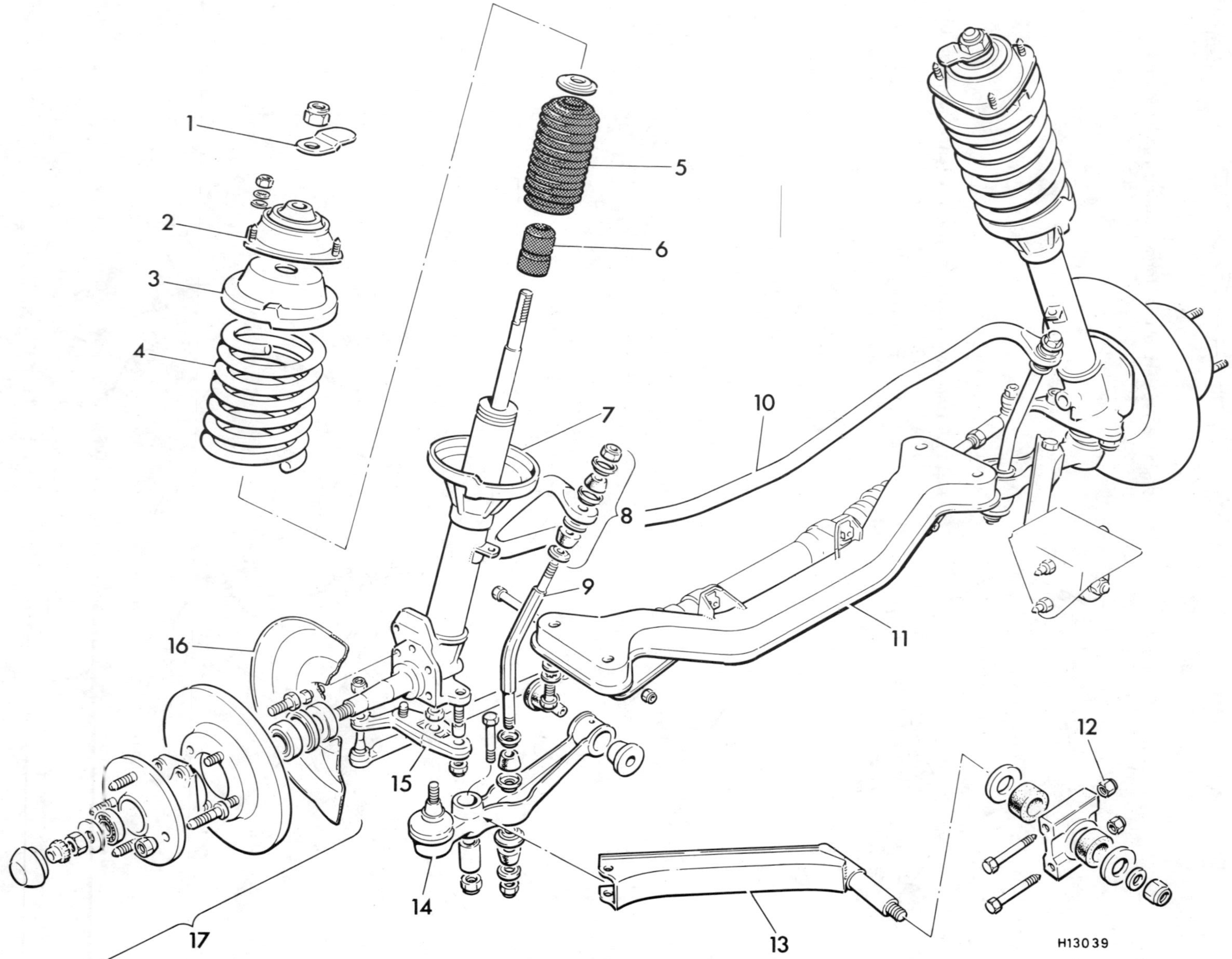

H13039

Fig. 11.8 Front suspension components (Sec. 8)

1 Rebound stop plate
2 Strut upper mounting
3 Spring upper cup
4 Coil spring
5 Gaiter
6 Bump stop
7 Strut
8 Drop link upper mounting
9 Drop link
10 Stabiliser bar
11 Crossmember
12 Tie-rod front mounting
13 Tie-rod
14 Track control arm
15 Steering arm
16 Shield
17 Hub/disc assembly

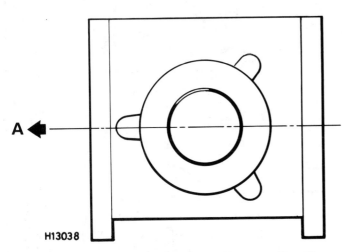

Fig. 11.9 Tie-bar case bracket viewed from rear (Sec. 7)
Projection must point inboard as shown (A)

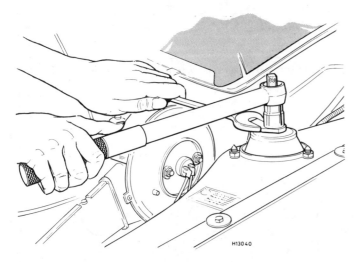

Fig. 11.10 Method of releasing and tightening strut damper nut
(Sec. 8)

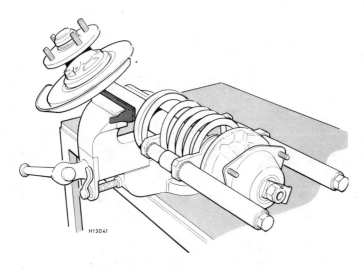

Fig. 11.11 Strut removal with spring clamps in position (Sec. 9)

through the holes in the inner wing. Fit the nuts finger-tight, making sure that the cable clip is located on the inner rear stud.

14 Prise the track control arm downwards and connect the steering arm to the strut. Fit new self-locking nuts to hold the steering arm to the strut and tighten to the specified torque.

15 Tighten the top mounting nuts to the specified torque.

16 Refit the brake caliper, the roadwheel and lower the car. Apply the brake pedal two or three times to position the disc pads against the disc.

17 If the damper rod nut was released (see paragraph 6), tighten the nut to the specified torque, holding the stop plate so that no twist is imposed on the rubber insert.

18 Check the front wheel alignment, see Section 29.

9 Front strut top mounting – removal and refitting

1 The strut top mountings are of rubber construction and must never be subjected to internal twist due to incorrect refitting of the strut or tightening of the damper rod nut.

2 Remove the complete strut assembly as described in Section 8.

3 Hold the strut carefully in a vice, taking care not to crush or distort the strut tubular casing.

4 Fit two spring compressors at opposite points and over the maximum number of coils.

5 Tighten both clamps equally until all spring pressure is removed from the spring upper cup.

6 Hold the rebound stop plate and unscrew and remove the unit which holds the top mounting to the strut.

7 Remove the rebound stop plate, top mounting and upper cup.

8 To refit, have the strut secured in the vice and fully extend the damper rod. Always fit a new rubber bump stop to the damper rod if it shows signs of deterioration.

9 Make sure that the convoluted gaiter is not twisted and the spring is correctly set in the lower cup.

10 Refit the spring upper cup, top mounting and rebound stop plate.

11 It is very important now to turn the mounting rubber so that one of its securing studs is in line with the stub axle. This will prevent any torsioned stress occurring in the mounting when the suspension leg is bolted to the wing valance.

12 Hold the rebound stop plate with an open-ended spanner. Screw the nut onto the damper rod over an equivalent number of threads to the depth of the nut.

13 Slowly and progressively unscrew and remove the spring compressors.

14 Refit the strut, brake caliper and roadwheels.

15 Set the roadwheels in the straight ahead position by pushing the car backwards and forwards so that the roadwheel revolves through at least one complete turn.

16 Again holding the rebound stop plate with an open-ended spanner, tighten the damper rod nut to the specified torque wrench setting.

17 Check the front wheel alignment – see Section 29.

10 Front coil springs – removal and refitting

1 Remove the strut and dismantle the top mounting as described in the previous Sections.

2 Withdraw the coil spring complete with the compressor clamps in position.

3 If the original springs are to be refitted, there is no need to remove the compressors but simply transfer the spring/compressor assembly to the new strut.

4 If new springs are to be fitted, gently release the compressors equally, and fit them to the new springs. Do not mix up the springs as they are different lengths from side to side. The right-hand spring is larger than that on the left of the car.

5 Refit the spring, top mounting and strut, by reversing the removal operations in this and the previous Sections.

11 Front crossmember – removal and refitting

1 Place the car over an inspection pit or on ramps.

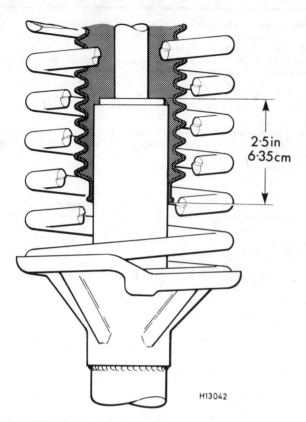

2·5in
6·35cm

Fig. 11.12 Strut gaiter refitting diagram (Sec. 9)

H13042

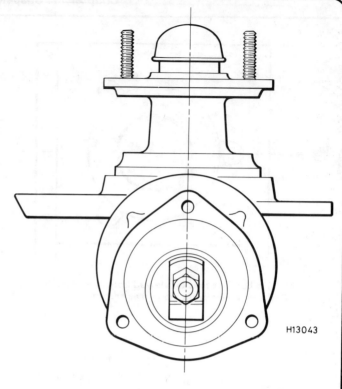

H13043

Fig. 11.13 Strut torsional rubber set ready for strut refitting (Sec. 9)

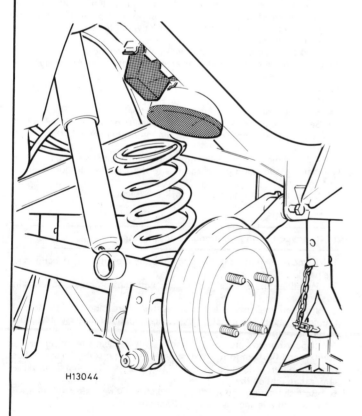

H13044

Fig. 11.14 Removing a rear coil spring (Sec. 14)

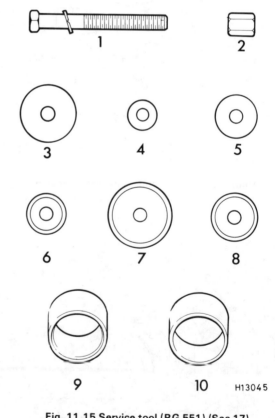

H13045

Fig. 11.15 Service tool (RG 551) (Sec 17)

1	Bolt	6	Cup
2	Nut	7	Cup
3	Washer	8	Cup
4	Washer	9	Sleeve
5	Washer	10	Sleeve

2 Apply the handbrake fully and disconnect the battery.

3 The weight of the engine must now be taken. This can be carried out in one of two ways. By either using a jack and wooden block under the sump or using a cross support bar and adjustable hook. If the latter method is used, attach the hook to the front engine lifting eye (heater hose attached to it) on 1300/1600 engines or to the lifting eye plate on 930 engines which is located adjacent to the alternator.

4 Raise the engine just enough to take its weight.

5 Unscrew and remove the engine mounting bracket nuts from below the crossmember. On some models, reinforcement stays are fitted (photo).

6 Unscrew the steering rack and pinion mounting bolts (see Section 28). Withdraw the clamp bracket from the side fitted with the rubber insulator.

7 Disconnect the drop link at the ends of the stabiliser bar. Twist the bar to clear the track control arm.

8 Unscrew and remove the bolts that secure the cast tie-rod bush mounting bracket to the bodyframe.

9 Unscrew and remove the four bolts that hold the crossmember to the bodyframe side members.

10 Pull the crossmember downwards and then remove the track control arm inboard bolts.

11 Prise the track control arms downwards so that the flexible bushes can be extracted.

12 Remove the crossmember from below the car.

13 Refitting is a reversal of removal.

12 Roadwheel studs – renewal

1 In the event of stud breakage or damage to threads occurring, the wheel securing studs must not be drifted out. They are an interference fit and removal other than by a balljoint remover or similar tool will cause bearing damage or hub distortion.

2 Refitting of a stud may be carried out by using a forked-end clamp or using a wheel nut and distance piece to draw it into position.

13 Rear shock absorbers – removal, testing and refitting

1 Do not attempt to remove a shock absorber with the car jacked up and the rear axle hanging free. Either remove a shock absorber with the car standing normally on its roadwheels or raised at the rear by jacks placed under the rear axle.

2 Open the hatchback and remove the floor covering and spare wheel cover.

3 Fold the rear seats and backrests forward.

4 Unscrew and remove the four cross-head screws from the loading floor flap hinge, also the single screw from the side load floor panel on the side of the car from which the shock absorber is to be removed.

5 If the right-hand side shock absorbers is being removed, take off the two grommets that cover the two nuts on the floor above the shock absorber top mounting.

6 Unscrew and remove the two locknuts from the top of the shock absorber mounting. On the right-hand side only, some models have reinforcement washers; extract these if they are fitted.

7 Disconnect the shock absorber lower mounting.

8 Remove the shock absorber from the car.

9 To test the shock absorber, grip its lower mounting eye in a vice with the unit in the vertical attitude. Fully extend the shock absorber and then fully retract it, eight or ten times in rapid succession. If the action is jerky or offers no resistance, renew the unit.

10 Inspect the outer casing for fluid leakage and if evident, renew the unit.

11 Check the mounting bushes for wear or deterioration and renew as necessary.

12 Before refitting a new shock absorber, it should be primed by gripping its lower end in a vice as described in paragraph 9 and fully extending and contracting it two or three times.

13 Refitting is a reversal of removal, but make sure that the rubber mounting bushes are correctly located and all nuts and bolts are tightened to the specified torque wrench settings.

14 Rear coil springs – removal and refitting

1 Jack up the rear of the car and support it securely under the body side member, just forward of the suspension link front bracket.

2 Remove the rear roadwheel.

3 Support the rear axle on a jack.

4 Disconnect the shock absorber lower mounting and compress the shock absorber upwards.

5 Slowly lower the jack under the axle until the coil springs can be withdrawn.

6 To refit the spring, first check that the upper insulator is fitted in the spring pan with its wider edge towards the rear.

7 Pull the rear axle down and place the spring in the lower link.

8 The help of an assistant will now be required to pull down on the top coil of the spring to set it in a curve, so that it can be engaged in the seat of the insulator.

9 Raise the axle jack and reconnect the shock absorber.

10 Refit the roadwheel, remove the stand and lower the jack.

11 Bounce the car up and down several times to settle the suspension. Tighten the shock absorber lower mounting bolt to the specified torque.

15 Rear suspension bump pads – renewal

1 These pads, located above the rear axle casing, are retained by tabs.

2 To remove them, lever the tabs away from the pad. After locating the new pads in position, tap the tabs back to grip the pads securely.

16 Rear suspension upper and lower links – removal and refitting

1 If all the links are to be removed together, then it is recommended that the rear axle is removed from the car (see Chapter 8).

2 Upper links may be removed from the car while it is standing on its roadwheels but only disconnect one link at a time to prevent the axle tipping forward.

3 The lower links can be removed after first having withdrawn the coil springs as described in Section 14.

4 To remove an upper link, detach the handbrake cable support clip from the link.

5 Unscrew the pivot nuts and extract the bolts.

6 Remove the link.

7 To remove a lower link, first withdraw the coil spring as described in Section 14.

8 Unscrew the link pivot nuts and withdraw the bolts. Lift away the link.

9 Refitting of both the upper and lower link is a reversal of removal but before tightening the pivot bolts to the specified torque, lower the car to the ground and bounce the car to settle the suspension bushes. Make sure that the bolts are inserted as shown in Fig. 11.2.

17 Rear suspension links – bush renewal

1 The rubber bushes fitted to the suspension links and their mounting points on the rear axle may be removed or replaced with the axle in position, provided only one link or mounting bush requires attention at the same time.

2 A service tool (RG 551) is available to cover all the bushes, but a screwed bolt with suitable distance piece and plates will be a good substitute. Always lubricate the new bushes with brake fluid or soft soap before fitting.

3 It is important that the bushes are withdrawn or inserted from the sides indicated in the illustrations. The method of extraction or insertion using the type of tool illustrated is obvious but the lower link rear bushes must have their 'ears' horizontally located when assembled.

18 Steering column – endfloat adjustment

1 This operation may be carried out with the steering column in the car.

2 Release the steering column lock and disconnect the battery.

3 Have an assistant push downwards on the steering wheel. Measure the gap between the face of the sprag washer and the thin washer adjacent to the bottom bush. If this is outside the tolerance indicated the adjustment must be carried out.

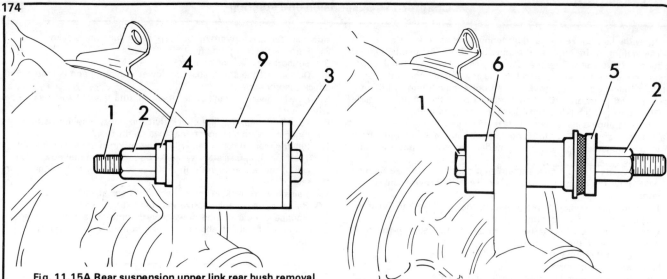

Fig. 11.15A Rear suspension upper link rear bush removal
(Refer to Fig. 11.15 for key) (Sec. 17)

Fig. 11.15B Rear suspension upper link rear bush refitting
(Refer to Fig. 11.15 for key) (Sec. 17)

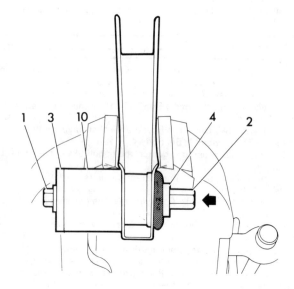

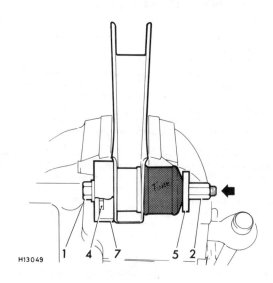

Fig. 11.15C Rear suspension upper link front bush removal
(Refer to Fig. 11.15 for key) (Sec. 17)

Fig. 11.15D Rear suspension upper link front bush refitting
(Refer to Fig. 11.15 for key) (Sec. 17)

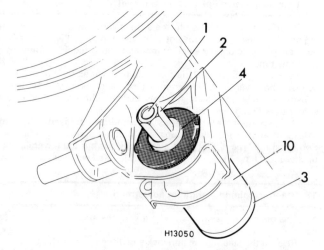

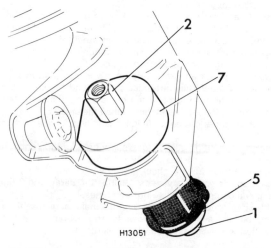

Fig. 11.15E Rear suspension lower link rear bush removal
(Refer to Fig. 11.15 for key) (Sec. 17)

Fig. 11.15F Rear suspension lower link rear bush refitting
(Refer to Fig. 11.15 for key) (Sec. 17)

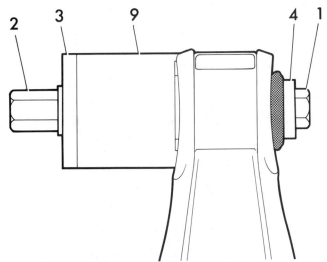

Fig. 11.15G Rear suspension lower link front bush removal
(Refer to Fig. 11.15 for key) (Sec. 17)

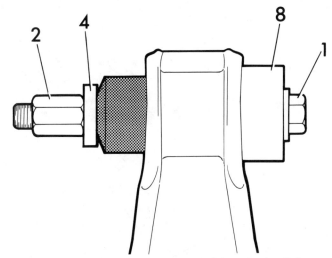

Fig. 11.15H Rear suspension lower link front bush refitting
(Refer to Fig. 11.15 for key) (Sec. 17)

4   Place the car over an inspection pit or on ramps.
5   If the endfloat is less than that specified, the sprag washer must be carefully sprung down the shaft. To do this, press a long drift under the radiator and over the front crossmember, so that it rests against the top yoke of the intermediate shaft joint. On no account apply the drift to the universal joint.
6   Tap the drift sharply to spring the sprag washer down the column. Recheck the gap.
7   If the endfloat is greater than that specified, then the sprag washer must be moved up the shaft. To do this, press a 21 mm open-ended spanner over the end of the column shaft, between the sprag washer and the yoke of the intermediate shaft universal joint. Cut a U-shaped shim of thickness equal to the specified clearance and insert this between the sprag washer and the thin washer. Levering against the spanner, prise the sprag washer carefully and evenly up the shaft until the column endfloat is reduced.

19 Steering column flexible coupling – removal and refitting

1   Release the steering column lock.
2   Unscrew but do not remove, the four nuts that secure the flexible coupling to the pinion shaft flange and intermediate yoke.
3   Remove the nuts and withdraw the bolts without disturbing the relative position of the inner column or steering gear pinion shaft flange.
4   Remove the flexible coupling.
5   Refitting is a reversal of removal. Make sure that the inner shaft or pinion shaft is not moved from its original position.
6   Refit the nuts and bolts and tighten to the specified torque.

20 Steering wheel – removal and refitting

1   Unlock the steering and then prise out the centre motif.
2   Slacken, but do not remove, the retaining nut from the top of the column (photo).
3   Pull the steering wheel upwards to break the tapered fit of the steering wheel hub to the shaft splines. If the wheel will not move, do not exert excessive force on the wheel or apply blows to the rear of the rim or spokes, as this may dislodge the sprag washer at the base of the steering column. Have an assistant apply reasonable force to the steering wheel in an upward direction while you give the inner column a sharp blow downward with a soft-faced mallet. Do not remove the nut during this operation as the threads may be damaged if struck, but unscrew the nut until it is flush with the end of the inner shaft.
4   To refit the steering wheel, apply a smear of grease to the splines and having checked that the roadwheels are in the 'straight ahead' position, fit the wheel with the spoke vertical and in the lower section of the rim. It should be possible to lock the steering in this position.

5   Tighten the steering wheel nut to the specified torque.
6   Check the steering column endfloat and adjust if necessary, as described in Section 18.
7   Refit the steering wheel motif.

21 Steering column top bush – renewal

1   Disconnect the battery and then remove the steering wheel as described in the preceding Section.
2   Remove the lighting and wiper switch assembly from the top of the column as described in Chapter 10.
3   Extract the circlip from the top of the column, retrieve the washer and lever out the top bush.
4   Refit the new bush, lightly smeared with grease, and then refit the remaining components.

22 Steering column intermediate shaft – removal and refitting

1   Disconnect the battery and set the front roadwheels to the straight ahead position.
2   Scribe alignment marks, bottom yoke to coupling and universal joint yoke to inner column (photo).
3   Remove the pinch bolt from the universal joint.
4   Remove the nuts from the bolts that secure the bottom yoke to the coupling. Extract the bolts.
5   Pull the intermediate shaft clear of the inner shaft.
6   Before refitting, smear the splines of the shaft with grease. Align the scribe marks or if new components are being refitted, transfer the marks to the same relative positions on the new parts.
7   Press the steering column assembly downward when pushing the intermediate shaft onto the inner column.
8   Tighten all nuts and bolts to the specified torque.
9   If a new intermediate shaft has been fitted, check the front wheel alignment (see Section 29).

23 Steering column lock – removal and refitting

1   The unit is a combined lock and ignition switch, secured by a special clamp with shear-head bolts. A key-operated peg engages in a slot in the inner steering column. In the event of loss of keys without a record having been kept of the number, or malfunction of the lock, then it should be removed as follows.
2   Disconnect the battery earth lead and steering column cowl.
3   Disconnect the ignition switch cables, identifying them for reconnection.
4   Centre punch each of the centres of the shear-head bolts. It may

Fig. 11.16 Steering column endfloat adjustment diagram (Sec. 18)

0·14 / 0·25mm (·005"/·010")

H13054

CAMBER **S.A.I.**

A B C

H13057

Fig. 11.17 Steering angles (Sec. 29)

A   Wheel angle
B   Verticals
C   Steering axis

H13055

H11872

Fig. 11.18 Steering column lock and key positions (Sec 23)

O   Steering column locked
I   Accessories (radio) on
II   Ignition on
III   Start position

be possible to unscrew the bolts by applying a punch to their edges to rotate them. If not, proceed to the next paragraph.

5 Drill out the centres of the shear-bolt heads $\frac{1}{8}$ in (3 mm) in depth using a $\frac{11}{32}$ in (9 mm) drill.

6 Release and withdraw the two halves of the unit.

7 Refitting is carried out by first setting the lock to the 'park' position so that the locking peg is disengaged.

8 Fit the new lock so that its locating tag engages correctly in the steering column hole and insert the shear-head bolts. Screw them in only finger tight at this stage.

9 Check the operation of the lock for smoothness and engagement by inserting the key and if necessary, giving the lock unit a slight twist in either direction. When satisfied that the unit is correctly positioned, fully tighten the shear-head bolts sufficiently to shear their heads.

10 Reconnect the ignition cable, the battery earth lead and refit the steering column cowl.

24 Track-rod end – removal and refitting

1 With the car over an inspection pit or the front end raised, slacken the locknut on the outer end of the track-rod by half a turn (photo).

2 Unscrew and remove the track-rod end ball stud nut. Using a suitable extractor, separate the track-rod end from the steering arm.

3 Clean, count and record the number of exposed threads on the track-rod and then holding the track-rod quite still, unscrew and remove the track-rod end.

4 Smear the threads with a little grease and screw on the new track-rod end until it is in its correct attitude, almost touching the locknut.

5 Engage the track-rod end ball-stud with the steering arm and screw on the securing nut to the specified torque.

6 Check that the balljoint is in its correct attitude, hold the track-rod quite still and tighten the locknut.

7 Check and adjust the front wheel alignment (Section 29) as soon as possible.

25 Rack and pinion flexible bellows – renewal

1 If on inspection, the bellows at either end of the rack and pinion housing are found to be split or perforated, they must be renewed immediately.

2 Remove the track-rod end and locknut as described in the preceding Section.

3 Place a container under the bellows to catch the oil which will drain out during the following operations.

4 Slacken the securing clips and slide off the damaged bellows.

5 Now jack up the car on the side opposite to the one from which the bellows were removed and then turn the steering from lock to lock. This will have the effect of causing the remaining bellows to pump out any oil remaining in the rack and pinion housing.

6 Fit the new bellows with clips but only tighten the inner clip.

7 Using a long spout oil can, inject $\frac{1}{4}$ pint (250 mls) of the specified oil into the rack and pinion housing. To do this, pass the spout under the smaller neck of the bellows (which has not yet been secured with

its clip) making sure that the spout passes over the rack ball-end fitting as shown.

8 Inject a small quantity of oil and then move the steering slowly from lock to lock to distribute the oil. Repeat until the oil in the can has all been injected. Remove the can and tighten the securing clip.

9 Lower the jack, refit and connect the track-rod end and then check the front wheel alignment (Section 29).

26 Steering column – removal and refitting

1 Disconnect the battery.

2 Raise the front of the car by positioning the jack under the crossmember. Set the roadwheels in the straight ahead position and then lock the steering column by removing the ignition key.

3 Peel back the floor covering from the footwell on the driver's side.

4 Remove the steering wheel, the cowls and the steering column switch.

5 Working inside the engine compartment, remove the four nuts from the floor plate which surrounds the outer column.

6 Remove the two nuts, washers and bolts from the lower yoke of the steering intermediate shaft at the flexible coupling. Disconnect the upper support and pedal support brackets and withdraw the steering column into the car.

7 Refit by reversing the removal operations. Apply a bead of sealant to the sealing face of the floor plate before bolting up.

8 If the roadwheels are in the straight-ahead attitude and the steering column locked, then the correct alignment of the column to the rack and pinion will automatically be assured.

9 Tighten all nuts and bolts to the specified torque wrench settings.

27 Steering column – dismantling and reassembly

1 Remove the column as described in the preceding Section.

2 Extract the circlip from its groove at the top of the inner shaft and remove the washer.

3 Disengage the steering column lock using the ignition key.

4 Grip the intermediate shaft and pull sharply to extract the inner shaft from the outer tube. The bottom bush will be dislodged at the same time.

5 Mark the relationship of the inner shaft to the intermediate shaft joint yoke. Unscrew the pinch bolt and pull off the intermediate shaft.

6 Remove the sprag washer, the plain washer and the bottom bush from the inner shaft.

7 Examine all components and renew as necessary. Smooth away any burrs resulting from removal of the sprag washer.

8 Commence reassembly by driving a new sprag washer onto the inner shaft. Use a piece of tubing to do this and locate the washer about $\frac{1}{8}$ in (3.0 mm) up the shaft.

9 Make sure that the steering column lock is unlocked, insert the inner shaft into the outer tube and locate the bottom bush.

10 Refit the top bush, washer and circlip.

11 Adjust the column endfloat as described in Section 18.

12 Apply grease to the inner shaft splines, engage the steering

20.2 Steering wheel retaining nut after motif removed

22.2 Steering column intermediate shaft

24.1 Track-rod end and suspension lower swivel

column lock and refit the intermediate shaft.

13 Tighten the coupling pinch bolt to the specified torque.

28 Rack and pinion steering gear – removal and refitting

1   With the car over an inspection pit, on ramps or jacked up under the front crossmember, disconnect both track-rod ends from the steering arms using a suitable extractor.

2   Disconnect the intermediate shaft at the flexible coupling.

3   Unscrew the two set-bolts from each rack mounting at the crossmember brackets.

4   Withdraw the complete rack and pinion assembly.

5   Dismantling and overhaul is not recommended and spare parts are not normally available. If a new assembly is to be fitted, it must first be drained of its storage/preservative oil and then refilled with $\frac{1}{4}$ pint (250 mls) of the specified lubricant. These operations are carried out by releasing the smaller neck of one set of bellows.

6   When refitting, inject the oil in stages and move the steering gear from one lock to the other between fillings. Hold the rack and pinion housing at 45° during the refilling operation.

7   To refit, set the roadwheels in the straight ahead position. To ensure this situation, place a long piece of wood along one side of the car so that it makes contact with all four tyre sidewalls. Repeat on the wheels on the opposite side of the car.

8   If the original gear is being refitted, bolt it into position and then turn the pinion shaft on the gear until the two track-rod end ball-studs will drop into the eyes of the steering arms without deflecting the arms from their previously set positions.

9   If a new rack and pinion gear is being fitted, bolt it into position and then centralise the rack. To do this, mark the edge of the pinion flange plate as a means of counting the number of turns from lock to

lock. Record the number and then turn the pinion flange exactly half this number of turns back from full lock. Screw on the track-rod ends and locknuts until their ball-studs will drop into the eyes of the steering arms, which will still be in the straight ahead position.

10 Tighten the track-rod end ball-stud nuts and locknuts to the specified torque.

11 Engage the steering column lock and with the roadwheels in the straight ahead position reconnect the intermediate shaft and coupling.

12 Only if new gear has been fitted, check the front wheel alignment (Section 29).

29 Steering angles and front wheel alignment

1   Accurate front wheel alignment is essential for good steering and tyre wear. Before considering the steering angles, check that the tyres are correctly inflated, that the front wheels are not buckled, the hub bearings are not worn or incorrectly adjusted and that the steering linkage is in good order, without slackness or wear at the joints.

2   Wheel alignment consists of four factors:

Camber is the angle at which the front wheels are set to the vertical when viewed from the front of the car. Positive camber is the amount (in degrees) that the wheels are tilted outwards at the top from the vertical.

Castor is the angle between the steering axis and a vertical line when viewed from each side of the car. Positive castor is when the steering axis is inclined rearward.

Steering axis inclination is the angle, when viewed from the front of the car, between the vertical and an imaginary line drawn between the upper and lower suspension leg pivots.

Toe-in is the amount by which the distance between the front inside edges of the road wheels (measured at hub height) is less than

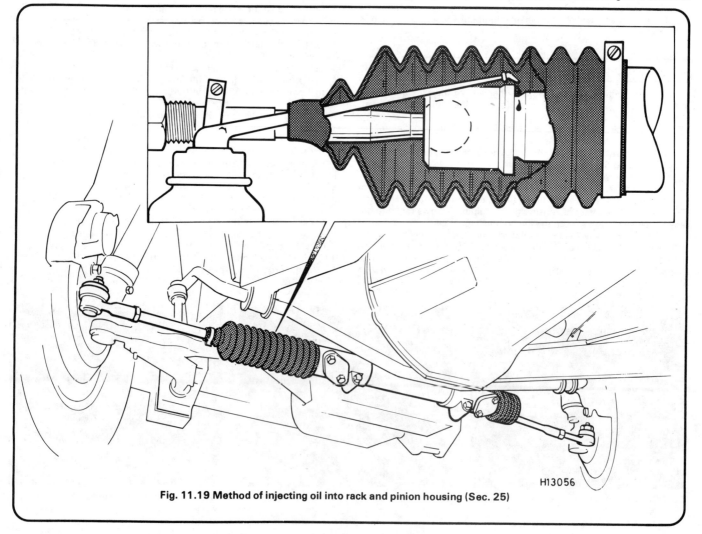

Fig. 11.19 Method of injecting oil into rack and pinion housing (Sec. 25)

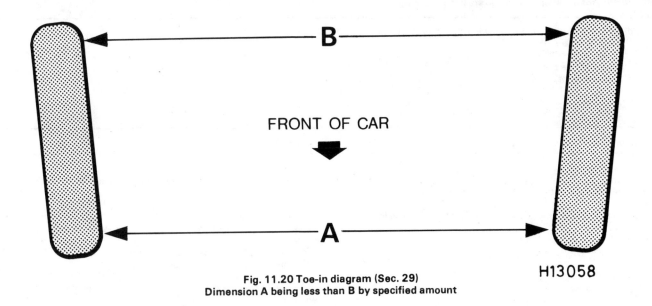

FRONT OF CAR

Fig. 11.20 Toe-in diagram (Sec. 29)
Dimension A being less than B by specified amount

H13058

the diametrically opposite distance measured between the rear inside edges of the front roadwheels.

3   The camber and castor angles are set in production and do not alter unless resulting from collision or accident damage. In these cases, the angles can only be checked out using very specialised gauges and weighting equipment – a job for your dealer. Front wheel tracking (toe-in) is also best carried out by your dealer but a reasonably accurate alternative and adjustment procedure may be carried out as follows:

4   Place the car on level ground with the wheels in the straight ahead position.

5   Obtain or make a toe-in gauge. One may be easily made from tubing, cranked to clear the sump and bellhousing, having an adjustable nut and setscrew at one end.

6   With the gauge, measure the distance between the two inner wheel rims at hub height at the rear of the wheel.

7   Rotate the roadwheel through 180° (half a turn) and measure the distance between the inner wheel rims at hub height at the front of the wheel. This measurement should be less by between $\frac{1}{32}$ and $\frac{1}{8}$ inch (1 to 3 mm). This represents the correct toe-in of the front wheels.

8   Where the toe-in is found to be incorrect, slacken both track-rod end locknuts and the outer clips on the rubber steering rack covers and ensure that the covers are not sticking to the track-rod.

9   Rotate both track-rods equally but in opposite directions until on re-checking, the toe-in is correct. It is imperative that the track-rods are maintained at equal lengths, otherwise the specified wheel angles on turns will be incorrect. Make sure that the bellows are not twisting.

10 If due to previously incorrect adjustment or the fitting of new components, the two track-rods are of unequal length (often indicated by the steering wheel spoke being in the incorrect attitude when the roadwheels are in the straight ahead position), then centralise the steering in the following way. Disconnect the track-rod ends from the steering arms.

11 Turn the steering wheel from lock to lock and count the number of turns. Now turn the steering wheel from one full lock position back half the number of turns just counted. Use a piece of tape on the steering

wheel rim against a marker on the instrument panel as a guide to the number of turns.

12 Check that the roadwheels are in the straight-ahead position. Release the track-rod end locknuts and adjust the position of the track-rod ends on the rods until the ball-studs will drop into the eyes of the steering arms without deflecting them.

13 Now adjust the toe-in as previously described in paragraph 9.

14 Tighten the track-rod end locknuts, making sure that the track-rod ends are held in the correct plane during tightening. Tighten the steering rack bellows outboard clips.

30 Wheels and tyres

1   The roadwheels are of the pressed steel type fitted with radial ply tyres.

2   Always check tyre pressures COLD, preferably first thing in the morning.

3   Periodically inspect the roadwheels for rust, both inside and out and clean and repaint them.

4   Do not mix fabric braced and steel braced tyres on the same car.

5   If the tyres have been balanced on the car, then always mark one wheel stud hole and the end of the stud before removing a roadwheel so that it can be refitted in the same relative position, otherwise the balance will be upset.

6   If the wheels have been balanced off the car then they may be moved periodically to even out tyre wear. Move the tyres from front to rear and rear to front on the same side of the car only, never from side to side as the same directional rotation must always be maintained with radial tyres.

7   At about half the useful life of the tyres, the roadwheels should be re-balanced to compensate for loss of tread which will probably have altered their balance.

8   Always have punctures professionally repaired and when purchasing a new tyre, have a new valve assembly fitted at the same time.

Fault Diagnosis overleaf

31 Fault diagnosis – suspension and steering

Before diagnosing faults from the following chart, check that any irregularities are not caused by:
  (a) Binding brakes
  (b) Incorrect 'mix' of tyres
  (c) Incorrect tyre pressures
  (d) Misalignment of the body frame

Symptom	Reason/s
Steering wheel can be moved considerably before any sign of movement of the wheels is apparent	Wear in the steering linkage, gear and column coupling
Vehicle difficult to steer in a consistent straight line – wandering	As above Wheel alignment incorrect (indicated by excessive or uneven tyre wear) Front wheel hub bearings loose or worn Worn suspension unit swivel joints
Steering stiff and heavy	Incorrect wheel alignment (indicated by excessive or uneven tyre wear) Excessive wear or seizure in one or more of the joints in the steering linkage or suspension unit balljoints Excessive wear in the steering gear unit
Steering knock (when traversing rough road)	Worn column top bush Worn rack and pinion gear Loose column coupling pinch bolt
Wheel wobble and vibration	Roadwheels out of balance Roadwheels buckled Wheel alignment incorrect Wear in the steering linkage, suspension unit bearings or track control arm bushes Broken or loose stabiliser bar
Excessive pitching and rolling on corners and during braking	Defective dampers

Chapter 12 Bodywork and fittings

For modifications, and information applicable to later models, see Supplement at end of manual

Contents

Specifications

Torque wrench settings

	lbf ft	Nm
Door hinge bolt to door and body pillar	20	27
Front/rear bumper back bars to body	20	27
Front/rear bumper back bars to bumper	6	9
Tailgate hinge nuts	11	15
Gas strut balljoint to glass	7	10
Gas strut balljoint to body	10	14

1 General description

The combined body and underframe is of welded all-steel con-struction. It is produced in a three-door hatchback style only, although different trim specifications are available according to model (LS, GL or S). All the usual refinements are standard equipment, including a heating/ventilation system, reclining front seats and inertia reel seat belts. On GL and S versions, the rear seat is of the divided type, permitting each seat back to be folded down independently of the other.

2 Maintenance – bodywork and underframe

1   The general condition of the car's bodywork is the one thing that

This sequence of photographs deals with the repair of the dent and paintwork damage shown in this photo. The procedure will be similar for the repair of a hole. It should be noted that the procedures given here are simplified — more explicit instructions will be found in the text

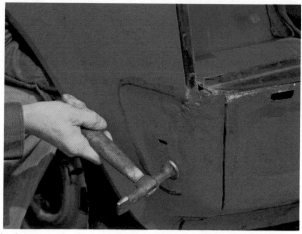

In the case of a dent the first job — after removing surrounding trim — is to hammer out the dent where access is possible. This will minimise filling. Here, the large dent having been hammered out, the damaged area is being made slightly concave

Now all paint must be removed from the damaged area, by rubbing with coarse abrasive paper. Alternatively, a wire brush or abrasive pad can be used in a power drill. Where the repair area meets good paintwork, the edge of the paintwork should be 'feathered', using a finer grade of abrasive paper

In the case of a hole caused by rusting, all damaged sheet-metal should be cut away before proceeding to this stage. Here, the damaged area is being treated with rust remover and inhibitor before being filled

Mix the body filler according to its manufacturer's instructions. In the case of corrosion damage, it will be necessary to block off any large holes before filling — this can be done with aluminium or plastic mesh, or aluminium tape. Make sure the area is absolutely clean before ...

... applying the filler. Filler should be applied with a flexible applicator, as shown, for best results; the wooden spatula being used for confined areas. Apply thin layers of filler at 20-minute intervals, until the surface of the filler is slightly proud of the surrounding bodywork

Initial shaping can be done with a Surform plane or Dreadnought file. Then, using progressively finer grades of wet-and-dry paper, wrapped around a sanding block, and copious amounts of clean water, rub down the filler until really smooth and flat. Again, feather the edges of adjoining paintwork

The whole repair area can now be sprayed or brush-painted with primer. If spraying, ensure adjoining areas are protected from over-spray. Note that at least one inch of the surrounding sound paintwork should be coated with primer. Primer has a 'thick' consistency, so will find small imperfections

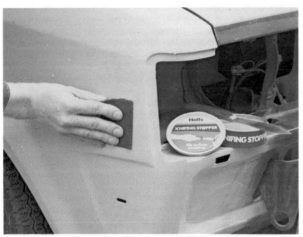

Again, using plenty of water, rub down the primer with a fine grade wet-and-dry paper (400 grade is probably best) until it is really smooth and well blended into the surrounding paintwork. Any remaining imperfections can now be filled by carefully applied knifing stopper paste

When the stopper has hardened, rub down the repair area again before applying the final coat of primer. Before rubbing down this last coat of primer, ensure the repair area is blemish-free – use more stopper if necessary. To ensure that the surface of the primer is really smooth use some finishing compound

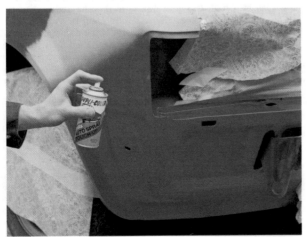

The top coat can now be applied. When working out of doors, pick a dry, warm and wind-free day. Ensure surrounding areas are protected from over-spray. Agitate the aerosol thoroughly, then spray the centre of the repair area, working outwards with a circular motion. Apply the paint as several thin coats

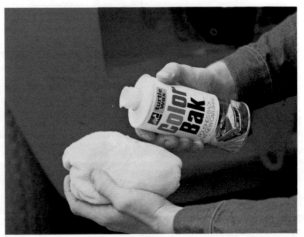

After a period of about two weeks, which the paint needs to harden fully, the surface of the repaired area can be 'cut' with a mild cutting compound prior to wax polishing. When carrying out bodywork repairs, remember that the quality of the finished job is proportional to the time and effort expended

significantly affects it value. Maintenance is easy but needs to be regular and particular. Neglect, particularly after minor damage, can quickly lead to further deterioration and costly repair bills. It is important to keep watch on those parts of the car not immediately visible; for example the underside, inside all the wheel arches and the lower part of the engine compartment. Keep the water drain holes clear at the bottom of the doors (photo).

2   The basic maintenance routine for the bodywork is washing, preferably with a lot of water from a hose. This will remove all the loose solids which may have stuck to the car. It is important to flush these off in such a way as to prevent grit from scratching the finish. The wheel arches and underbody need washing in the same way to remove any accumulated mud which will retain moisture and tend to encourage rust. Paradoxically enough, the best time to clean the underbody and wheel arches is in wet weather when the mud is thoroughly wet and soft. In very wet weather the underbody is usually cleaned of large accumulations automatically, and this is a good time for inspection.

3   Periodically, it is a good idea to have the whole of the underside of the car steam cleaned, engine compartment included, so that a thorough inspection can be carried out to see what minor repairs and renovations are necessary. Steam cleaning is available at many garages and is necessary for removal of accumulation of oily grime which sometimes is allowed to cake thick in certain areas near the engine, gearbox and back axle. If steam facilities are not available, there are one or two excellent grease solvents available which can be brush applied. The dirt can then be simply hosed off.

4   After washing paintwork, wipe it off with a chamois leather to give an unspotted clear finish. A coat of clear wax polish will give added protection against chemical pollutants in the 'air. If the paintwork sheen has dulled or oxidised, use a cleaner/polisher combination to restore the brilliance of the shine. This requires a little effort, but is usually caused because regular washing has been neglected. Always check that the door and ventilator opening drain holes and pipes are completely clear so that water can drain out. Brightwork should be treated in the same way as paintwork. Windscreens and windows can be kept clear of the smeary film which often appears, if a little ammonia is added to the water. If they are scratched, a good rub with a proprietary metal polish will often clear them. Never use any form of wax or other body or chromium polish on glass.

3   Maintenance – upholstery and carpets

Mats and carpets should be brushed or vacuum cleaned regularly to keep them free of grit. If they are badly stained, remove them from the car for scrubbing or sponging and make quite sure that they are dry before replacement. Seat and interior trim panels can be kept clean with a wipe over with a damp cloth. If they do become stained (which

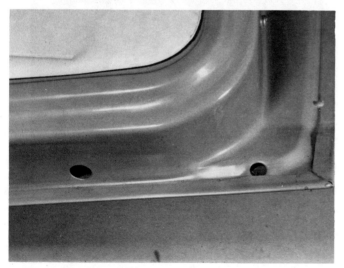

2.1 Water drain holes in door

can be more apparent on light coloured upholstery) use a little liquid detergent and a soft nail brush to scour the grime out of the grain of the material. Do not forget to keep the head lining clean in the same way as the upholstery. When using liquid cleaners inside the car do not over-wet the surfaces being cleaned. Excessive damp could get into the upholstery seams and padded interior, causing stains, offensive odours or even rot. If the inside of the car gets wet accidentally, it is worthwhile taking some trouble to dry it out properly. *Do NOT use oil or electric heaters inside the car.*

4   Minor body repairs

See photo sequences on pages 182 and 183.

Repair of minor scratches in the vehicle's bodywork

If the scratch is very superficial, and does not penetrate to the metal of the bodywork, repair is very simple. Lightly rub the area of the scratch with a paintwork renovator, or a very fine cutting paste, to remove the loose paint from the scratch and to clear the surrounding bodywork of wax polish. Rinse the area with clean water.

Apply touch-up paint to the scratch using a thin paint brush; continue to apply thin layers of paint until the surface of the paint in the scratch is level with the surrounding paintwork. Allow the new paint at least two weeks to harden, then, blend it into the surrounding paintwork by rubbing the paintwork in the scratch area with a paintwork renovator, or a very fine cutting paste. Finally apply wax polish.

Where the scratch has penetrated right through to the metal of the bodywork, causing the metal to rust, a different repair technique is required. Remove any loose rust from the bottom of the scratch with a penknife; then apply rust inhibitor paint to prevent the formation of rust in the future. Using a rubber or nylon applicator, fill the scratch with bodystopper paste. If required, this paste can be mixed with a cellulose thinner to provide a very thin paste which is ideal for filling narrow scratches. Before the stopper paste on the scratch hardens, wrap a piece of smooth cotton rag around the top of a finger: Dip the finger in cellulose thinners and then quickly sweep it across the surface of the stopper-paste in the scratch; this will ensure that the surface of the stopper-paste is slightly hollowed. The scratch can now be painted over as described earlier in this Section.

Repair of dents in the vehicle's bodywork

When deep denting of the vehicle's bodywork has taken place the first task is to pull the dent out, until the affected bodywork almost attains its original shape. There is little point in trying to restore the original shape completely, as the metal in the damaged area will have stretched on impact and cannot be reshaped fully to its original contour. It is better to bring the level of the dent up to a point which is about $\frac{1}{8}$ in (3 mm) below the level of the surrounding bodywork. In cases where the dent is very shallow anyway, it is not worth trying to pull it out at all.

If the underside of the dent is accessible, it can be hammered out gently from behind, using a mallet with a wooden or plastic head. Whilst doing this, hold a suitable block of wood firmly against the impact from the hammer blows and thus prevent a large area of the bodywork from being 'belled out'.

Should the dent be in a section of the bodywork which has double skin or some other factor making it inaccessible from behind, a different technique is called for. Drill several small holes through the metal inside the dent area, particularly in the deeper section. Then screw long selftapping screws into the holes just sufficiently for them to gain a good purchase in the metal. Now the dent can be pulled out by pulling on the protruding heads of the screws with a pair of pliers.

The next stage of the repair is the removal of the paint from the damaged area, and from an inch or so of the surrounding undamaged bodywork. This is accomplished more easily by using a wire brush or abrasive pad on a power drill, although it can be done just as effectively by hand using sheets of abrasive paper. To complete the preparations for filling, score the surface of the bare metal with a screwdriver or the tang of a file, or alternatively, drill small holes in the affected area. This will provide a really good key for the filler paste. To complete the repair see the Section on filling and re-spraying.

Repair of rust holes or gashes in the vehicle's bodywork

Remove all paint from the affected area and from an inch or so of the surrounding sound bodywork, using an abrasive pad or a wire brush on a power drill. If these are not available a few sheets of abrasive paper will do the job just as effectively. With the paint removed you will be able to gauge the severity of the corrosion and therefore decide whether to renew the whole panel (if this is possible) or to repair the affected area. New body panels are not as expensive as most people think and it is often quicker and more satisfactory to fit a new panel than to attempt to repair large areas of corrosion.

Remove all fittings from the affected area except those which will act as a guide to the original shape of the damaged bodywork (eg headlamp shells etc). Then, using tin snips or a hacksaw blade, remove all loose metal and any other metal badly affected by corrosion. Hammer the edges of the hole inwards in order to create a slight depression for the filler paste.

Wire brush the affected area to remove the powdery rust from the surface of the remaining metal. Paint the affected area with rust inhibiting paint; if the back of the rusted area is accessible treat this also.

Before filling can take place it will be necessary to block the hole in some way. This can be achieved by the use of one of the following materials: zinc gauze, aluminium tape or polyurethane foam.

Zinc gauze is probably the best material to use for a large hole. Cut a piece to the approximate size and shape of the hole to be filled, then position it in the hole so that its edges are below the level of the surrounding bodywork. It can be retained in position by several blobs of filler paste around its periphery.

Aluminium tape should be used for small or very narrow holes. Pull a piece off the roll and trim it to the approximate size and shape required, then pull off the backing paper (if used) and stick the tape over the hole; it can be overlapped if the thickness of one piece is insufficient. Burnish down the edges of the tape with the handle of a screwdriver, or similar, to ensure that the tape is securely attached to the metal underneath.

Polyurethane foam is best used where the hole is situated in a section of bodywork of complex shape, backed by a small box section (eg where the sill panel meets the rear wheel arch – most vehicles). The usual mixing procedure for this foam is as follows: Put equal amounts of fluid from each of the two cans provided in the kit, into one container. Stir until the mixture begins to thicken, then quickly pour this mixture into the hole, and hold a piece of cardboard over the larger apertures. Almost immediately the polyurethane will begin to expand, gushing frantically out of any small holes left unblocked. When the foam hardens it can be cut back to just below the level of the surrounding bodywork with a hacksaw blade.

Having blocked off the hole, the affected area must now be filled and sprayed. See Section on bodywork filling and respraying.

Bodywork repairs – filling and respraying

Before using this Section, see the Sections on dent, deep scratch, rust hole and gash repairs.

Many types of bodyfiller are available, but generally speaking those proprietary kits which contain a tin of filler paste and a tube of resin hardener are best for this type of repair. A wide, flexible plastic or nylon applicator will be found invaluable for imparting a smooth and well contoured finish to the surface of the filler.

Mix up a little filler on a clean piece of card or board. Use the hardener sparingly (follow the maker's instructions on the packet) otherwise the filler will set very rapidly.

Using the applicator, apply the filler paste to the prepared area; draw the applicator across the surface of the filler to achieve the correct contour and to level the filler surface. As soon as a contour that approximates the correct one is achieved, stop working the paste. If you carry on too long the paste will become sticky and begin to 'pick up' on the applicator.

Continue to add thin layers of filler paste at twenty minute intervals until the level of the filler is just proud of the surrounding bodywork.

Once the filler has hardened, excess can be removed using a plane or file. From then on, progressively finer grades of abrasive paper should be used, starting with a 40 grade 'wet or dry' paper. Always wrap the abrasive paper around a flat rubber cork or wooden block,

otherwise the surface of the filler will not be completely flat. During the smoothing of the filler surface the 'wet or dry' paper should be periodically rinsed in water, this will ensure that a very smooth finish is imparted to the filler at the final stage.

At this stage the dent should be surrounded by a ring of bare metal, which in turn should be encircled by the finely 'feathered' edge of the good paintwork. Rinse the repair area with clean water, until all of the dust produced by the rubbing-down operation is gone.

Spray the whole repair area with a light coat of grey primer; this will show up any imperfections in the surface of the filler. Repair these imperfections with fresh filler paste or bodystopper, and once more smooth the surface with abrasive paper. If bodystopper is used, it can be mixed with cellulose thinners to form a really thin paste which is ideal for filling small holes. Repeat this spray and repair procedure until you are satisfied that the surface of the filler and the feathered edge of the paintwork are perfect. Clean the repair area with clean water and allow to dry fully.

The repair area is now ready for spraying. Paint spraying must be carried out in a warm, dry, windless and dust free atmosphere. This condition can be created artificially if you have access to a large indoor working area, but if you are forced to work in the open, you will have to pick your day very carefully. If you are working indoors, dousing the floor in the work area with water will settle the dust which would otherwise be in the atmosphere. If the repair area is confined to one body panel, mask off the surrounding panels; this will help to minimise the effects of a slight mis-matching in paint colours. Bodywork fittings (eg. chrome strips, door handles etc) will also need to be masked off. Use genuine masking tape and several thicknesses of newspaper for the masking operation.

Before commencing to spray, agitate the aerosol can thoroughly, then spray a test area (an old tin, or similar) until the technique is mastered. Cover the repair area with a thick coat of primer; the thickness should be built up using several thin layers of paint rather than one thick one. Using 400 grade 'wet or dry' paper, rub down the surface of the primer until it is really smooth. While doing this, the work area should be thoroughly doused with water. Allow to dry before spraying on more paint.

Spray on the top coat, again building up the thickness by using several thin layers of paint. Start spraying in the centre of the repair area and then using a circular motion, work outwards until the whole repair area and about 2 inches of the surrounding original paintwork is covered. Remove all masking material 10 to 15 minutes after spraying on the final coat of paint. Allow the new paint at least two weeks to harden fully; then, using a paintwork renovator or a very fine cutting paste, blend the edges of the new paint into the existing paintwork. Finally, apply wax polish.

5 Major body repairs

Where serious damage has occurred or large areas need renewal due to neglect, it means certainly that completely new sections or panels will need welding in and this is best left to professionals. If the damage is due to impact it will also be necessary to completely check the alignment of the body shell structure. Due to the principle of construction the strength and shape of the whole can be affected by damage to a part. In such instances the services of a Chrysler agent with specialist checking jigs are essential. If a body is left misaligned it is first of all dangerous as the car will not handle properly and secondly, uneven stresses will be imposed on the steering, engine and transmission, causing abnormal wear or complete failure.

6 Maintenance – hinges and locks

1   Oil the hinges of the bonnet, boot and doors, with a drop or two of light oil periodically. A good time is after the car has been washed.
2   Oil the bonnet release catch pivot pin and safety catch pivot pin periodically.
3   Do not over lubricate door latches and strikers. Normally a little oil on the rotary cam spindle alone is sufficient.

7 Front bumper – removal and refitting

1   The bumper extension can be removed independently of the main bumper assembly. To do this, reach under the front wing and extract

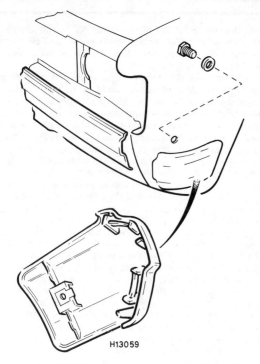

H13059

Fig. 12.1 Front bumper extension (Sec. 7)

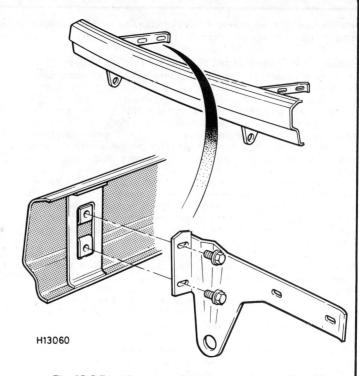

H13060

Fig. 12.2 Front bumper to back bar attachment (Sec. 7)

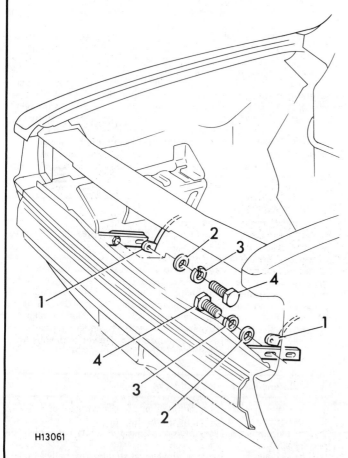

H13061

Fig. 12.3 Front bumper back bar assembly (Sec. 7)

1   Earth tag
2   Plain washer
3   Spring washer
4   Setscrew

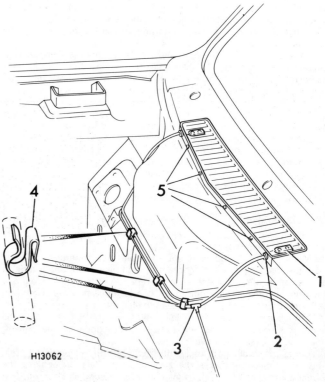

H13062

Fig. 12.4 Air intake grille (Sec. 11)

1   Washer jet
2   Grommet
3   T-connector
4   Spring clip
5   Plastic stud

the selftapping screw and washer which holds the extension to the wing.

2   The extension is held in position on the bumper by two mouldings that fit over two protrusions on the inner face of the bumper. Using a screwdriver as a lever, ease the mouldings over the protrusions and withdraw the extension.

3   To remove the bumper complete, extract the selftapping screws that secure the bumper extension from under the front wings.

4   Unscrew and remove the four bolts that hold the bumper to the support bars.

5   The support bars can be removed by unbolting them from the bodyframe. Note particularly the position of the earth tags.

6   Refitting of all components is a reversal of removal.

8   Radiator grille – removal and refitting

1   Open the bonnet. On models equipped with headlamp wash/wipe, remove the wiper arms and disconnect the pipes from the washer jets.

2   Remove the four selftapping screws, washers and spring clips from the top of the grille. Ease the top of the grille forward and lift it from the car. The base of the grille is held in position by four lugs engaged in cutouts.

3   To refit, reverse the removal operation.

9   Bonnet – removal and refitting

1   Open the bonnet and place protective covers on the top of the wings.

2   Disconnect the battery, also the engine compartment lamp (where fitted).

3   Mark the position of the hinge brackets on the bonnet. Masking tape is useful for this and prevents damaging the paint, as would happen if scribe marks were made (photo).

4   Have an assistant support the bonnet and then unscrew and remove the set-screws that hold the brackets to the bonnet. Remove

the bonnet from the car.

5   Refitting is a reversal of removal. Align the bonnet if necessary before the hinge bolts are fully tightened, to give an equal clearance at both sides and at the rear.

10   Bonnet lock – removal, refitting and adjustment

1   If the bonnet release cable should break, the bonnet can be opened by inserting a suitable rod through the radiator grille above the badge, to operate the release catch. Open the bonnet.

2   Disconnect the battery and the engine compartment interior lamp (where fitted).

3   Remove the radiator grille as described in Section 8.

4   Disconnect the bonnet release cable from the lock (photo).

5   Unscrew the three set set-screws that hold the lock to the locking platform and remove the lock.

6   Release the locknut which secures the release handle to the scuttle bracket.

7   Disengage the cable grommet from the engine compartment rear bulkhead and withdraw the cable assembly.

8   If necessary, the lock striker can be removed by releasing the locknut.

9   Refitting all components is a reversal of removal. Adjust the closure of the bonnet by releasing the striker locknut and screwing the striker in or out. When correctly adjusted, the bonnet should have some free movement in the locked position.

11   Air intake grille – removal and refitting

1   Open the bonnet and disconnect the shorter screen wash pipe from the T-connector.

2   Unclip the longer pipe from the spring retaining clips.

3   Withdraw the plastic pipe grommets from the front lip of the grille.

4   Using a small screwdriver, carefully ease the jets from the slots in the grille and withdraw the complete jet/pipe assemblies.

9.3 Bonnet hinge bracket

10.4 The bonnet lock

13.2 Window regulator handle showing spring clip

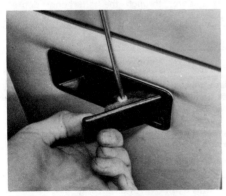
13.3 Extracting door interior handle screw

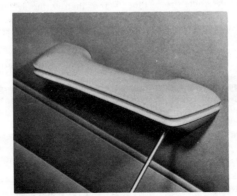
13.4 Extracting an armrest screw

13.7 Door with trim panel removed

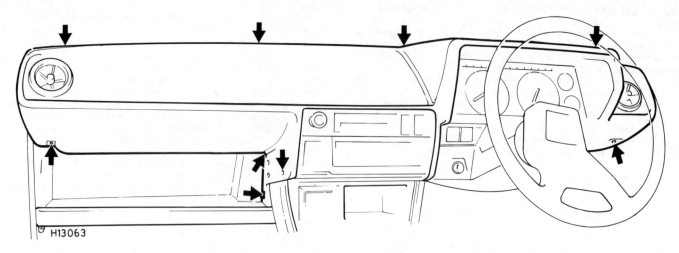

Fig. 12.5 Facia securing screws (Sec. 12)

5   Remove the four plastic studs that secure the grille to the body.
6   Ease the front edge of the panel upwards and remove the panel.
7   Refitting is a reversal of removal.

12 Facia panel – removal and refitting

1   Disconnect the battery.
2   Extract the seven screws that secure the bottom half of the steering column cowl. Lower the cowl complete with choke control.
3   Unscrew and remove the two nuts and washers that secure the outer legs of the steering column upper support bracket.
4   Unscrew and remove the two nuts and washers that secure the steering column lower support.
5   Lower the steering column and support it by allowing the steering wheel to rest on the driver's seat.
6   Reach up behind the instrument panel and disconnect the speedometer cable.
7   If fitted, withdraw the tailgate wash/wipe switch. To do this, mark the position of the wires and then disconnect them from the switch.
8   Extract the six screws that secure the lower switch panel. Pull the panel forward and disconnect the switches and panel lights. Remove the panel and finisher strip.
9   Remove the cigar lighter and pull off the heater control knobs.
10 If a radio is fitted, remove the control knob and the trim plate, disconnect the aerial lead, power and speaker leads, extract the mounting screws and withdraw the radio.
11 Extract the four screws from the centre control panel. Pull the panel forward, noting the wiring connections to the switches and bulb holders, disconnect them and withdraw the panel.
12 Remove the two securing bolts at the heater control bracket.
13 Disconnect the left-hand and right-hand air ducts from the ventilators at the extreme end of the facia panel.
14 Remove the four cross-head screws with their plain washers from the top of the facia.
15 Remove the two cross-head screws, washers and nuts which are located one at each lower end of the facia.
16 Extract the screws that secure the inner end of the parcel shelf.
17 Pull the facia, complete with instrument panel forward, until the multi-socket connector at each side of the instrument panel printed circuit can be disconnected. Disconnect the choke warning plug.
18 Withdraw the facia panel out through the passenger door.
19 Refitting is a reversal of removal but make quite sure that the electrical sockets, plugs and wires are correctly connected.

13 Door interior trim panel – removal and refitting

1   Using a thin wide-bladed tool, prise the window regulator handle away from the escutcheon.

2   Using a hooked piece of wire, pull out the regulator handle securing clip and withdraw the handle (photo).
3   To remove the door interior handle, pull the handle until the cross-head screw is visible. Extract the screw and remove the handle (photo).
4   To remove the armrest, extract the two concealed screws and withdraw it (photo).
5   If a door pocket is fitted, slide the two small plastic cover screws outwards and extract the screws. Do not attempt to pull the pocket from the door.
6   Slide a wide-bladed tool between the trim panel and the door at its lower edge. Slide the blade along until it touches one of the clips and then twist the blade to release the clip. Now insert the fingers and release the clips progressively. This will be found easier if a sharp jerk is given at each clip.
7   Remove the trim panel (photo).
8   The door pocket can be removed if required, by pinching in the side until the securing tags disengage.
9   Refitting of all components is a reversal of removal. Do not over-tighten the arm rest screws or the plastic insert threads may strip.

14 Window regulator assembly – removal and refitting

1   Close the window fully and secure the glass with small rubber or wooden wedges.
2   Remove the door interior trim panel as described in the preceding Section.
3   Unscrew and remove the four screws that hold the window regulator to the door.
4   Extract the two cross-head screws that secure the lower guide channel and remove the channel.
5   Disengage the regulator rollers from the window glass channels and then withdraw the regulator through the large door pocket aperture. Take care not to tear the waterproof sheet.
6   Refitting is a reversal of removal.

15 Window lower guide channel – removal and refitting

1   Wind the window glass fully up.
2   Extract the two cross-head screws that secure the channel to the door structure. Withdraw the guide channel through the lower rear aperture.
3   Refitting is a reversal of removal but check that the glass closes correctly. If not, the window regulator and guide channel can be adjusted within the limits of their slotted securing screw holes.

16 Door waist seals and trim – removal and refitting

1   Remove the door interior trim panel as described in the preceding Section.

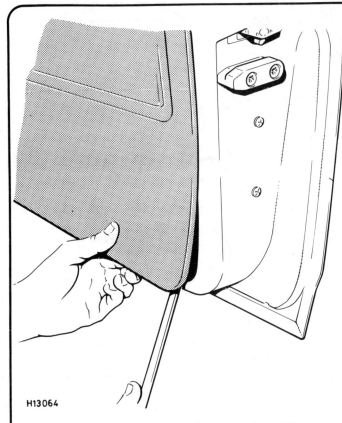

H13064

Fig. 12.6 Removing door trim panel (Sec. 13)

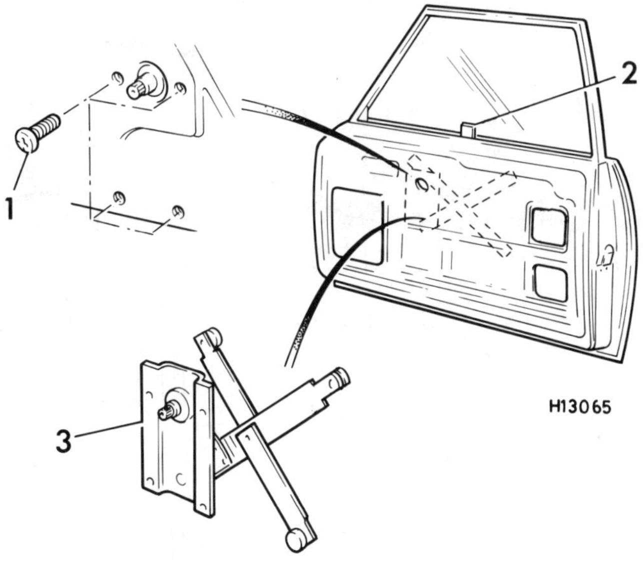

Fig. 12.7 Window regulator assembly (Sec. 14)

1   Screw
2   Wedge
3   Regulator

H13065

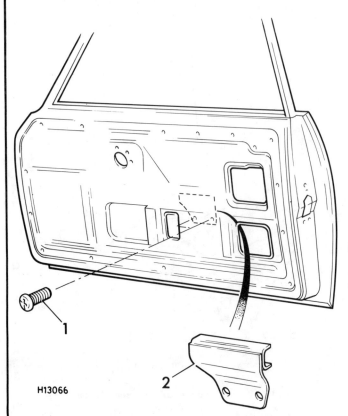

H13066

Fig. 12.8 Window regulator lower guide channel (Sec. 14)

1   Screw
2   Lower guide channel

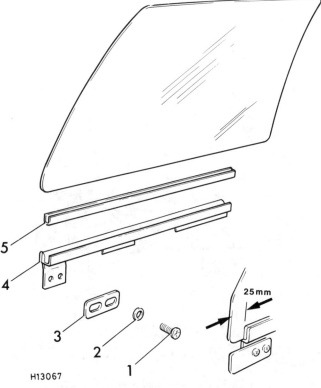

H13067

Fig. 12.9 Window glazing strip and channel guide (Sec. 17)

1   Screw
2   Washer
3   Extension bracket
4   Channel guide
5   Glazing strip

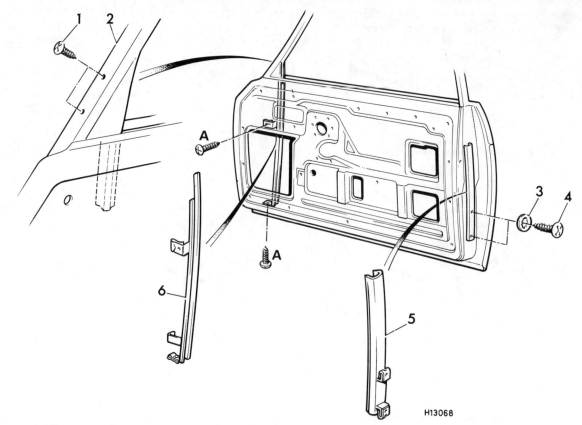

Fig. 12.10 Front and rear glass channel guides (Sec. 19)

1	Screw	3	Washer	5	Rear guide	A	Adjusting screws
2	Fillet	4	Screw	6	Front guide		

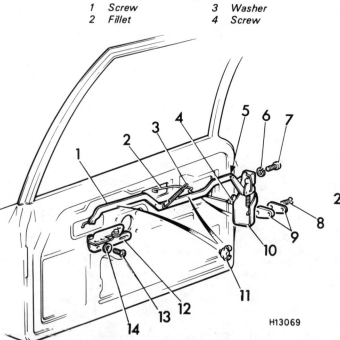

Fig. 12.11 Door lock mechanism (Sec. 20)

1	Remote control lever	9	Dovetail
2	Locking rod	10	Door lock
3	Return spring	11	Anti-rattle clip
4	Spring clip	12	Remote control lever
5	Circlip	13	Screw
6	Washer	14	Washer
7 and 8 Screws			

Fig. 12.12 Exterior door handle assembly (Sec. 21)

1	Connecting rod	4	Seal
2	Handle	5	Bracket
3	Screw	6	Screw

2   Wind the window glass fully down.
3   To remove the inner and outer waist seals, dislodge the securing clips and then partially close the window and retrieve the clips from the door interior.
4   Remove the seal from the door.
5   To fit the new seal, locate it firmly in position. Bend a hook on the end of a piece of flat strip steel to support a clip and pull the tool upwards to fit a clip into each indentation in the seal.
6   To remove the waist trim and inner seal, drill the three pop rivets from the waist trim finisher clips and remove the finisher. The inner seal is fastened to the waist trim with six spring clips.
7   Refitting is a reversal of removal but make sure that the trim finisher is correctly aligned before pop riveting it.

17 Door window glass – removal and refitting

1   Raise the window fully and support in this position with small rubber or wooden wedges.
2   Remove the regulator assembly and the door waist trim and inner seal (if fitted) as described in earlier Sections.
3   Remove the temporary wedges and carefully lower the glass, tilting the front edge of the glass downward through 45°, until the glass can be withdrawn from the door interior.
4   If new glass is to be fitted, remove the channel guide and glazing strip from the old window. If the reason for renewal is because the old window has broken, then clean out all the glass crystals from the door interior, retrieve the glass channel guide and glazing strip and remove the waist trim, inner seal and the regulator assembly.
5   Fit the glazing strip to the new glass and smear its outer surface with soapy water.
6   Tap the channel onto the strip using a rubber mallet.
7   Refitting is a reversal of removal. If necessary adjust the front channel guide to ensure correct closure.

18 Door glass run channel – renewal

1   Remove the door interior panel, the waist trim and inner seal, the regulator and window glass all as previously described.
2   Start by pulling out the channel from the bottom on the hinged side and then peel it away completely and remove it.
3   Insert the new channel at the top rear corner of the door frame first. Refit the other components by reversing the removal operations.

19 Door glass channel guides – removal and refitting

1   Access to these guides is obtained after removing the door interior panel.
2   Remove the waist seals, the window regulator, the window glass and the glass run channel, all as described in earlier Sections of this Chapter.
3   Extract the three cross-head screws that secure the channel to the door.
4   Extract the cross-head screw which holds the channel guide to the door fillet.
5   Withdraw the guide through the door pocket aperture.
6   Extract the two cross-head screws that secure the rear channel guide to the door structure and then withdraw the guide through the lower rear aperture.
7   Refitting is a reversal of removal. Ensure that the spire nuts are fitted securely in the channel guides. Any adjustment necessary to ensure smooth closure of the window glass can be carried out by moving the position of the front guide within the limits of the slotted securing screw holes.

20 Door lock – removal and refitting

1   Close the window fully and then remove the interior trim pad as described in Section 13.
2   Remove the glass run channel from the rear channel guide.
3   Extract the two cross-head screws that hold the rear channel guide to the doorframe and remove the guide.
4   Disconnect the rod which connects the private lock to the door

lock at its lower end.
5   Unclip the rod which connects the exterior handle to the door lock at its lower end and then disengage the rod from the lock.
6   Release the locking rod from the two plastic clips.
7   Remove the two cross-head screws that secure the remote control lever.
8   Unhook the return spring from the remote control rod (photo).
9   Release the two anti-rattle clips on the remote control rod (photos).
10 Extract the cross-head screws that hold the dovetail and lock assembly to the door edge (photo).
11 Withdraw the lock, rod and remote control lever through the upper rear aperture.
12 Disconnect the remote control lever circlip and remove the lever.
13 Disconnect the spring clip which secures the locking rod and remove the rod (photo).
14 Extract the two remaining locking clips from the lock.
15 Refitting is a reversal of removal.

21 Door exterior handle – removal and refitting

1   Close the window fully.
2   Remove the door interior handle as described in Section 13.
3   Working through the rear upper aperture in the door, unclip the connecting rod which runs between the door handle and the door lock at its lower end. Disengage the rod from the lock.
4   Unscrew the handle rear screw two or three turns. This is accessible after prising out the rubber sealing plug.
5   Now extract the screw and retaining bracket from the front of the handle. Slide the handle towards the front of the car until it disengages from the door panel. Withdraw the handle complete with seal and rod.
6   Refitting is a reversal of removal but if any adjustment is required, release the clip and screw the connecting rod in or out until the hooked part of the rod lines up with the operating rod when in the free standing position. Refasten the clip.

22 Door private lock – removal and refitting

1   Remove the door interior trim panel as described in Section 13.
2   Disconnect the rod which connects the private lock to the door lock at its lower end.
3   Using a hooked rod, extract the spring clip from around the private lock. Withdraw the lock from the door outer panel.
4   Refitting is a reversal of removal.

23 Door – removal and refitting

1   Open the door to its fullest extent and support its lower edge on blocks with pads of cloth as insulators.
2   Unscrew and remove the set-screws that secure the hinges to the edge of the door and lift the door away.
3   If the door hinges must be removed from the body pillar, first mark their position so that they can be refitted in their original places. The upper hinge is accessible after withdrawing the parcels shelf and scuttle trim pad but to reach the lower hinge, release the bottom of the wing and pull it away from the body pillar. The wing is secured by a self-tapping screw and washer located under a rubber plug.
4   When unscrewing the hinge nuts from the body pillar, stuff a piece of rag into the aperture at the base of the body pillar in case one of the nuts should be dropped and lost inside the sill.
5   Refitting is a reversal of removal. Any adjustment required to provide even clearance all round the door edge, or to make the outer surface of the door flush with adjacent body panels, can be made by moving the door within the limits of the oversize fixing holes on the body pillar, or by inserting packing shims between the hinge plates and the body pillar.
6   Any adjustment of the door hinges will necessitate re-positioning of the striker. To do this, partially release the securing screws.

24 Tailgate – removal and refitting

1   Disconnect the battery.

20.8 Door remote control rod return spring

20.9A Door remote control rod anti-rattle clip

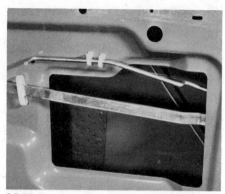

20.9B Door remote control rod and locking rod anti-rattle clips

20.10 Door lock and dovetail

20.13 Door locking slide viewed from inner face of trim panel

27.4 A tailgate latch

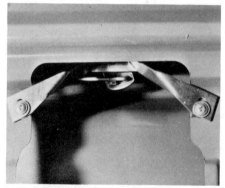

27.5 Tailgate lock support bracket

2   Open the tailgate to its fullest extent.
3   Disconnect the leads to the window heating element at the base of the gas-filled support strut.
4   Where fitted, remove the wiper wheel box (see Chapter 10).
5   Extract the locking pins from the bottom of each strut. Have an assistant support the tailgate and then disconnect the hinges from the glass and lift it away.
6   Refitting is a reversal of removal.

25 Tailgate gas-filled strut – removal and refitting

1   Open the tailgate and have an assistant support it. As an aid, your assistant can use a wooden prop suitably padded at its upper end to support the tailgate; but use care on this all-glass assembly.
2   Disconnect the leads from the tailgate heating element at the top and bottom of the strut.
3   Extract the locking pins from the top and bottom of the strut by

inserting a thin screwdriver blade into the locking pin groove and easing out the pin.
4   Disconnect the strut.
5   Refit by reversing the removal operations.

26 Tailgate attachments – removal and refitting

1   It is imperative that the hinges and lock striker are removed from the tailgate glass with great care and refitting is always carried out by tightening nuts and bolts to the specified torque only.
2   If after removal of the tailgate, the hinges are to be removed from the body, first withdraw the cross-head screw and collect the support plate, the sealing washer and the distance tube.
3   Remove the hinge cover to gain access to the hinge nuts and washers.
4   The gas-filled strut balljoints can be removed after withdrawal of the strut itself. Note the earth cable under the right-hand balljoint.

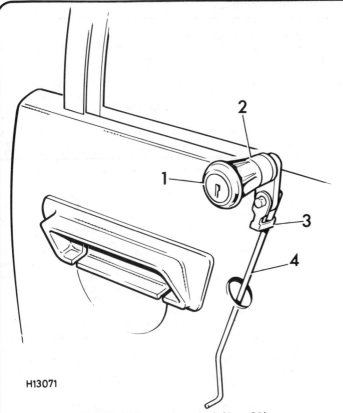

H13071

Fig. 12.13 Door private lock (Sec. 22)

1   Lock   3   Link
2   Spring clip   4   Connecting rod

H13072

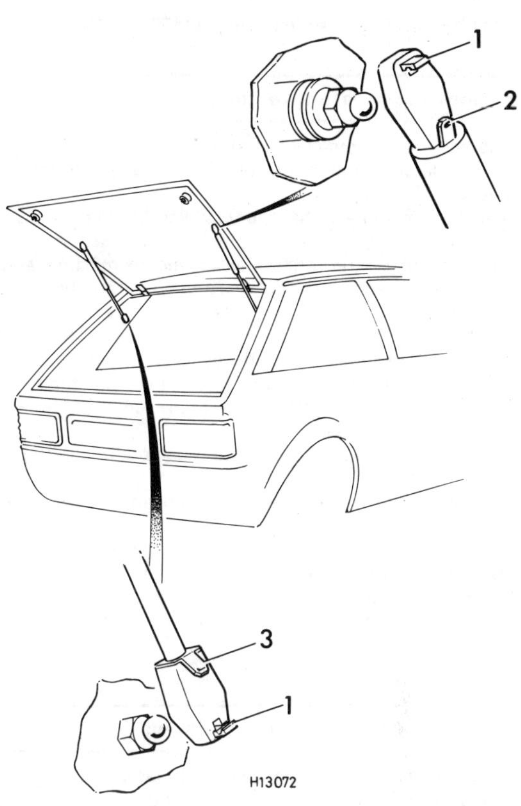

Fig. 12.14 Tailgate gas-filled strut attachment (Sec. 25)

1   Locking pin
2 and 3 Heated window terminals

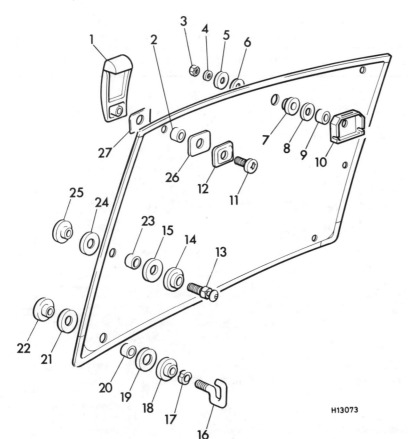

H13073

Fig. 12.15 Tailgate components (Sec. 26)

1   Hinge
2   Spacer
3   Nut
4   Cover plate
5   Escutcheon plate
6 and 7 Seals
8   Washer
9   Spacer
10 Wheelbox
11 Screw
12 Support plate
13 Balljoint
14 Attachment plate
15 Seal
16 Striker
17 Locknut
18 Attachment plate
19 Seal
20 Spacer
21 Seal
22 Escutcheon pin
23 Spacer
24 Seal
25 Escutcheon plate
26 and 27 Seals

5   The wiper motor can be removed by reference to Chapter 10.

27 Tailgate lock – removal and refitting

1   Open the tailgate and remove the trim panel from it.
2   Unscrew the latch trunnion rods enough to be able to remove the connecting rods.
3   Where fitted, disconnect the courtesy/warning lamp plug to the left-hand latch.
4   Mark the outline of the latches as an aid to refitting and then extract the screws that secure the latches and withdraw them (photo).
5   Extract the screws that retain the lock support bracket and remove the bracket (photo).
6   Remove the lock assembly pin and washer.
7   Withdraw the connecting rod cam assembly from the tail lamp. Note the plastic sleeve on the offside rod to prevent a short circuit on the rear number plate terminal.
8   Unhook the clips from the connecting rods and then withdraw the rods.
9   Prise off the circular spring retaining clip and remove the turn button lock.
10   Refitting is a reversal of removal, but refit the latches only finger tight initially and close the tailgate to centralise them. With the latches in the closed position, pull the connecting rods through the trunnion so that they locate against the ends of the cam slots. Tighten the trunnion screws.

28 Tailgate drain tubes – removal and refitting

1   Disconnect the battery and remove the rear lamp asembly.
2   Withdraw the drain tube from the grommet and the floor panel. Prise out the grommet and then remove the tube insert.
3   Refitting is a reversal of removal.
4   Always keep the drain tubes clear of obstruction by probing periodically.

29 Rear bumper – removal and refitting

1   Prise out the plug from the bumper extension.

2   Unscrew the self-tapping screw and washer.
3   Unscrew and remove the back bar set-screws and withdraw the bumper complete with back bar assembly.
4   The bumper can be dismantled after removal.
5   The extension is held in position on the bumper by two mouldings which fit over the protrusions on the inner face of the bumper. The extension can be removed leaving the main bumper assembly in position on the car.
6   Reassembly and refitting are reversals of removal and dismantling.

30 Windscreen glass – removal and refitting

1   Where a windscreen is to be renewed due to shattering, the facia air vents should be covered before attempting removal. Adhesive sheeting is useful to stick to the outside of the glass to enable large areas of crystallised glass to be removed. Remove the wiper arms.
2   Where the screen is to be removed intact then an assistant will be required. First release the rubber surround from the bodywork by running a blunt, small screwdriver around and under the rubber weatherstrip both inside and outside the car. This operation will break the adhesion of the sealer originally used. Take care not to damage the paintwork or cut the rubber surround with the screwdriver.
3   Have your assistant push the inner lip of the rubber surround off the flange of the windscreen body aperture. Once the rubber surround starts to peel off the flange, the screen may be forced gently outwards by careful hand pressure. The second person should support and remove the screen complete with rubber surround and metal beading as it comes out.
4   Remove the beading from the rubber surround.
5   Before fitting a windscreen, ensure that the rubber surround is completely free from old sealant, glass fragments and has not hardened or cracked. Fit the rubber surround to the glass.
6   Cut a piece of strong cord, greater in length than the periphery of the glass and insert it into the body flange locating channel of the rubber surround. Apply a coating of suitable sealer to the body mating face of the rubber surround.
7   Offer the windscreen up to the body aperture and pass the ends of the cord at the bottom centre into the car. Press the windscreen into place at the same time pulling on the ends of the cords simultaneously to engage the rubber surround lip over the body flange.
8   Refit the bright moulding and joining caps to the rubber surround. A special tool suitably made up to facilitate this operation is necessary.

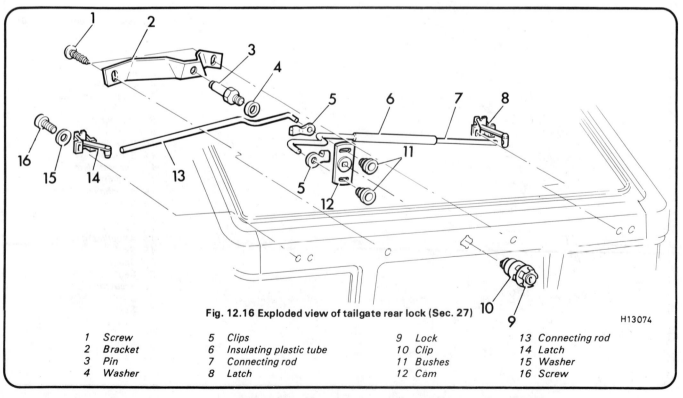

Fig. 12.16 Exploded view of tailgate rear lock (Sec. 27)

H13074

1	Screw	5	Clips	9	Lock	13	Connecting rod
2	Bracket	6	Insulating plastic tube	10	Clip	14	Latch
3	Pin	7	Connecting rod	11	Bushes	15	Washer
4	Washer	8	Latch	12	Cam	16	Screw

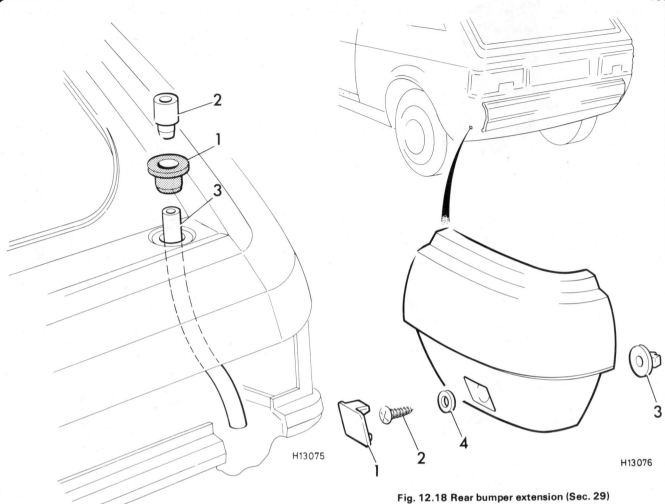

H13075

Fig. 12.17 Tailgate drain tube (Sec. 28)

1 Grommet
2 Insert
3 Tube

H13076

Fig. 12.18 Rear bumper extension (Sec. 29)

1 Blanking plug
2 Self-tapping screw
3 Nut
4 Washer

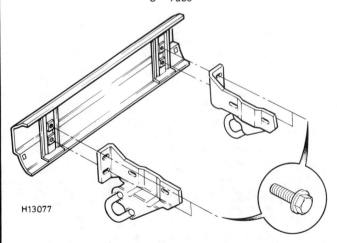

H13077

Fig. 12.19 Rear bumper back bar assembly (Sec. 29)

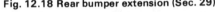

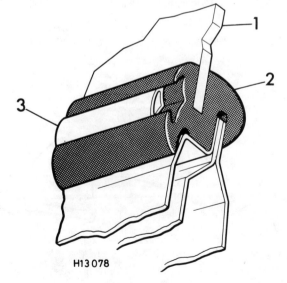

H13 078

Fig. 12.20 Sectional view of windscreen weatherseal (Sec. 30)

1 Windscreen
2 Weatherseal
3 Beading

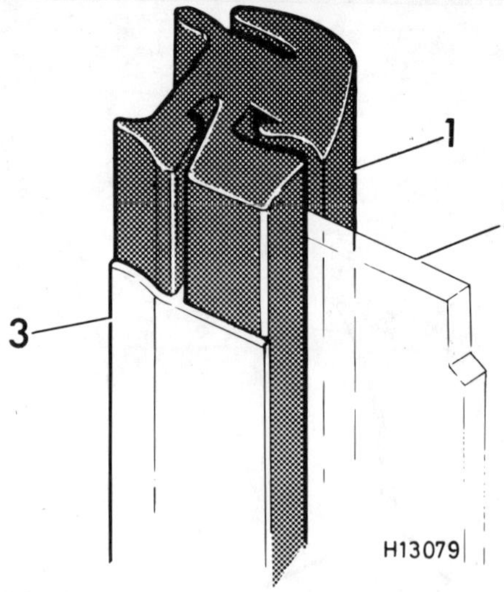

Fig. 12.21 Sectional view of rear quarter glass weatherseal (Sec. 31)

1	Weatherseal	2	Glass	3	Finisher

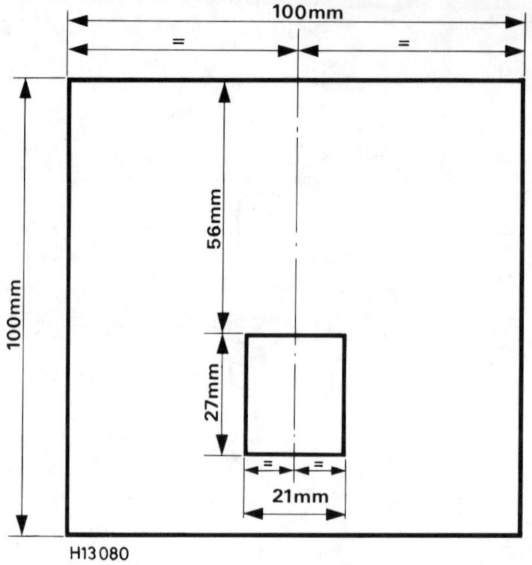

Fig. 12.22 Interior mirror mounting template (Sec. 32)

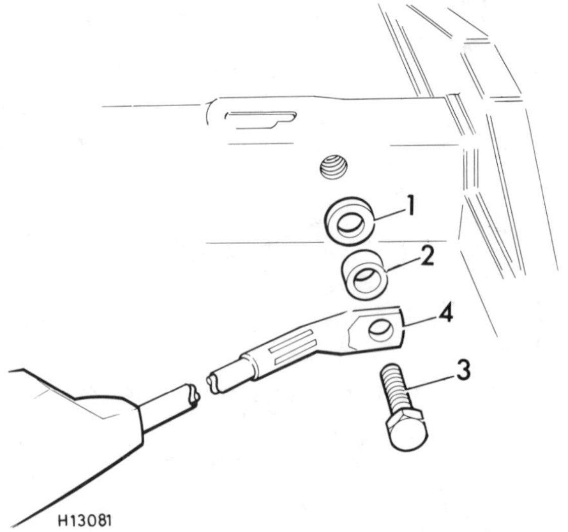

Fig. 12.23 Safety belt stalk anchorage (Sec. 33)

1 Washer   3 Setscrew
2 Spacer   4 Buckle stalk

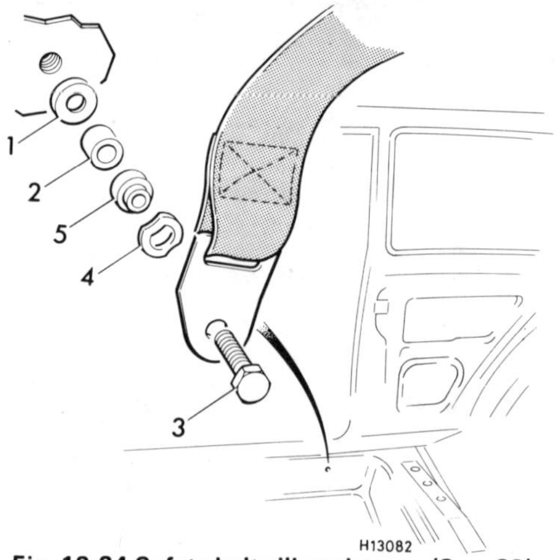

Fig. 12.24 Safety belt sill anchorage (Sec. 33)

1 Washer   4 Wave washer
2 Spacer   5 Collar
3 Setscrew

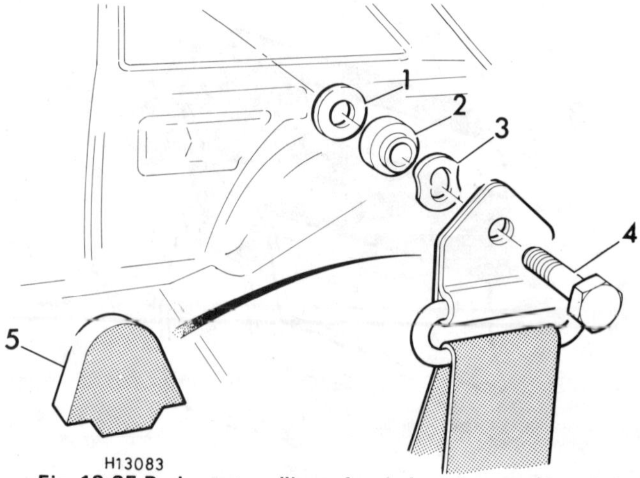

Fig. 12.25 Body centre pillar safety belt anchorage (Sec. 33)

1 Washer   4 Setscrew
2 Collar   5 Plastic cover
3 Wave washer

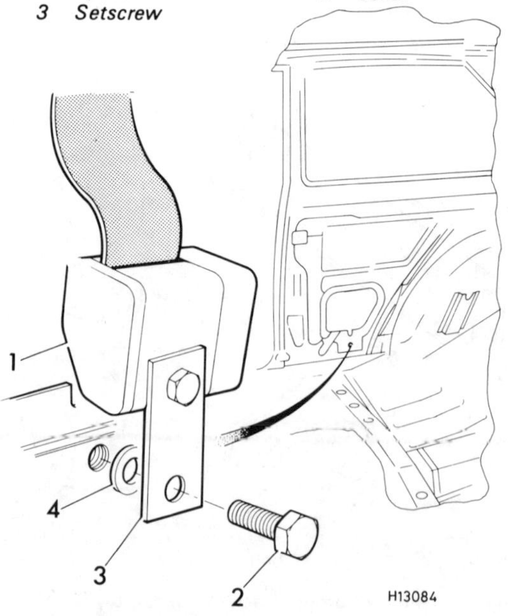

Fig. 12.26 Safety belt reel anchorage (Sec. 33)

1 Inertia reel   3 Bracket
2 Setscrew   4 Washer

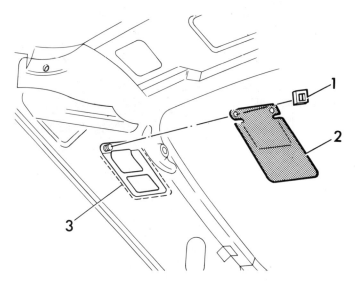

Fig. 12.27 Air extraction flap components (Sec. 34)

1 Spring clip
2 Air box flap
3 Location of air box flap

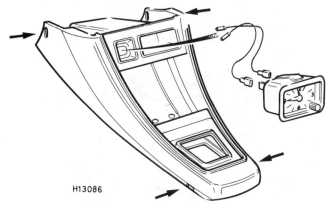

Fig. 12.28 Centre console mounting screws (Sec. 34)

31 Rear quarter fixed glass – removal and refitting

1   The operations are similar to those described for renewal of the windscreen glass using the help of an assistant.
2   When refitting the rubber weatherstrip, make sure that the finisher is fitted beforehand.

32 Interior rear view mirror – refitting

1   The interior rear view mirror is bonded to the windscreen glass. If the mirror bracket should break or a new windscreen is fitted, it will be necessary to bond a new mirror to the glass, unless it is decided to fit a more practical type of mirror using a bracket screwed directly to the roof panel. This type of mirror is available as an accessory from independent manufacturers.
2   Rub the base of the new bracket with emery paper to roughen it.
3   Clean the windscreen glass free from old bonding material by very careful scraping. No solvent has yet been produced to remove this type of bonding material.
4   If a new screen has been fitted, a template should be made up in strong paper and the position for fitting the mirror outlined in masking tape.
5   If possible, warm the bonding area with warm air from a hair dryer.
6   The official bonding method is to apply Loctite 312 NF activator to the glass and bracket contact areas and allow to dry for 30 seconds; then apply a thin film of Loctite 312 adhesive to the bracket base.
7   Press the bracket base to the screen so that the slots in the bracket are towards the top of the screen. Apply pressure for thirty seconds. Allow the adhesive to cure for 5 minutes before fitting the mirror to the bracket.
8   Provided both contact surfaces are perfectly clean, equally good bonding results are obtainable using one of the new instant glues. Four or five equally spaced drops are enough.

33 Safety belts – care and anchorage points

1   The inertia reel type safety belts normally require no attention other than occasionally wiping them free from dirt with warm soapy water.
2   Occasionally inspect the belts for chafing and renew if evident.
3   To test the operation of the inertia reel, drive the car at between 10 and 15 mph (16 and 24 kph) and apply the footbrake sharply. If the reel mechanism is operating correctly, the occupant will be restrained

from moving forward.
4   Never make any alteration to the belts or fixings. If the belts are removed for any body maintenance work or if new belts are fitted, it is essential that the anchorage components are always assembled as shown in the illustrations.

34 Body internal components – removal and refitting

Air extraction flap valve
1   Remove the gas-filled strut used to support the tailgate.
2   Remove the gas-filled strut balljoint.
3   Raise the tailgate sealing rubber at the base of the trim to release the rear quarter trim fixing.
4   Remove the rear seat belt anchorage or blanking plug.
5   Ease the front of the quarter trim from under the lip of the quarter light weather seal.
6   Remove the rubber flap seal which covers the air box aperture.
7   Extract the two clips that secure the air box flap. Ease the flap from the two locating pegs and remove the flap.
8   Refitting is a reversal of removal but tuck the flap inside the air box aperture.

Air extraction grille
9   This is secured to the body by four locating studs, one of which has a self-threading nut.
10   To remove the grille, withdraw the nut and carefully prise off the grille. Refitting is a reversal of removal.

Sun visor
11   The visor itself can be removed after extracting the three mounting screws.
12   If the visor storage hook is to be removed, only partially push the dowel locking pin inward. The hook can then be withdrawn from the headlining. If the dowel pin is pushed in too far, it will be lost and a completely new hook assembly will have to be fitted. Refitting is a reversal of removal.

Centre console
13   If a clock is fitted, disconnect the battery and withdraw the clock (press fit only) far enough to be able to disconnect the Lucar connectors.
14   Remove the gear lever knob.
15   Extract the two screws from the console tray, the single screw from the inner end of the parcel tray and the two at the rear of the console. Refitting is a reversal of removal.

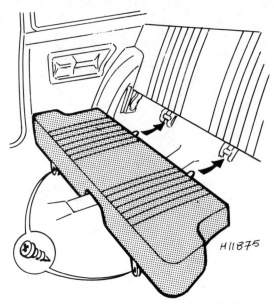

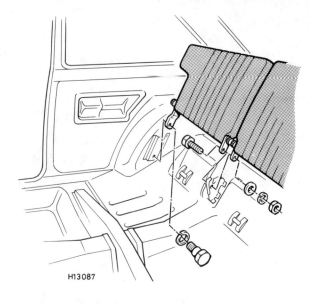

Fig. 12.29 Seat cushion and backrest arrangement

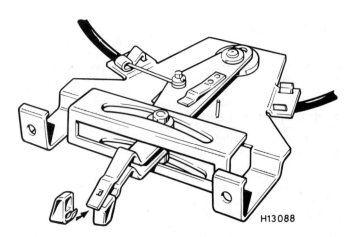

Fig. 12.30 Heater control assembly (Sec. 37)

35 Rear seats – removal and refitting

One piece type backrest

1   Move the front seats as far forward as possible and fold down their backrests.
2   Working on the rear seat, extract the two cross-head screws that secure the front of the cushion. Ease the front of the cushion upward and forward, so releasing the wire tongues from the pan attachments. Remove the cushion, taking care not to tear the headlining.
3   Remove the now exposed shouldered bolt and spring washer which hold each of the backrest hinges to the side brackets.
4   Ease the backrest upward to free it from the hinges.

Split type backrest

5   Remove the rear seat cushion as described in paragraphs 1 and 2.
6   Remove the set screw, nut and washers from the centre hinge bracket. Swing the link forward and upwards to clear the centre hinge bracket.
7   Ease each backrest upwards to free it from its hinge brackets and remove from the car interior.
8   Refitting of all components is a reversal of removal.

36 Heater and ventilation system – general description

1   The heater system delivers fresh air to the windscreen for demisting purposes and to the car interior. The flow to each may be varied in respect of volume and temperature by the two facia mounted controls. A flow-through fresh air ventilation system is fitted. This delivers unheated air through the two facia mounted controllable ducts and exhausts the stale air through the flap valves at the rear of the rear side windows.
2   The heater assembly comprises a matrix heated by water from the engine cooling system and a booster fan controlled by a two-position switch located on the facia panel. During normal forward motion of the car, air is forced through the air intake just forward of the windscreen and passes through the heater matrix, absorbing heat and carrying it to the car interior. When the car is stationary or travelling at low speed then the booster fan may be actuated.

37 Heater – removal and refitting

1   Disconnect the battery.
2   Drain the cooling system and disconnect the heater hoses at the engine compartment rear bulkhead.
3   Where fitted, remove the centre console and the radio.
4   Using a small screwdriver, compress the spring retainer and pull off the heater control knobs.
5   Extract the two securing screws and withdraw the heater control panel.
6   Extract the two screws that hold the control bracket and ease the control assembly forward and downward.
7   Unclip each cable at the heater end, release the flap valve cable from its trunnion and unhook the water valve cable from its lever.
8   Withdraw the complete control assembly with cables from under the facia.
9   Remove the facia and instrument panel as described in Section 12.
10   Disconnect the multi-plug to the heater blower motor and the handbrake warning switch wiring connector.
11   Lift out the demister ducts.
12   Disconnect the fresh air hoses from the heater centre duct. Withdraw the centre duct and seal from the heater.
13   Peel away the strips of tape that secure the wiring harness to the front of the heater.
14   Extract the heater upper mounting screws. Lower the heater assembly and remove it from the car. Take care not to spill any of the coolant which remains in the heater interior.
15   Refitting is a reversal of removal. Adjust the controls as described in Section 39 and refill the cooling system.

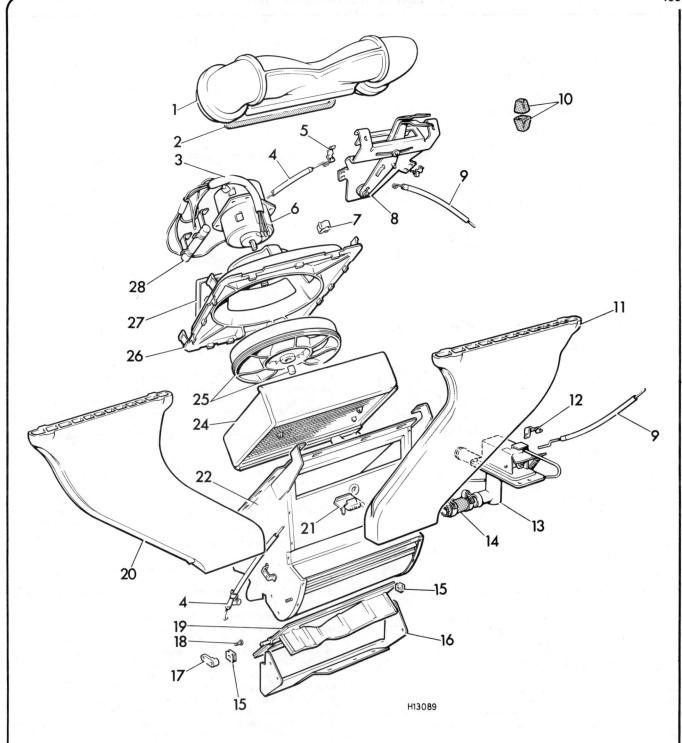

Fig. 12.31 Exploded view of the heater (Sec. 38)

H13089

1 Centre duct	9 Valve control cable	15 Flap valve bearing	22 Casing
2 Seal	10 Control lever knobs	16 Deflector plate	23 Capillary tube clips
3 Fan harness	11 Demist duct	17 Flap control lever	24 Matrix
4 Flap control cable	12 Clip	18 Cable trunnion	25 Fan
5 Clip	13 Thermostatic valve and	19 Flap valve	26 Top cover
6 Blower motor	capillary tube	20 Demist duct	27 Seal
7 Clip	14 Hose and clips	21 Wiring socket	28 Resistor
8 Control bracket			

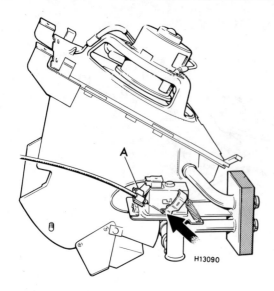

Fig. 12.32 Water valve cable adjustment (see text) (Sec 39)

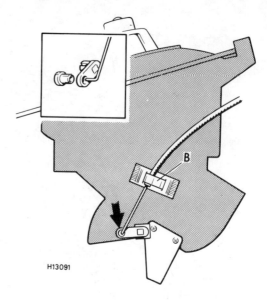

Fig. 12.33 Flap valve cable adjustment (see text) (Sec. 39)

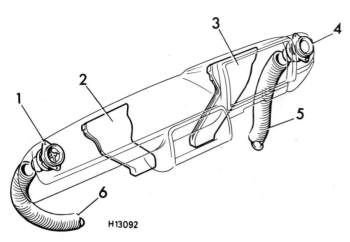

Fig. 12.34 Fresh air vents and demister ducts (Sec. 40)

1   Air vent (ball socket type)
2 and 3 Demister ducts
4   Air vent (alternative pivot
      plate type)
5 and 6 Flexible hoses

38 Heater – dismantling and reassembly

1   Refer to Fig. 12.31 and release the blower harness plastic socket (2).
2   Release the eight plastic clips that retain the heater top cover assembly (26) and lift it off.
3   Remove the seven selftapping screws from the deflector plate (16) and withdraw it.
4   Note the position of each flap valve bearing (15) (the wider slot accommodates the deflector plate) and having set the flap valve to its mid position, prise out the bearings and withdraw the flap valve assembly.
5   Carefully release the capillary tube from the four clips (23). Release the water valve to heater block inlet pipe hose clip (14) and remove the bulkhead seal.
6   Release the water valve (13) which is retained by four screws. Withdraw the valve and capillary assembly as far as possible.

7   Turn the heater casing over and withdraw the heater block. The water valve and capillary may now be removed.
8   Carefully prise off the fan securing clip and detach the fan.
9   Disconnect the motor cables, detach the motor securing clips and withdraw the motor.
10 Reassembly is a reversal of dismantling but carefully observe the following points: The three fan motor cables should be connected in the correct positions: green/yellow adjacent to the endplate groove, black in the centre and green/brown in the remaining location.
11 Where a replacement water valve and capillary assembly is being fitted, then the capillary tube must conform to the shape of the original and must be refitted correctly. If the original capillary tube was distorted during removal, then a template may be made up as a former for the new tube, using a piece of wooden board and small sections of dowel to form an elementary type of tube bender.

39 Heater – adjustments

1   The heat control and the air distribution flap valve control do not normally require alteration or adjustment, unless the clips A or B have been disturbed or the heater unit removed or dismantled.
2   Where necessary, release clip A and set the heater facia control to the cold position (extreme left) – blue.
3   Set the lever on the heater unit fully clockwise as shown by the arrow (Fig. 12.32) and refit the clip A and the outer cable. Snap it closed while holding the lever in its previously set position.
4   To adjust the air distribution flap valve, release clip B (Fig. 12.33) and set the upper facia control to the off position, marked O.
5   Set the heater unit lever fully anti-clockwise as indicated by the arrow and secure clip B to the outer cable.

40 Fresh air ventilator, hoses and ducts – removal and refitting

1   Reach up under the facia panel and disconnect the flexible hoses from the facia ventilators.
2   Remove the facia as described in Section 12.
3   Remove the two demisting ducts from the heater.
4   Remove the two ventilator hoses from the heater centre duct.
5   Release the two spring retainers that secure each of the facia ventilators. Withdraw the ventilators.
6   The flexible hoses should be renewed or taped if split.
7   Refitting is a reversal of removal.

Chapter 13 Supplement:
Revisions and information on later models

Contents

1 Introduction

This Supplement covers the more important changes which have been made to the Sunbeam range after 1979.

The 1.6l Ti model is also included. This car has a higher compression ratio, twin Weber dual venturi carburettors and suspension changes, when compared with other versions in this range. The Ti is recognisable by its black air dam and bumpers, and rear spoiler.

2 Specifications

The Specifications listed here are revisions of, or additional to, the main Specifications at the beginning of each Chapter

Engine (1.6 Ti)
Power output (max)	100 bhp (DIN) at 4800 rpm
Torque (max)	96 lbf ft at 2900 rpm
Compression ratio	9.4 : 1

Fuel system
Zenith Stromberg carburettor (B series)

Engine		Carburettor number	Carburettor type
(a)	930	S 4103	1.50 CD3
(b)	1300 LC	S 3912 B	1.50 CD3
(c)	1300 HC	S 3908 B	1.75 CD3
(d)	1300 HC	S 4013	1.50 CD3
(e)	1600 LC	S 3913 B	1.50 CD3
(f)	1600 HC	S 3909	1.75 CD3
(g)	1600 HC	S 4012	1.50 CD3

Carburettor specifications
As listed in above section:

	Needle type	Piston spring	Cam type	Fast idle gap in (mm)	Idle speed (rpm)
(a)	B5ET	Blue	G	0.025 to 0.030 (0.6 to 0.75)	820 to 880
(b)	B5DK	Blue	M	0.025 to 0.035 (0.6 to 0.9)	770 to 830
(c)	B1EB	Plain	VA	0.025 to 0.035 (0.6 to 0.9)	870 to 930
(d)	B5DV	Blue	M	0.025 to 0.035 (0.6 to 0.9)	770 to 830
(e)	B5DK	Blue	M	0.025 to 0.035 (0.6 to 0.9)	770 to 830
(f)	B1EC	Plain	VA	0.025 to 0.035 (0.6 to 0.9)	870 to 930
(g)	B5DU	Blue	M	0.025 to 0.035 (0.6 to 0.9)	770 to 830

Weber carburettor (9, A and B series Ti models)

Carburettor number:	
Front	126
Rear	127
Primary venturi	32 mm
Secondary venturi	3.5 mm
Emulsion tube	F49
Main jet	115
Air correction jet	135
Idle jet	50 – F26
Fuel inlet needle valve	1.5 mm
Pump jet	40
Pump spring	Medium
Pump bleed	0.6 mm
Pump stroke:	
9 and A series	16 mm
B series	18.5 mm
Internal vent	8 mm diameter
Float level	7.5 mm
Starting jet:	
9 and A series	70F5
B series	F950

Ignition system

Ignition timing, 1600 Ti (dynamic, with vacuum pipe disconnected)

Engine speed (rpm)	BTDC
950	7° to 9°
3000	28° to 30°

Electrical system

Fuses

Number	Fuse rating	Circuit protected
1	Red 16A	Heated rear window relay and element
2	White 8A	Horn(s)
3	White 8A	Heater blower motor and switch
4	White 8A	Interior lamps and door switches Console connections OR clock and cigar lighter Load compartment lamp Pressure differential warning actuator
5	White 8A	Direction indicator flasher unit
6	White 8A	Reverse lamps and switch Stop lamps and switch Heated rear window switch and relay Brake pad wear indicator and switch Windscreen wiper motor, switch and pump Rear window wiper motor and pump Electronic oil level control unit and sensor Selector gate illumination, auto transmission Headlamp wash/wipe motors and pump
7	White 8A	Headlamp main beam, right hand
8	White 8A	Headlamp dip beam, right hand
9	White 8A	Side and tail lamps, right hand Rear number plate lamps Switch panel illumination Instrument panel illumination
10	White 8A	Side and tail lamps, left hand Console connection OR clock illumination Heater control illumination Rear fog lamps and switch Under bonnet lamp
11	White 8A	Headlamp dip beam, left hand Headlamp wash/wipe relay
12	White 8A	Headlamp main beam, left hand
In-line	Blue/yellow 10A	Engine cooling fan motor and switch

Suspension

Coil spring identification (front)

Model	Right-hand side		Left-hand side	
	Colour	Free length in (mm)	Colour	Free length in (mm)
1.0 Standard	Green	16.6 (423)	Pink	15.9 (404)
1.0 Heavy duty	Brown	15.9 (403)	Yellow	15.2 (385)
1.3/1.6 Standard	White	16.9 (429)	Blue	16.8 (411)
1.3/1.6 Heavy duty	Red	15.5 (394)	Red + Red	15.0 (379)

Coil spring identification (rear)

Model	Colour	Free length in (mm)
1.0 Standard	Plain	11.7 (296)
1.0 Heavy duty	Blue	11.3 (288)
1.3/1.6 Standard	Plain	11.7 (296)
1.3/1.6 Heavy duty	Blue	11.3 (288)

---

3   Engine

Bolts and screws (930 engine)

1   Some engine components are secured or connected by means of 'Taptite' self-tapping screws. As these screws form their own threads, some of the affected components (coolant pump/impeller housing, etc) are supplied new with plain drilled holes to accept the 'Taptite' screws.
2   As previously emphasised, great care must be taken when tightening bolts into their threaded holes in the light alloy engine in order to avoid the risk of stripping the threads. The use of a torque wrench is essential.
3   Where a thread has been stripped, Helicoil inserts can be fitted in accordance with the makers' (Armstrong Patents Co. Ltd, Beverley, Yorkshire) instructions.

---

4   Cooling system

No-loss cooling system – description

1   This system is fitted to certain models; it includes an expansion tank with a pressure cap mounted on the left-hand inner wing panel under the bonnet.
2   Topping up should only be carried out by removing the cap from the expansion tank.
3   Always observe the normal safety precautions of covering the cap with a cloth and releasing it slowly if the engine is hot. Maintain the coolant level in the expansion tank at the level mark.

No loss cooling system – draining

4   Remove the pressure cap from the expansion tank. Set the heater control to HOT and remove the radiator cap.
5   Unscrew the radiator drain tap and the cylinder block drain plug.

No-loss cooling system – refilling

6   Make sure that the heater control is still set to HOT. Close the drain tap and screw in the drain plug.
7   Refill the system through the radiator filler neck with the specified anti-freeze mixture or corrosion inhibiting mixture as appropriate, according to climatic conditions.
8   When the radiator is brim full, screw on the radiator cap. Wet the rubber sealing ring in the cap before tightening to reduce the strain on the radiator.
9   Pour coolant into the expansion tank until it reaches the correct level.
10   Run the engine until it reaches normal temperature and then allow it to cool.
11   Top up the level in the expansion tank to its correct level. The level will drop initially after starting the engine as air is expelled from the system but thereafter should not alter.

---

5   Fuel system

Weber carburettors – description.

1   Two Weber 40 DCOE dual barrel carburettors are fitted to Ti models, using individual throttle barrel connections to the four inlet ports of the cylinder head.

Fig. 13.1 Cooling system expansion tank (Sec 4)

2   The carburettors are fitted with a manually-operated choke and an accelerator pump.

Weber carburettors – removal and refitting

3   Remove the air cleaner and casing. The air cleaner cover is retained at the top by two clips and secured at its base by four projections.
4   Remove the asbestos heat shield which is located between the carburettor and the air cleaner.
5   Disconnect the carburettor fuel pipes by unscrewing the banjo union bolts.
6   Extract the float chamber screw from the front carburettor in order to move the fuel pipes to one side, then refit the screw.
7   Release the choke inner and outer cables from the carburettors and tie them to one side.
8   Disconnect the accelerator control rod balljoint from the carburettor operating lever.
9   Remove the carburettor mounting pads and washers.
10   Withdraw the carburettors then separate them.
11   Remove the heat shield retaining plate and asbestos heat shield.
12   Refitting is a reversal of removal but tighten all mounting nuts to 10 lbf ft (13 Nm).
13   Check that the earth bond between the front carburettor and the thermostat housing is in position.

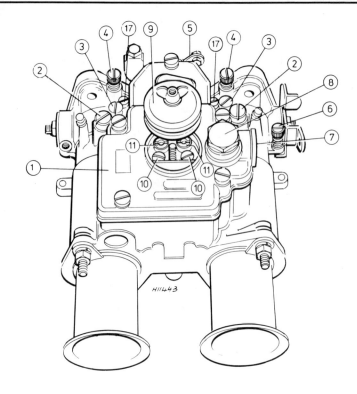

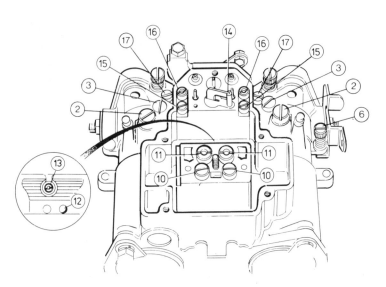

Fig. 13.2 Weber 40 DCOE carburettor (Sec 5)

1   Float chamber cover
2   Accelerator pump jets
3   Progression hole inspection cover
    screws
4   Idle mixture control screws
5   Cold start device operating lever
6   Idle speed adjusting screws
7   Fuel inlet
8   Fuel filter cover plug
9   Removable cover
10 Slow running jets
11 Main jet/emulsion tube/air
    correction jet assemblies
12 Feed holes to well below main and
    slow running jets
13 Accelerator pump inlet valve
14 Accelerator pump
15 Accelerator pump outlet valves
16 Starter jets
17 Blanking plugs

Weber carburettors – idle speed adjustment

14 Before any adjustments are carried out, make sure that the ignition system and spark plugs are correctly adjusted, and the valve clearances are set to the specified tolerance.

15 Check the specified idle speed for your particular model and engine (see Specifications at the front of this Supplement or refer to Chapter 3).

16 Turn the idle speed screw (A) until the engine is idling at the specified level. If the engine does not idle smoothly, then the carburettors may require synchronizing or the mixture adjusted as described in the following paragraphs.

Weber carburettors – synchronizing

17 Remove the air intake box from the carburettors.

18 Use a balance meter or manometer carefully following the instructions supplied with the test kit.

Weber carburettors – idle mixture adjustment

19 Make sure that the air cleaner is correctly in position and a tachometer is connected to the engine.

20 Prise out the tamperproof plugs.

21 Turn both idle mixture screws gently fully in and then unscrew them $2\frac{1}{2}$ turns each.

22 Start the engine and set it to idle at its specified idling speed of 950 rev/min.

23 Adjust each of the mixture screws until the engine speed reaches its highest level.

24 Re-adjust the idle speed to 950 rev/min.

25 To check the adjustment, short out each spark plug in turn. The drop in engine speed should be equal for each cylinder.

Weber carburettors – cleaning, overhaul and adjustment.

26 The only dismantling required is very occasional cleaning, and this

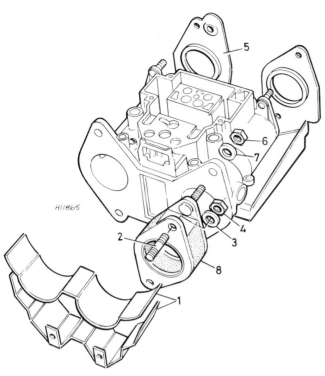

Fig. 13.3 Weber carburettor mounting details (Sec 5)

1 Heat shield mounting plate	5 Heat shield
2 Stud	6 Nut
3 Washer	7 Washer
4 Nut	8 Carburettor mounting

can be carried out without the need to remove the carburettors from the engine.

27 If a carburettor is worn, it is very often more economical to exchange the complete unit for a reconditioned or new one; consult your carburettor specialist about this.

28 To clean a carburettor, first slacken the fuel inlet filter cover plug. Disconnect the fuel pipe.

29 Remove the five screws which secure the float chamber cover to the carburettor body. Retain the brass washers located under the spring washers.

30 Lift off the float chamber cover, taking care not to damage the float or arm.

31 Remove the fuel inlet cover and filter. Clean the filter in fuel.

32 With the floats hanging fully down, use air pressure to clean out the fuel feed hole which is normally covered by the gauze filter mesh.

33 Use a syringe to syphon fuel from the float chamber and the well below the main jets.

34 Remove the slow running jet assembly followed by the main jet, the emulsion tube, the air correction jet assembly, the starter jets and the accelerator pump jets.

35 Clean out the jets with air pressure; never be tempted to use wire or the jet calibration will be ruined.

36 Reassembly is a reversal of dismantling, but check the float level setting in the following way.

Weber carburettors – float level setting

37 Check that the fuel inlet needle valve is screwed tightly into its housing and that the spring-loaded needle slides freely.

38 Hold the carburettor cover vertically so that the floats hang down and the float arm just contacts the needle valve without depressing the

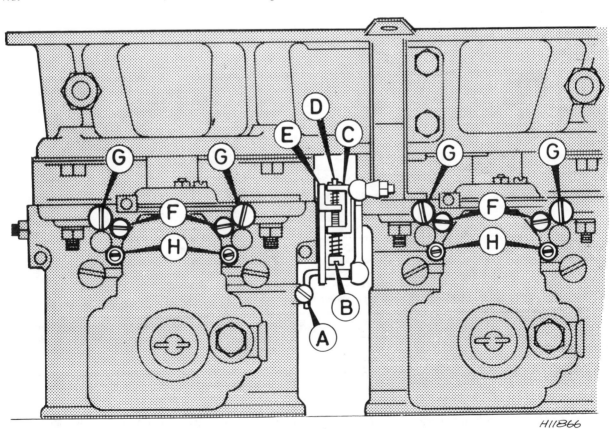

Fig. 13.4 Weber carburettor adjusting screws (Sec 5)

A Idle speed screw	E Throttle lever (front)
B Balance screw	F Vacuum plugs
C Throttle lever (rear)	G Idle mixture screws
D Spring plunger	H By-pass screws

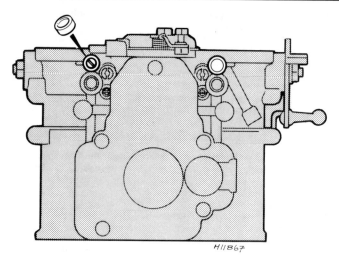

Fig. 13.5 Location of tamperproof plugs (Weber carburettor)
(Sec 5)

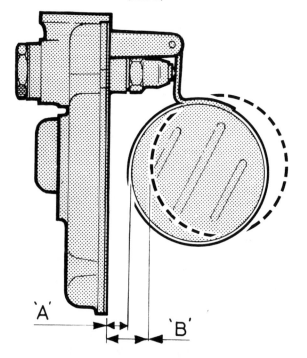

Fig. 13.6 Float level setting diagram (Weber carburettor) (Sec 5)

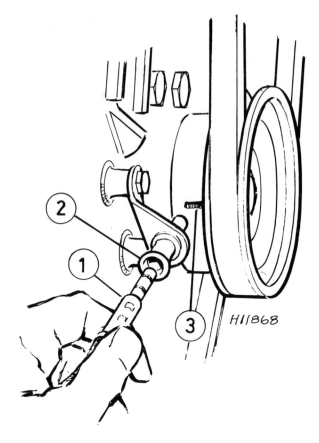

Fig. 13.7 Location of dynamic timing tester probe (Sec 6)

1   Timing probe   3   Crankshaft pulley slots
2   Probe locating sleeve

impulses are compared by the dynamic timing tester with the firing
point of each cylinder registered by the coil primary winding. The
dynamic timing tester averages the readings from the four cylinders
and indicates the result as a reading on the meter of the instrument
being used.
4   A special ten-pin socket connector is mounted on the right-hand
wing valance within the engine compartment, above the battery.
5   The socket connections include:

1   Earth
2   Automatic transmission
3   HT coil (positive)
4   Alternator field supply
5   Earth
6   Supply to starter motor solenoid
7   HT coil (negative)
8   Alternator IND field output
9   Supply to starter motor
10   Battery (positive)

6   The diagnostic connector provides a simple connection for the
dynamic ignition timing tester.
7   With the connection of suitable diagnostic equipment, fault tracing
and rectification is made quick and simple by service stations so
equipped.

spring-loaded end of the valve needle. Under these conditions,
distance A (float to surface of cover gasket) should be 8.5 mm. Check
both floats at the same time.
39   If adjustment is required, bend the tab on the float arm.
40   Now check the float stroke which should be 6.5 mm. The best
method of doing this is to take measurement B (cover gasket surface
to float in its lowest position) which should be 15.0 mm. Where
necessary, bend the float arm stop lug.

6   Ignition system

Electromagnetic timing probe and diagnostic connector
1   On later models, provision is made for reading of the individual
cylinder firing points by the timing probe of a dynamic timing tester.
2   Basically, the engine has been modified to incorporate slots in the
crankshaft pulley at 20° ATDC for all cylinders together with a sleeve
mounted on the timing cover.
3   With the engine running, the timing probe is inserted into the
sleeve and produces an impulse as each reference slot passes. These

7   Braking system

Bleeding the hydraulic system − general
1   In addition to the two-man method of bleeding the brakes
described in Chapter 9, Section 11, the following alternative methods
are recommended.
2   If the master cylinder has been disconnected and reconnected, the

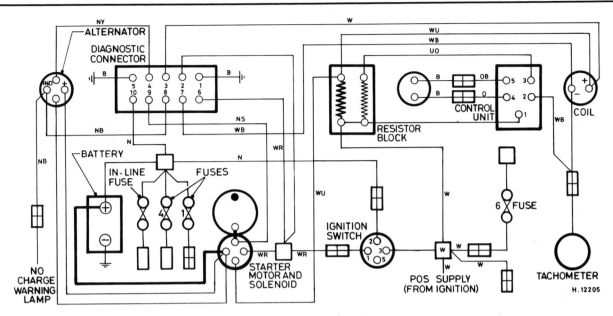

Fig. 13.8 Diagnostic connector circuit diagram (Sec 6)

complete system (both circuits) must be bled.

3   If only a component of one circuit has been disturbed, only that particular circuit need be bled.

4   If the entire system is being bled, the sequence of bleeding should be carried out by starting at the bleed screw furthest from the master cylinder and finishing at the one nearest to it. Unless the pressure bleeding method is being used, do not forget to keep the fluid level in the master cylinder reservoir topped up to prevent air from being drawn into the system which would make any work done worthless.

5   Before commencing operations, check that all system hoses and pipes are in good condition, with all unions tight and free from leaks.

6   Take great care not to allow hydraulic fluid to come into contact with the vehicle paintwork as it is an effective paint stripper. Wash off any spilled fluid immediately with cold water.

7   Destroy the servo vacuum by giving several applications of the brake pedal in quick succession.

Bleeding the hydraulic system – using a one-way valve kit

8   There are several one-man, one-way, brake bleeding kits available from motor accessory shops. It is recommended that one of these kits is used wherever possible as it will greatly simplify the bleeding operations and also reduce the risk of air or fluid being drawn back into the system, quite apart from being able to do the work without the help of an assistant.

9   To use the kit, connect the tube to the bleed screw and open the screw half a turn.

10 Depress the brake pedal fully and slowly release it. The one-way valve in the kit will prevent expelled air and fluid from returning at the end of each pedal downstroke. Repeat this operation several times to be sure of ejecting all air from the system. Some kits include a translucent container which can be positioned so that the air bubbles and fluid can actually be seen being ejected from the system.

11 Tighten the bleed screw, remove the tube and repeat the operations on the remaining brakes.

12 On completion, depress the brake pedal. If it still feels spongy repeat the bleeding operations as air must still be trapped in the system.

Bleeding the hydraulic system – using a pressure bleeding kit

13 These kits too are available from motor accessory shops and are usually operated by air pressure from the spare tyre.

14 By connecting a pressurised container to the master cylinder fluid reservoir, bleeding is then carried out by simply opening each bleed screw in turn and allowing the fluid to run out, rather like turning on a tap, until no air is visible in the expelled fluid.

15 By using this method, the large reserve of hydraulic fluid provides a safeguard against air being drawn into the master cylinder during

bleeding which often occurs if the fluid level in the reservoir is not maintained.

16 Pressure bleeding is particularly effective when bleeding 'difficult' systems, or when bleeding the complete system at time of routine fluid renewal.

All bleeding methods

17 When bleeding is completed, check and top up the fluid level in the master cylinder reservoir.

18 Check the feel of the brake pedal. If it feels at all spongy, air must still be present in the system and further bleeding is indicated. Failure to bleed satisfactorily after a reasonable repetition of the bleeding operations may be due to worn master cylinder seals.

19 Discard brake fluid which has been expelled. It is almost certain to be contaminated with moisture, air and dirt making it unsuitable for further use. Clean fluid should always be stored in an air tight container as it is hygroscopic (absorbs moisture readily), which lowers its boiling point and could affect braking performance under severe conditions.

Disc pad wear warning system

20 On some models, a sensor is embedded in each disc pad which, when the friction material wears down to a pre-determined level, makes contact with the brake disc and completes a warning lamp circuit.

21 The warning lamp will illuminate as a reminder to renew the pads immediately.

22 A test switch is incorporated in the circuit; this should be depressed periodically to illuminate the bulb which is a means of verifying the correct operation of the circuit. Testing the circuit can only be carried out with the ignition switch ON.

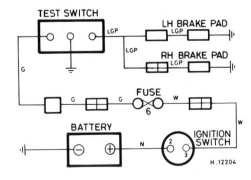

Fig. 13.9 Disc pad wear warning system (Sec 7)

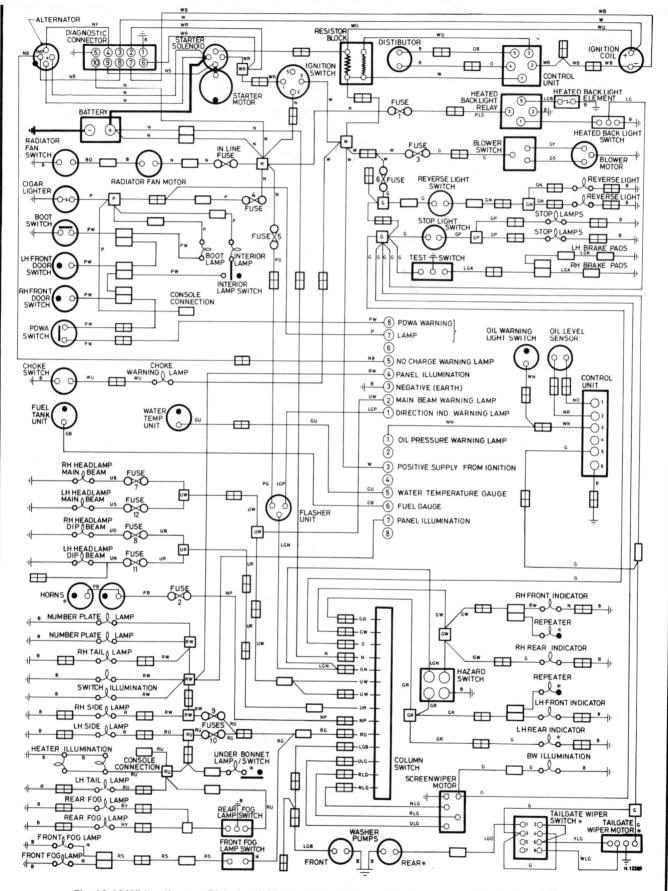

Fig. 13.10 Wiring diagram. Right-hand drive models with two-dial instrument panel, 9 Series onwards
Refer to page 158 for key

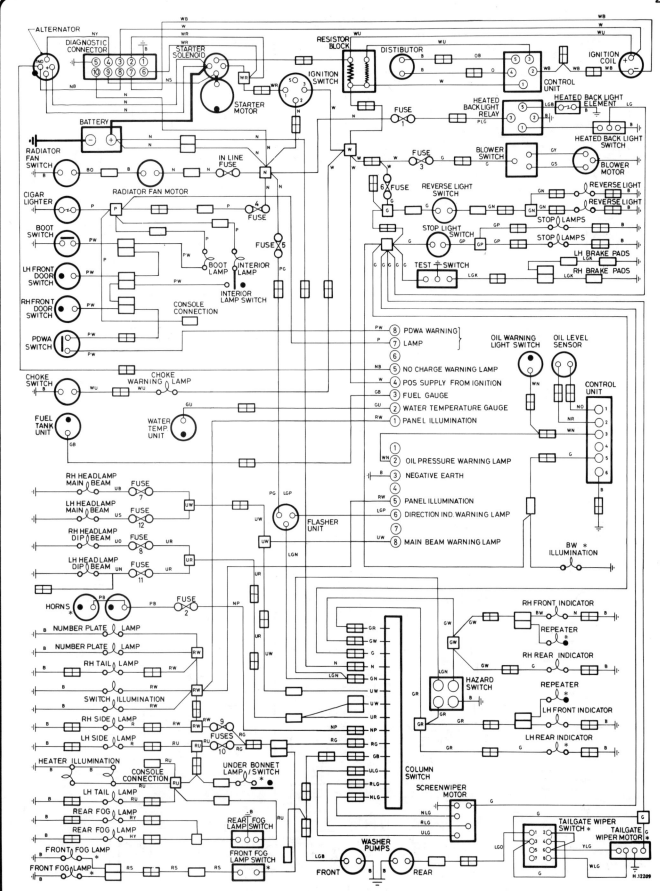

Fig. 13.11 Wiring diagram. Left-hand drive models with two-dial instrument panel, 9 Series onwards
Refer to page 158 for key

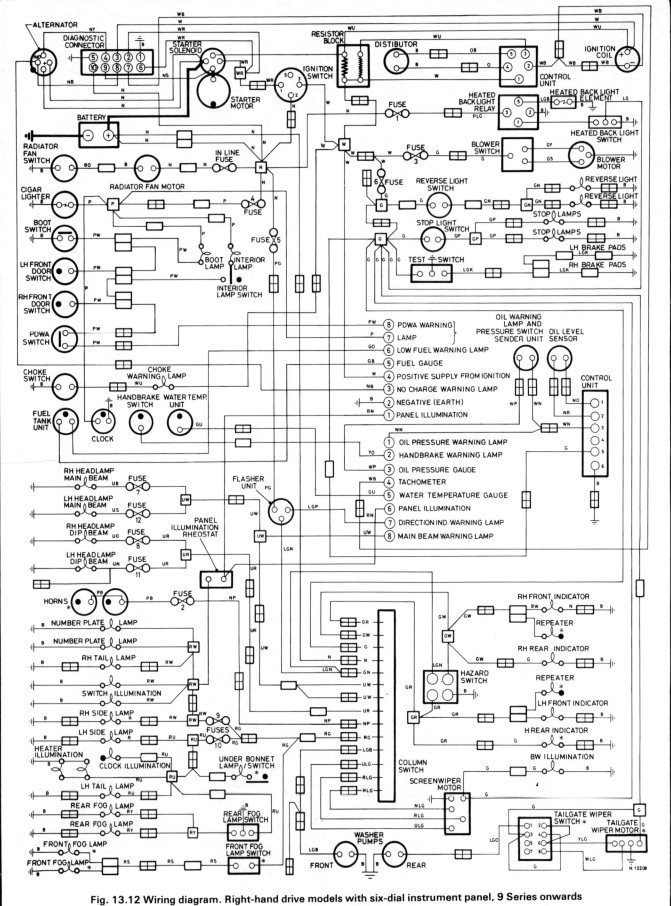

Fig. 13.12 Wiring diagram. Right-hand drive models with six-dial instrument panel, 9 Series onwards

Refer to page 158 for key

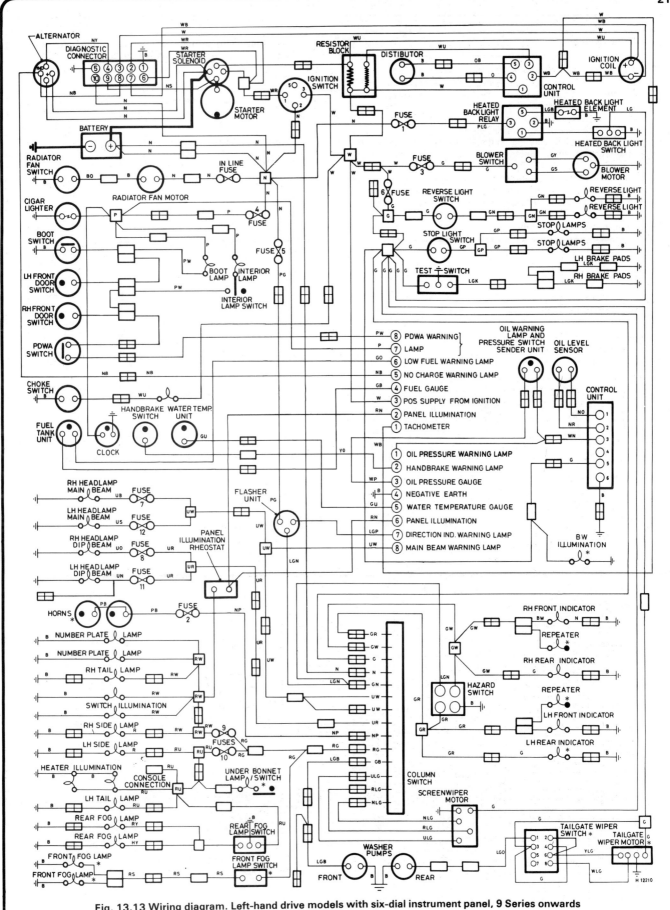

Fig. 13.13 Wiring diagram. Left-hand drive models with six-dial instrument panel, 9 Series onwards
Refer to page 158 for key

8 Electrical system

Electronic engine oil level indicator – description

1   The electronic oil level indicator system consists of a sensor in the dipstick, a control unit mounted under the dash, a warning light on the instrument panel and associated wiring. The circuit diagram is included in the wiring diagrams.

2   The dipstick sensor is a resistor which will be completely or partially immersed in oil depending on the level in the sump. When the engine is started, a small electric current is passed through the resistor, causing its temperature to rise. If the oil level in the sump is correct, the resistor will be completely submerged in oil which will dissipate the heat. The temperature increase will therefore be very small. If the level is too low, the resistor will not be cooled and a large increase in temperature will occur. This will cause an increase in resistance of the sensor and thus of the voltage at its terminals in the

control unit. The voltage increase will trigger an electronic circuit in the control unit, causing the warning light on the instrument panel to flash, thus informing the driver of low oil level in the sump.

9 Bodywork

Parcels shelf – removal and refitting

1   Pull the draught seal from the edge of the door aperture at the point where the parcels shelf joins the side panel.

2   Using a knife or screwdriver blade, prise out the retaining clip (A).

3   Extract all the shelf fixing screws (five on models without centre console, six where a centre console is fitted).

4   Remove the shelf.

5   Refitting is a reversal of the removal procedure.

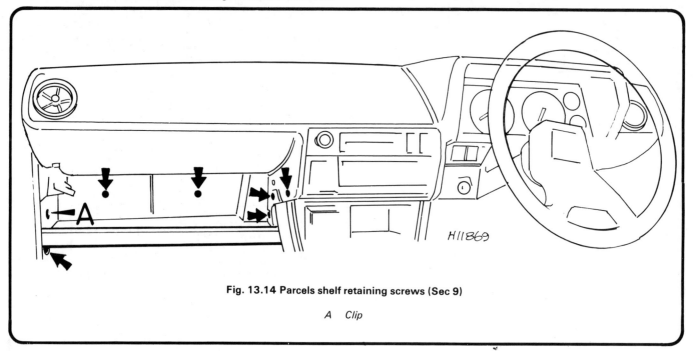

Fig. 13.14 Parcels shelf retaining screws (Sec 9)

A   Clip

Safety first!

Professional motor mechanics are trained in safe working procedures. However enthusiastic you may be about getting on with the job in hand, do take the time to ensure that your safety is not put at risk. A moment's lack of attention can result in an accident, as can failure to observe certain elementary precautions.

There will always be new ways of having accidents, and the following points do not pretend to be a comprehensive list of all dangers; they are intended rather to make you aware of the risks and to encourage a safety-conscious approach to all work you carry out on your vehicle.

Essential DOs and DON'Ts

DON'T rely on a single jack when working underneath the vehicle. Always use reliable additional means of support, such as axle stands, securely placed under a part of the vehicle that you know will not give way.

DON'T attempt to loosen or tighten high-torque nuts (e.g. wheel hub nuts) while the vehicle is on a jack; it may be pulled off.

DON'T start the engine without first ascertaining that the transmission is in neutral (or 'Park' where applicable) and the parking brake applied.

DON'T suddenly remove the filler cap from a hot cooling system – cover it with a cloth and release the pressure gradually first, or you may get scalded by escaping coolant.

DON'T attempt to drain oil until you are sure it has cooled sufficiently to avoid scalding you.

DON'T grasp any part of the engine, exhaust or catalytic converter without first ascertaining that it is sufficiently cool to avoid burning you.

DON'T allow brake fluid or antifreeze to contact vehicle paintwork.

DON'T syphon toxic liquids such as fuel, brake fluid or antifreeze by mouth, or allow them to remain on your skin.

DON'T inhale dust – it may be injurious to health (see *Asbestos* below).

DON'T allow any spilt oil or grease to remain on the floor – wipe it up straight away, before someone slips on it.

DON'T use ill-fitting spanners or other tools which may slip and cause injury.

DON'T attempt to lift a heavy component which may be beyond your capability – get assistance.

DON'T rush to finish a job, or take unverified short cuts.

DON'T allow children or animals in or around an unattended vehicle.

DO wear eye protection when using power tools such as drill, sander, bench grinder etc, and when working under the vehicle.

DO use a barrier cream on your hands prior to undertaking dirty jobs – it will protect your skin from infection as well as making the dirt easier to remove afterwards; but make sure your hands aren't left slippery.

DO keep loose clothing (cuffs, tie etc) and long hair well out of the way of moving mechanical parts.

DO remove rings, wristwatch etc, before working on the vehicle – especially the electrical system.

DO ensure that any lifting tackle used has a safe working load rating adequate for the job.

DO keep your work area tidy – it is only too easy to fall over articles left lying around.

DO get someone to check periodically that all is well, when working alone on the vehicle.

DO carry out work in a logical sequence and check that everything is correctly assembled and tightened afterwards.

DO remember that your vehicle's safety affects that of yourself and others. If in doubt on any point, get specialist advice.

IF, in spite of following these precautions, you are unfortunate enough to injure yourself, seek medical attention as soon as possible.

Asbestos

Certain friction, insulating, sealing, and other products – such as brake linings, brake bands, clutch linings, torque converters, gaskets, etc – contain asbestos. *Extreme care must be taken to avoid inhalation of dust from such products since it is hazardous to health*. If in doubt, assume that they *do* contain asbestos.

Fire

Remember at all times that petrol (gasoline) is highly flammable. Never smoke, or have any kind of naked flame around, when working on the vehicle. But the risk does not end there – a spark caused by an electrical short-circuit, by two metal surfaces contacting each other, by careless use of tools, or even by static electricity built up in your body under certain conditions, can ignite petrol vapour, which in a confined space is highly explosive.

Always disconnect the battery earth (ground) terminal before working on any part of the fuel or electrical system, and never risk spilling fuel on to a hot engine or exhaust.

It is recommended that a fire extinguisher of a type suitable for fuel and electrical fires is kept handy in the garage or workplace at all times. Never try to extinguish a fuel or electrical fire with water.

Fumes

Certain fumes are highly toxic and can quickly cause unconsciousness and even death if inhaled to any extent. Petrol (gasoline) vapour comes into this category, as do the vapours from certain solvents such as trichloroethylene. Any draining or pouring of such volatile fluids should be done in a well ventilated area.

When using cleaning fluids and solvents, read the instructions carefully. Never use materials from unmarked containers – they may give off poisonous vapours.

Never run the engine of a motor vehicle in an enclosed space such as a garage. Exhaust fumes contain carbon monoxide which is extremely poisonous; if you need to run the engine, always do so in the open air or at least have the rear of the vehicle outside the workplace.

If you are fortunate enough to have the use of an inspection pit, never drain or pour petrol, and never run the engine, while the vehicle is standing over it; the fumes, being heavier than air, will concentrate in the pit with possibly lethal results.

The battery

Never cause a spark, or allow a naked light, near the vehicle's battery. It will normally be giving off a certain amount of hydrogen gas, which is highly explosive.

Always disconnect the battery earth (ground) terminal before working on the fuel or electrical systems.

If possible, loosen the filler plugs or cover when charging the battery from an external source. Do not charge at an excessive rate or the battery may burst.

Take care when topping up and when carrying the battery. The acid electrolyte, even when diluted, is very corrosive and should not be allowed to contact the eyes or skin.

If you ever need to prepare electrolyte yourself, always add the acid slowly to the water, and never the other way round. Protect against splashes by wearing rubber gloves and goggles.

When jump starting a car using a booster battery, for negative earth (ground) vehicles, connect the jump leads in the following sequence: First connect one jump lead between the positive (+) terminals of the two batteries. Then connect the other jump lead first to the negative (–) terminal of the booster battery, and then to a good earthing (ground) point on the vehicle to be started, at least 18 in (45 cm) from the battery if possible. Ensure that hands and jump leads are clear of any moving parts, and that the two vehicles do not touch. Disconnect the leads in the reverse order.

Mains electricity

When using an electric power tool, inspection light etc, which works from the mains, always ensure that the appliance is correctly connected to its plug and that, where necessary, it is properly earthed (grounded). Do not use such appliances in damp conditions and, again, beware of creating a spark or applying excessive heat in the vicinity of fuel or fuel vapour.

Ignition HT voltage

A severe electric shock can result from touching certain parts of the ignition system, such as the HT leads, when the engine is running or being cranked, particularly if components are damp or the insulation is defective. Where an electronic ignition system is fitted, the HT voltage is much higher and could prove fatal.

Fault diagnosis

Introduction

The vehicle owner who does his or her own maintenance according to the recommended schedules should not have to use this section of the manual very often. Modern component reliability is such that, provided those items subject to wear or deterioration are inspected or renewed at the specified intervals, sudden failure is comparatively rare. Faults do not usually just happen as a result of sudden failure, but develop over a period of time. Major mechanical failures in particular are usually preceded by characteristic symptoms over hundreds or even thousands of miles. Those components which do occasionally fail without warning are often small and easily carried in the vehicle.

With any fault finding, the first step is to decide where to begin investigations. Sometimes this is obvious, but on other occasions a little detective work will be necessary. The owner who makes half a dozen haphazard adjustments or replacements may be successful in curing a fault (or its symptoms), but he will be none the wiser if the fault recurs and he may well have spent more time and money than was necessary. A calm and logical approach will be found to be more satisfactory in the long run. Always take into account any warning signs or abnormalities that may have been noticed in the period preceding the fault – power loss, high or low gauge readings, unusual noises or smells, etc – and remember that failure of components such as fuses or spark plugs may only be pointers to some underlying fault.

The pages which follow here are intended to help in cases of failure to start or breakdown on the road. There is also a Fault Diagnosis Section at the end of each Chapter which should be consulted if the preliminary checks prove unfruitful. Whatever the fault, certain basic principles apply. These are as follows:

Verify the fault. This is simply a matter of being sure that you know what the symptoms are before starting work. This is particularly important if you are investigating a fault for someone else who may not have described it very accurately.

Don't overlook the obvious. For example, if the vehicle won't start, is there petrol in the tank? (Don't take anyone else's word on this particular point, and don't trust the fuel gauge either!) If an electrical fault is indicated, look for loose or broken wires before digging out the test gear.

Cure the disease, not the symptom. Substituting a flat battery with a fully charged one will get you off the hard shoulder, but if the underlying cause is not attended to, the new battery will go the same way. Similarly, changing oil-fouled spark plugs for a new set will get you moving again, but remember that the reason for the fouling (if it wasn't simply an incorrect grade of plug) will have to be established and corrected.

Don't take anything for granted. Particularly, don't forget that a 'new' component may itself be defective (especially if it's been rattling round in the boot for months), and don't leave components out of a fault diagnosis sequence just because they are new or recently fitted. When you do finally diagnose a difficult fault, you'll probably realise that all the evidence was there from the start.

Electrical faults

Electrical faults can be more puzzling than straightforward mechanical failures, but they are no less susceptible to logical analysis if the basic principles of operation are understood. Vehicle electrical wiring exists in extremely unfavourable conditions – heat, vibration and chemical attack – and the first things to look for are loose or corroded connections and broken or chafed wires, especially where the wires pass through holes in the bodywork or are subject to vibration.

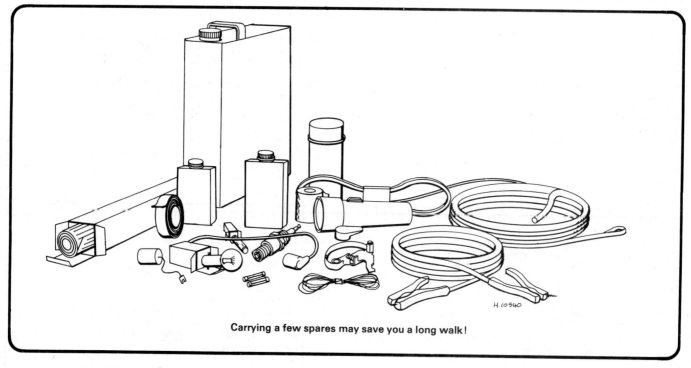

H.10540

Carrying a few spares may save you a long walk!

All metal-bodied vehicles in current production have one pole of the battery 'earthed', ie connected to the vehicle bodywork, and in nearly all modern vehicles it is the negative (–) terminal. The various electrical components – motors, bulb holders etc – are also connected to earth, either by means of a lead or directly by their mountings. Electric current flows through the component and then back to the battery via the bodywork. If the component mounting is loose or corroded, or if a good path back to the battery is not available, the circuit will be incomplete and malfunction will result. The engine and/or gearbox are also earthed by means of flexible metal straps to the body or subframe; if these straps are loose or missing, starter motor, generator and ignition trouble may result.

Assuming the earth return to be satisfactory, electrical faults will be due either to component malfunction or to defects in the current supply. Individual components are dealt with in Chapter 10. If supply wires are broken or cracked internally this results in an open-circuit, and the easiest way to check for this is to bypass the suspect wire temporarily with a length of wire having a crocodile clip or suitable connector at each end. Alternatively, a 12V test lamp can be used to verify the presence of supply voltage at various points along the wire and the break can be thus isolated.

If a bare portion of a live wire touches the bodywork or other earthed metal part, the electricity will take the low-resistance path thus formed back to the battery: this is known as a short-circuit. Hopefully a short-circuit will blow a fuse, but otherwise it may cause burning of the insulation (and possibly further short-circuits) or even a fire. This is why it is inadvisable to bypass persistently blowing fuses with silver foil or wire.

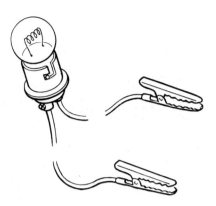

A simple test lamp is useful for investigating electrical faults

Spares and tool kit

Most vehicles are supplied only with sufficient tools for wheel changing; the *Maintenance and minor repair* tool kit detailed in *Tools and working facilities*, with the addition of a hammer, is probably sufficient for those repairs that most motorists would consider attempting at the roadside. In addition a few items which can be fitted without too much trouble in the event of a breakdown should be carried. Experience and available space will modify the list below, but the following may save having to call on professional assistance:

Spark plugs, clean and correctly gapped
HT lead and plug cap – long enough to reach the plug furthest from the distributor
Distributor rotor
Drivebelt – emergency type may suffice
Spare fuses
Set of principal light bulbs
Hose clips
Tin of radiator sealer and hose bandage
Tube of filler paste
Exhaust bandage
Roll of insulating tape
Length of soft iron wire
Length of electrical flex
Torch or inspection lamp (can double as test lamp)
Battery jump leads
Tow-rope
Ignition waterproofing aerosol
Litre of engine oil
Sealed can of hydraulic fluid
Emergency windscreen
Tyre valve core

If spare fuel is carried, a can designed for the purpose should be used to minimise risks of leakage and collision damage. A first aid kit and a warning triangle, whilst not at present compulsory in the UK, are obviously sensible items to carry in addition to the above.

When touring abroad it may be advisable to carry additional spares which, even if you cannot fit them yourself, could save having to wait while parts are obtained. The items below may be worth considering:

Cylinder head gasket
Alternator brushes
Fuel pump repair kit
Clutch and throttle cables

One of the motoring organisations will be able to advise on availability of fuel etc in foreign countries.

Engine will not start

Engine fails to turn when starter operated
Flat battery (recharge, use jump leads, or push start)
Battery terminals loose or corroded
Battery earth to body defective
Engine earth strap loose or broken
Starter motor (or solenoid) wiring loose or broken
Automatic transmission selector in wrong position, or inhibitor switch faulty
Ignition/starter switch faulty
Major mechanical failure (seizure) or long disuse (piston rings rusted to bores)
Starter or solenoid internal fault (see Chapter 10)

Starter motor turns engine slowly
Partially discharged battery (recharge, use jump leads, or push start)
Battery terminals loose or corroded
Battery earth to body defective
Engine earth strap loose
Starter motor (or solenoid) wiring loose
Starter motor internal fault (see Chapter 10)

Starter motor spins without turning engine
Flat battery
Starter motor pinion sticking on sleeve
Flywheel gear teeth damaged or worn
Starter motor mounting bolts loose

Engine turns normally but fails to start
Damp or dirty HT leads and distributor cap (crank engine and check for spark)
No fuel in tank (check for delivery at carburettor)
Excessive choke (hot engine) or insufficient choke (cold engine)
Fouled or incorrectly gapped spark plugs (remove, clean and regap)
Other ignition system fault (see Chapter 4)
Other fuel system fault (see Chapter 3)
Poor compression (see Chapter 1)
Major mechanical failure (eg camshaft drive)

Engine fires but will not run
Insufficient choke (cold engine)
Air leaks at carburettor or inlet manifold
Fuel starvation (see Chapter 3)
Ballast resistor defective, or other ignition fault (see Chapter 4)

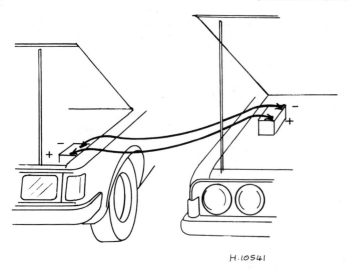

Correctly connected jump leads. Do not allow car bodies to touch!

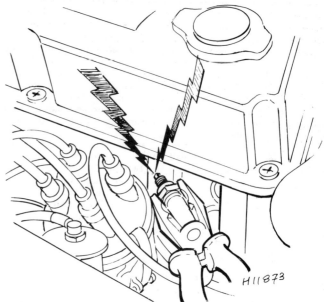

Crank engine and check for spark. Note use of insulated pliers – dry cloth or a rubber glove will suffice

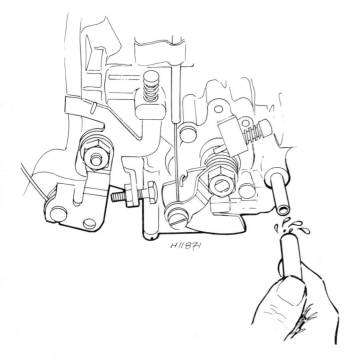

Remove fuel pipe from carburettor and check that fuel is being delivered

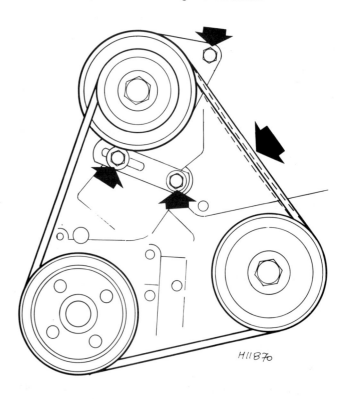

A slack drivebelt may cause overheating and battery charging problems. Slacken bolts arrowed to adjust

---

Engine cuts out and will not restart

Engine cuts out suddenly – ignition fault
    Loose or disconnected LT wires
    Wet HT leads or distributor cap (after traversing water splash)
    Coil or condenser failure (check for spark)
    Other ignition fault (see Chapter 4)

Engine misfires before cutting out – fuel fault
    Fuel tank empty
    Fuel pump defective or filter blocked (check for delivery)
    Fuel tank filler vent blocked (suction will be evident on releasing cap)
    Carburettor needle valve sticking

Carburettor jets blocked, where applicable
(fuel contaminated)
Other fuel system fault (see Chapter 3)

Engine cuts out – other causes
    Serious overheating
    Major mechanical failure (eg camshaft drive)

Engine overheats

Ignition (no-charge) warning light illuminated
Slack or broken drivebelt – retension or renew (Chapter 2)

Ignition warning light not illuminated
Coolant loss due to internal or external leakage (see Chapter 2)
Thermostat defective
Low oil level
Brakes binding
Radiator clogged externally or internally
Electric cooling fan not operating correctly
Engine waterways clogged
Ignition timing incorrect or automatic advance malfunctioning
Mixture too weak
Slack or broken drivebelt

Note: *Do not add cold water to an overheated engine or damage may result*

Low engine oil pressure

Gauge reads low or warning light illuminated with engine running
Oil level low or incorrect grade
Defective gauge or sender unit
Wire to sender unit earthed
Engine overheating
Oil filter clogged or bypass valve defective
Oil pressure relief valve defective
Oil pick-up strainer clogged
Oil pump worn or mountings loose
Worn main or big-end bearings

Note: *Low oil pressure in a high-mileage engine at tickover is not necessarily a cause for concern. Sudden pressure loss at speed is far more significant. In any event, check the gauge or warning light sender before condemning the engine.*

Engine noises

Pre-ignition (pinking) on acceleration
Incorrect grade of fuel
Ignition timing incorrect
Distributor faulty or worn
Worn or maladjusted carburettor
Excessive carbon build-up in engine

Whistling or wheezing noises
Leaking vacuum hose
Leaking carburettor or manifold gasket
Blowing head gasket

Tapping or rattling
Incorrect valve clearances
Worn valve gear
Worn timing chain
Broken piston ring (ticking noise)

Knocking or thumping
Unintentional mechanical contact (eg fan blades)
Worn drivebelt
Peripheral component fault (generator, water pump etc)
Worn big-end bearings (regular heavy knocking, perhaps less under load)
Worn main bearings (rumbling and knocking, perhaps worsening under load)
Piston slap (most noticeable when cold)

Conversion factors

Length (distance)

Inches (in)	X	25.4	= Millimetres (mm)	X	0.0394	= Inches (in)
Feet (ft)	X	0.305	= Metres (m)	X	3.281	= Feet (ft)
Miles	X	1.609	= Kilometres (km)	X	0.621	= Miles

Volume (capacity)

Cubic inches (cu in; in³)   X 16.387 = Cubic centimetres (cc; cm³)   X 0.061 = Cubic inches (cu in; in³)
Imperial pints (Imp pt)   X 0.568 = Litres (l)   X 1.76 = Imperial pints (Imp pt)
Imperial quarts (Imp qt)   X 1.137 = Litres (l)   X 0.88 = Imperial quarts (Imp qt)
Imperial quarts (Imp qt)   X 1.201 = US quarts (US qt)   X 0.833 = Imperial quarts (Imp qt)
US quarts (US qt)   X 0.946 = Litres (l)   X 1.057 = US quarts (US qt)
Imperial gallons (Imp gal)   X 4.546 = Litres (l)   X 0.22 = Imperial gallons (Imp gal)
Imperial gallons (Imp gal)   X 1.201 = US gallons (US gal)   X 0.833 = Imperial gallons (Imp gal)
US gallons (US gal)   X 3.785 = Litres (l)   X 0.264 = US gallons (US gal)

Mass (weight)

Ounces (oz)   X 28.35 = Grams (g)   X 0.035 = Ounces (oz)
Pounds (lb)   X 0.454 = Kilograms (kg)   X 2.205 = Pounds (lb)

Force

Ounces-force (ozf; oz)   X 0.278 = Newtons (N)   X 3.6 = Ounces-force (ozf; oz)
Pounds-force (lbf; lb)   X 4.448 = Newtons (N)   X 0.225 = Pounds-force (lbf; lb)
Newtons (N)   X 0.1 = Kilograms-force (kgf; kg)   X 9.81 = Newtons (N)

Pressure

Pounds-force per square inch (psi; lbf/in²; lb/in²)   X 0.070 = Kilograms-force per square centimetre (kgf/cm²; kg/cm²)   X 14.223 = Pounds-force per square inch (psi; lbf/in²; lb/in²)
Pounds-force per square inch (psi; lbf/in²; lb/in²)   X 0.068 = Atmospheres (atm)   X 14.696 = Pounds-force per square inch (psi; lbf/in²; lb/in²)
Pounds-force per square inch (psi; lbf/in²; lb/in²)   X 0.069 = Bars   X 14.5 = Pounds-force per square inch (psi; lbf/in²; lb/in²)
Pounds-force per square inch (psi; lbf/in²; lb/in²)   X 6.895 = Kilopascals (kPa)   X 0.145 = Pounds-force per square inch (psi; lbf/in²; lb/in²)
Kilopascals (kPa)   X 0.01 = Kilograms-force per square centimetre (kgf/cm²; kg/cm²)   X 98.1 = Kilopascals (kPa)

Torque (moment of force)

Pounds-force inches (lbf in; lb in)   X 1.152 = Kilograms-force centimetre (kgf cm; kg cm)   X 0.868 = Pounds-force inches (lbf in; lb in)
Pounds-force inches (lbf in; lb in)   X 0.113 = Newton metres (Nm)   X 8.85 = Pounds-force inches (lbf in; lb in)
Pounds-force inches (lbf in; lb in)   X 0.083 = Pounds-force feet (lbf ft; lb ft)   X 12 = Pounds-force inches (lbf in; lb in)
Pounds-force feet (lbf ft; lb ft)   X 0.138 = Kilograms-force metres (kgf m; kg m)   X 7.233 = Pounds-force feet (lbf ft; lb ft)
Pounds-force feet (lbf ft; lb ft)   X 1.356 = Newton metres (Nm)   X 0.738 = Pounds-force feet (lbf ft; lb ft)
Newton metres (Nm)   X 0.102 = Kilograms-force metres (kgf m; kg m)   X 9.804 = Newton metres (Nm)

Power

Horsepower (hp)   X 745.7 = Watts (W)   X 0.0013 = Horsepower (hp)

Velocity (speed)

Miles per hour (miles/hr; mph)   X 1.609 = Kilometres per hour (km/hr; kph)   X 0.621 = Miles per hour (miles/hr; mph)

*Fuel consumption**

Miles per gallon, Imperial (mpg)   X 0.354 = Kilometres per litre (km/l)   X 2.825 = Miles per gallon, Imperial (mpg)
Miles per gallon, US (mpg)   X 0.425 = Kilometres per litre (km/l)   X 2.352 = Miles per gallon, US (mpg)

Temperature

Degrees Fahrenheit = (°C x 1.8) + 32   Degrees Celsius (Degrees Centigrade; °C) = (°F - 32) x 0.56

It is common practice to convert from miles per gallon (mpg) to litres/100 kilometres (l/100km), where mpg (Imperial) x l/100 km = 282 and mpg (US) x l/100 km = 235

Index

Printed by
J H Haynes & Co Ltd
Sparkford Nr Yeovil
Somerset BA22 7JJ England